TAYYAR OZKAN

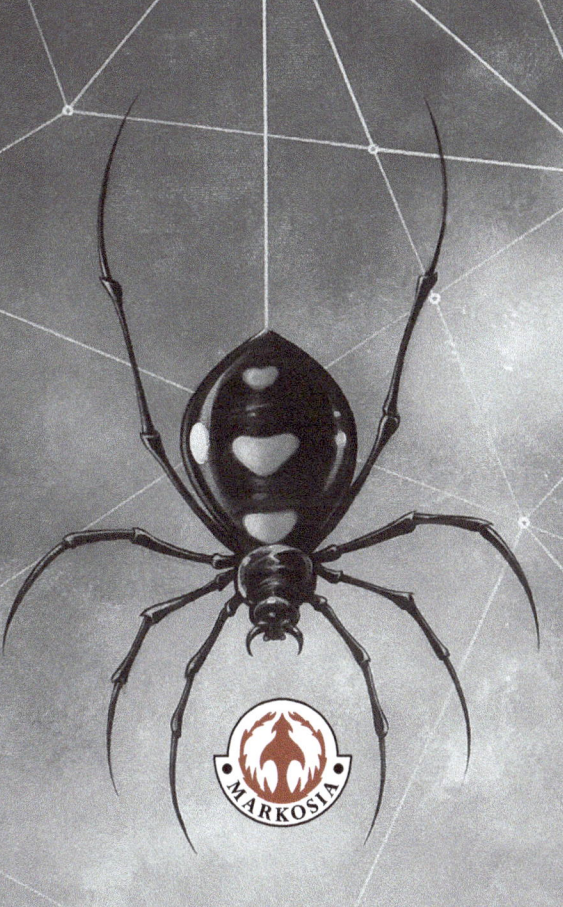

Art Anthology

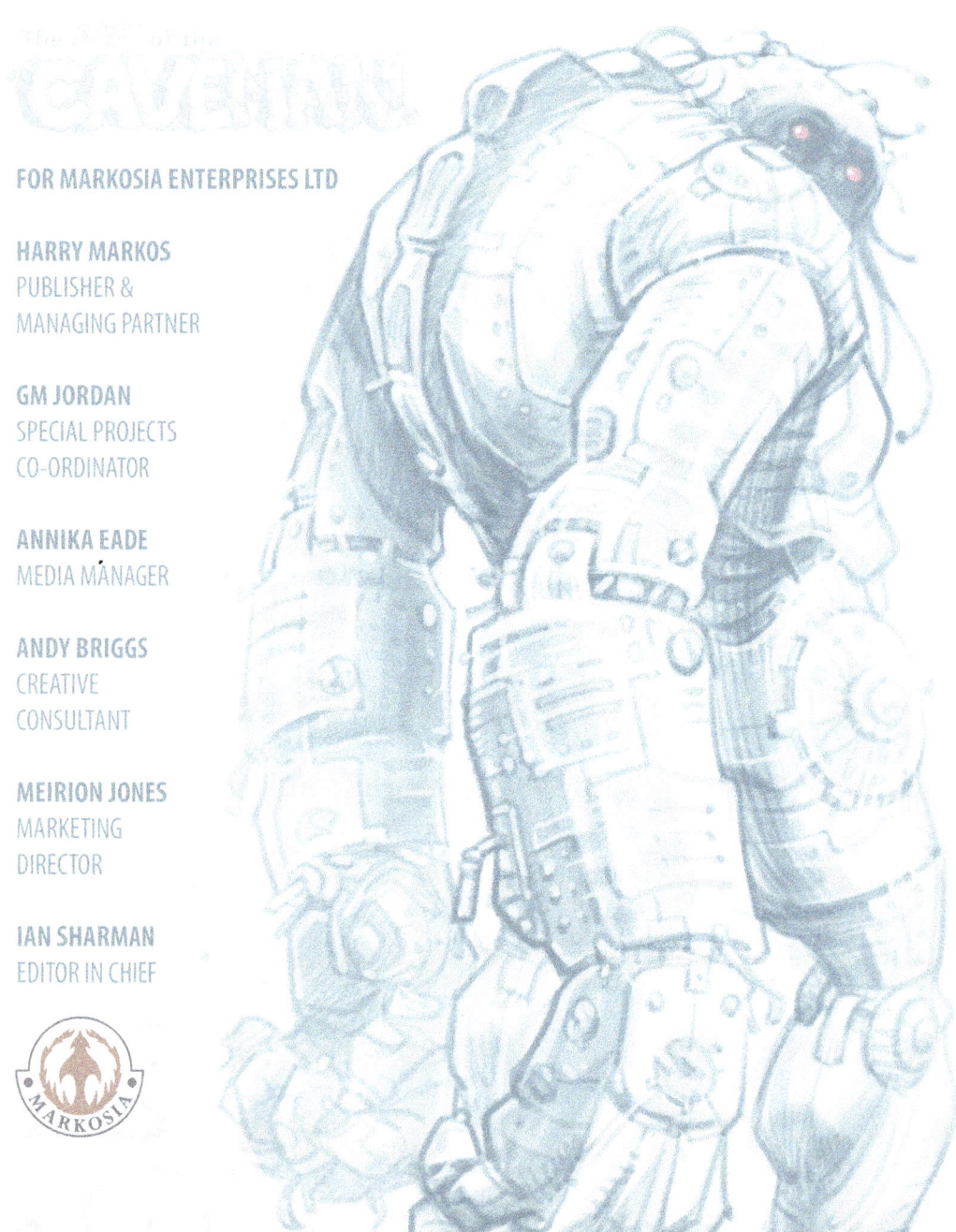

FOR MARKOSIA ENTERPRISES LTD

HARRY MARKOS
PUBLISHER &
MANAGING PARTNER

GM JORDAN
SPECIAL PROJECTS
CO-ORDINATOR

ANNIKA EADE
MEDIA MANAGER

ANDY BRIGGS
CREATIVE
CONSULTANT

MEIRION JONES
MARKETING
DIRECTOR

IAN SHARMAN
EDITOR IN CHIEF

ISBN 978-1-915387-02-8

www.markosia.com

Early
Drawings

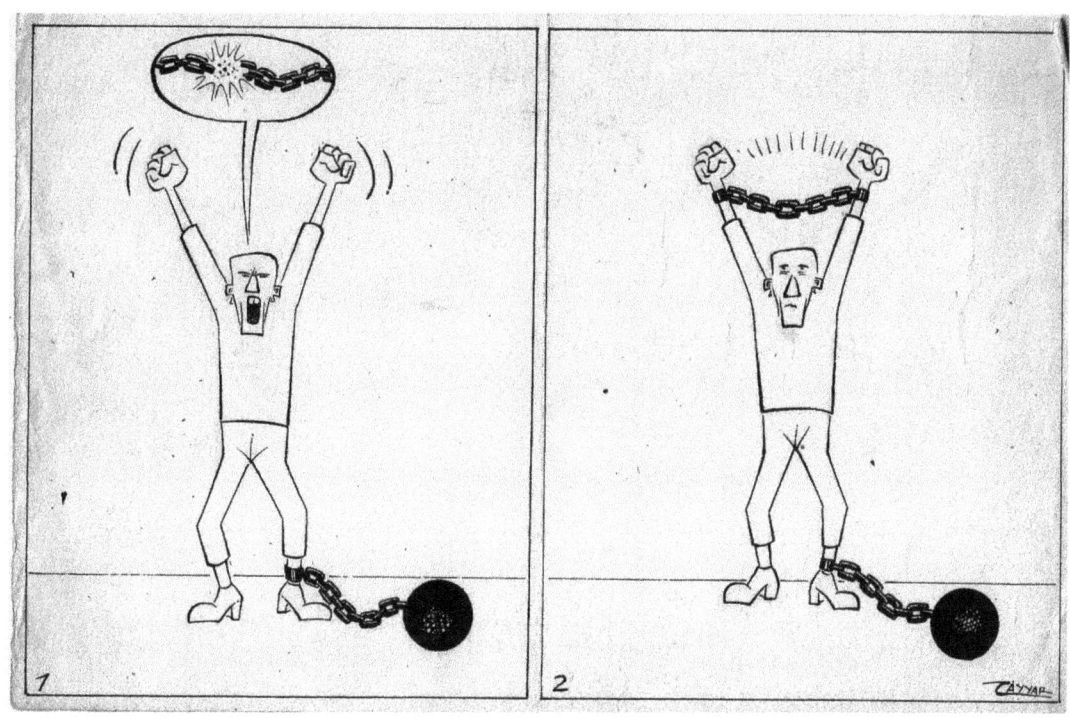

These are my **very early period** of time drawings in **Turkey**.
Most of them are drawn for the political syndicate magazines in between
1975-79 before my Fine Art Academy years.

We were very **active teens** in the 70s.

After the **military took over** the government **in 1980**, all political movements
were blocked.

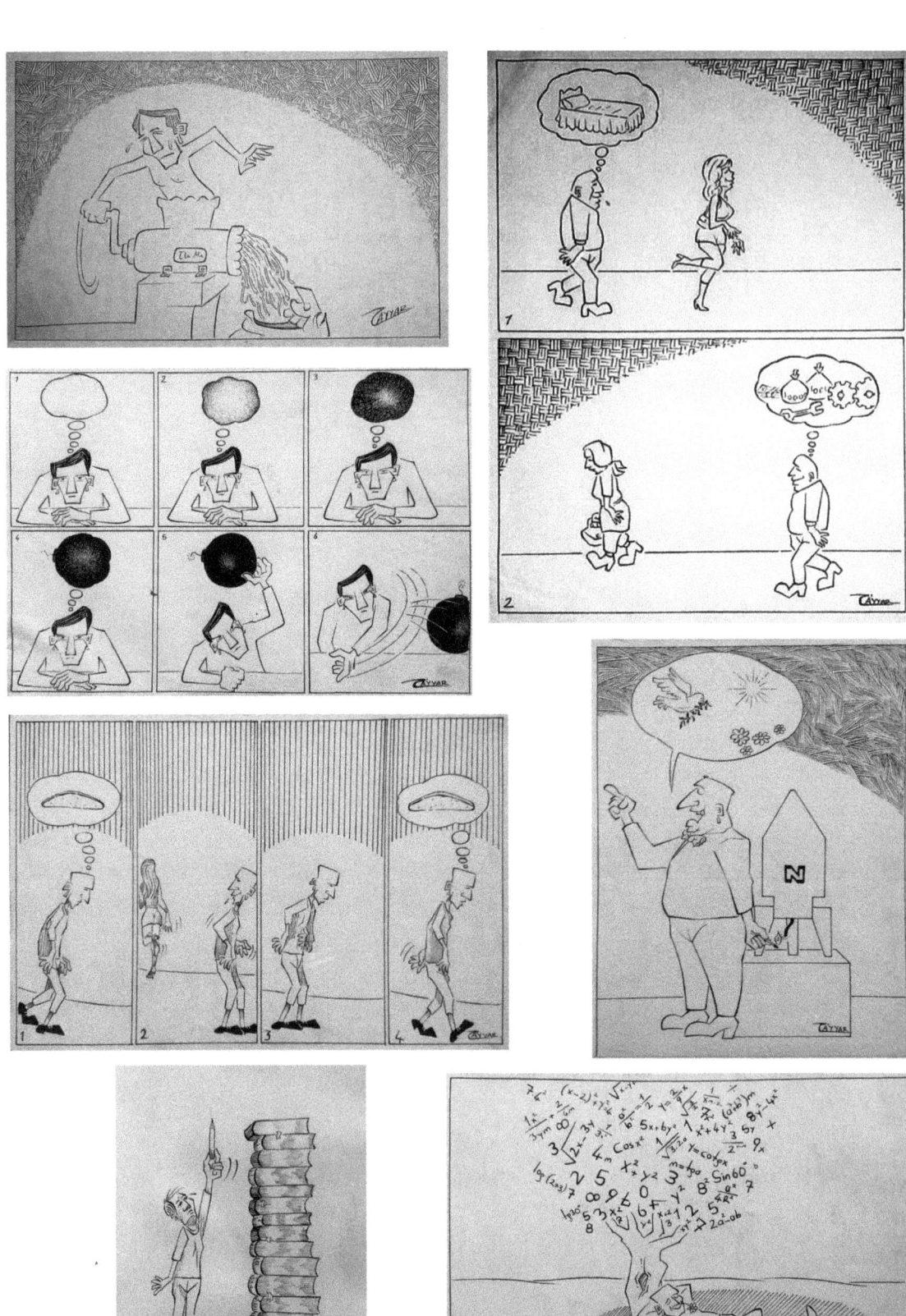

*Drawn for some **political syndicate magazines** in between 1975-76.*

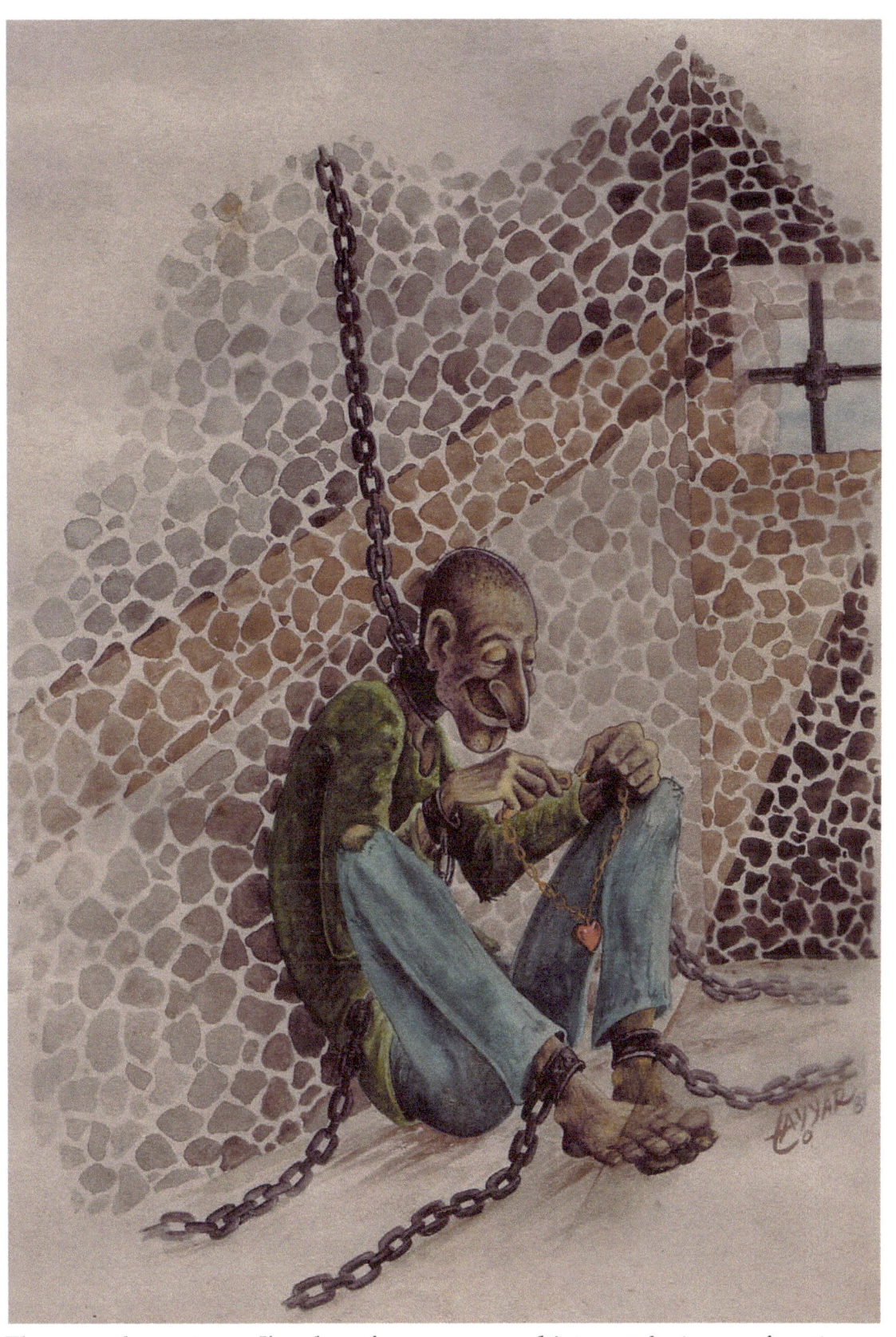

These are the *cartoons* I've done for my *personal interest* during my free times
in the late 70s - early 80s..

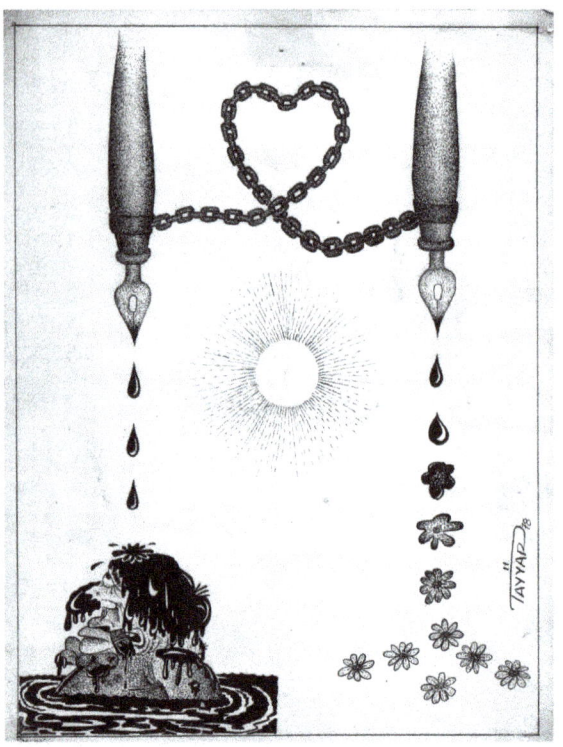

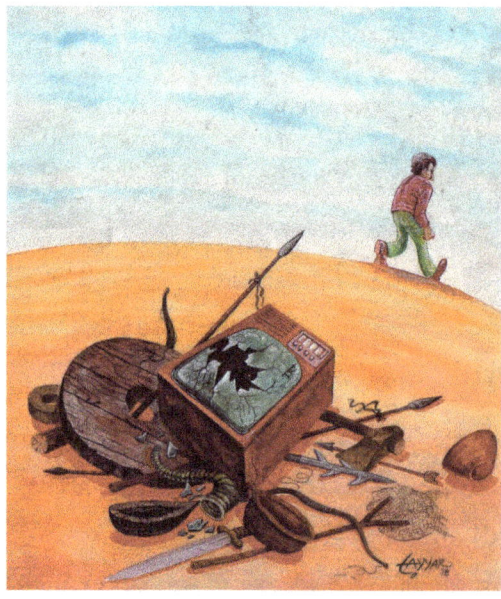

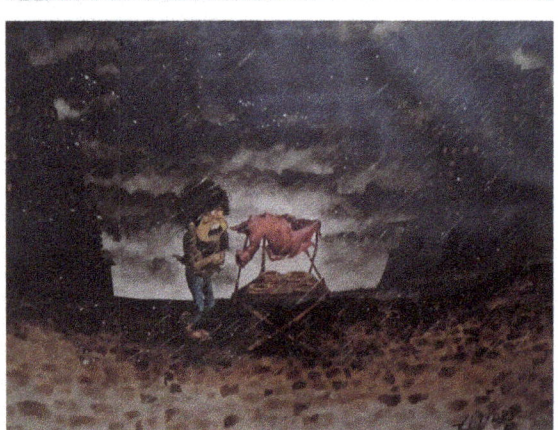

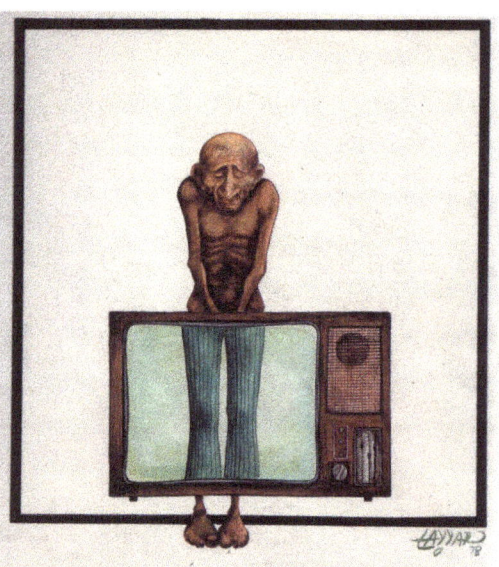

More *cartoons* I've done in the late 70s - early 80s.

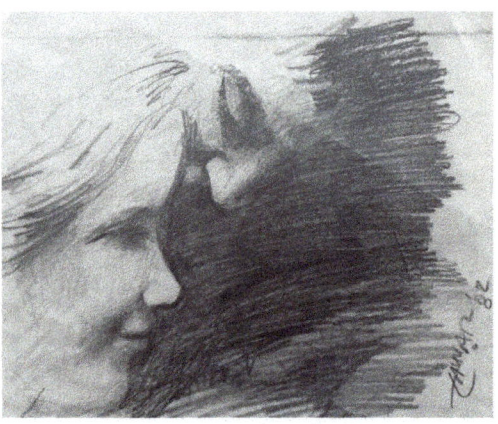

*-Pencil **sketch** in 1982.*

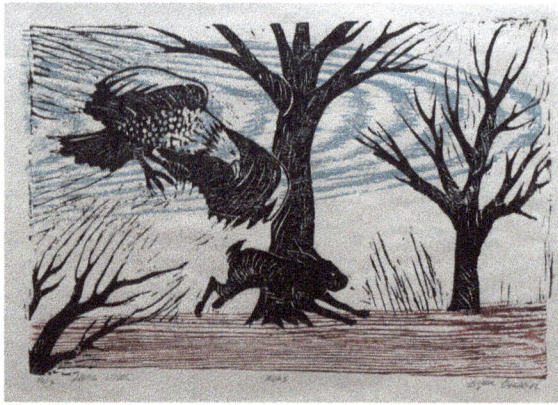

*-Linoleum print for the **school homework** in 1982.*

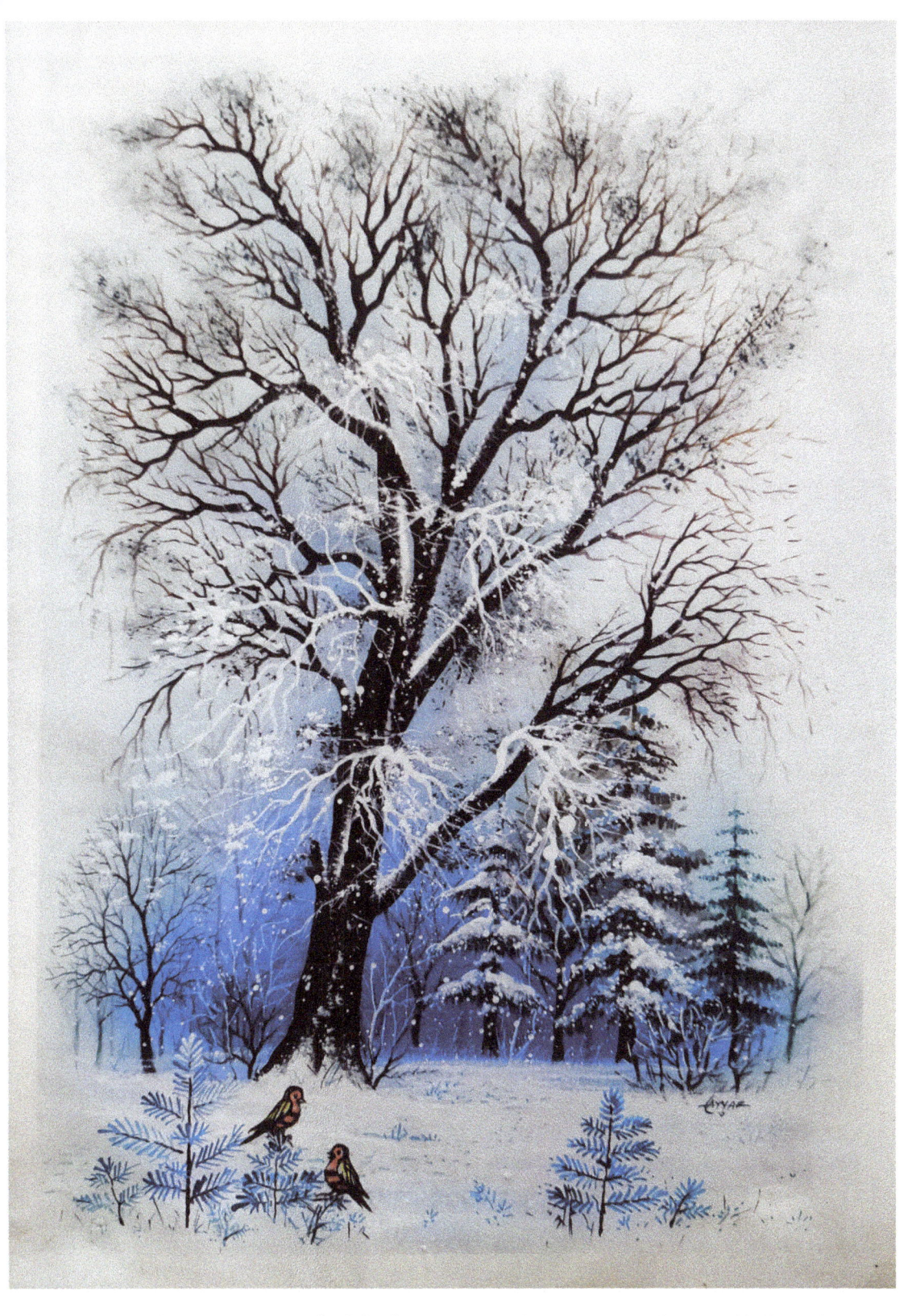

While I was living in *Istanbul*, before I moved to *New York* in *1989* I've done many *greeting cards* with gouache and acrylic on papers.

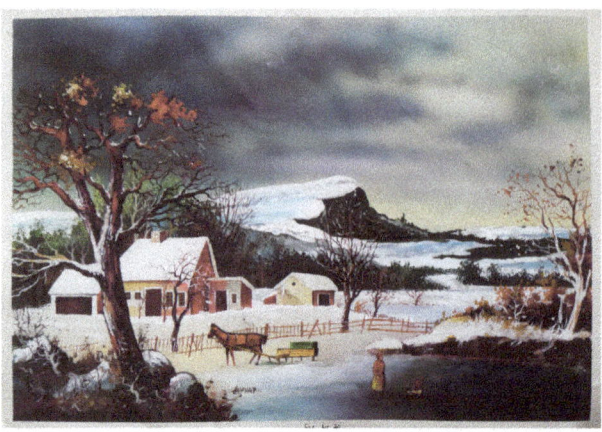
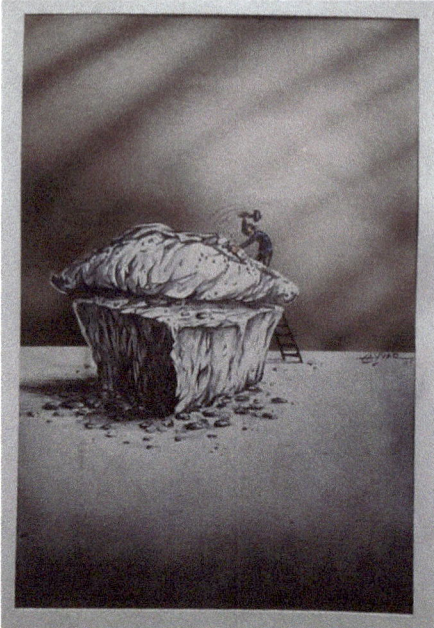
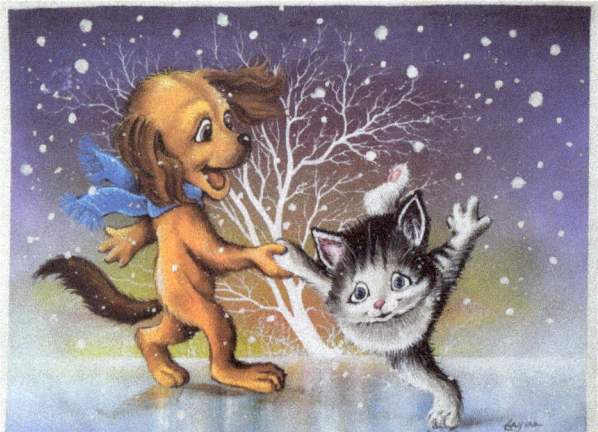
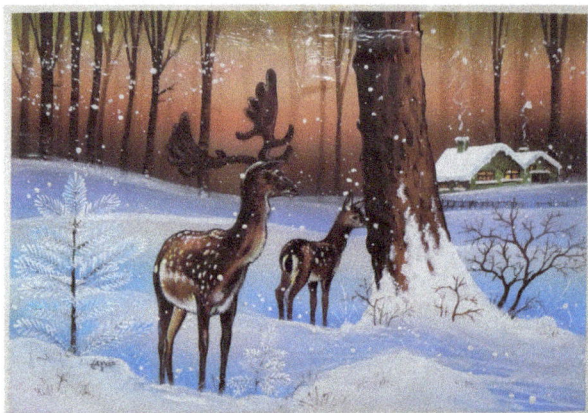
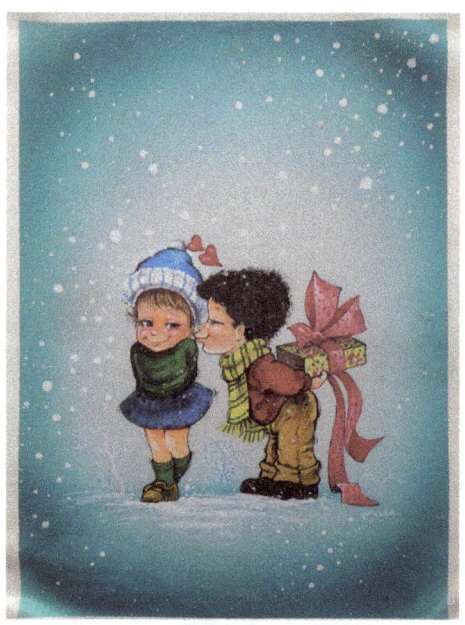
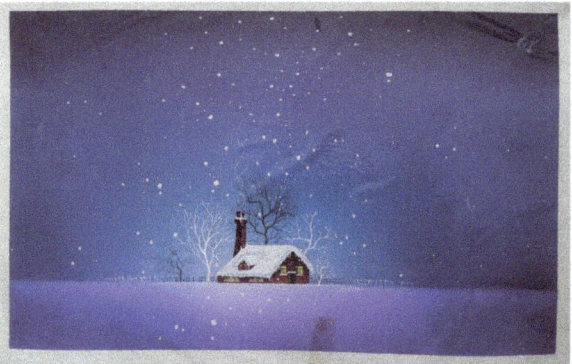
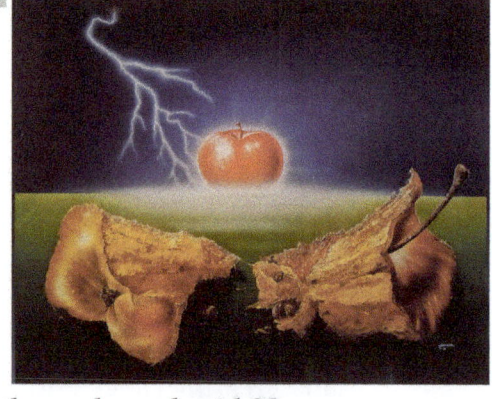

More *greeting cards* during the early and mid 80s.

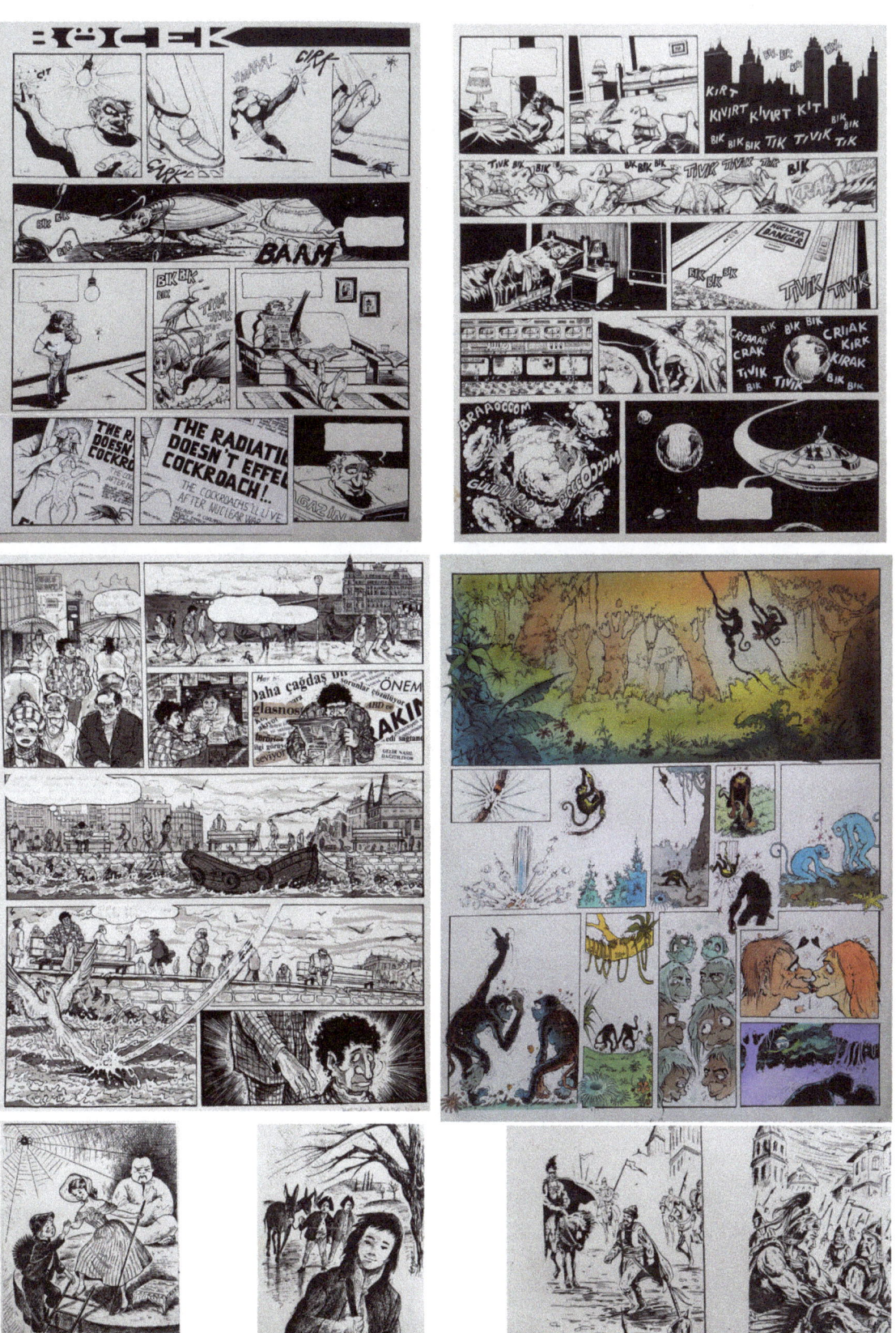

In the very *early 80s* some *comic pages* and drawings for the *Turkish* newspapers and magazines.

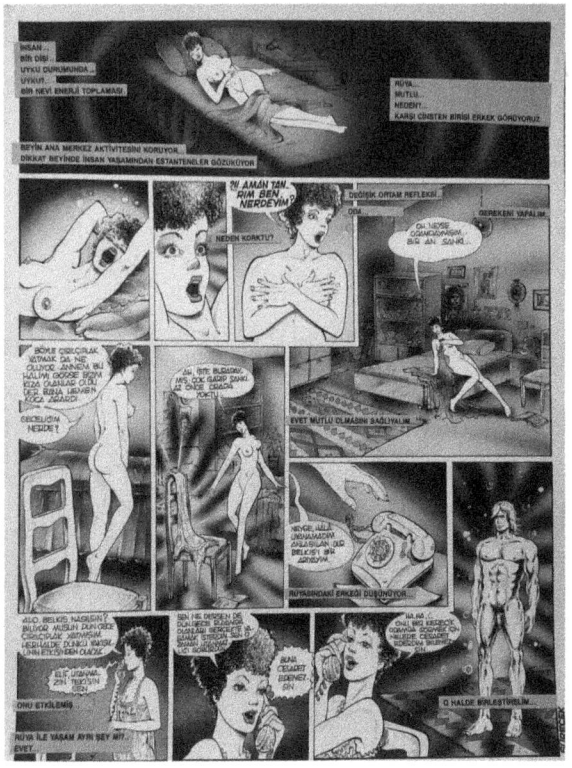

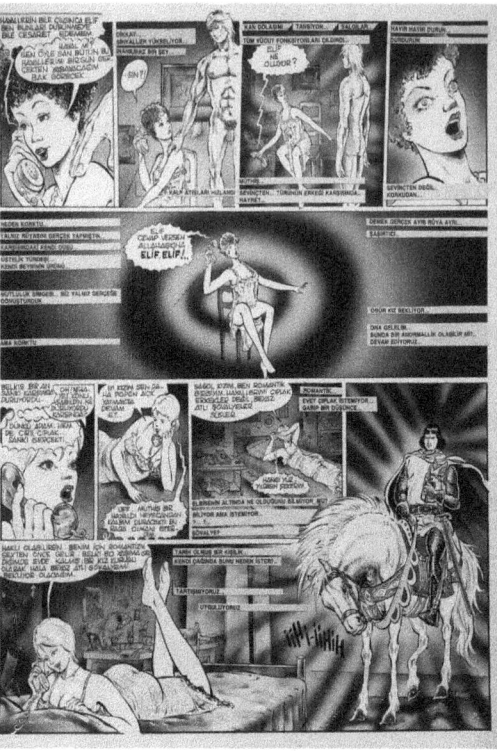

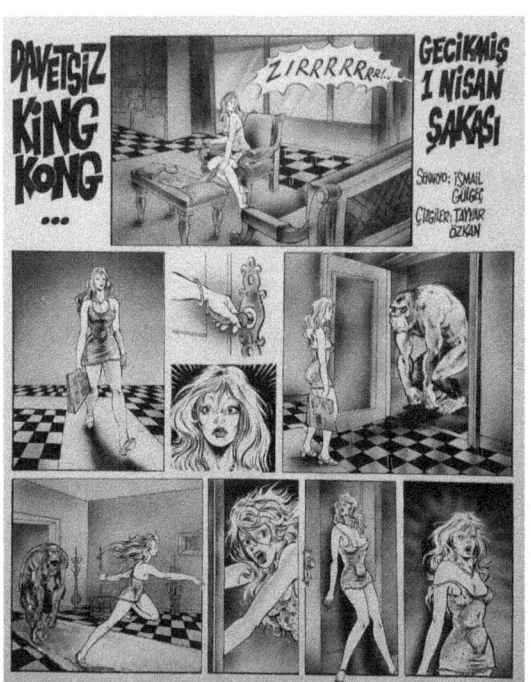

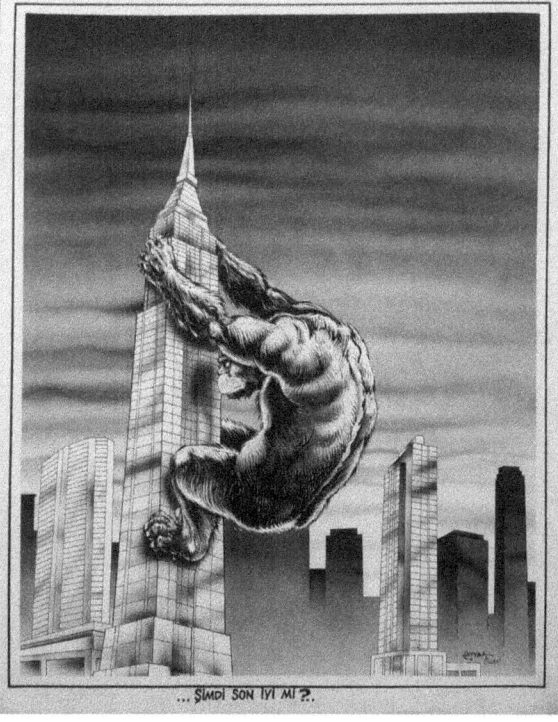

More *comic pages* for the *Turkish* newspapers and magazines in the early 80s.

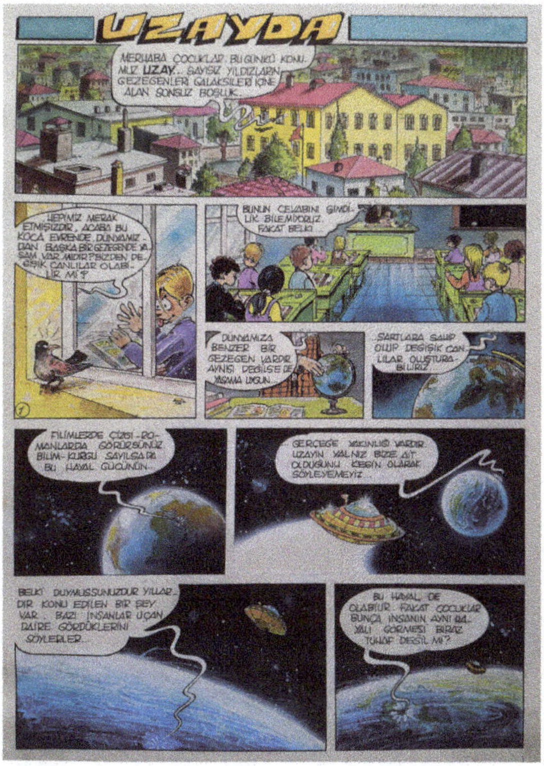

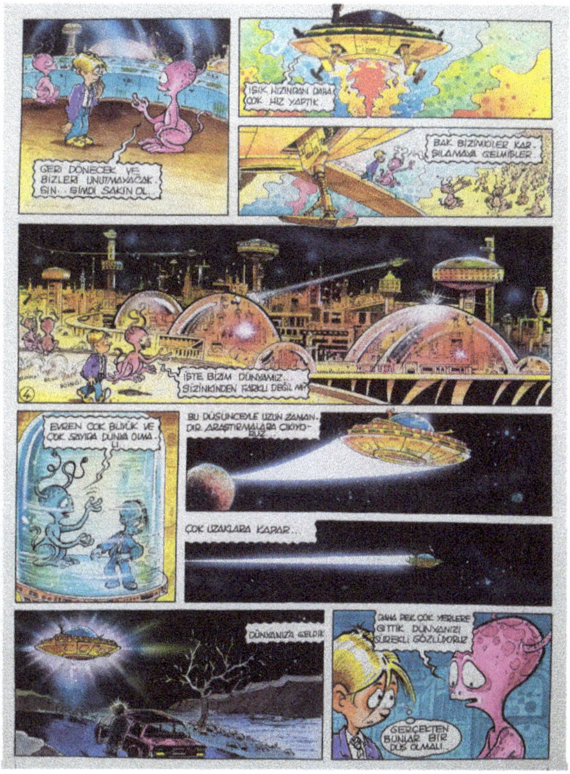

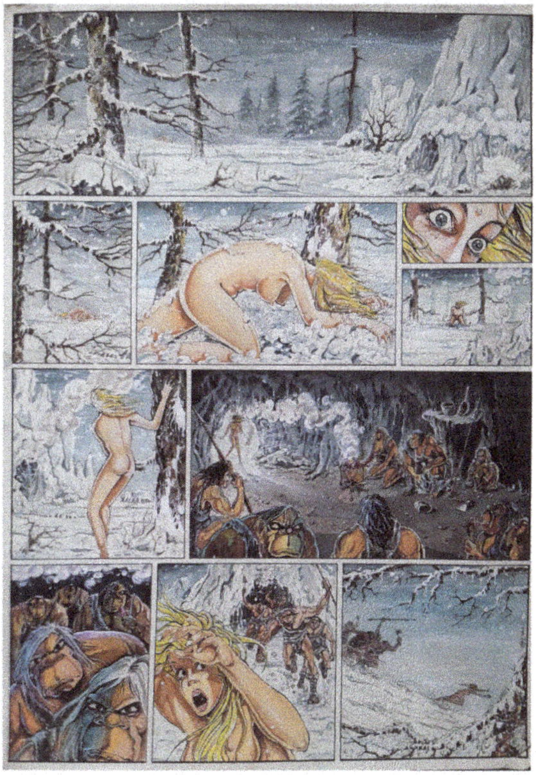

-First colored **CAVEMAN** story published in the Turkish **Playboy** Magazine in 1986.

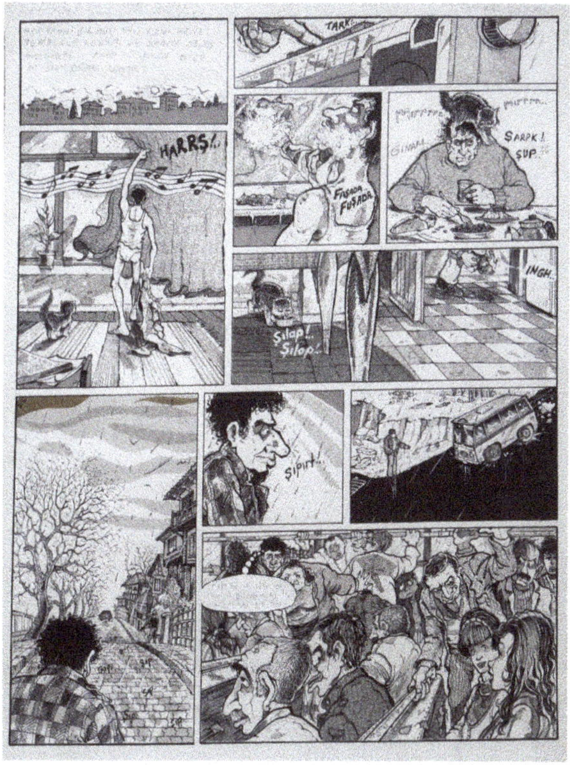

Variation of *comic pages* for the *Turkish* newspapers and magazines in the very early *80*s .

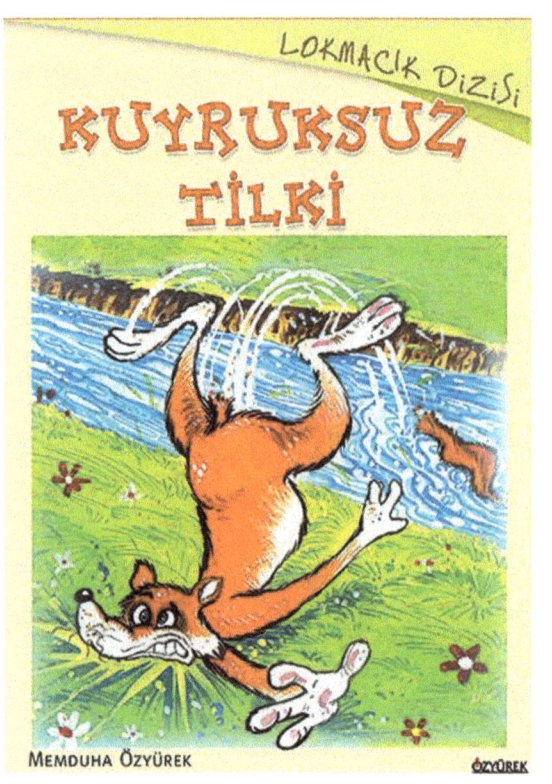

KUYRUKSUZ TİLKİ

Memduha Özyürek

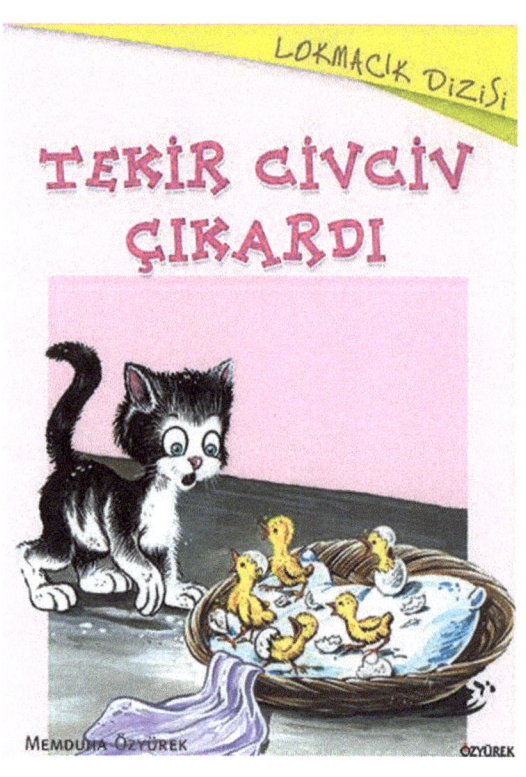

TEKİR CİVCİV ÇIKARDI

Memduha Özyürek

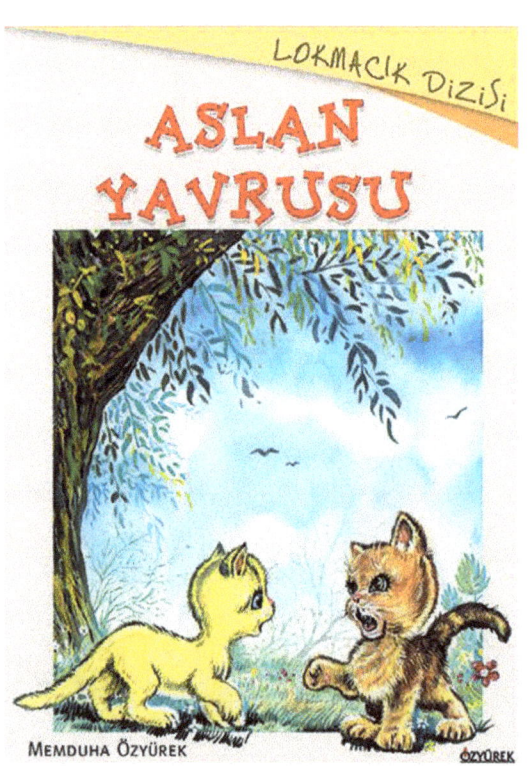

ASLAN YAVRUSU

Memduha Özyürek

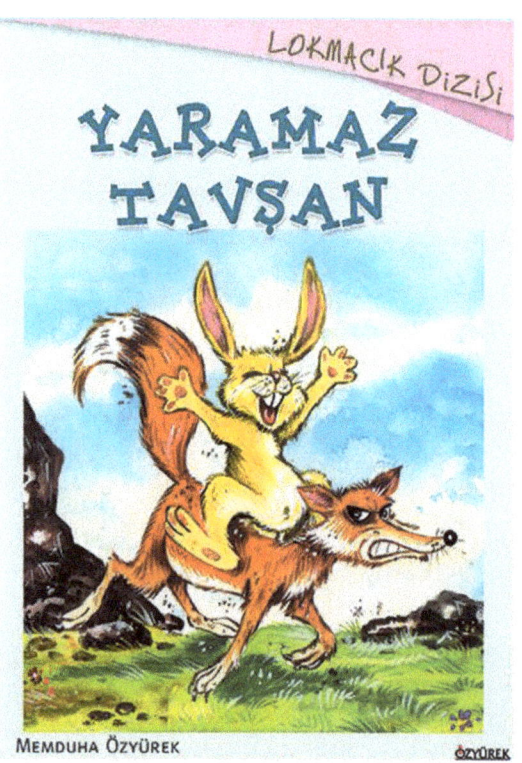

YARAMAZ TAVŞAN

Memduha Özyürek

-*Some of my first **children's books** which I've illustrated in the early 80s.*

While I was a ***student*** I was already ***working*** on many different projects in the ***publishing*** market.

COMICS

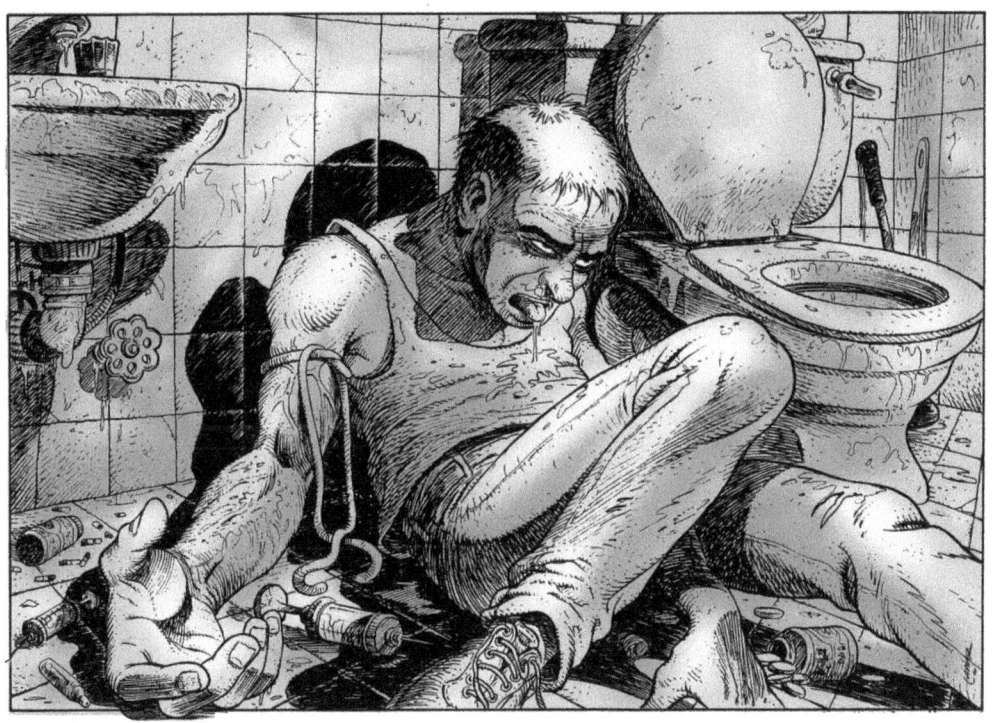

From here these are the *comic book work* I've done after I moved to *USA* in 1989.

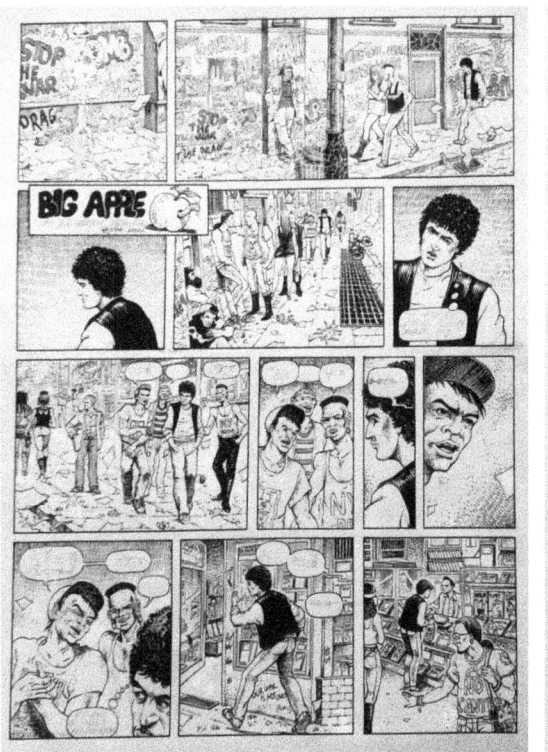
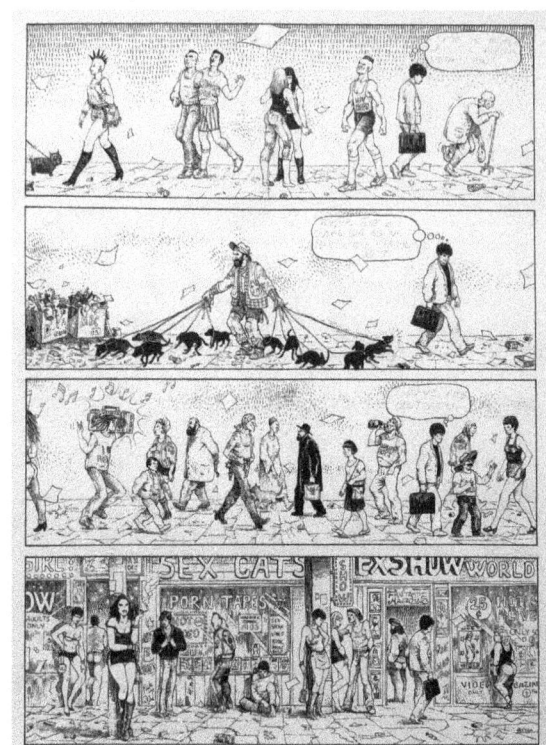
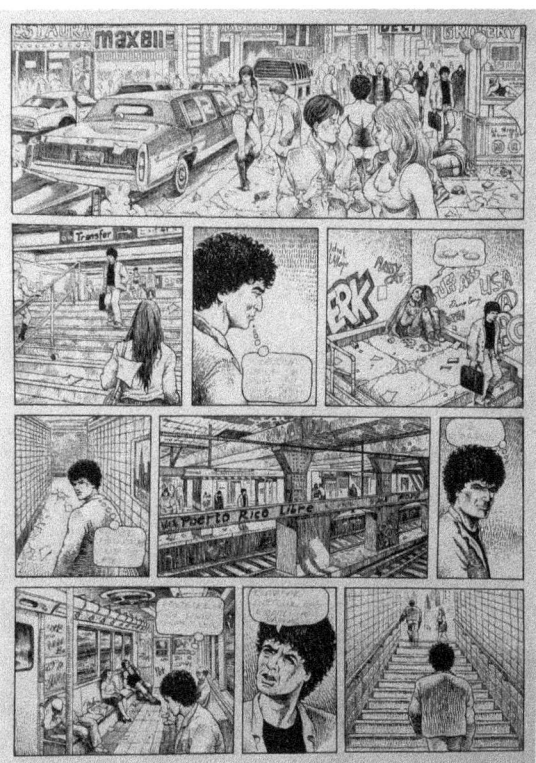
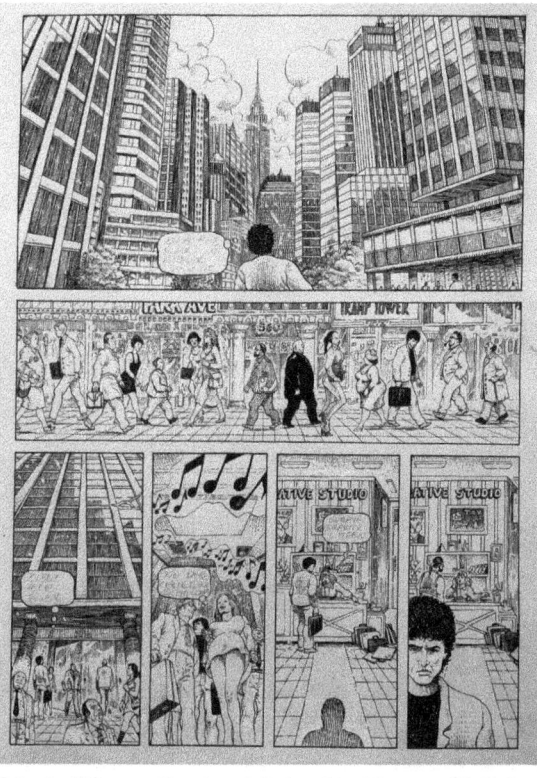

-I drew this 10 pages story after I moved to **New York City** and got published in **Heavy Metal Illustrated Magazine** in 1993. At the following years my well known CAVEMAN started to be published in the same magazine regularly for almost 20 years.

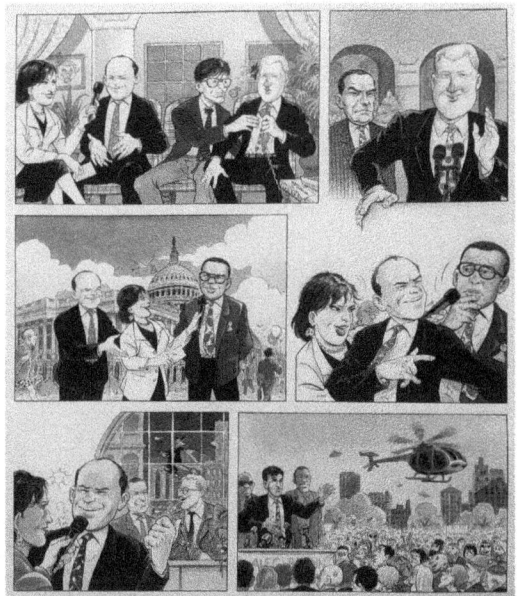

-For '**MAD**' Magazine.

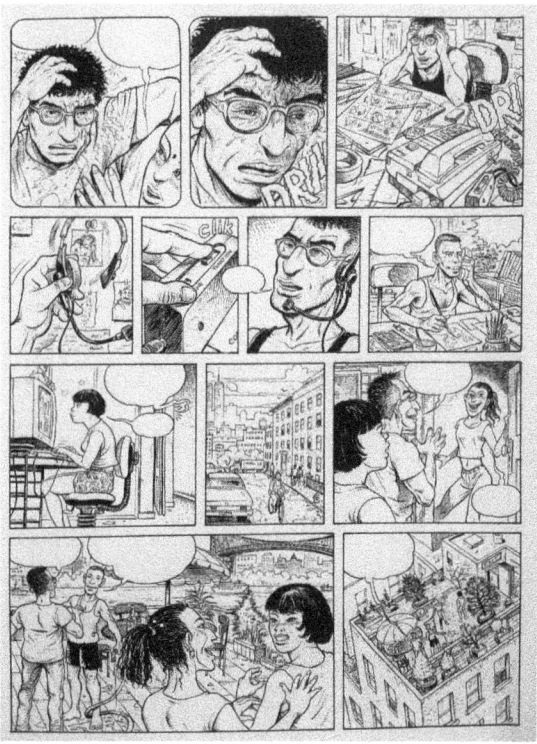

-For '**CRACKED**' Magazine.

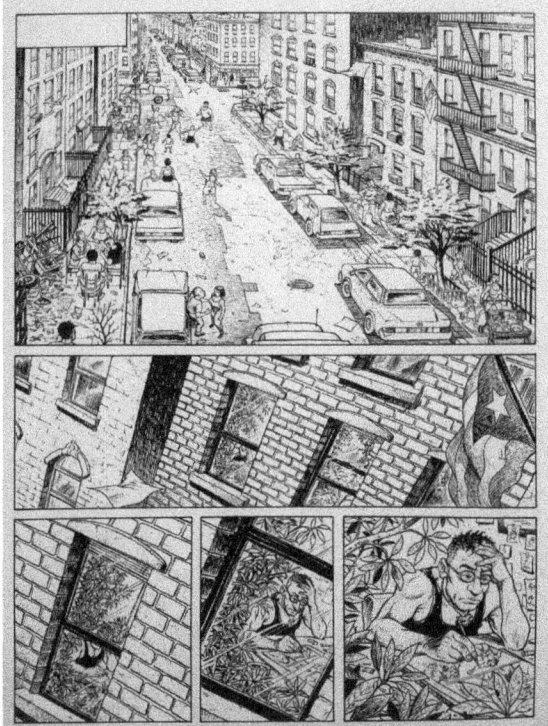

-This is the 90 pages **uncompleded** story about my life in New York.

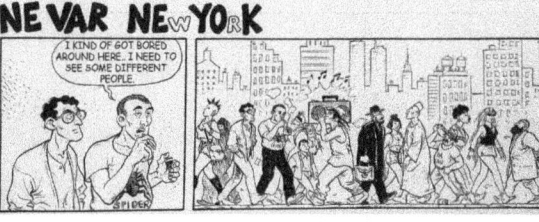

-Comic strips done for **some** newspapers.

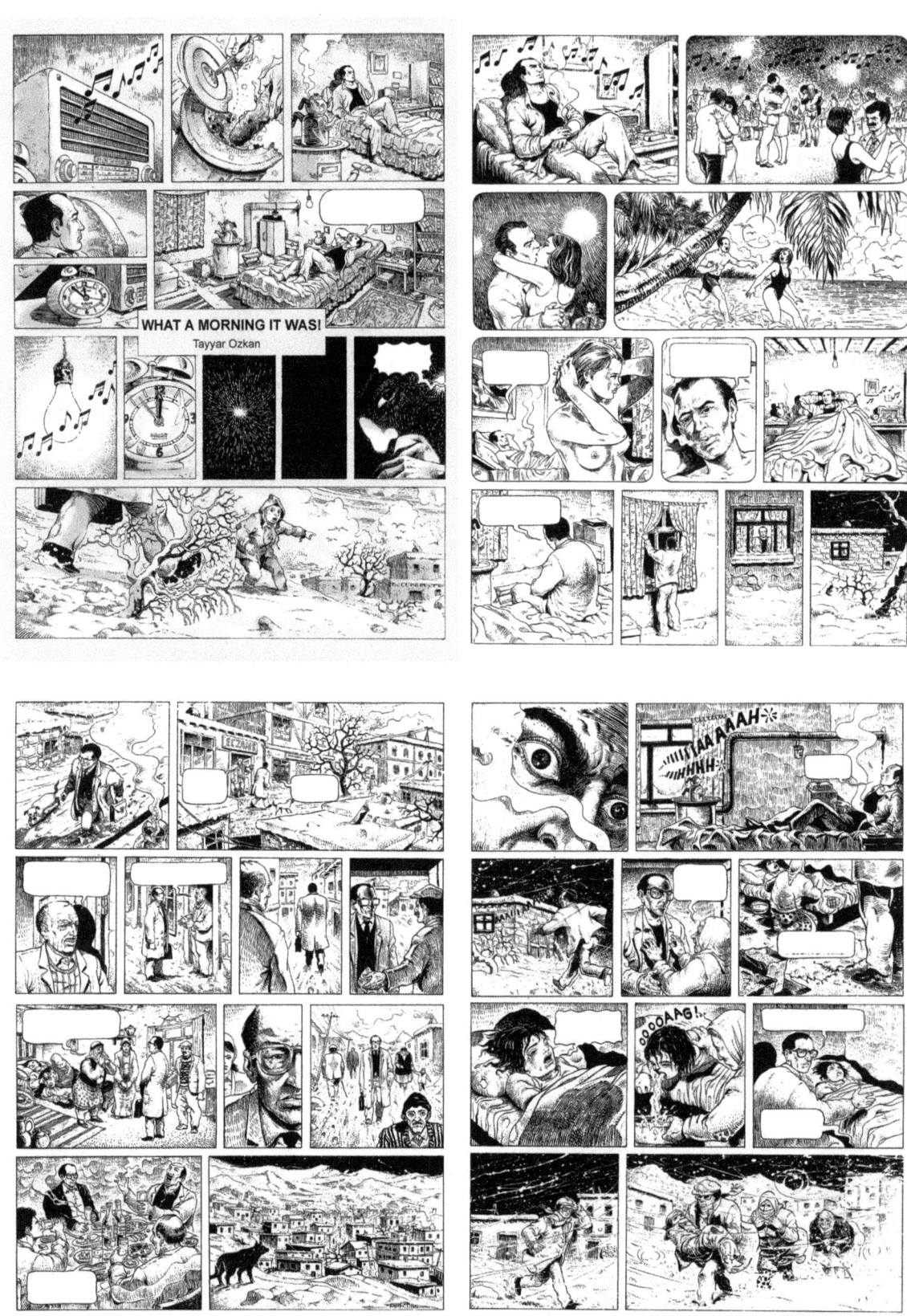

-WHAT A MORNING IT WAS. 10 Pages story.
Drawn for *WW3 Illustrated Magazine* in New York -1992

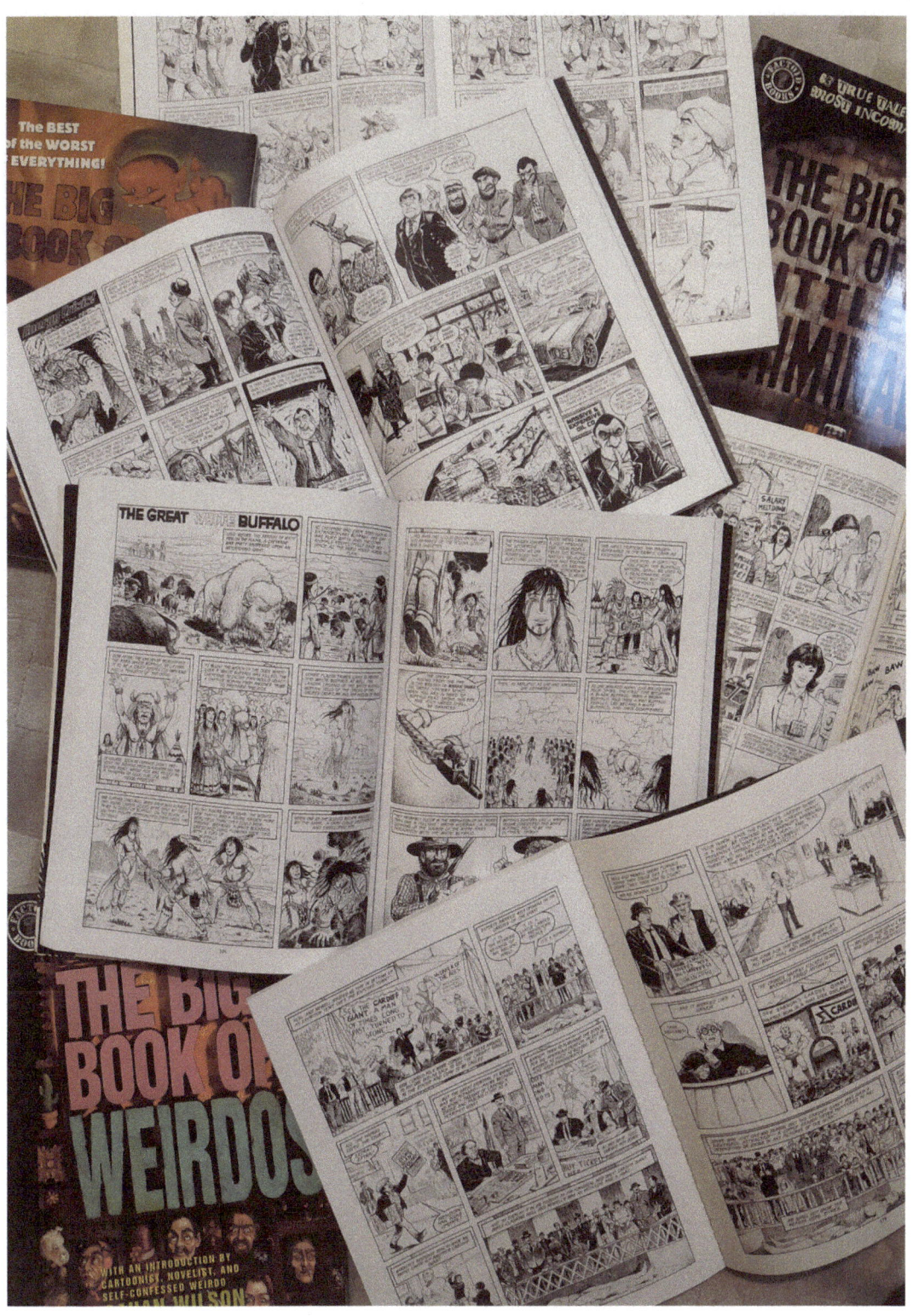

The pages from *"The Big Book of.."* series published by
Paradox Press/DC Comics in 1994-96 periof of time.
I've done drawings for every book of this series.

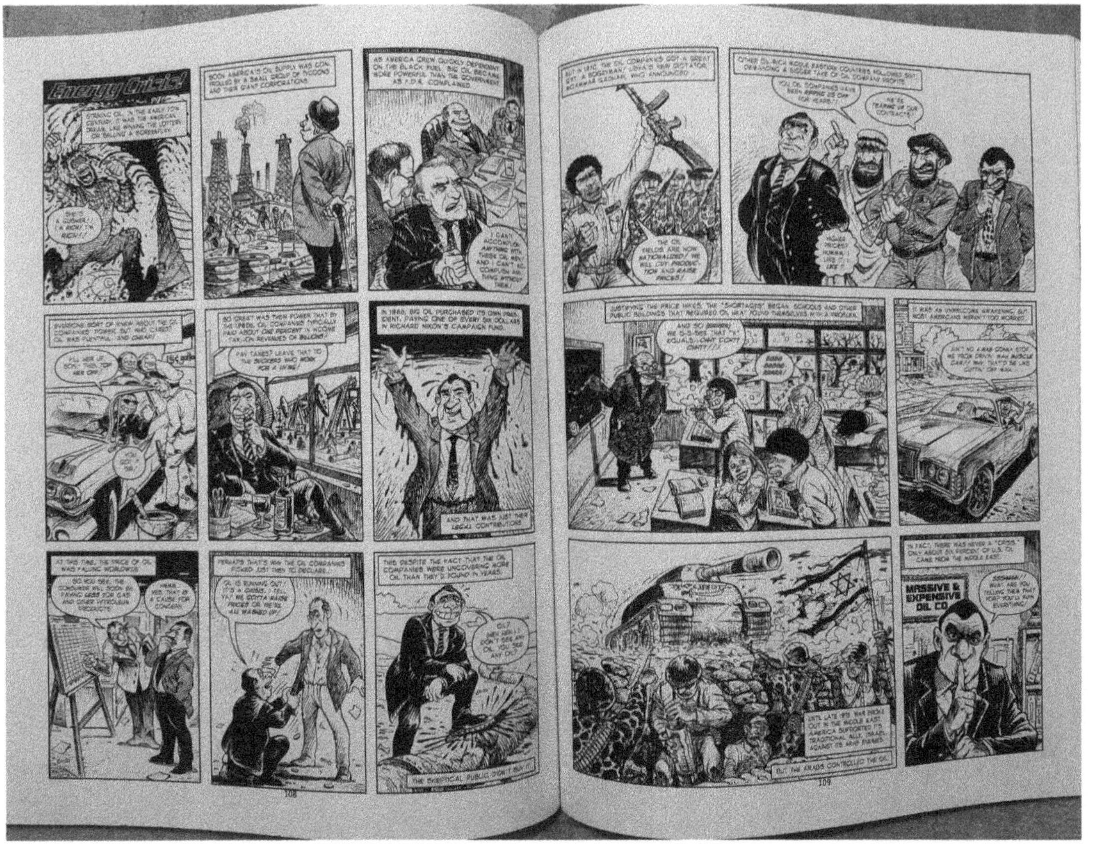

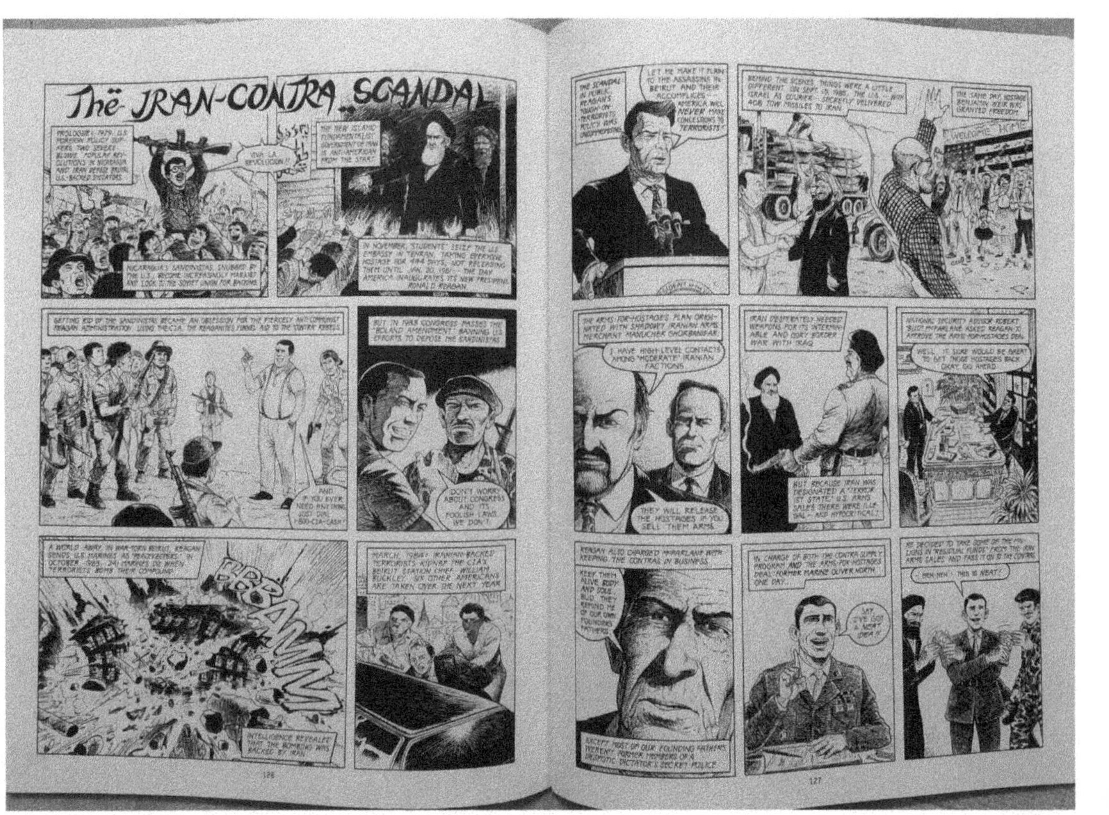

*-More printed pages from "**The Big Book of..**" series.*

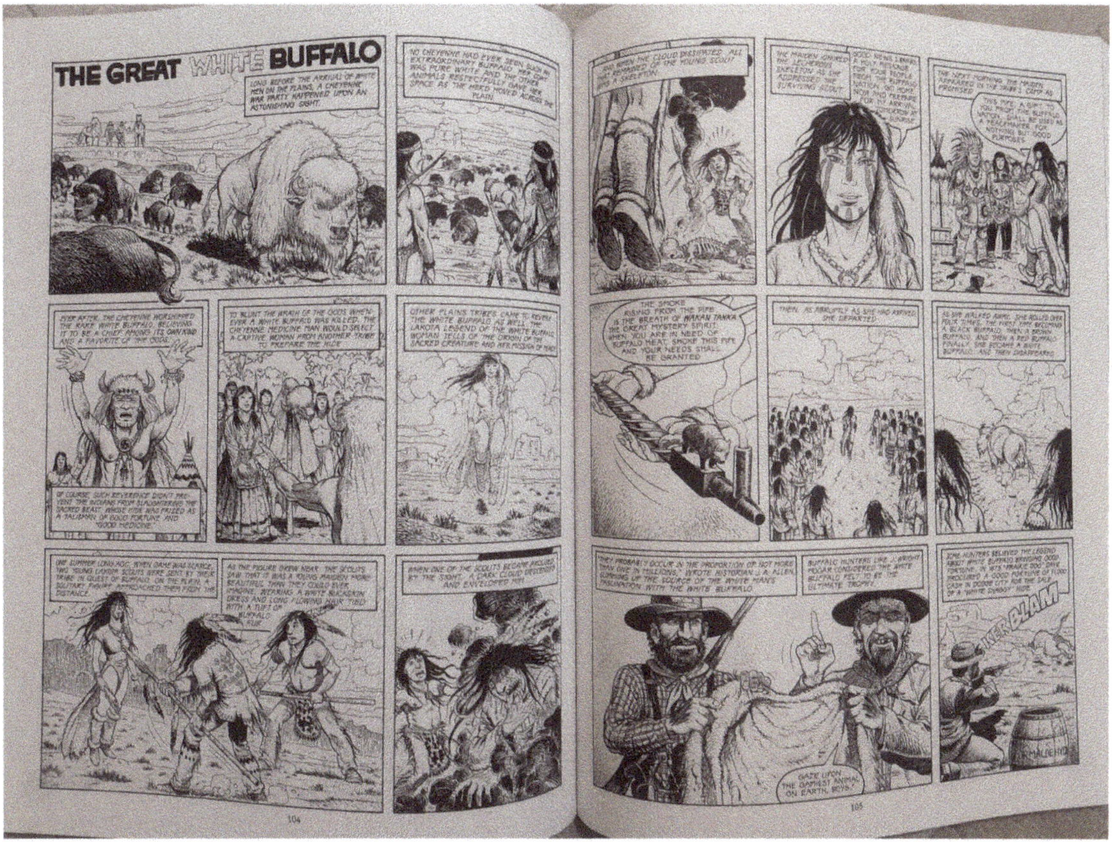

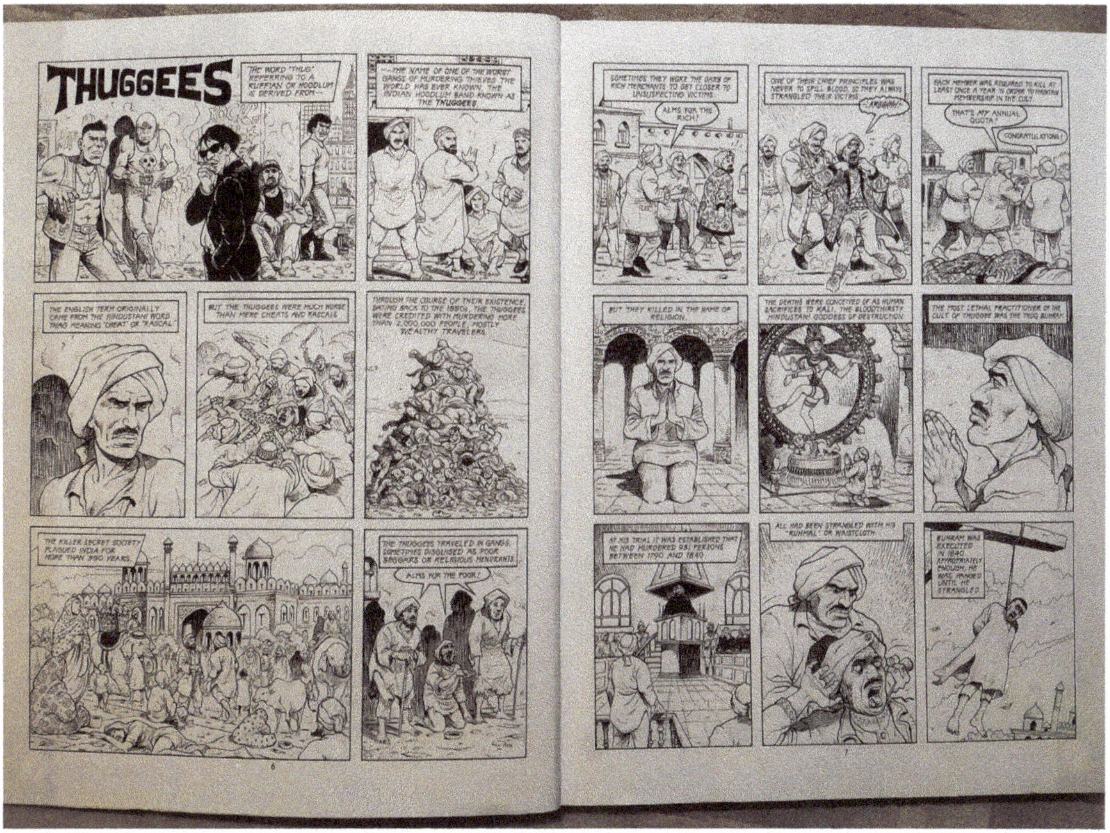

*-Printed pages from "**The Big Book of..**" series.*

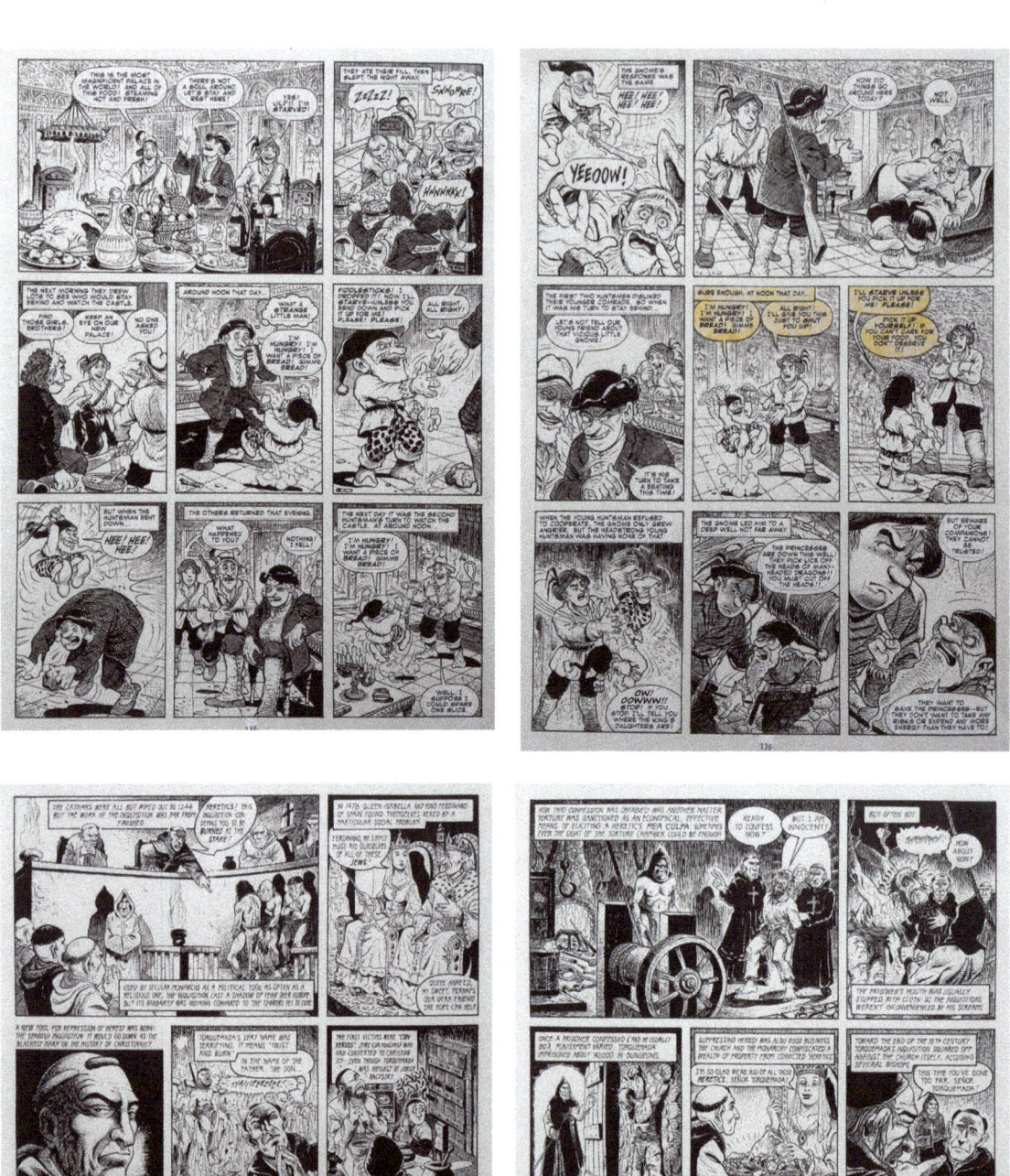

-More pages from "**The Big of Book..**" series.

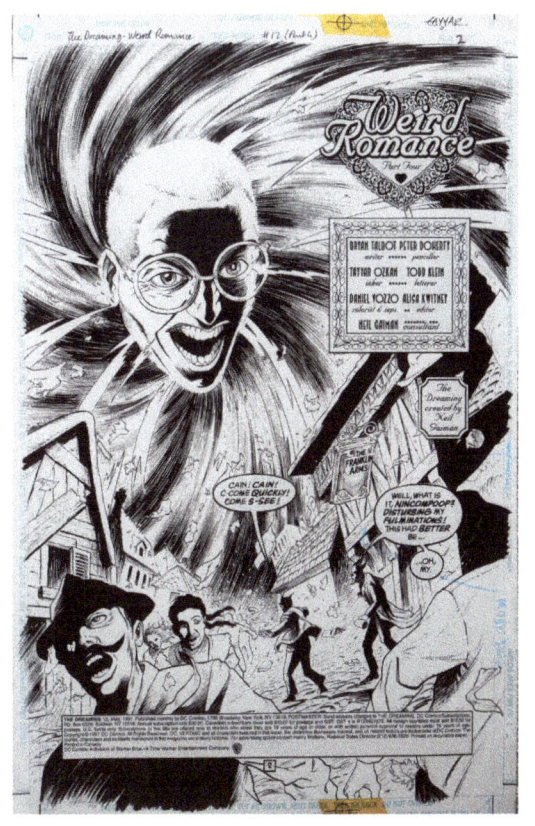

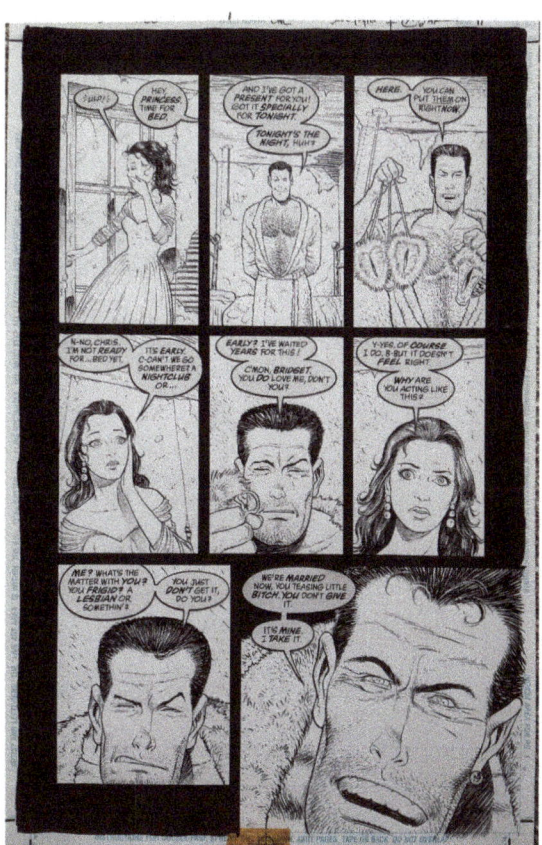

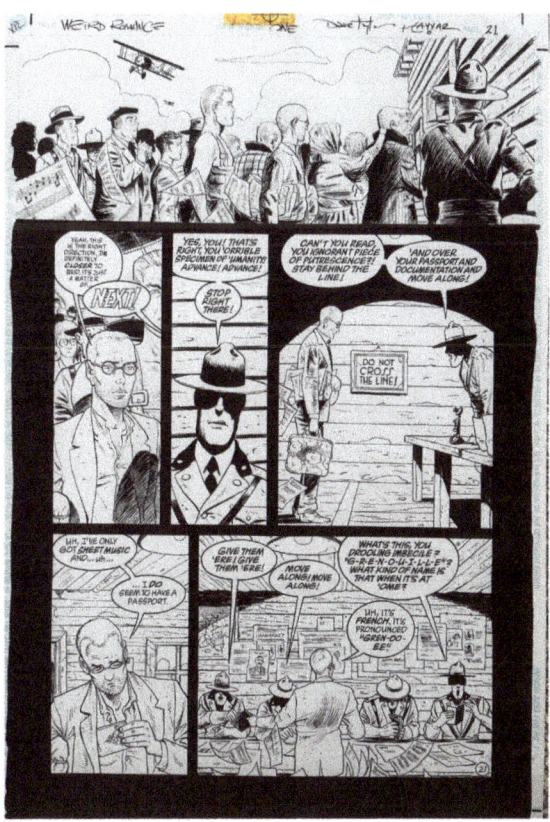

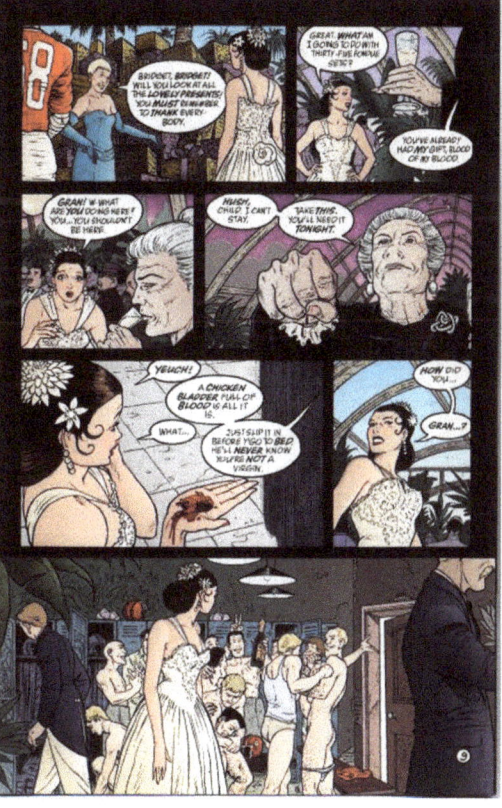

-I inked 4 issues of "*The Dreaming*" for *Vertigo/DC Comics* in 1997.

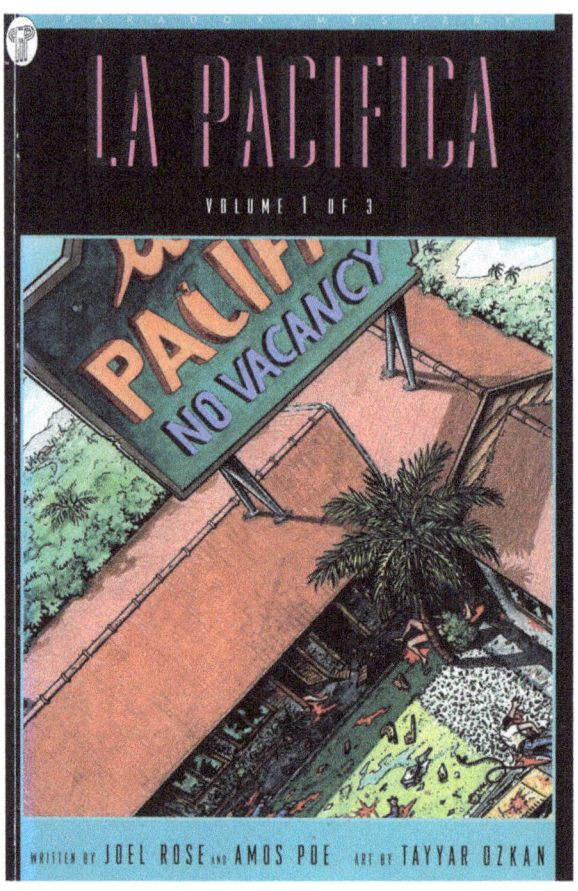

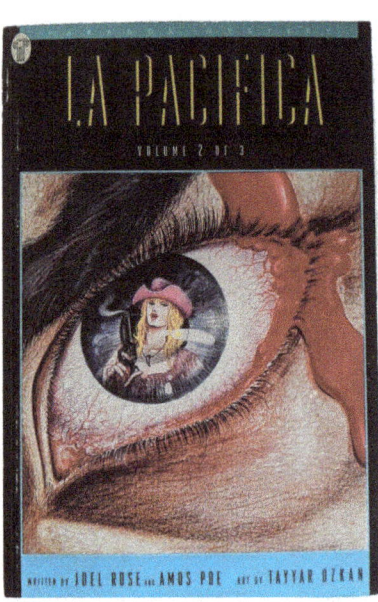

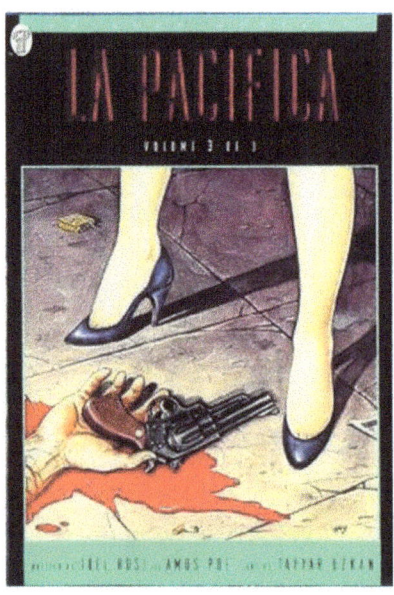

LA PACIFICA, graphic mystery written by *Joel Rose,* and *Amos Poe*..
drawn by *me*. Published by *Paradox Press/DC* (1994).
282 pages, 3 volumes, B&W.

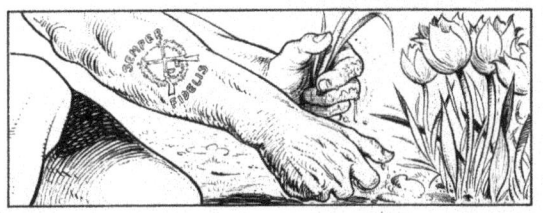

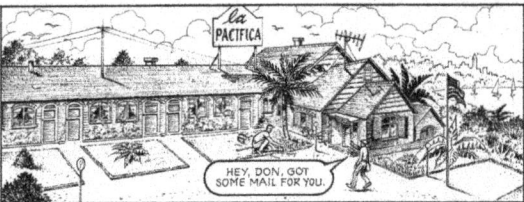

HEY, DON, GOT SOME MAIL FOR YOU.

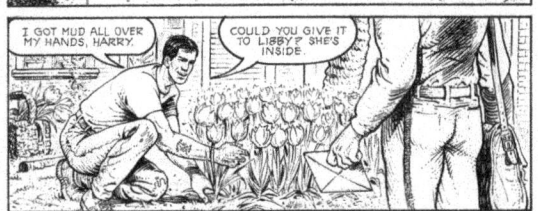

I GOT MUD ALL OVER MY HANDS, HARRY.

COULD YOU GIVE IT TO LIBBY? SHE'S INSIDE.

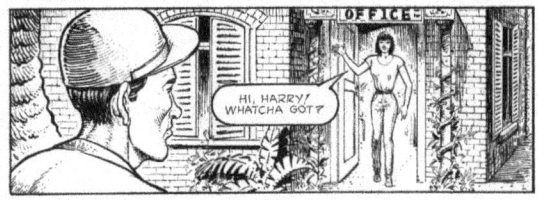

HI, HARRY! WHATCHA GOT?

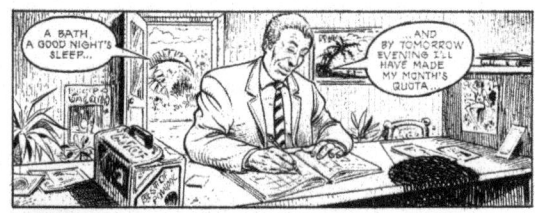

A BATH, A GOOD NIGHT'S SLEEP...

...AND BY TOMORROW EVENING I'LL HAVE MADE MY MONTH'S QUOTA.

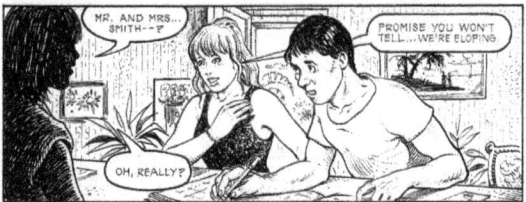

MR. AND MRS... SMITH--?

PROMISE YOU WON'T TELL...WE'RE ELOPING.

OH, REALLY?

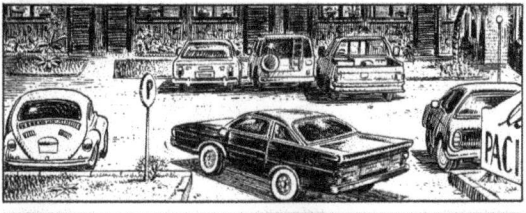

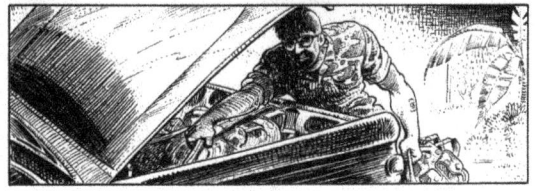

-LA PACIFICA pages.

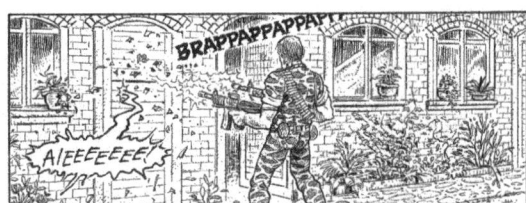

BRAPPAPPAPPAPP!

AIEEEEEEE!

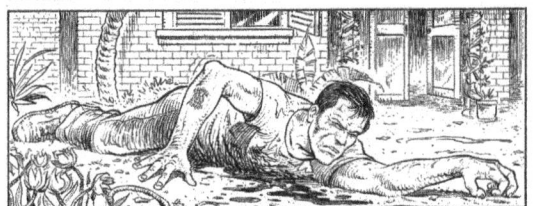

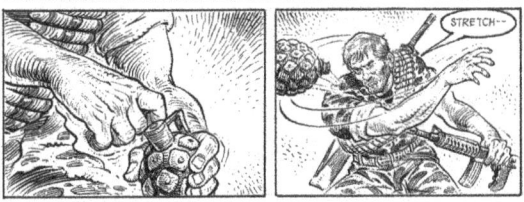

STRETCH--

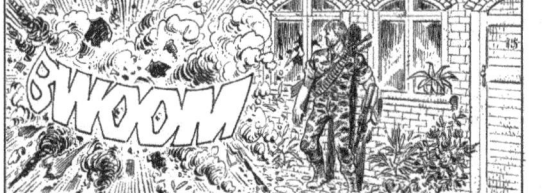

BWOOM

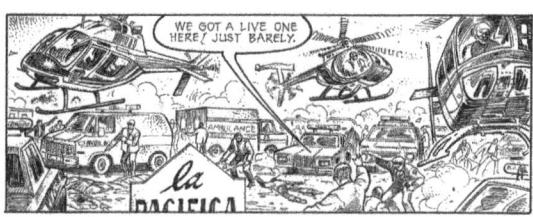

WE GOT A LIVE ONE HERE! JUST BARELY.

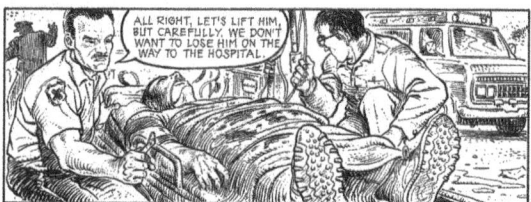

ALL RIGHT, LET'S LIFT HIM, BUT CAREFULLY. WE DON'T WANT TO LOSE HIM ON THE WAY TO THE HOSPITAL.

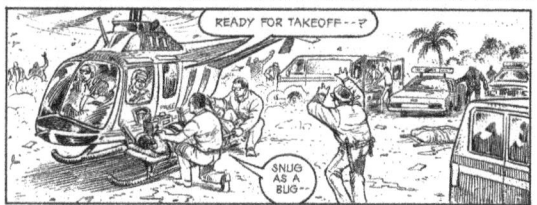

READY FOR TAKEOFF--?

SNUG AS A BUG--

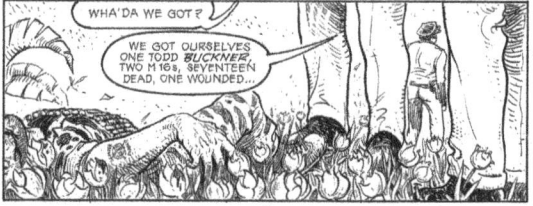

WHA'DA WE GOT?

WE GOT OURSELVES ONE TODD BUCKNER, TWO M16'S, SEVENTEEN DEAD, ONE WOUNDED...

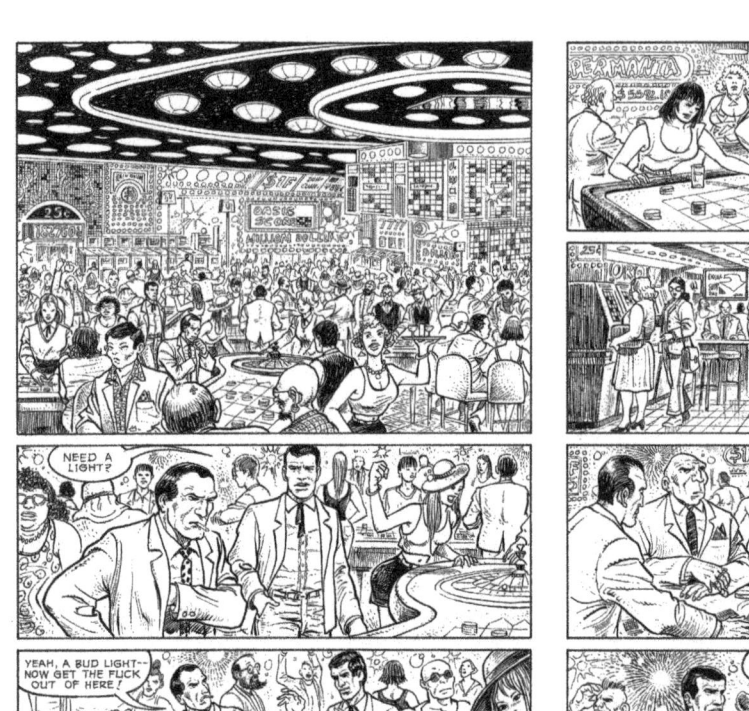

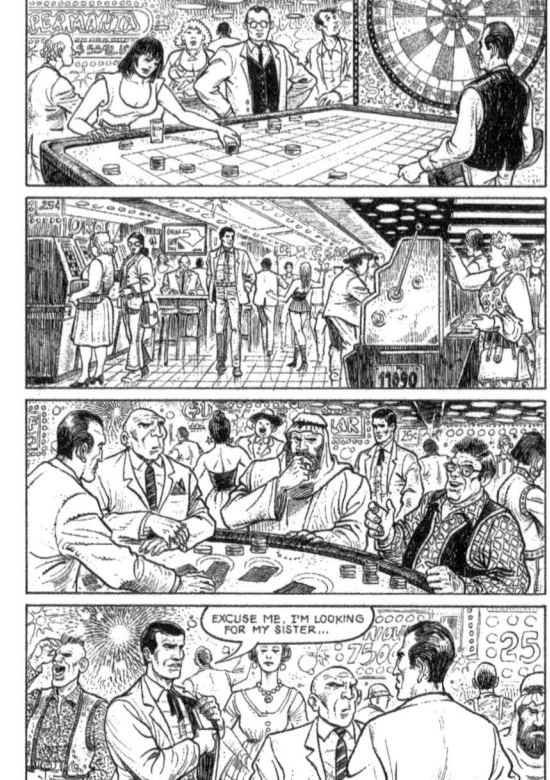

NEED A LIGHT?

YEAH, A BUD LIGHT-- NOW GET THE FUCK OUT OF HERE!

EXCUSE ME, I'M LOOKING FOR MY SISTER...

47

-*LA PACIFICA* pages.

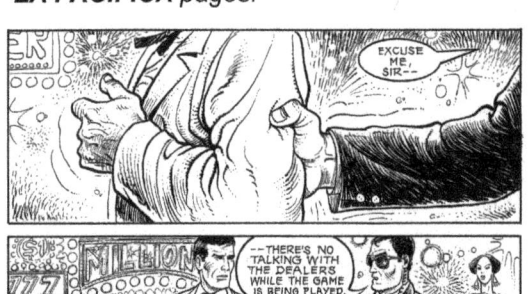

EXCUSE ME, SIR--

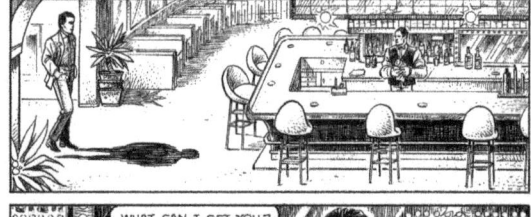

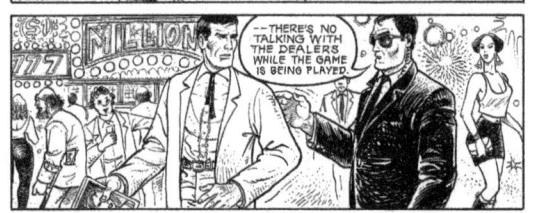

--THERE'S NO TALKING WITH THE DEALERS WHILE THE GAME IS BEING PLAYED.

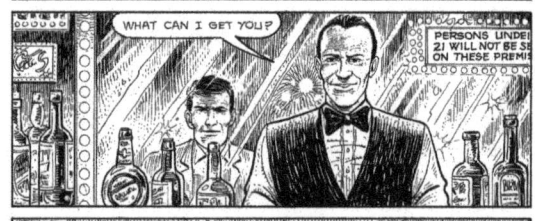

WHAT CAN I GET YOU?

PERSONS UNDER 21 WILL NOT BE SE ON THESE PREMIS

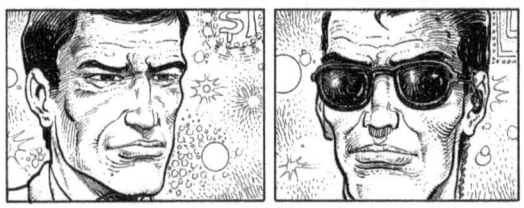

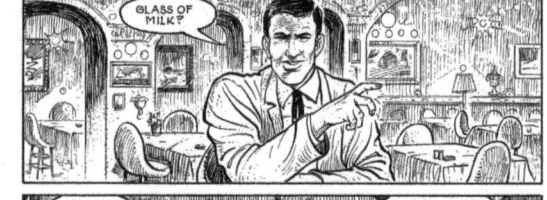

GLASS OF MILK?

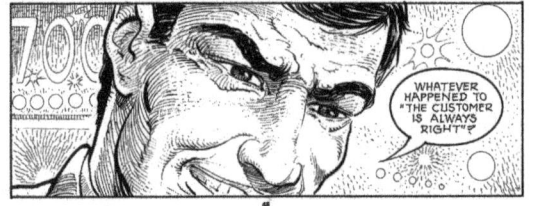

WHATEVER HAPPENED TO "THE CUSTOMER IS ALWAYS RIGHT"?

48

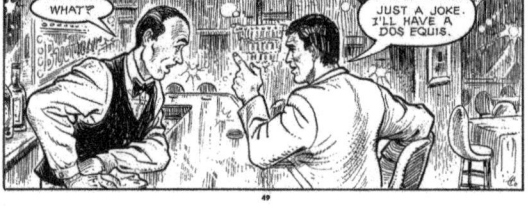

WHAT?

JUST A JOKE. I'LL HAVE A DOS EQUIS.

49

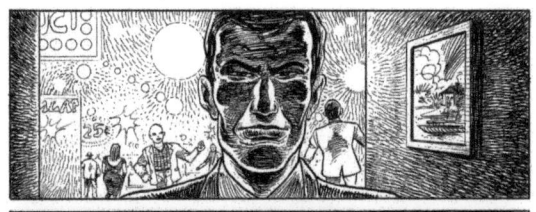

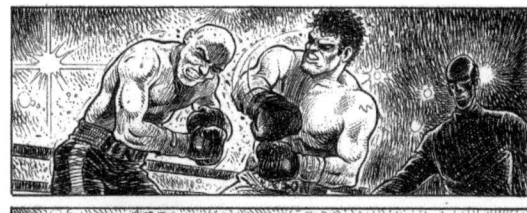

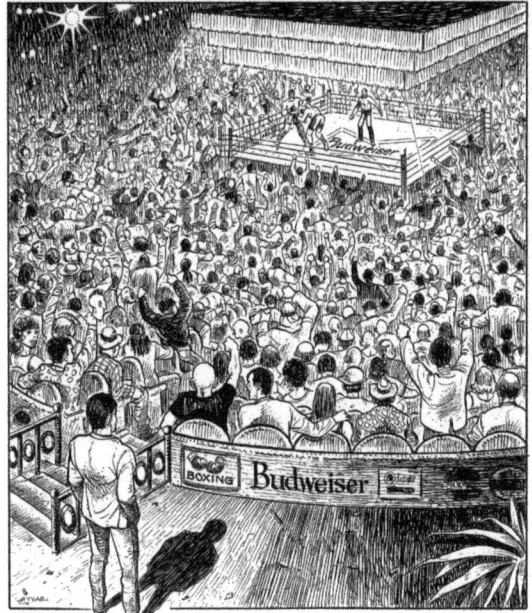

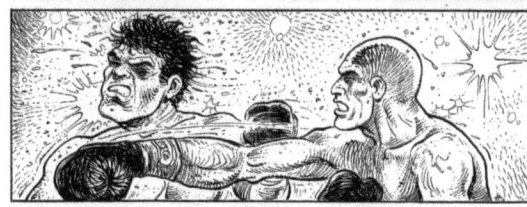

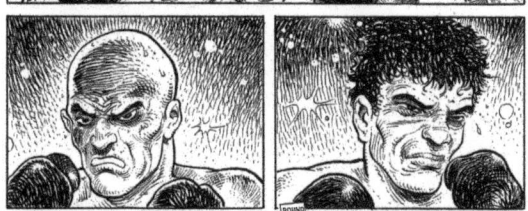

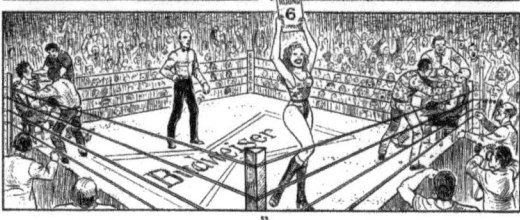

-LA PACIFICA pages goes on..

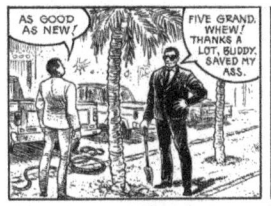

AS GOOD AS NEW!

FIVE GRAND. WHEW! THANKS A LOT, BUDDY. SAVED MY ASS.

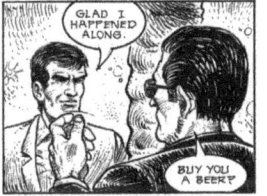

GLAD I HAPPENED ALONG.

BUY YOU A BEER?

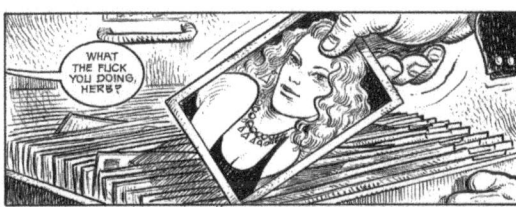

WHAT THE FUCK YOU DOING, HERB?

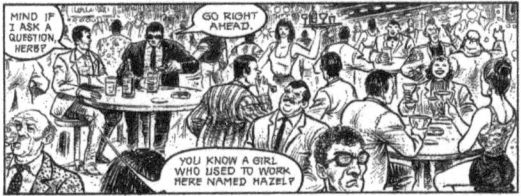

MIND IF I ASK A QUESTION, HERB?

GO RIGHT AHEAD.

YOU KNOW A GIRL WHO USED TO WORK HERE NAMED HAZEL?

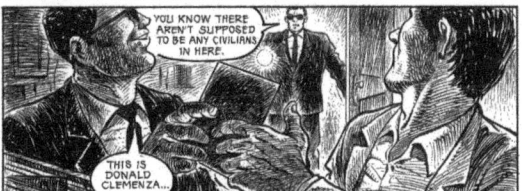

YOU KNOW THERE AREN'T SUPPOSED TO BE ANY CIVILIANS IN HERE.

THIS IS DONALD CLEMENZA...

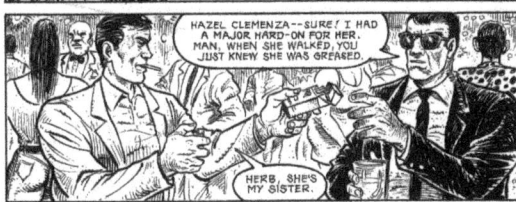

HAZEL CLEMENZA--SURE! I HAD A MAJOR HARD-ON FOR HER, MAN, WHEN SHE WALKED, YOU JUST KNEW SHE WAS GREASED.

HERB, SHE'S MY SISTER.

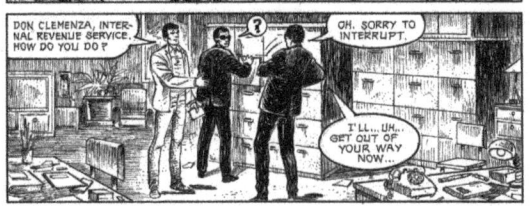

DON CLEMENZA, INTERNAL REVENUE SERVICE. HOW DO YOU DO?

OH, SORRY TO INTERRUPT.

I'LL...UH... GET OUT OF YOUR WAY NOW...

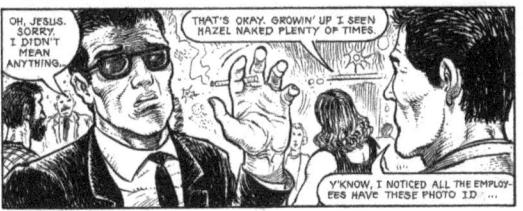

OH, JESUS. SORRY. I DIDN'T MEAN ANYTHING...

THAT'S OKAY. GROWIN' UP I SEEN HAZEL NAKED PLENTY OF TIMES.

Y'KNOW, I NOTICED ALL THE EMPLOYEES HAVE THESE PHOTO I.D. ...

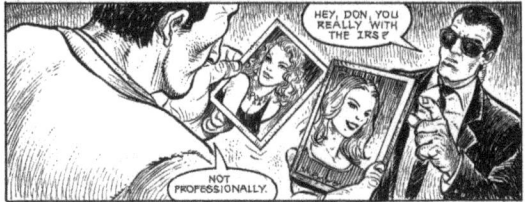

HEY, DON, YOU REALLY WITH THE IRS?

NOT PROFESSIONALLY.

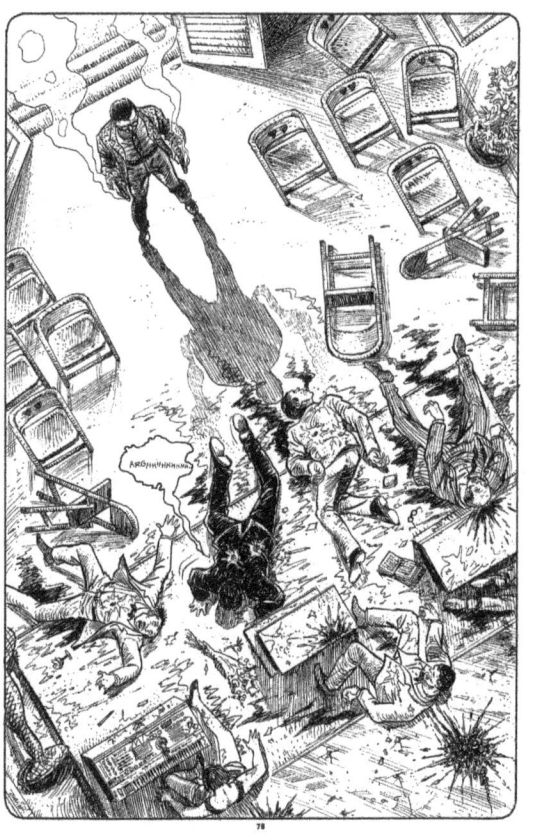

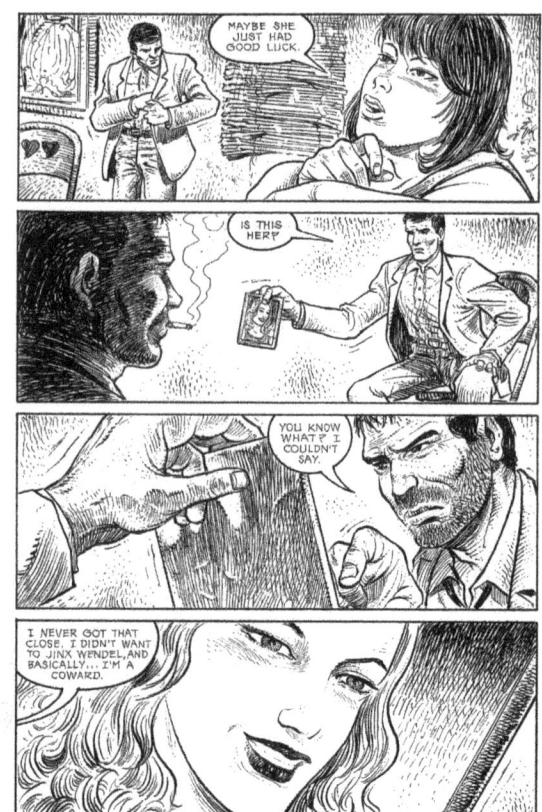

-More **LA PACIFICA** pages.

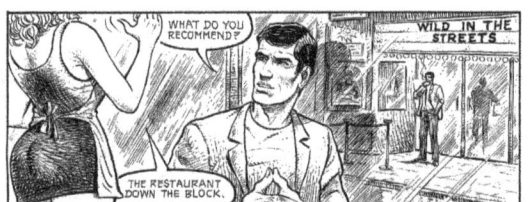

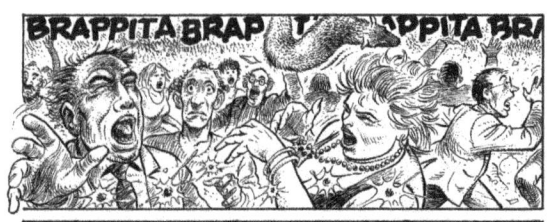

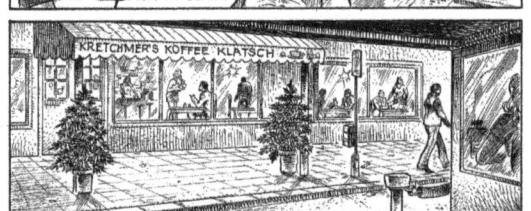

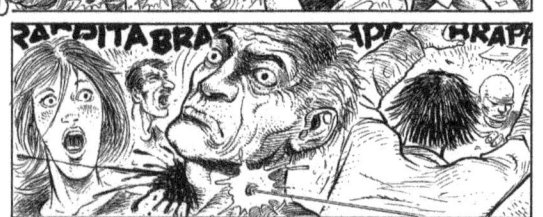

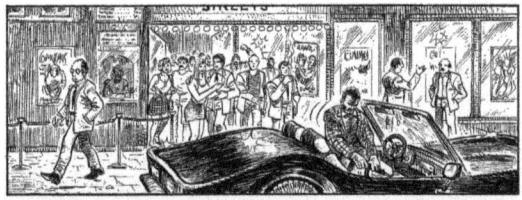

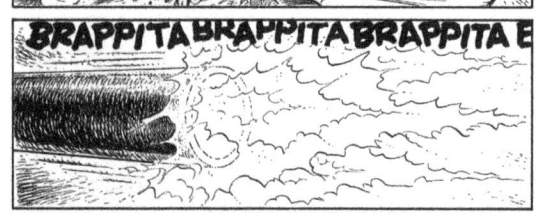

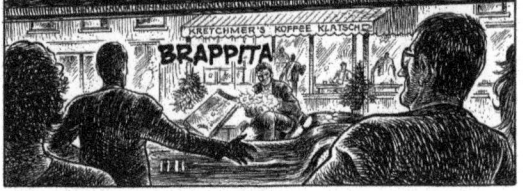

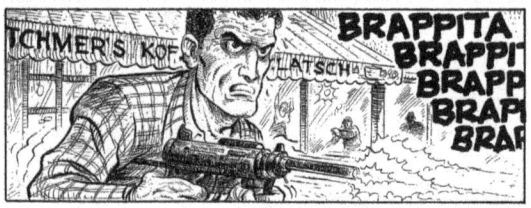

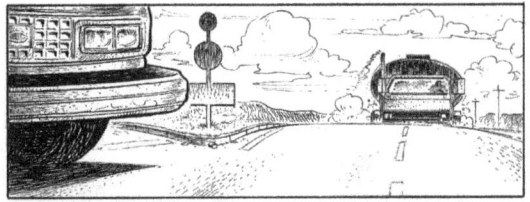

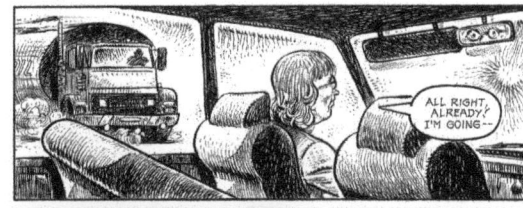

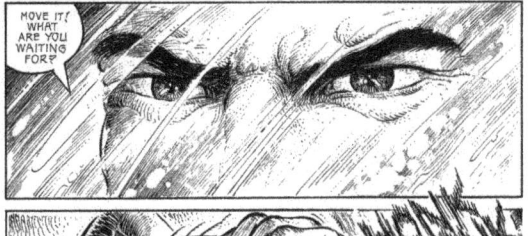

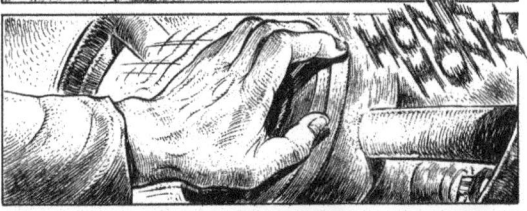

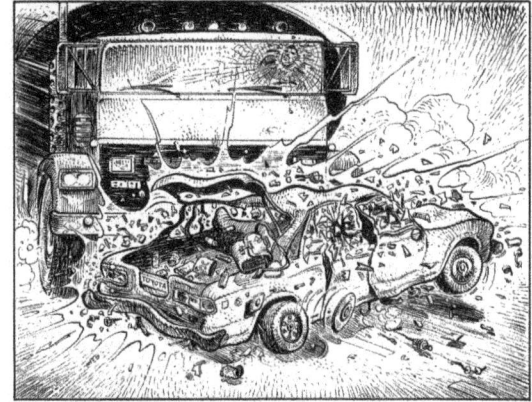

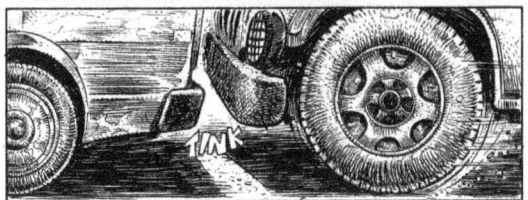

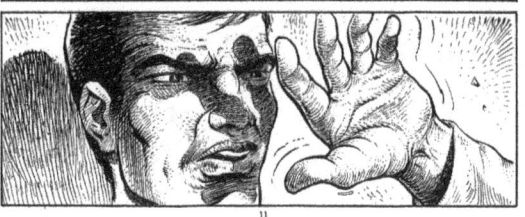

-LA PACIFICA pages.

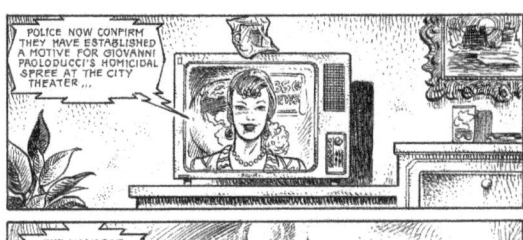

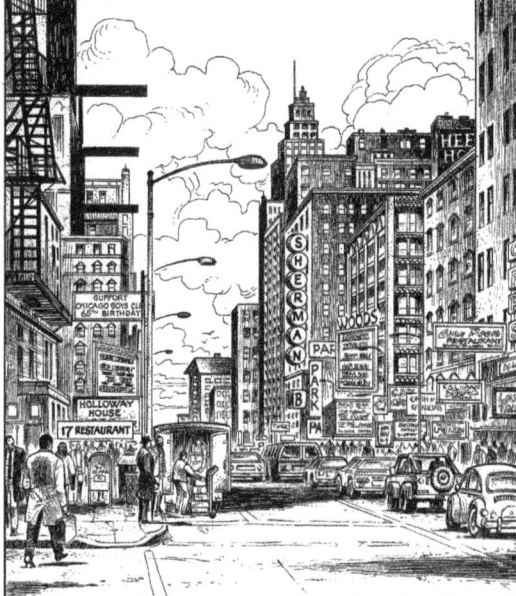

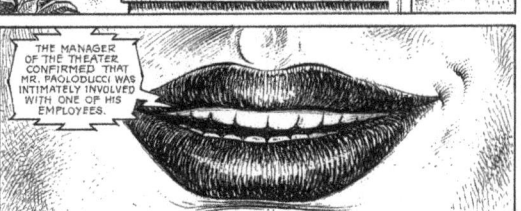

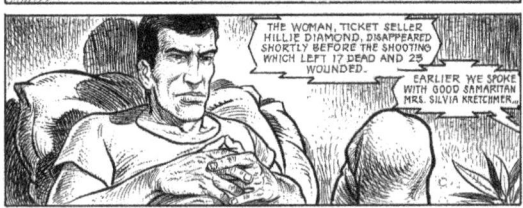

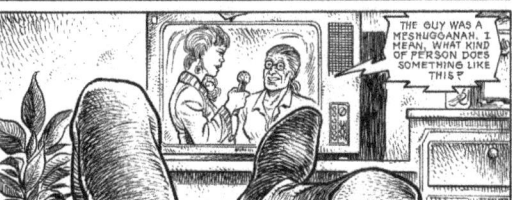

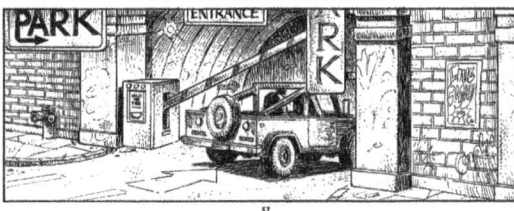

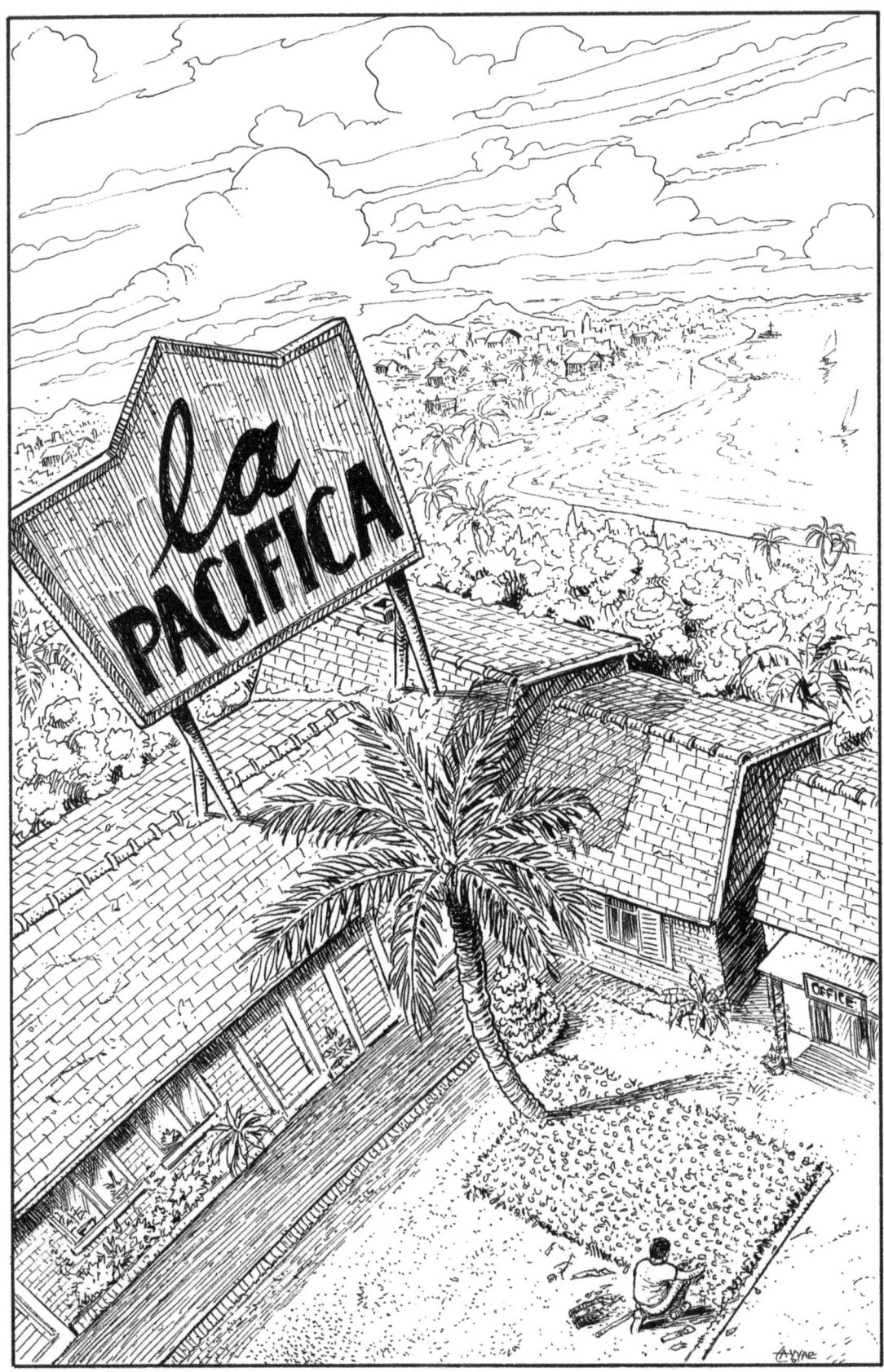

-LA PACIFICA full page.

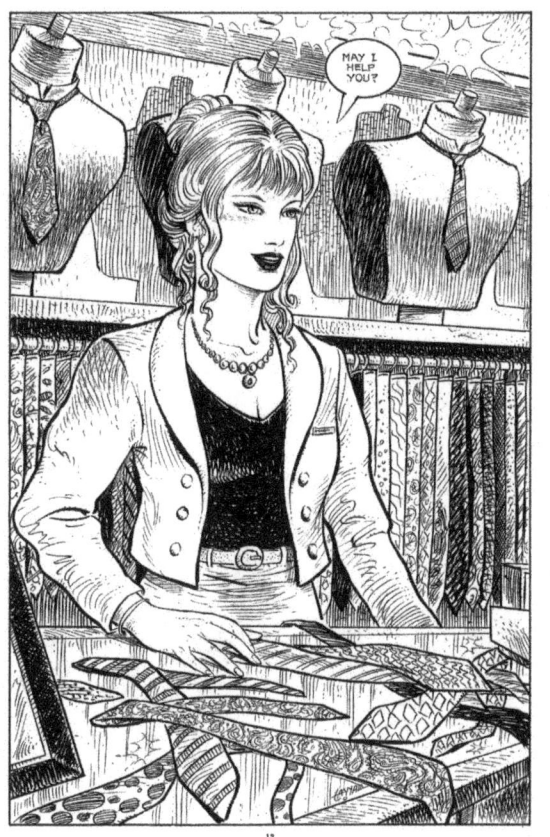

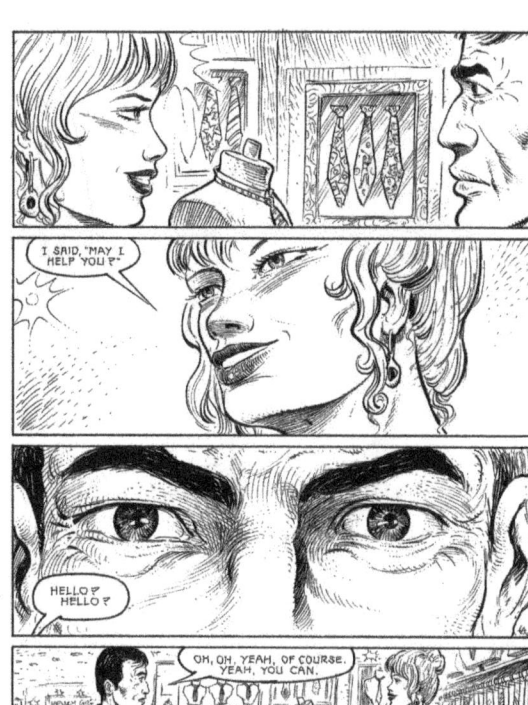

-*LA PACIFICA* pages.

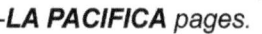

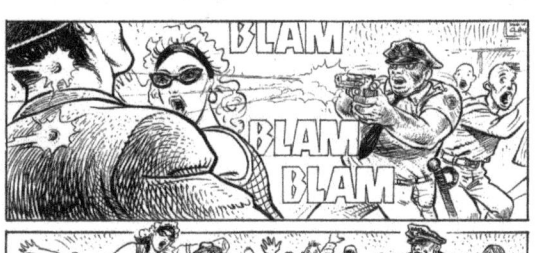

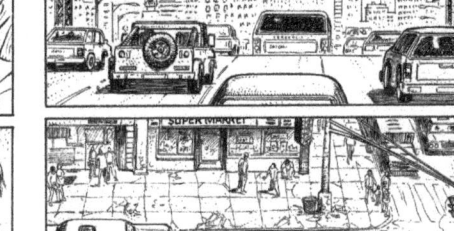

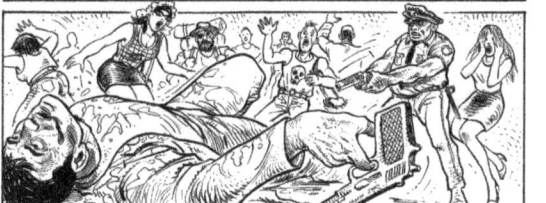

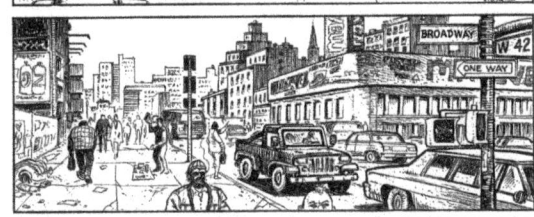

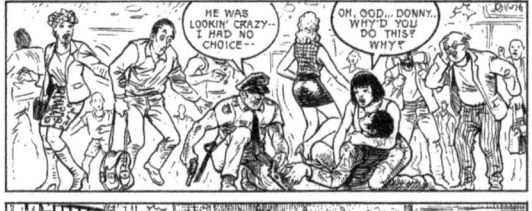

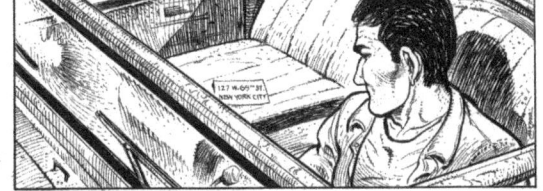

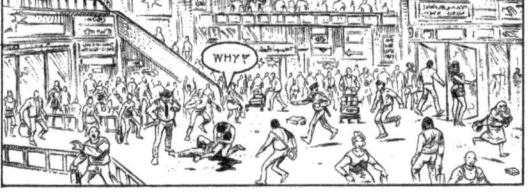

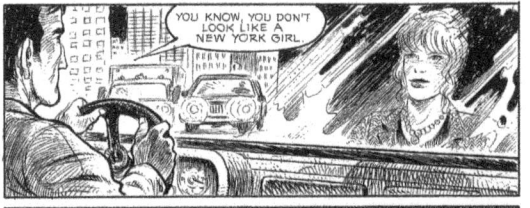

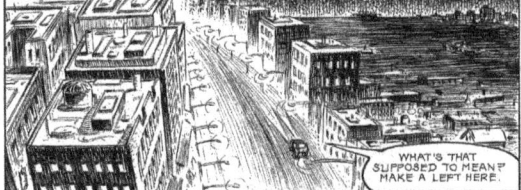

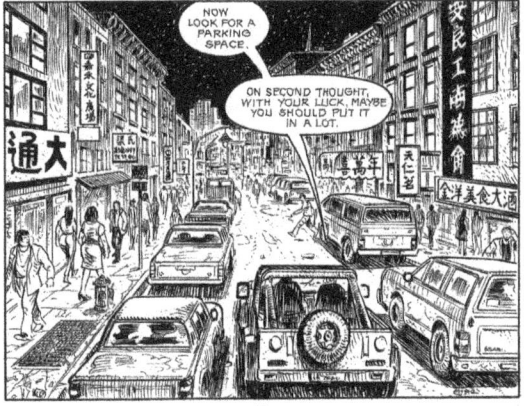

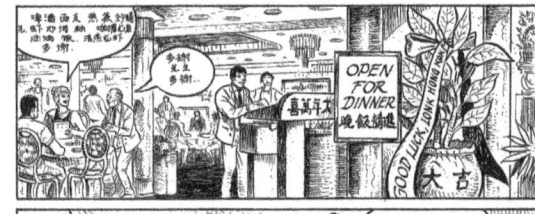

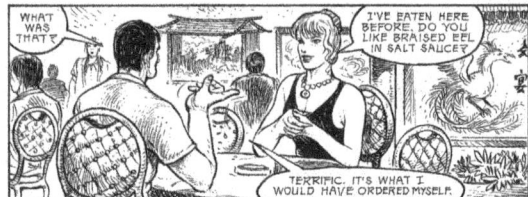

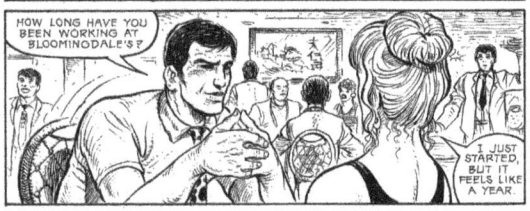

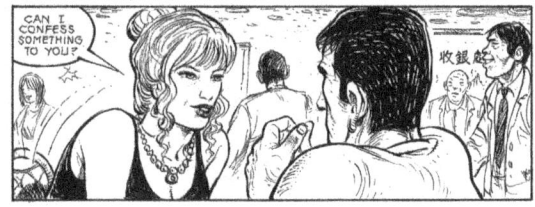

-LA PACIFICA pages.

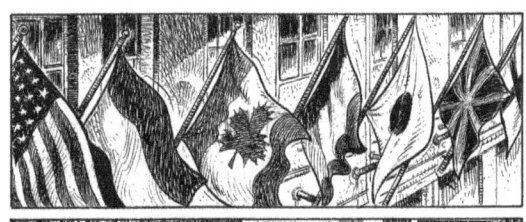

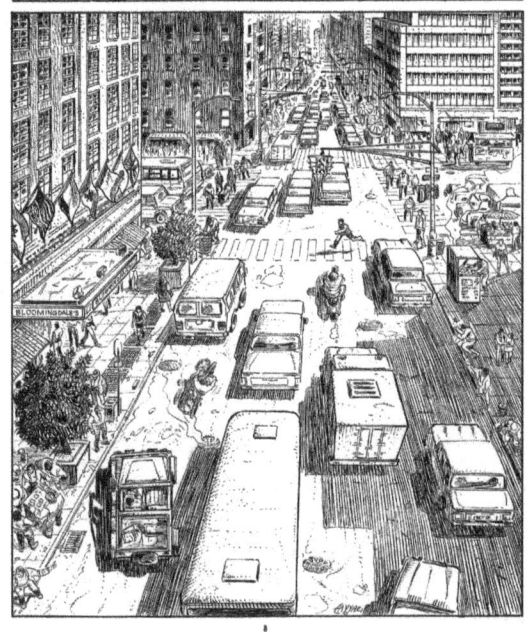

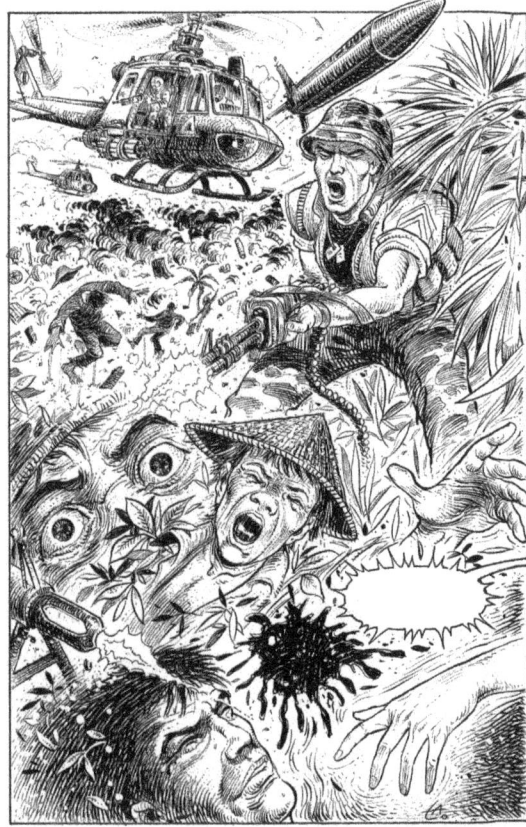

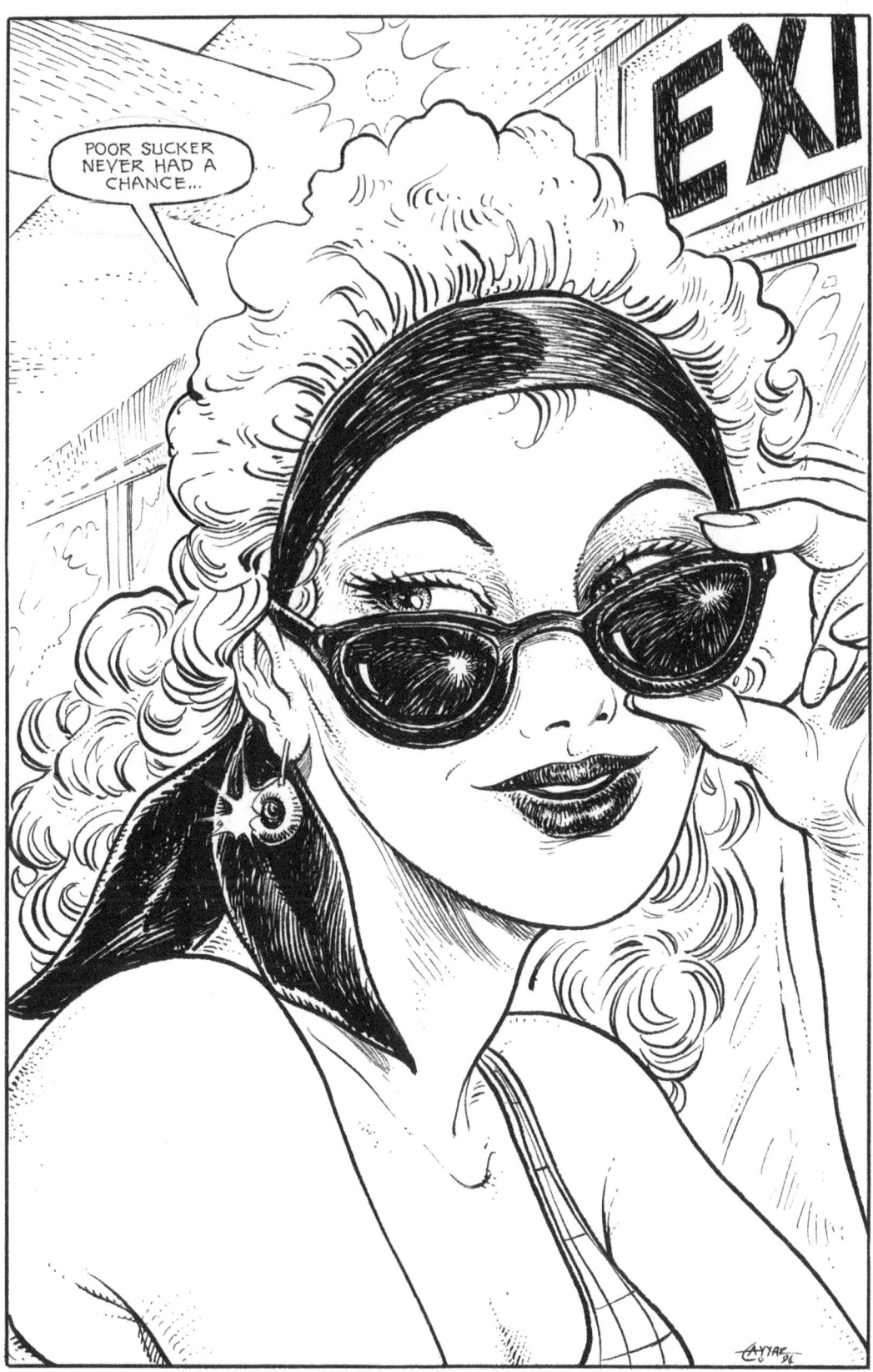

-*LA PACIFICA* full page.

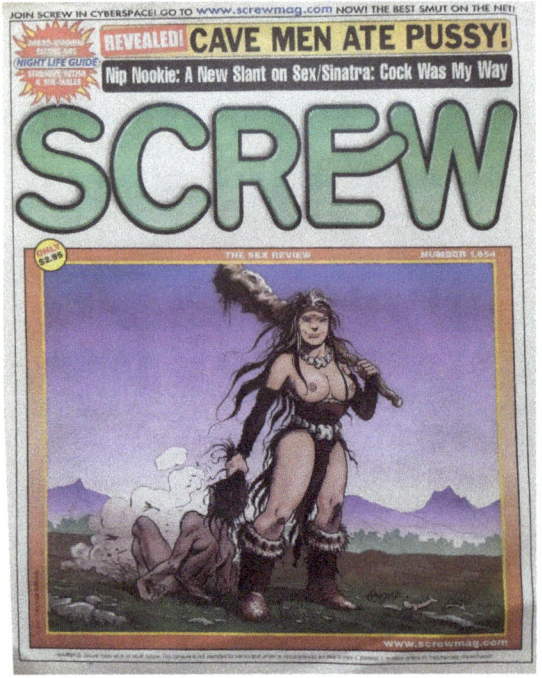

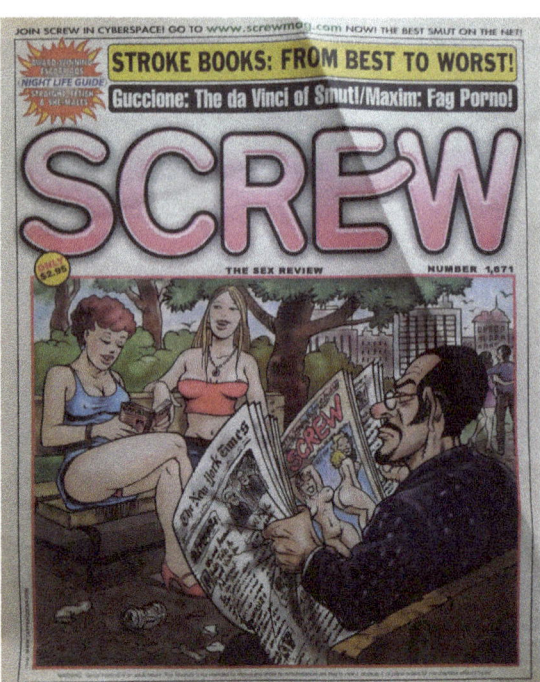

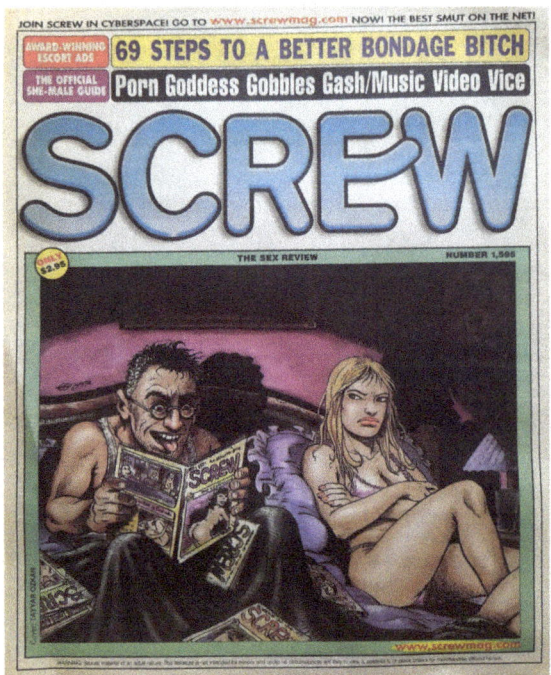

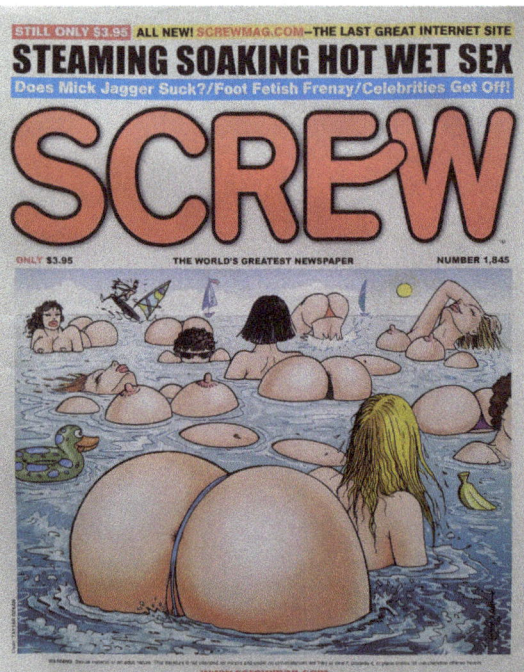

*-Some of the **cover drawings** for the popular erotic magazine '**SCREW**' in **NYC**.*

During the mid 90s *erotic publication* market grabbed my attention.
I've done many work in *USA* and *Europe* in that field.

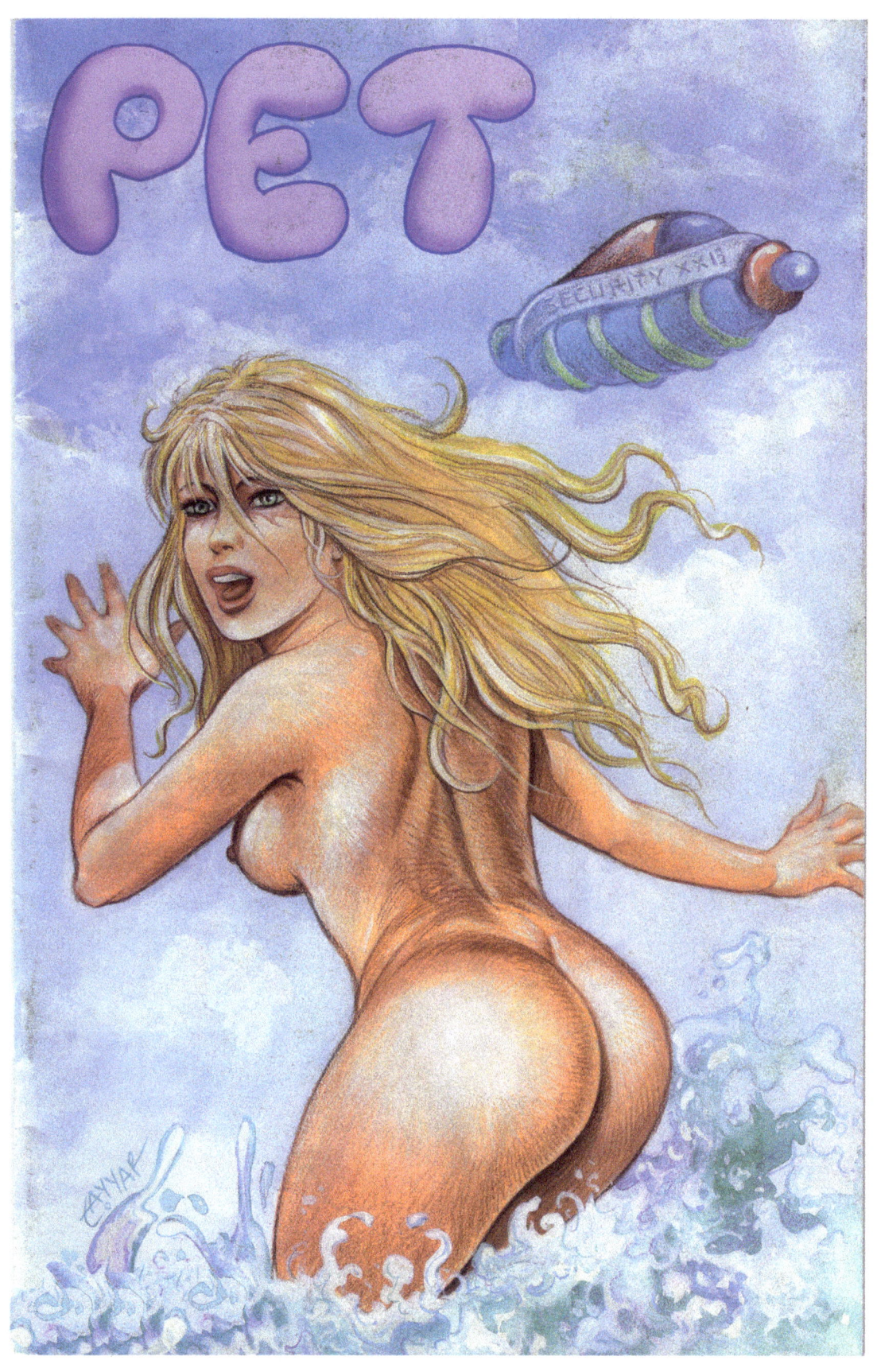

PET drawn for *Eros Comix*. 24 pages -1998

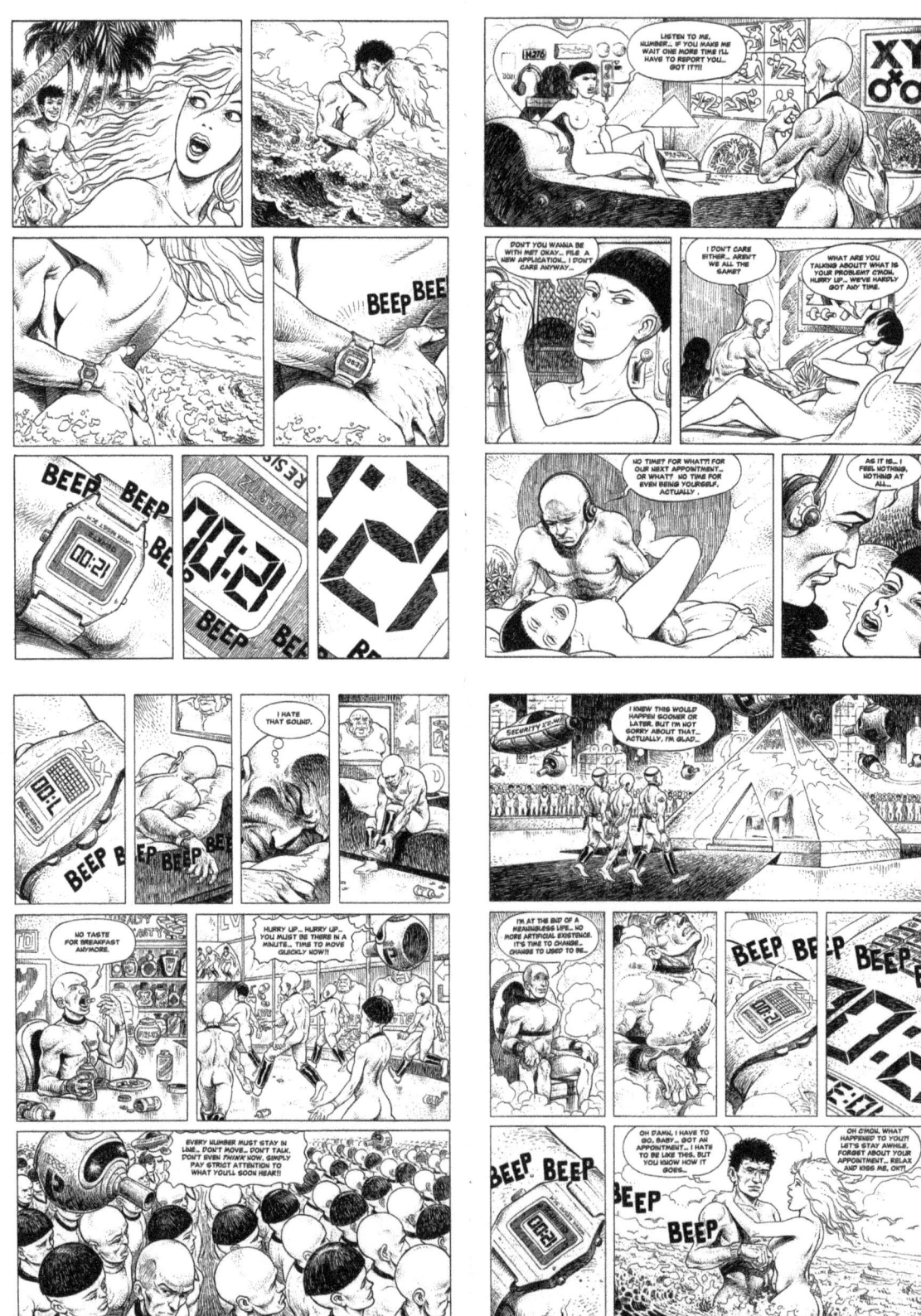

-PET pages.

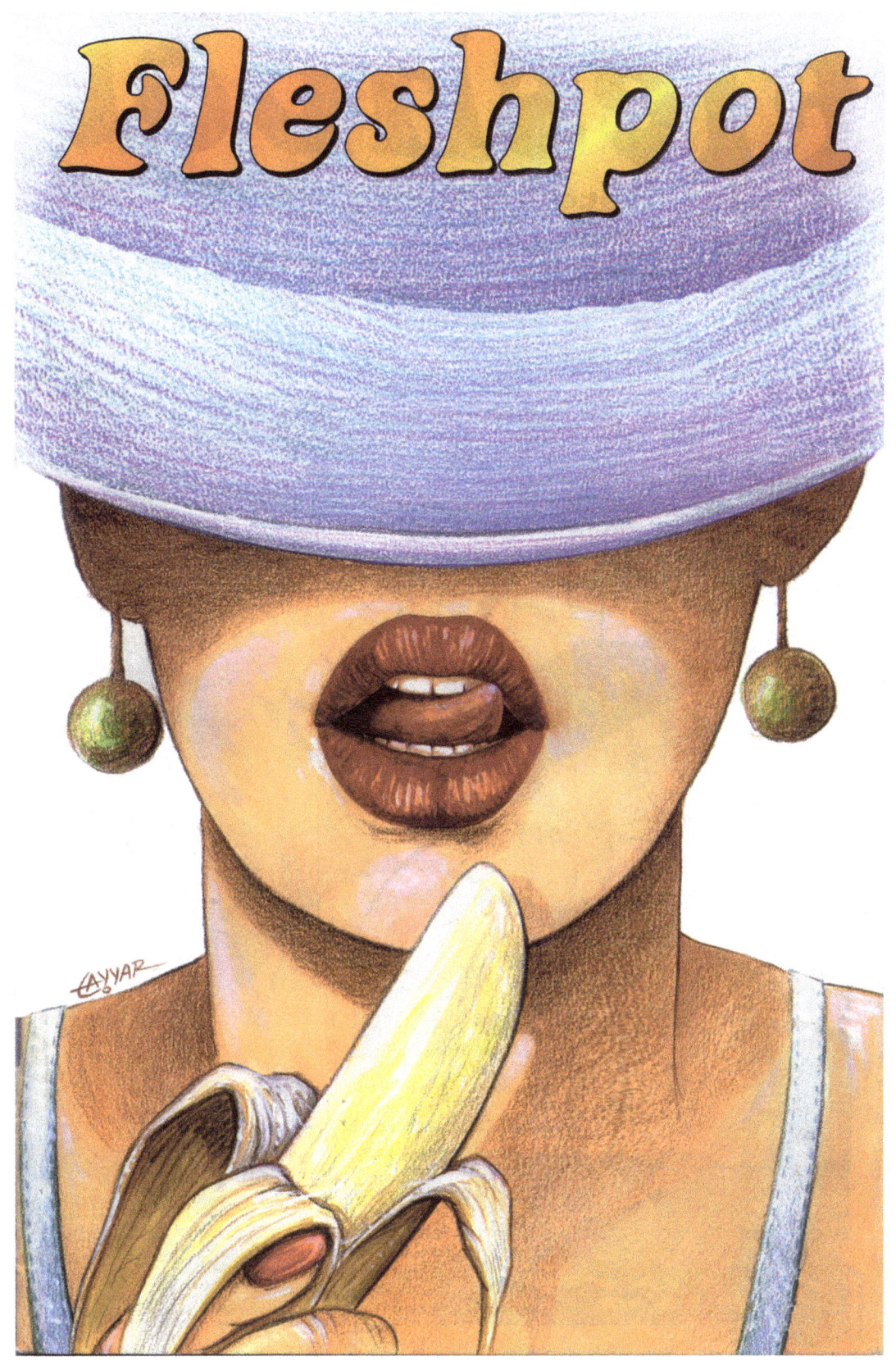

FLESHPOT drawn for *Eros Comix*. 24 pages -1997.

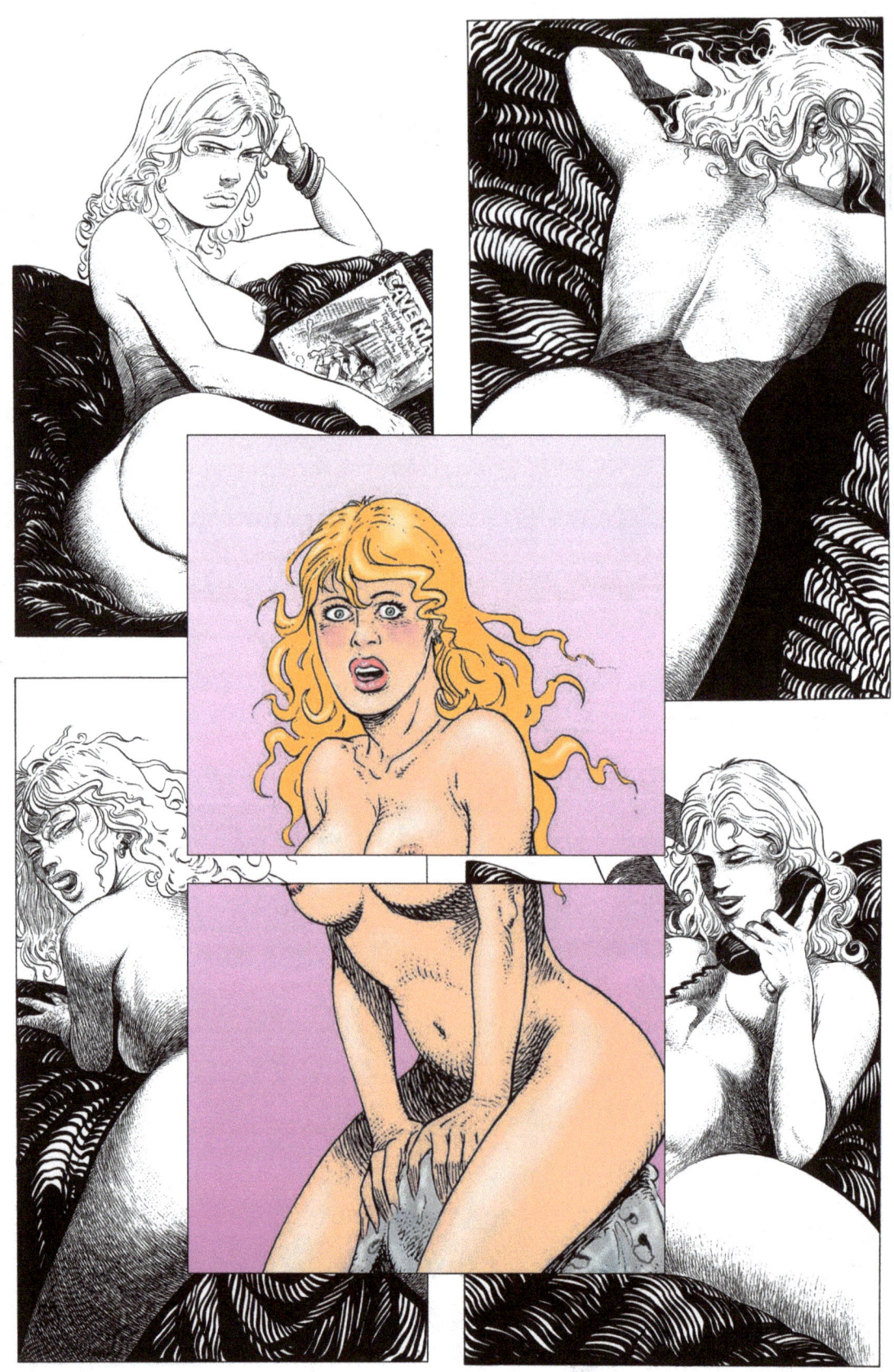

-FLESHPOT pages.

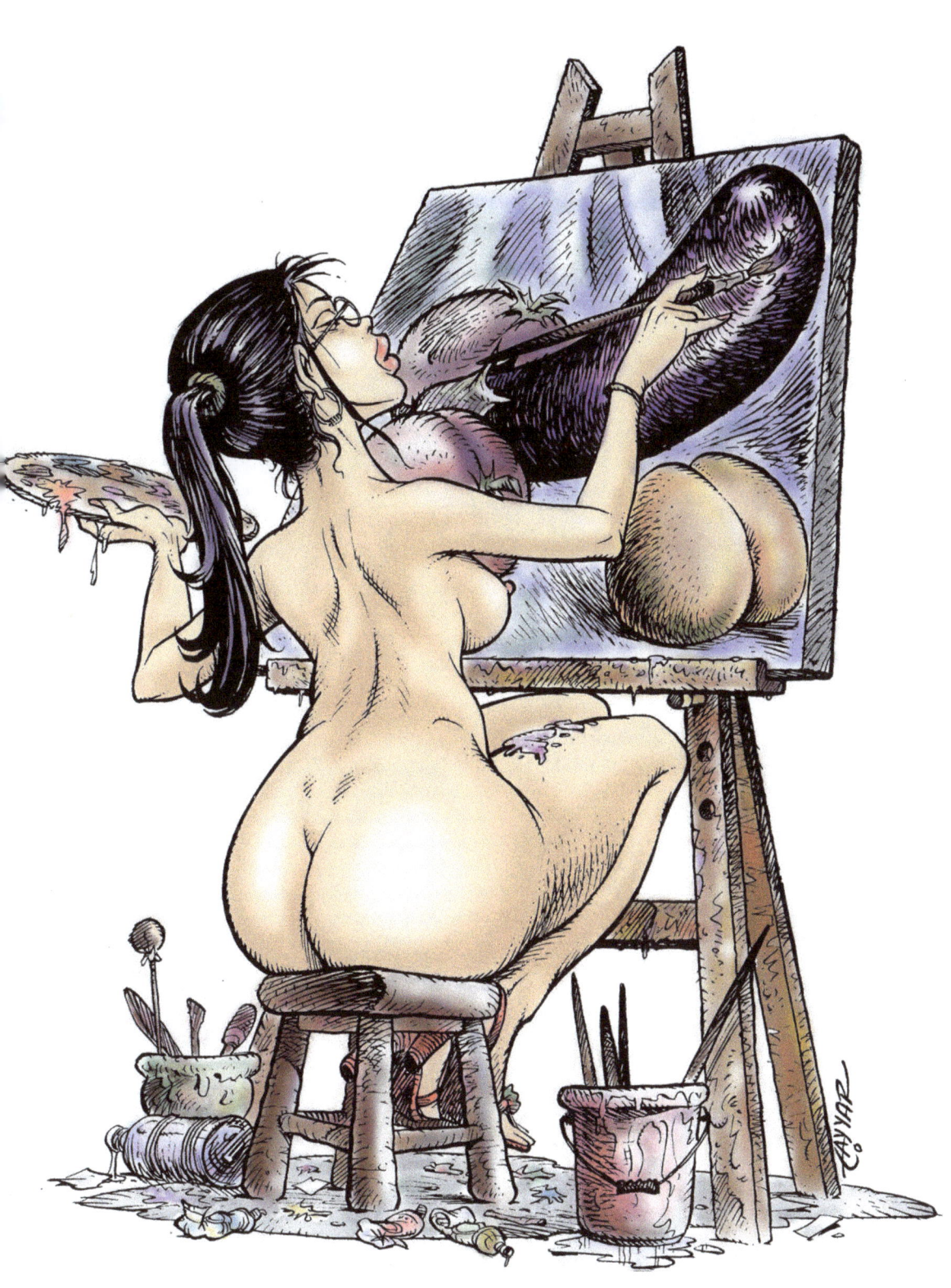

ORIENT SEXPRESS-1 drawn for *Eros Comix* while I was in *China* -2001

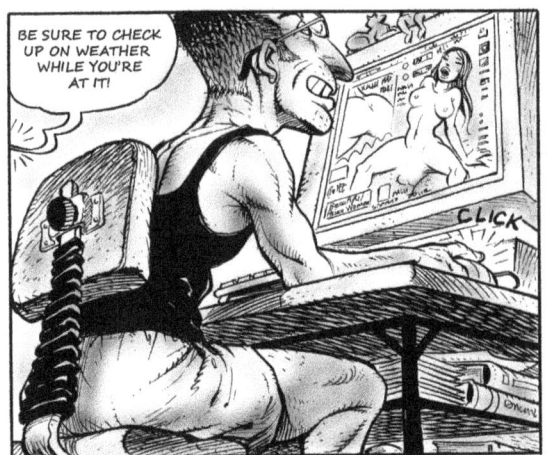

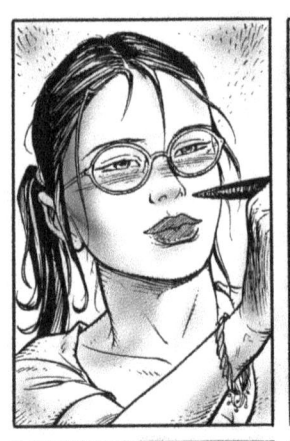

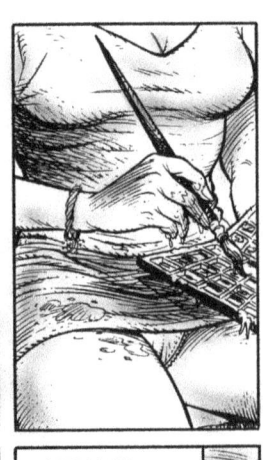

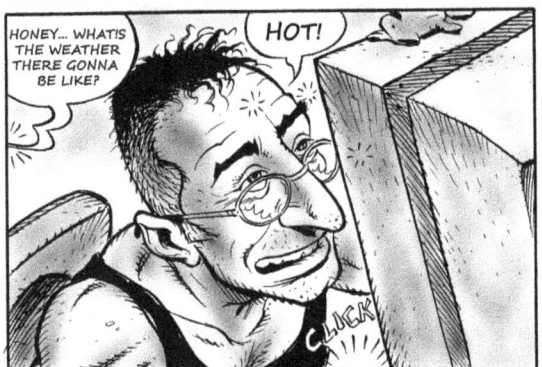

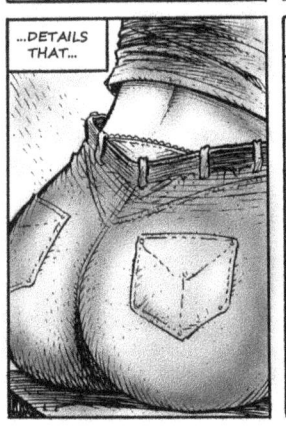

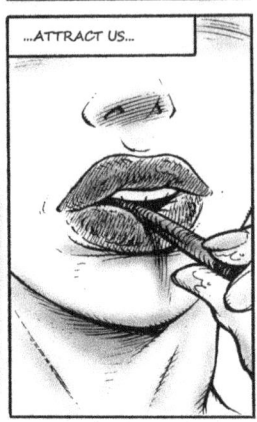

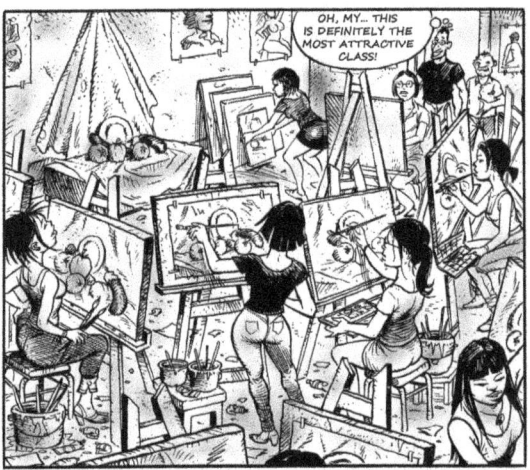

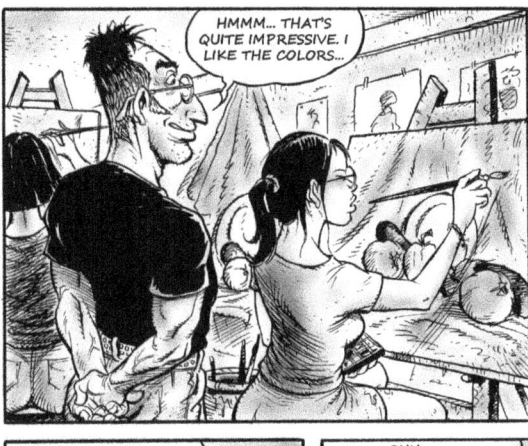

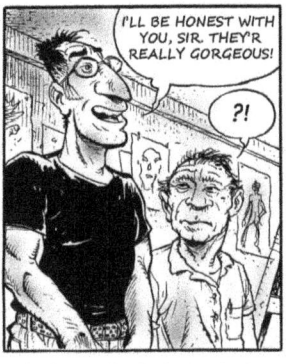

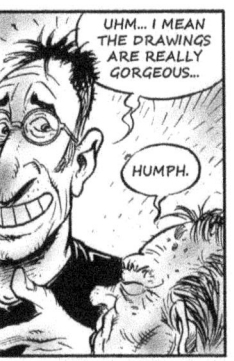

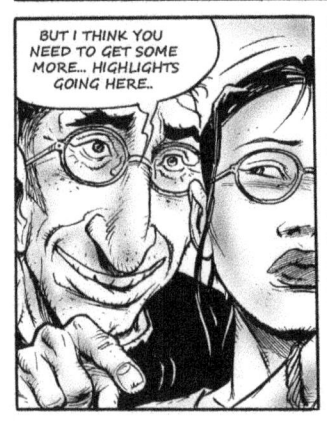

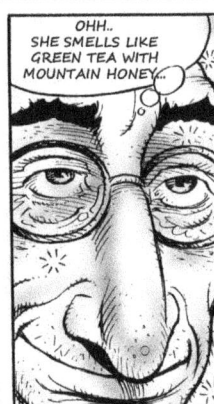

-ORIENT SEXPRESS-1 random pages.

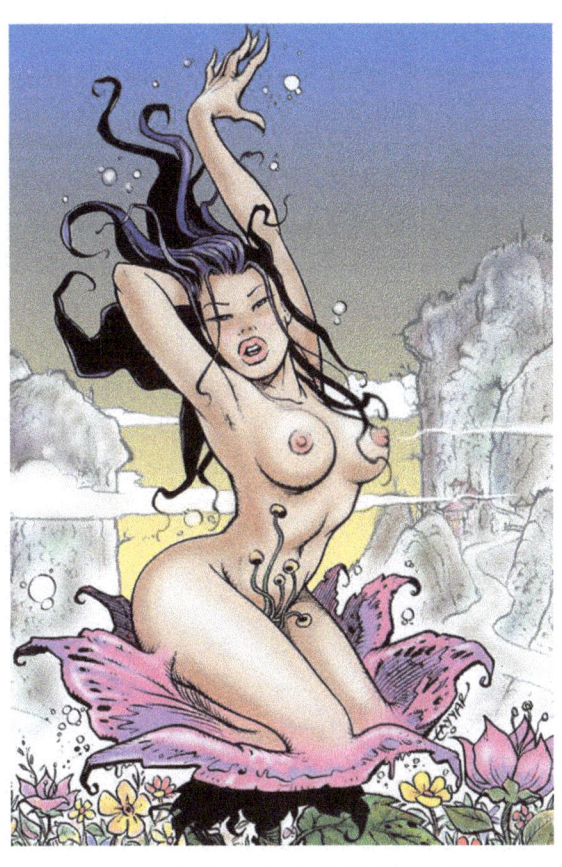

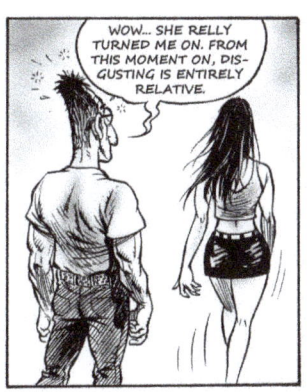

WOW... SHE RELLY TURNED ME ON. FROM THIS MOMENT ON, DISGUSTING IS ENTIRELY RELATIVE.

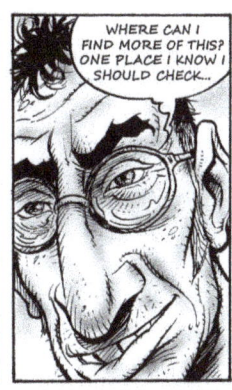

WHERE CAN I FIND MORE OF THIS? ONE PLACE I KNOW I SHOULD CHECK...

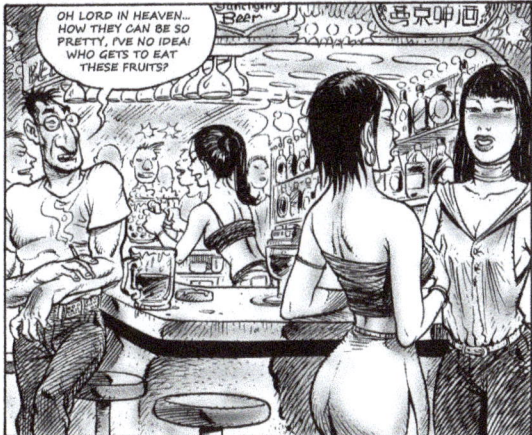

OH LORD IN HEAVEN... HOW THEY CAN BE SO PRETTY, I'VE NO IDEA! WHO GETS TO EAT THESE FRUITS?

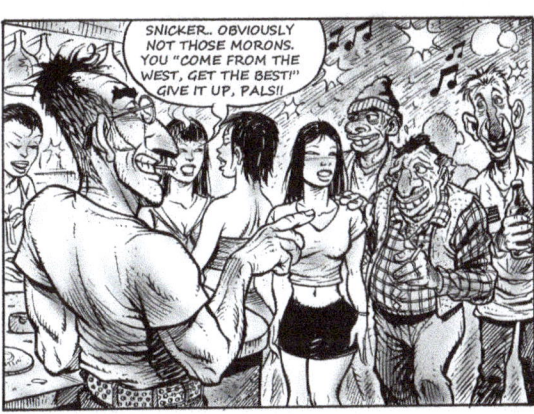

SNICKER... OBVIOUSLY NOT THOSE MORONS. YOU "COME FROM THE WEST, GET THE BEST!" GIVE IT UP, PALS!!

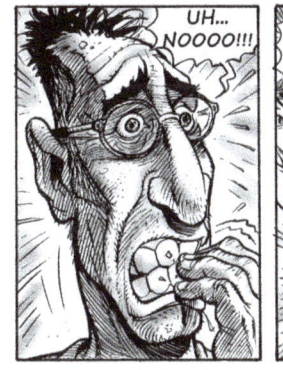

UH... NOOOO!!!!

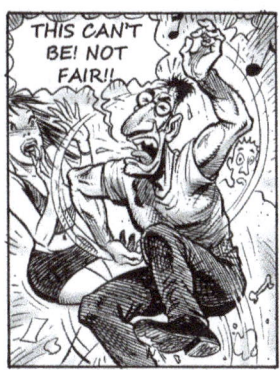

THIS CAN'T BE! NOT FAIR!!

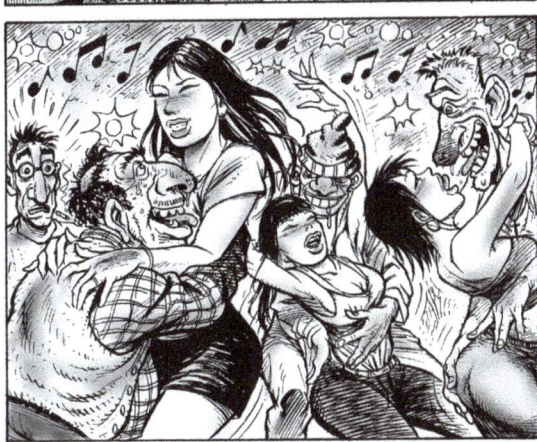

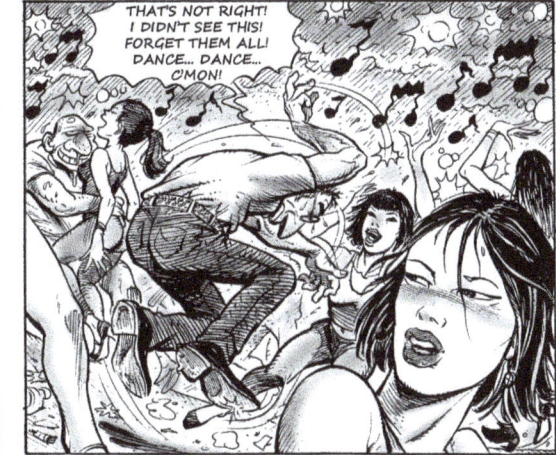

THAT'S NOT RIGHT! I DIDN'T SEE THIS! FORGET THEM ALL! DANCE... DANCE... C'MON!

-ORIENT SEXPRESS-2 Drawn for **Eros Comix** while I was in **China** as well -2001

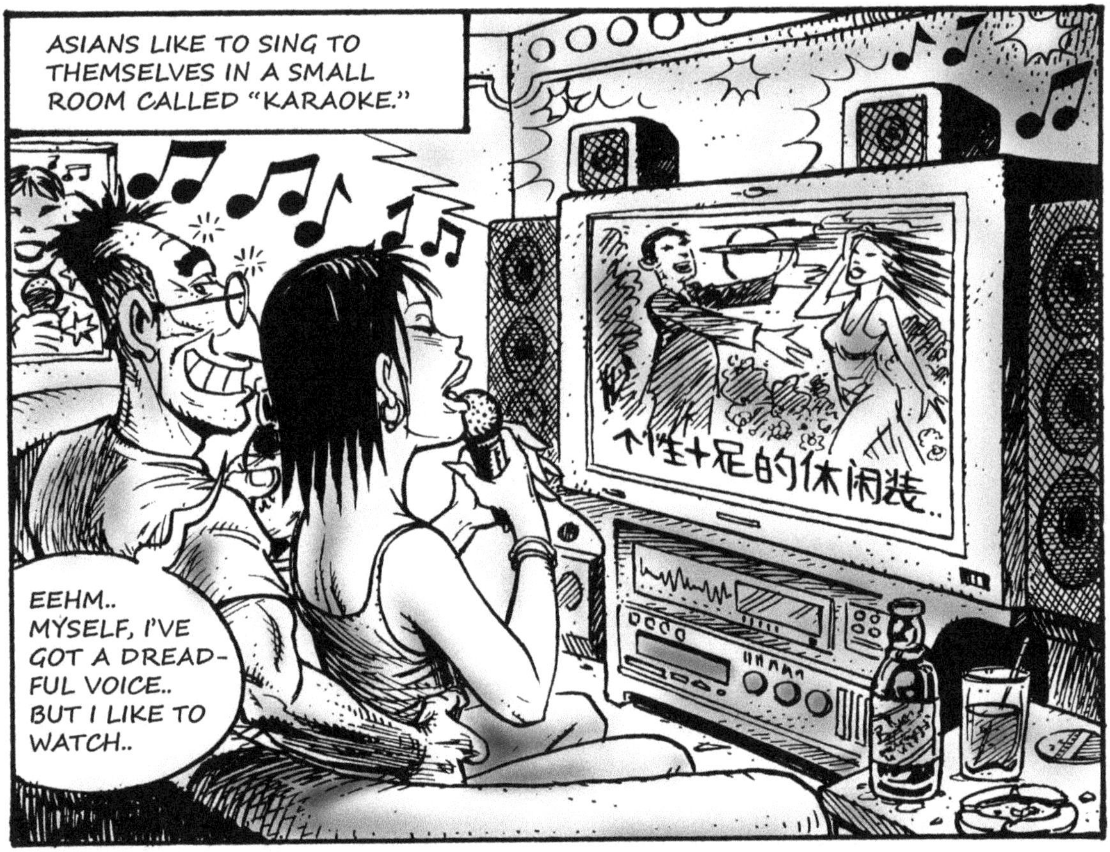

ASIANS LIKE TO SING TO THEMSELVES IN A SMALL ROOM CALLED "KARAOKE."

EEHM.. MYSELF, I'VE GOT A DREADFUL VOICE.. BUT I LIKE TO WATCH..

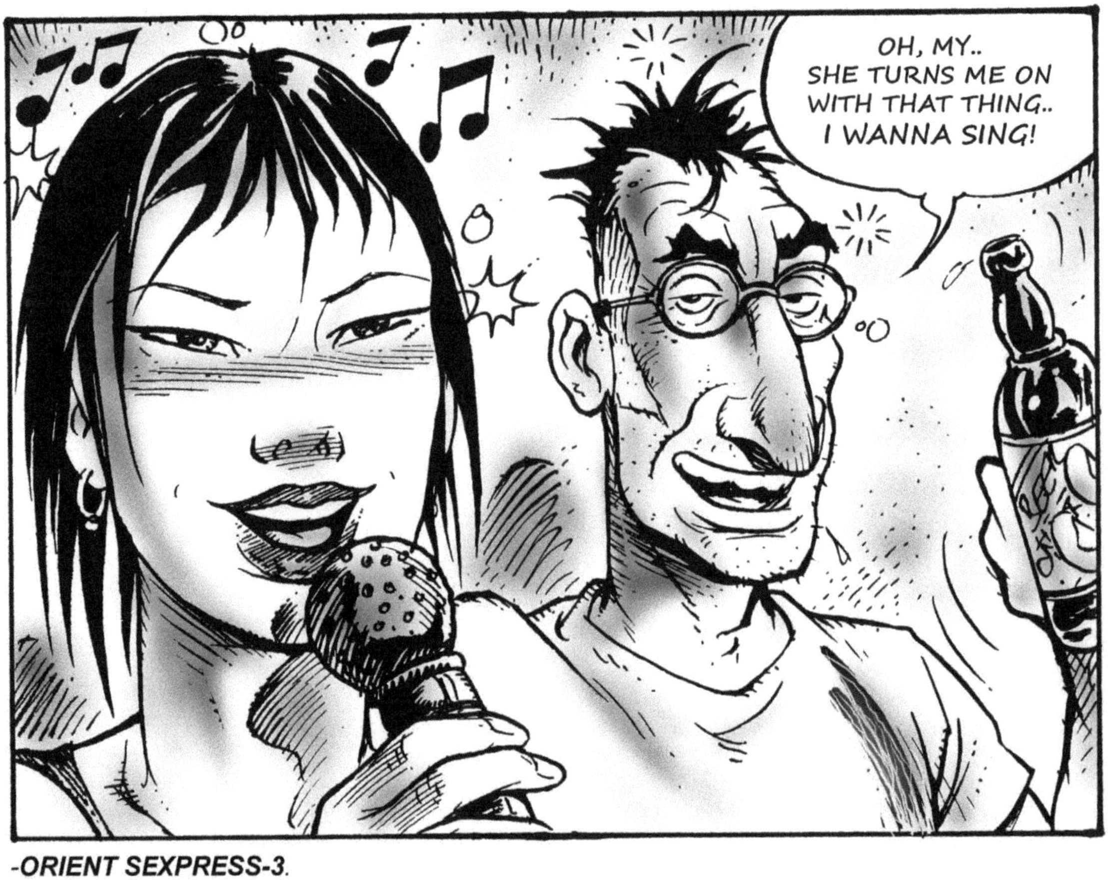

OH, MY.. SHE TURNS ME ON WITH THAT THING.. I WANNA SING!

-ORIENT SEXPRESS-3.

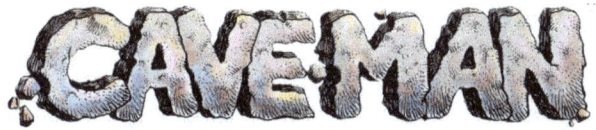

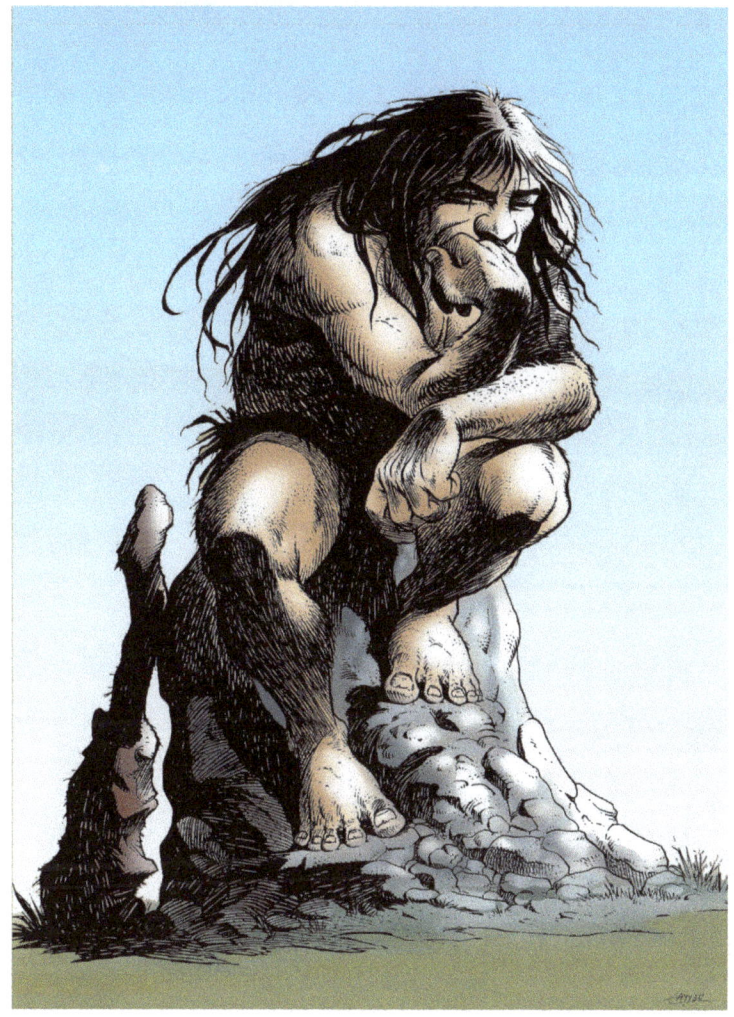

-These are the pages from my well know comic strips
called *CAVEMAN*.
I've been drawing this comic character since 1986.
All stories are *published* in the *world wide market* in many papers and
magazines (such as famous *Heavy Metal Illustrated Magazine*).
They all are also collected as a graphic novels in many countries for decades.
I still continue working on the character under the title of
"The AGE of the CAVEMAN".

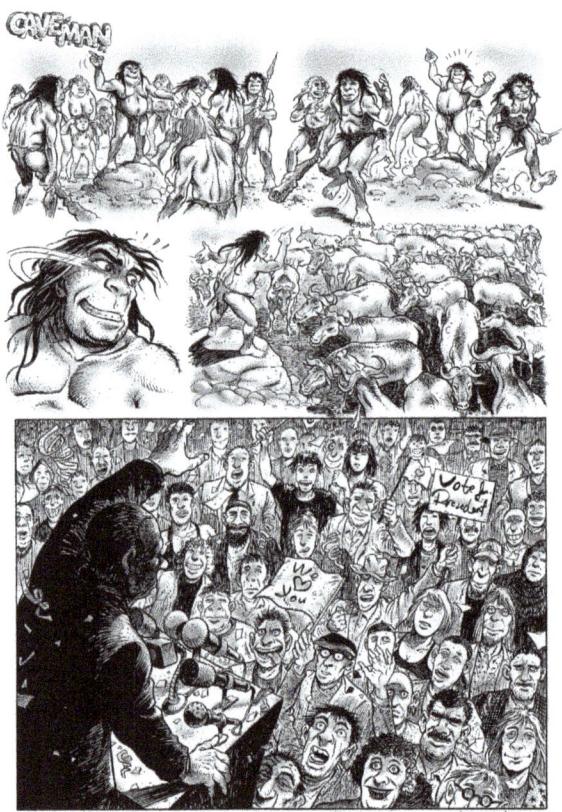

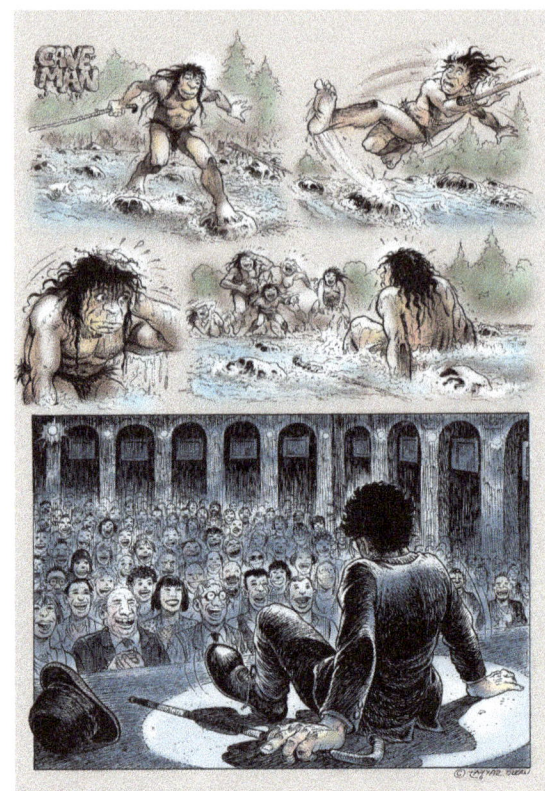

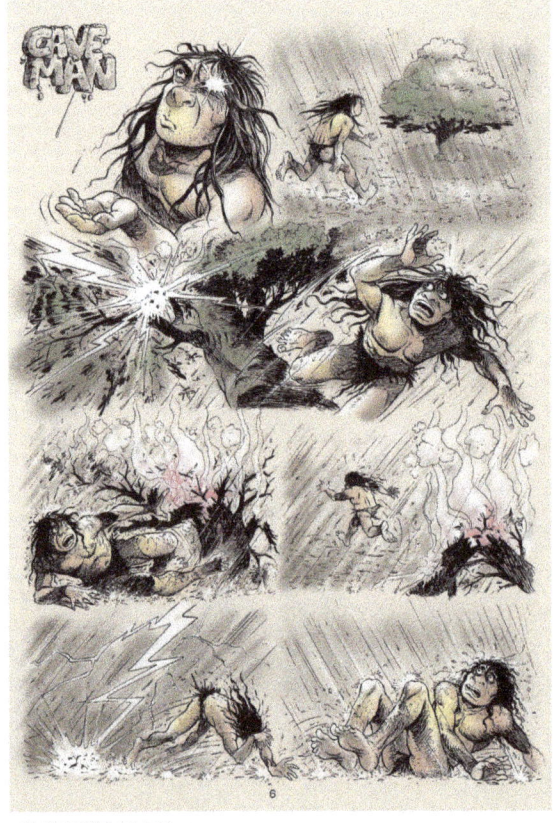

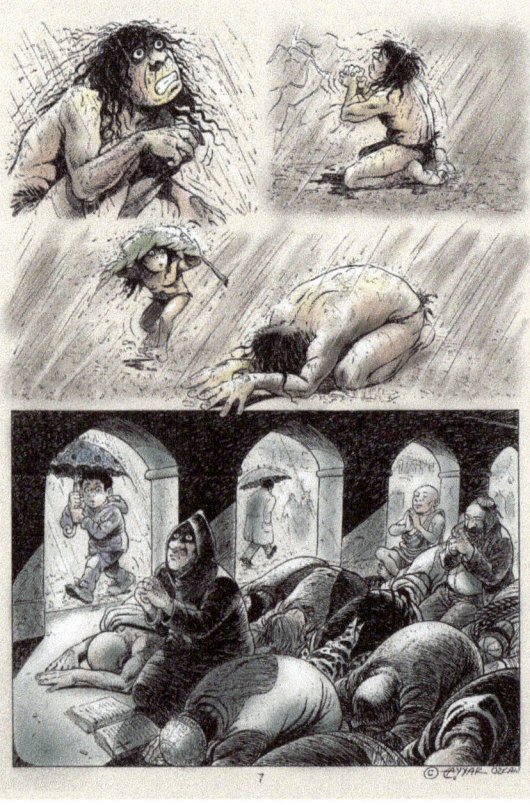

-*CAVEMAN* Pages..

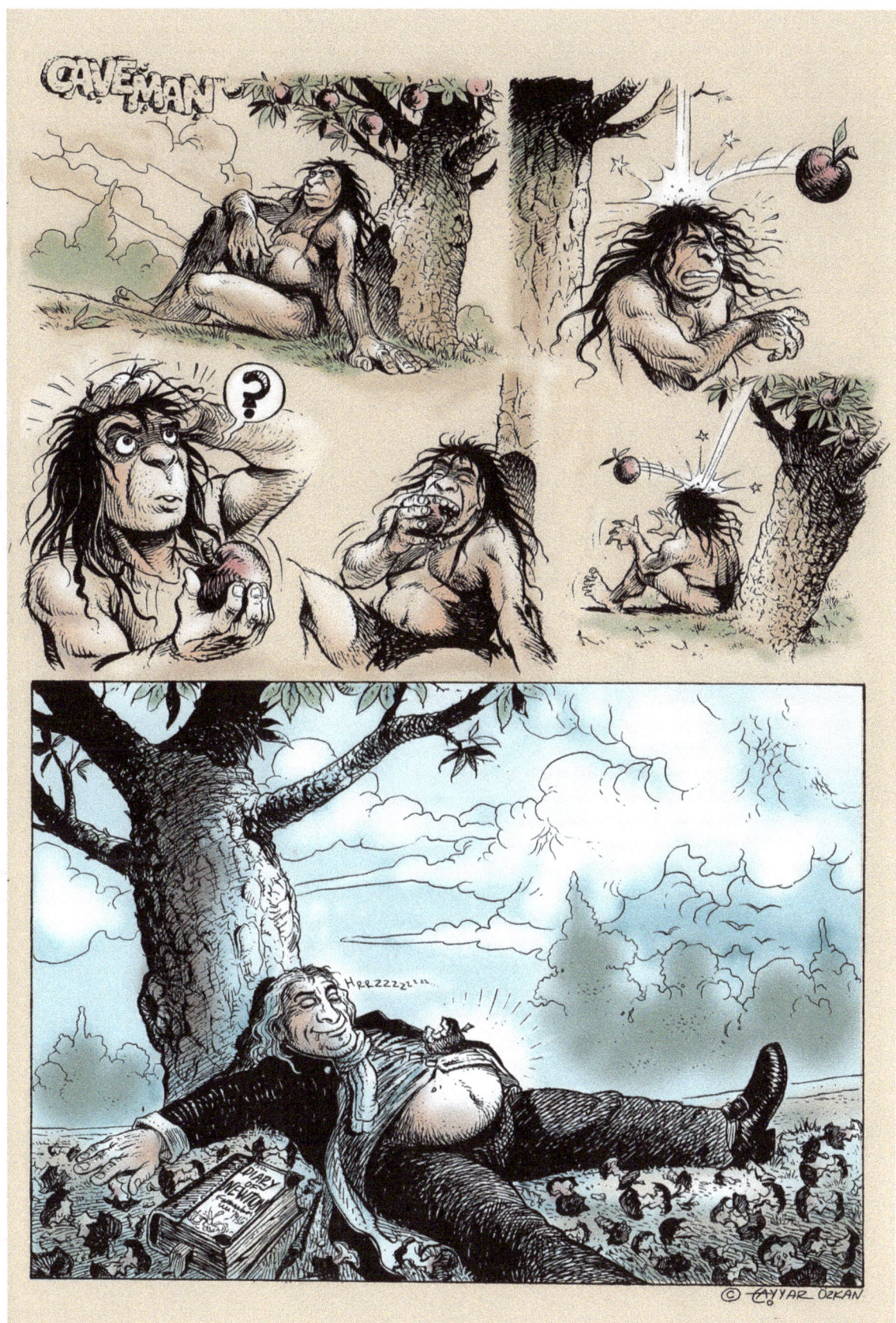

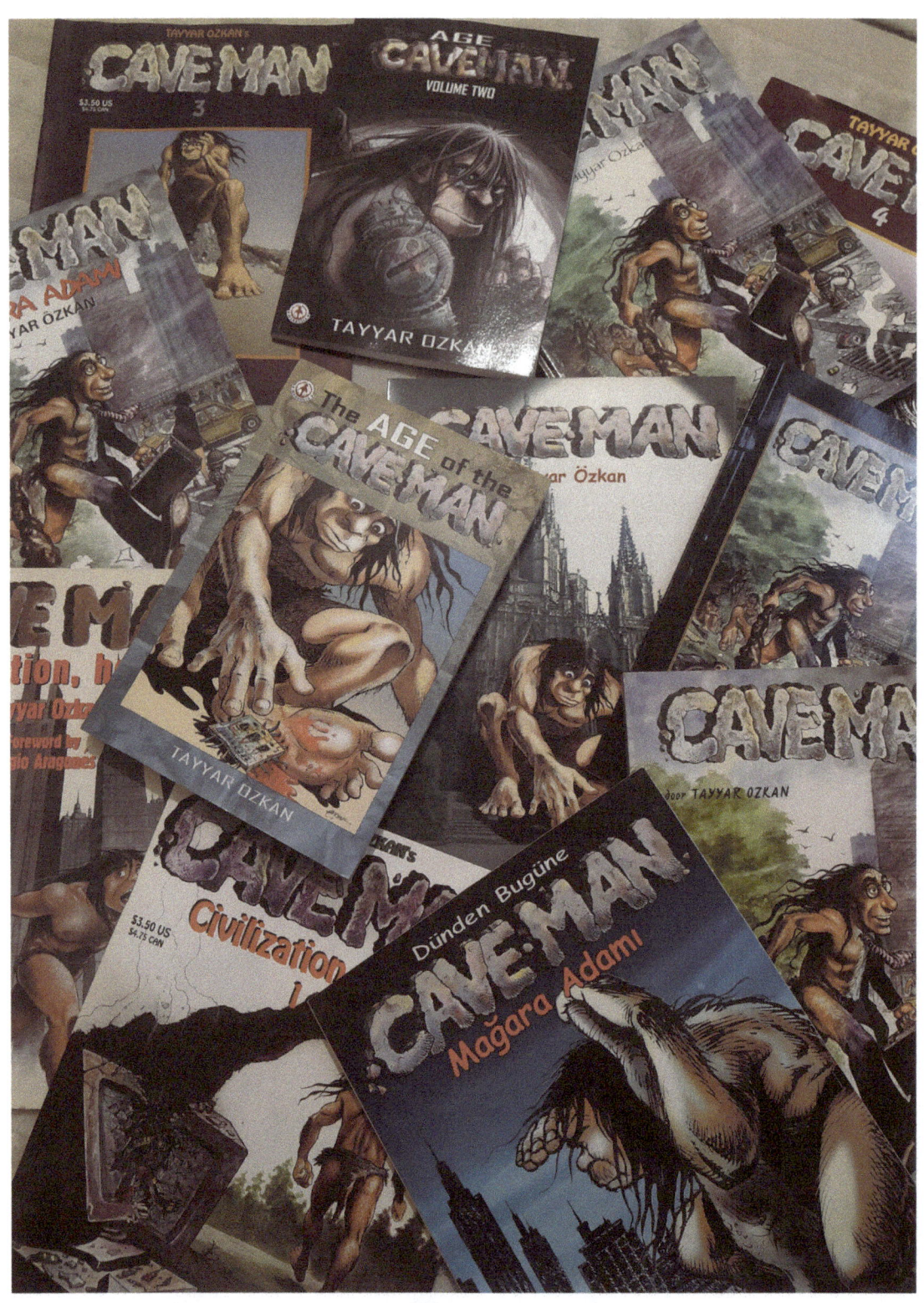

CAVEMAN books.. they all got *published* in the
different *counrtries* in different *times*.

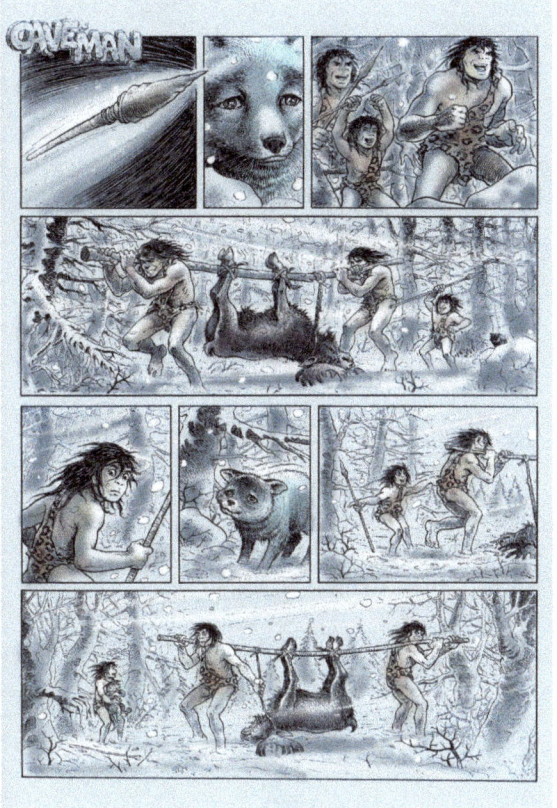

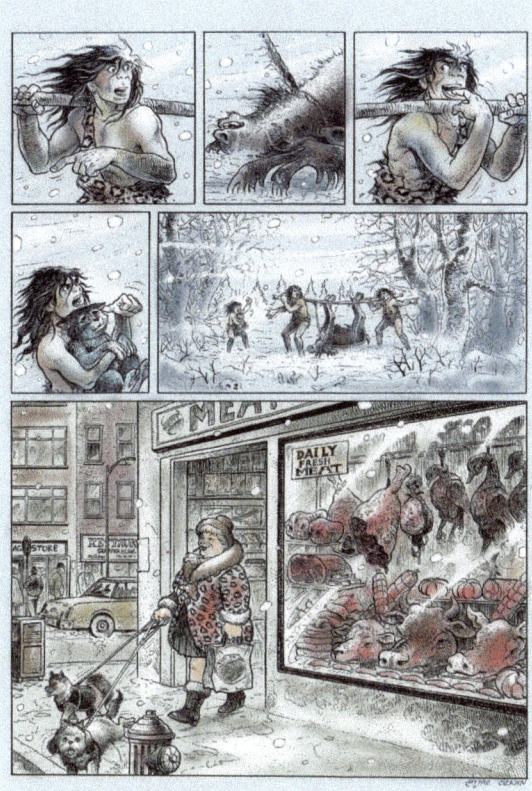

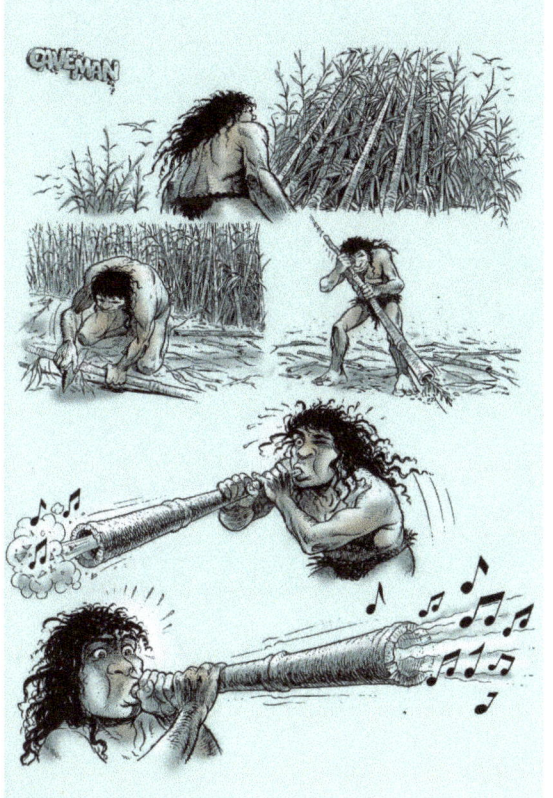

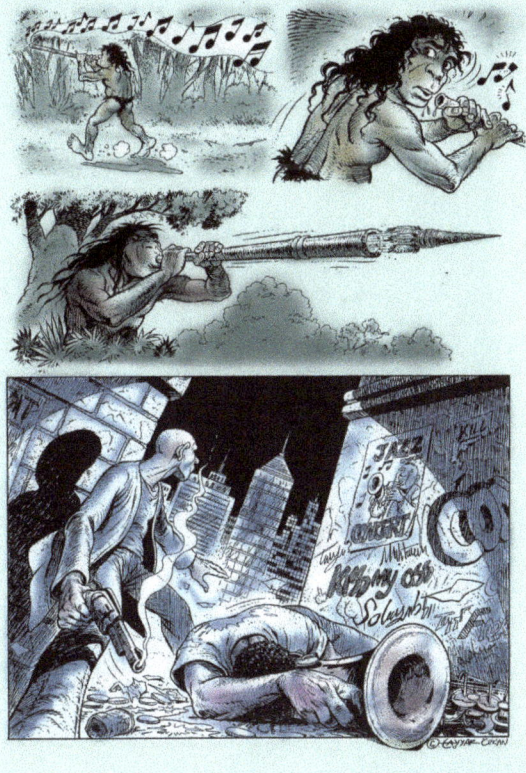

CAVEMAN *Pages..*

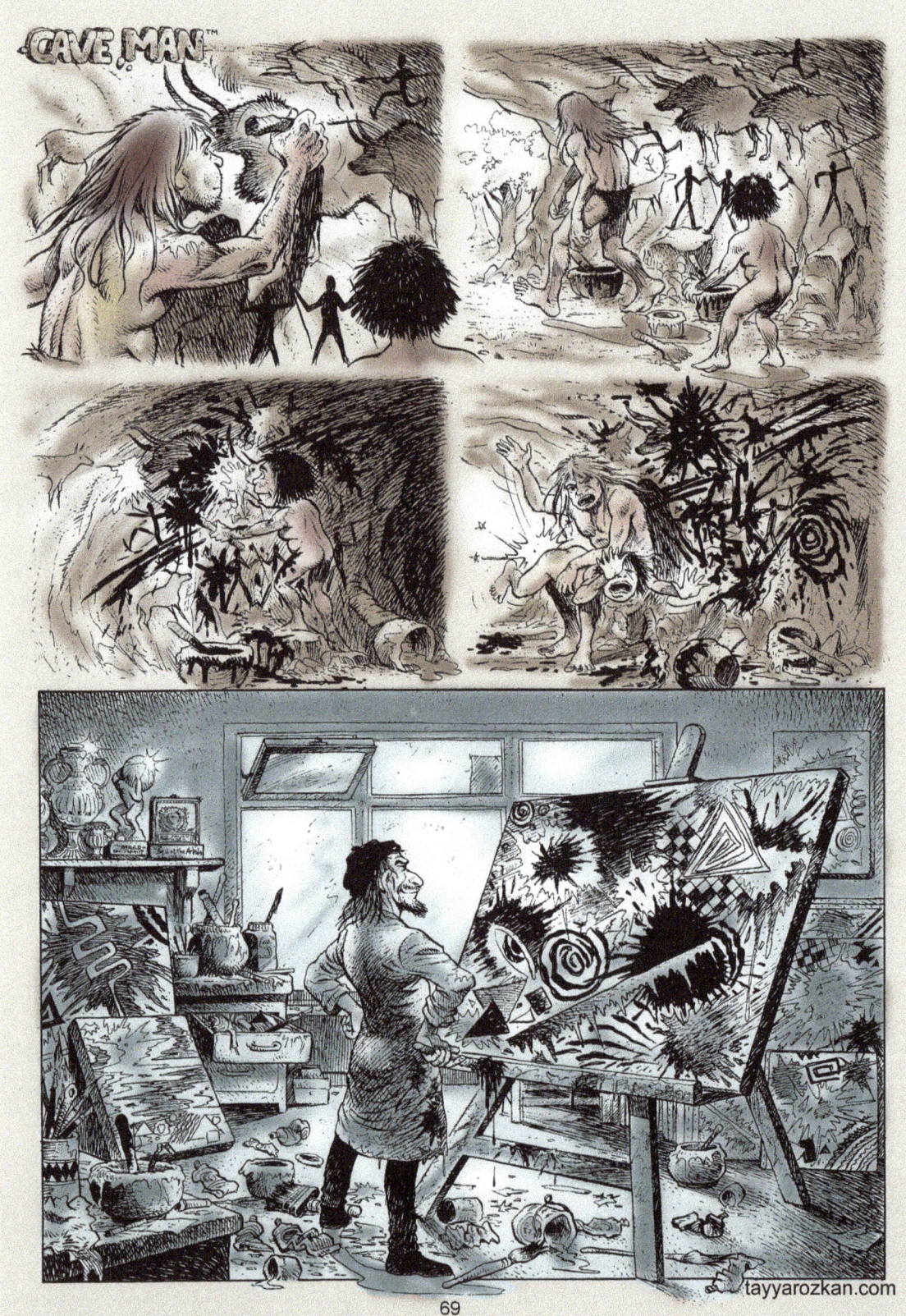

tayyarozkan.com

-*CAVEMAN* Page.

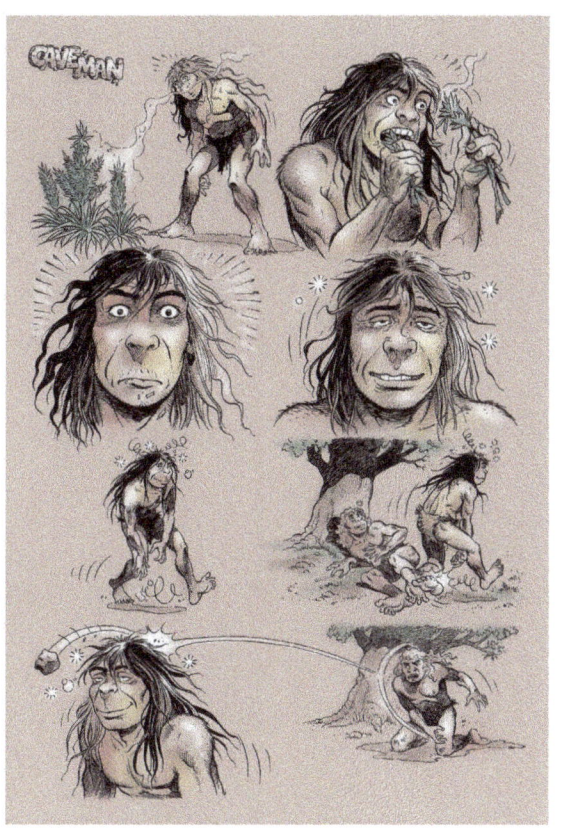

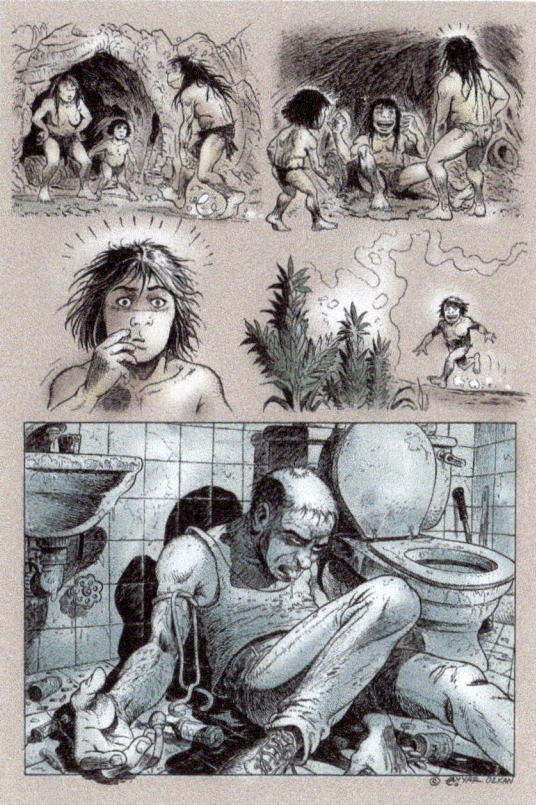

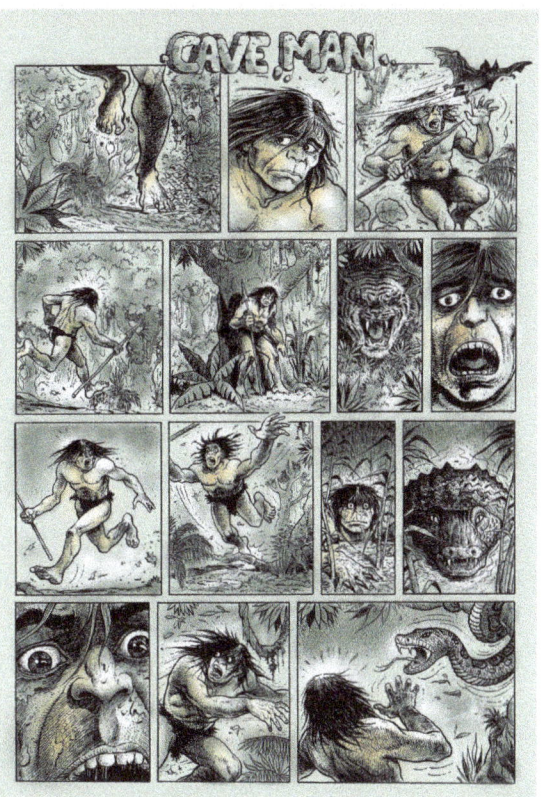

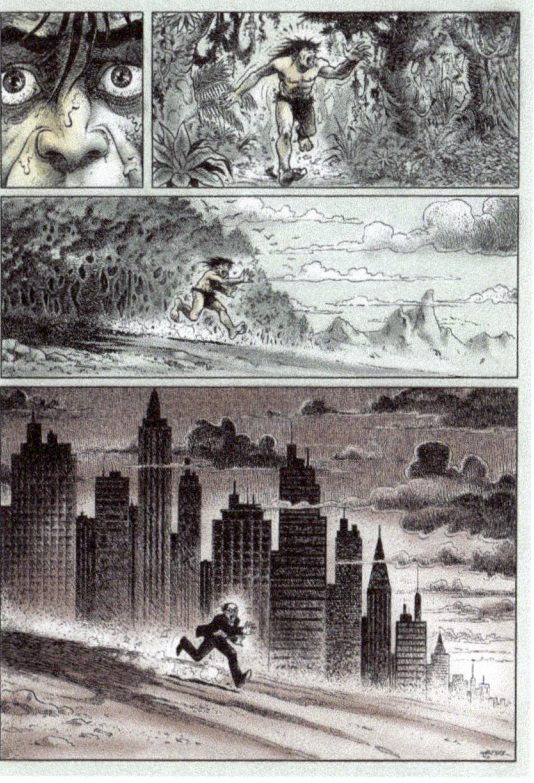

-*CAVEMAN* Pages..

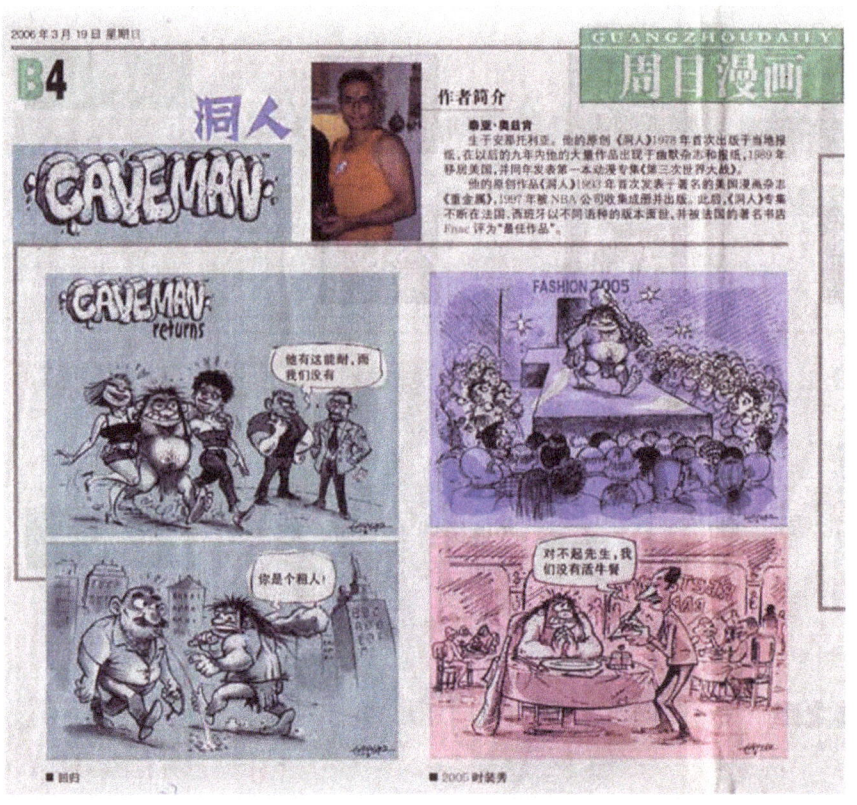

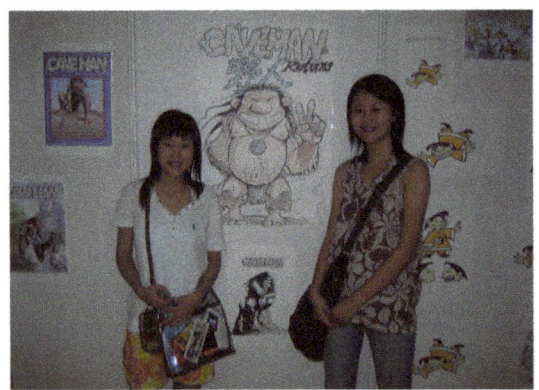

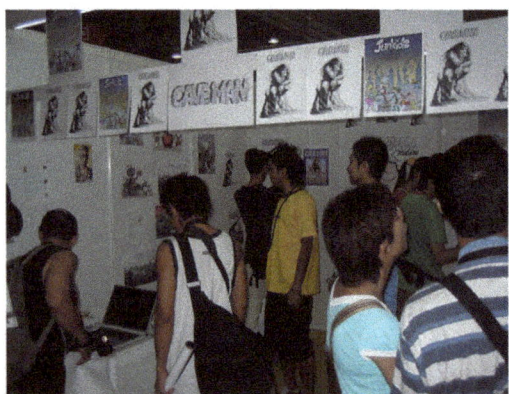

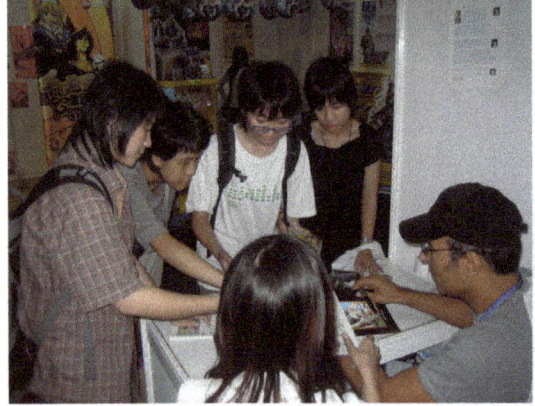

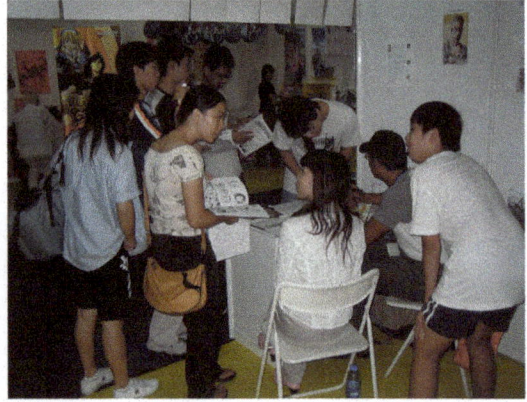

CAVEMAN was in *China* in 2005.

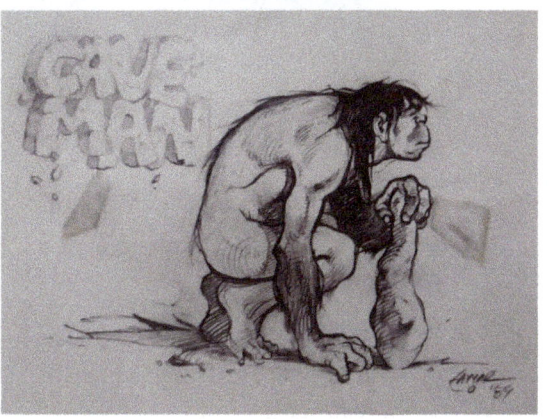

-*Self **portrait***.

Foreword
by Sergio Aragonés

great advantages of being a cartoonist
different countries, is being invit-
fairs, cartoon festivals and comic
nventions all over the
igh the years I've gone to
ain, Germany, Malaysia,
xico, among others...but
very special. In the late
s invited by HURRIYET,
daily newspaper, with four
onists from different coun-
a judge in their famous inter-
MAUI CARTOON COMPETI-
only were we treated like royalty,
had the opportunity to see Istanbul
different perspective by meeting peo-
what we do, other cartoonists.
us trip I had the same view
urists have, museums, temples,
arkets, but not until you meet
nd have a chance to compare, to
ings to talk "shop" with col-
nd better

equiva-
Society.
hem an
to be
neeting
tio with
ered around the fountain to sip tea and
ve... not only the quality, but the amount

-**Sergio Aragones**'s forward for my first
Caveman **graphic novel** -1996.

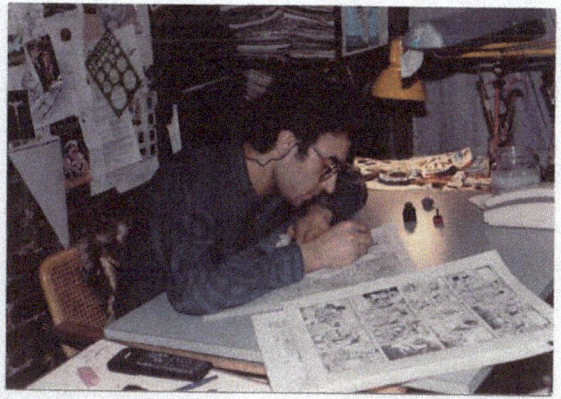

-The **first Caveman** sketching with a **title**
on it -1989.

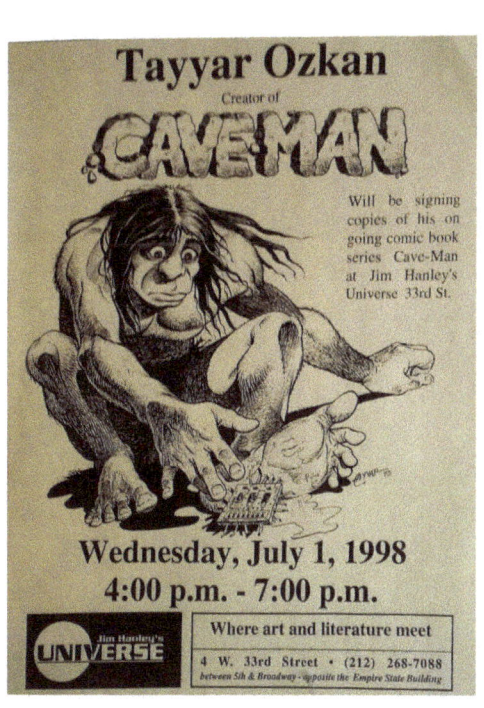

-A book **signing flyer** in NYC.

-My small **table** where I used to spent my
most of the time in **New York City** -1989.

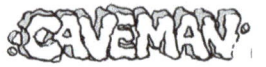
Tayyar Özkan

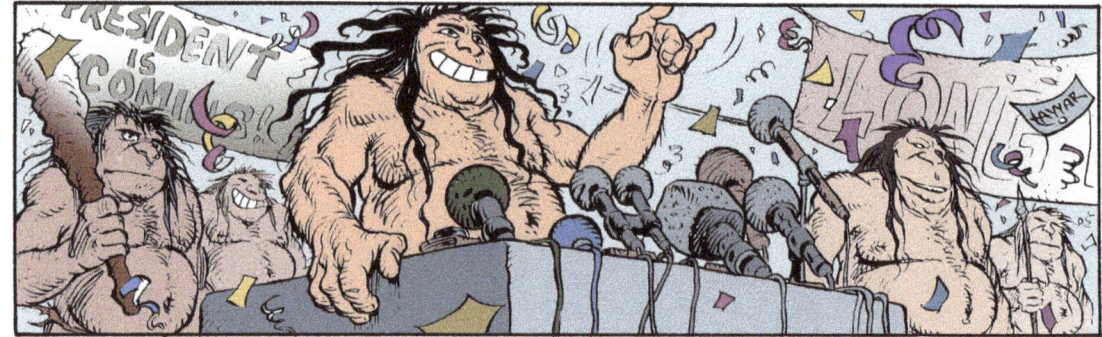
Tayyar Özkan

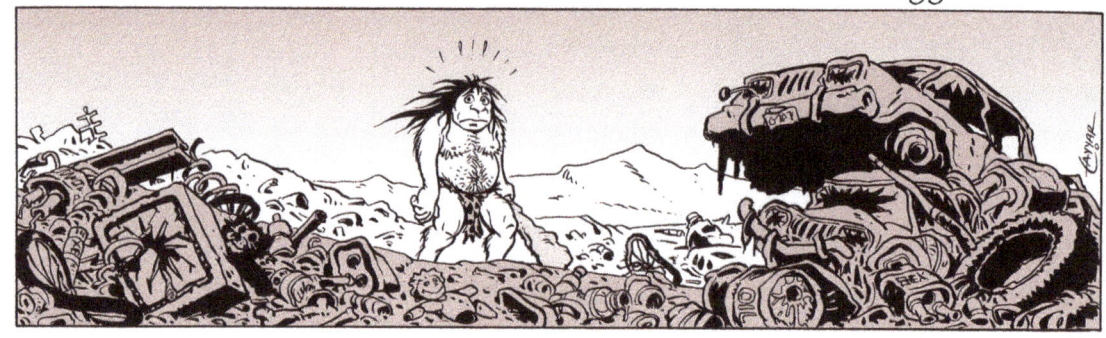
Tayyar Özkan

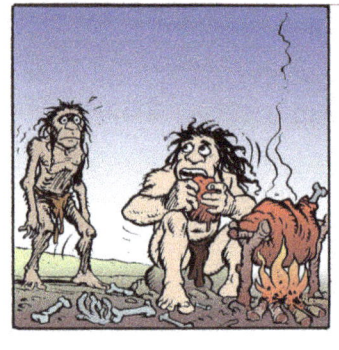
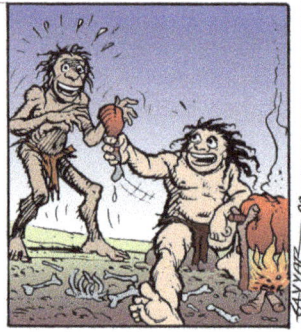
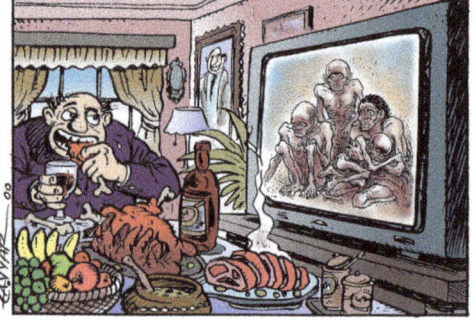
Tayyar Özkan

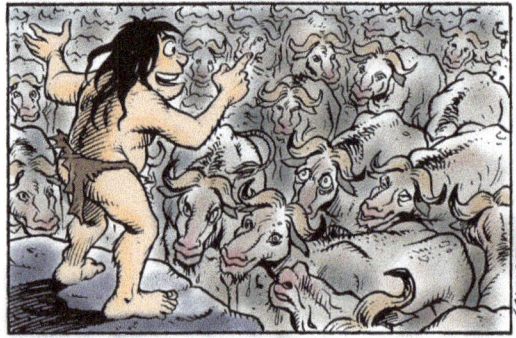
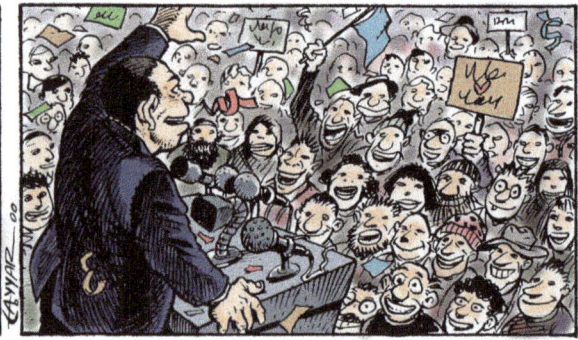
Tayyar Özkan

-*CAVEMAN* single comic strips.

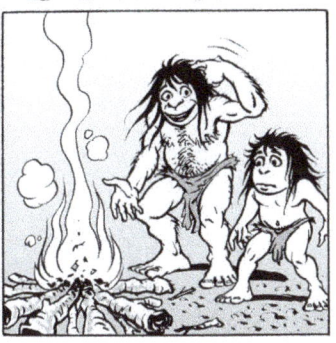
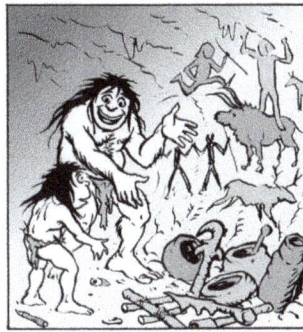
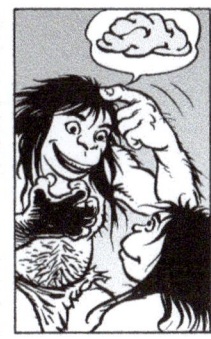
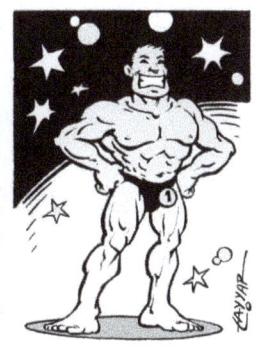

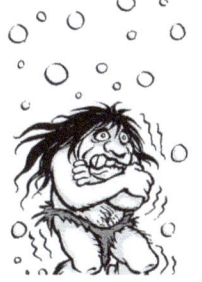
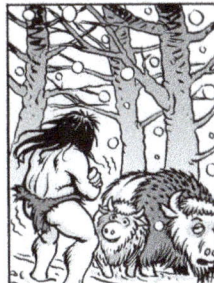
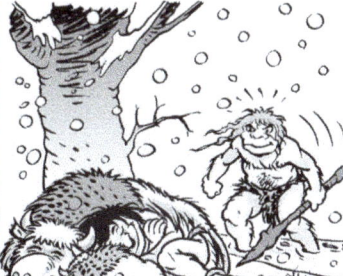
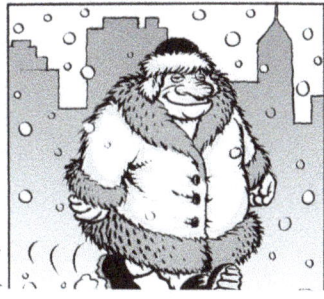

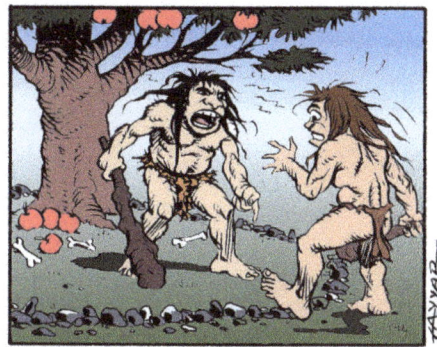
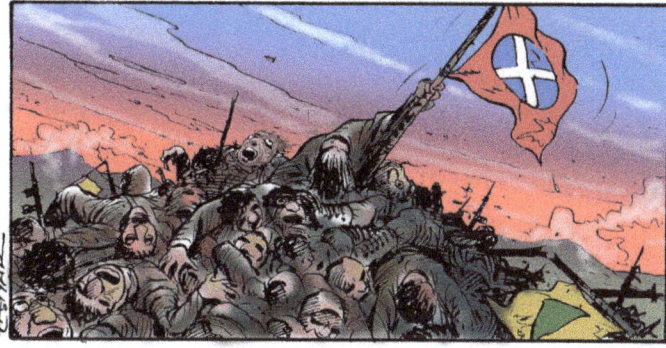

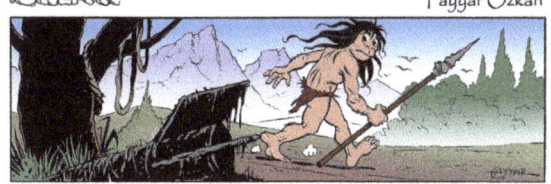

Tayyar Özkan

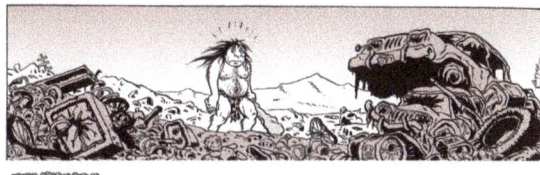

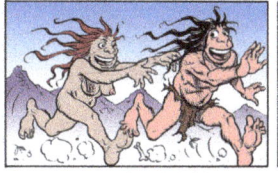
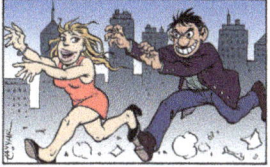

Tayyar Özkan

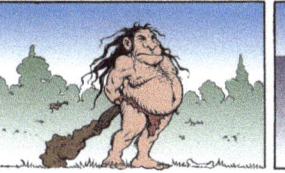
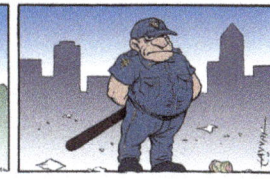

-More **CAVEMAN** comic strips.

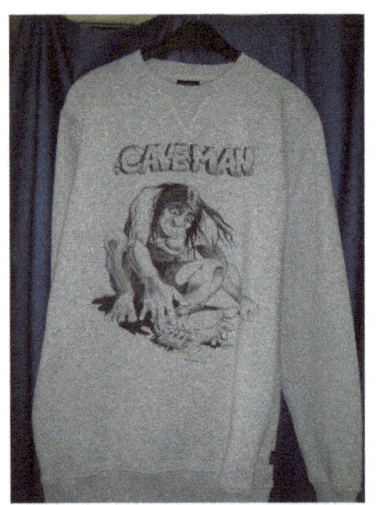
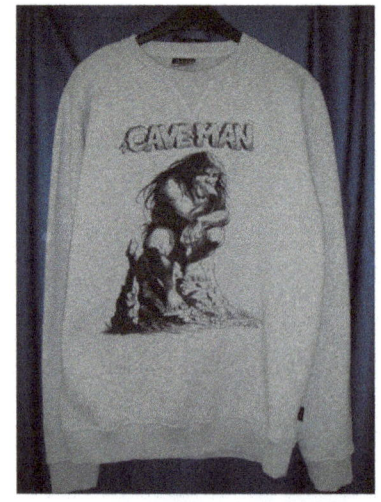

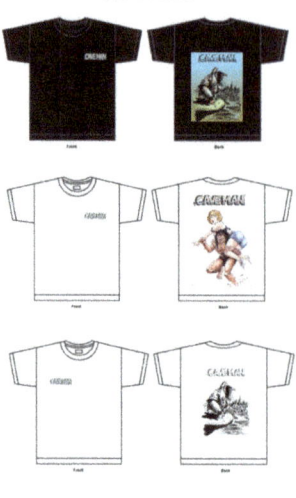

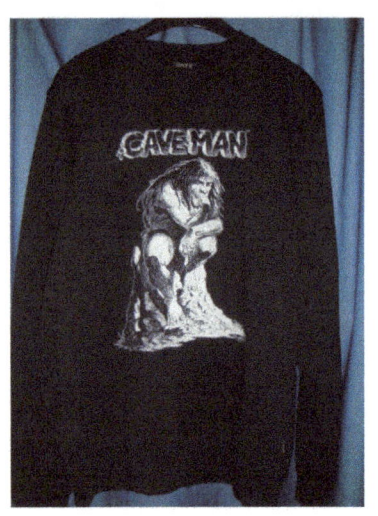
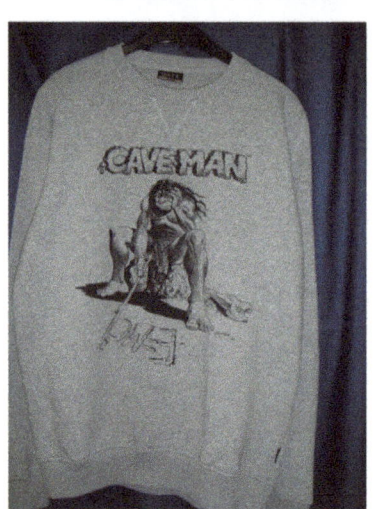

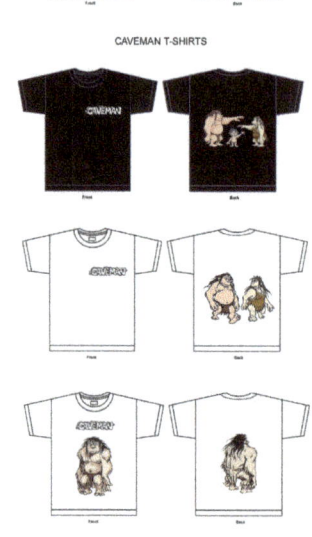

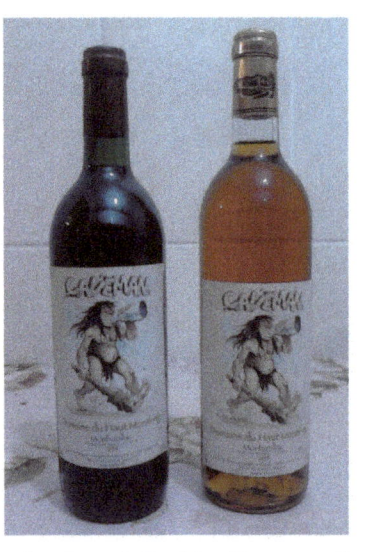
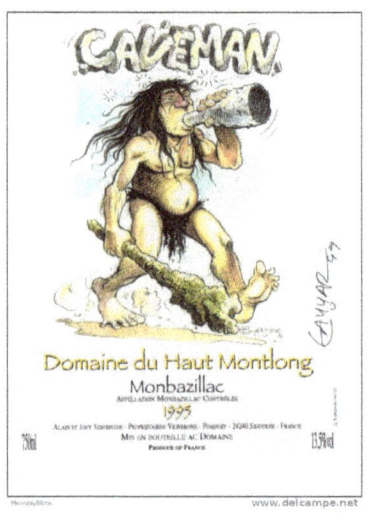

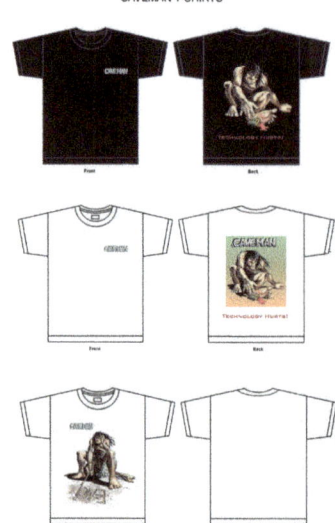

*-A wine **label** in **France** in 1995.*

CAVEMAN PRODUCTIONS.

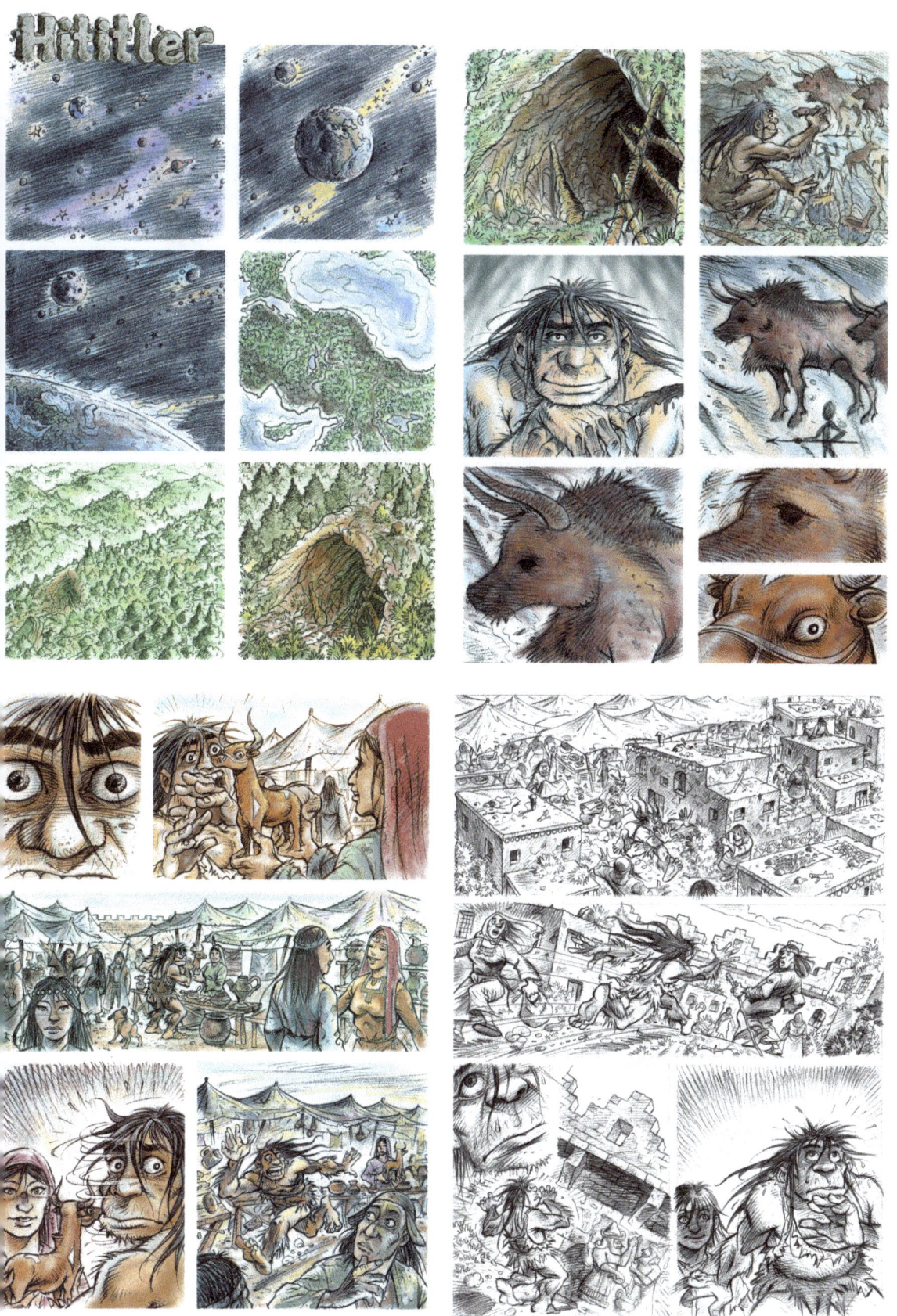

A project never got a chance to complete; *Caveman* goes to *Hittites* time.

THE AGE of the CAVEMAN

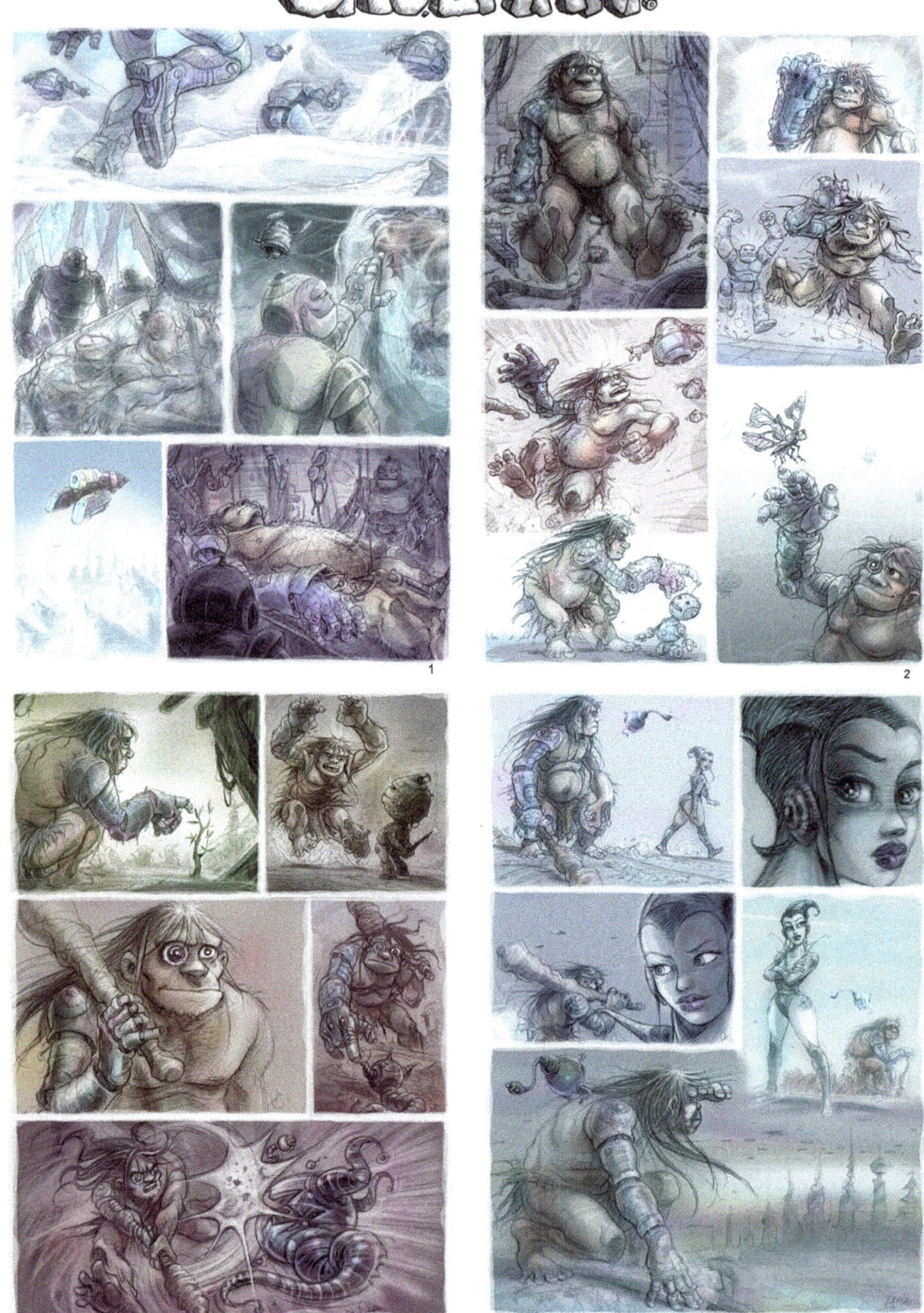

tayyar@tayyarozkan.com

CAVEMAN goes to the future.

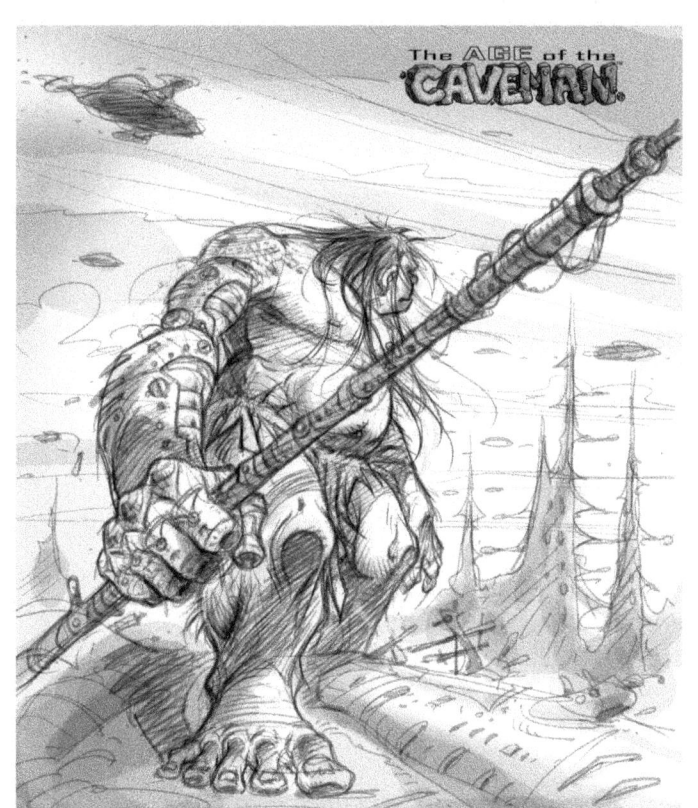

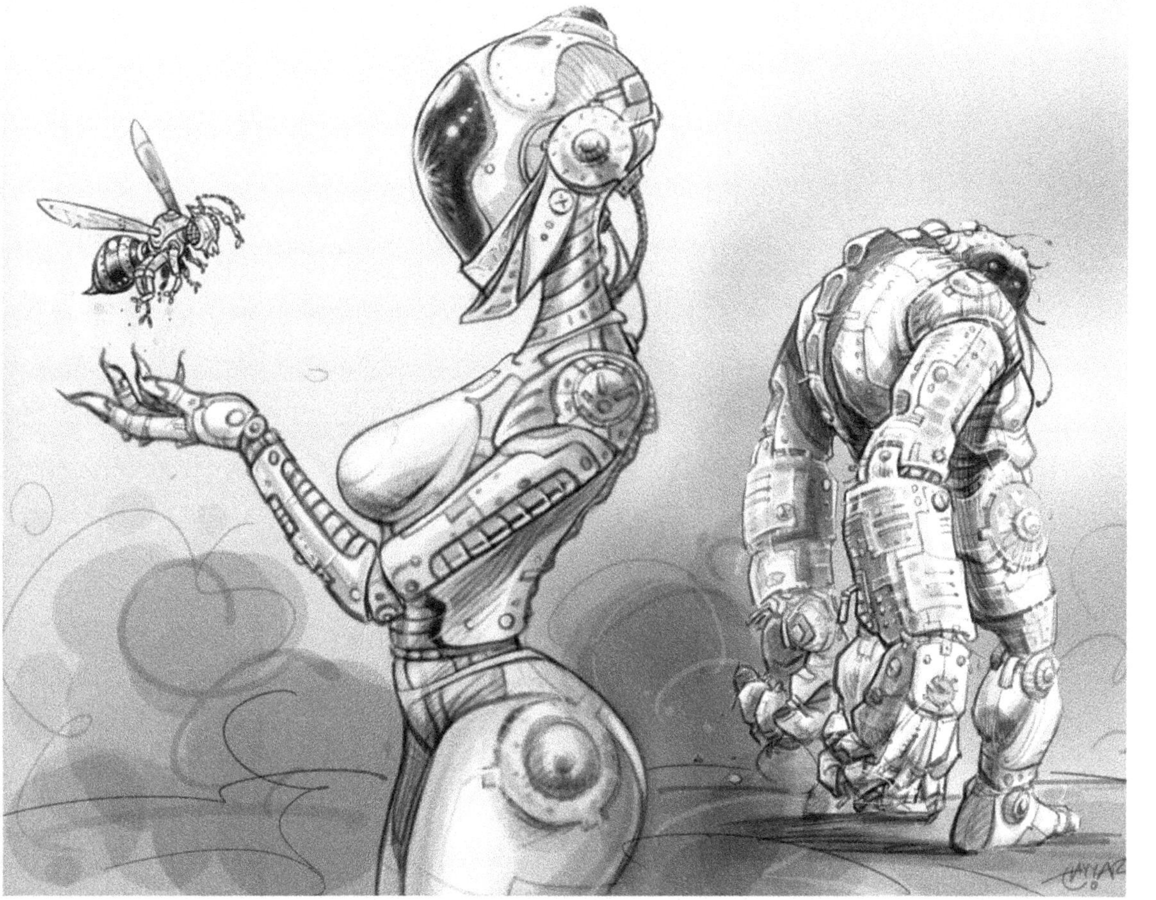

SKETCHES.

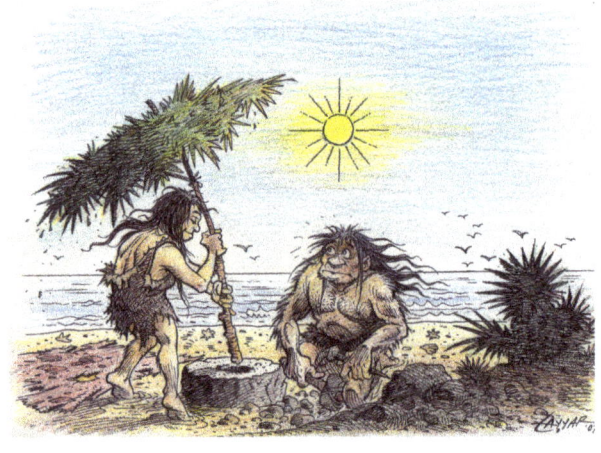
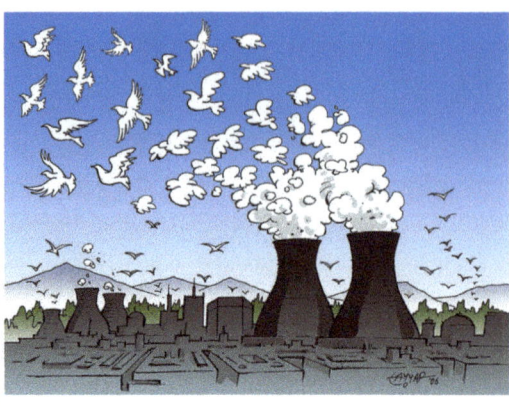
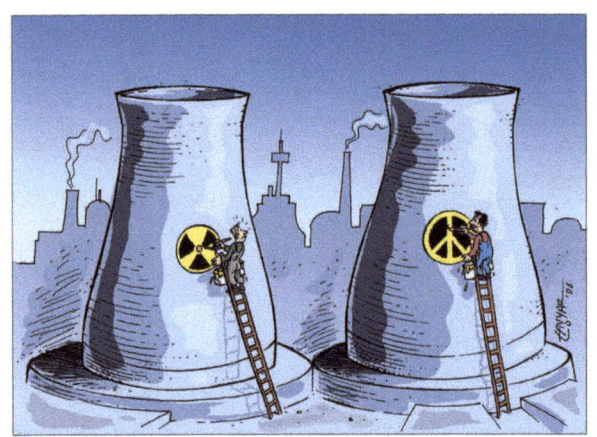
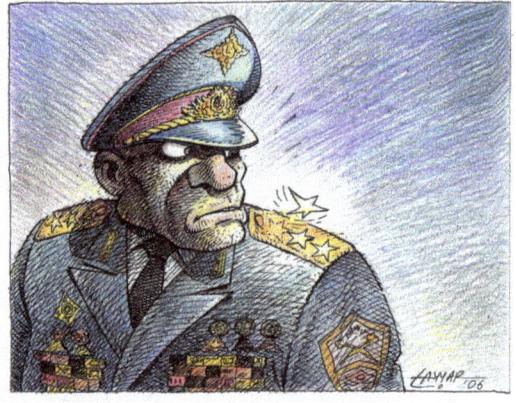
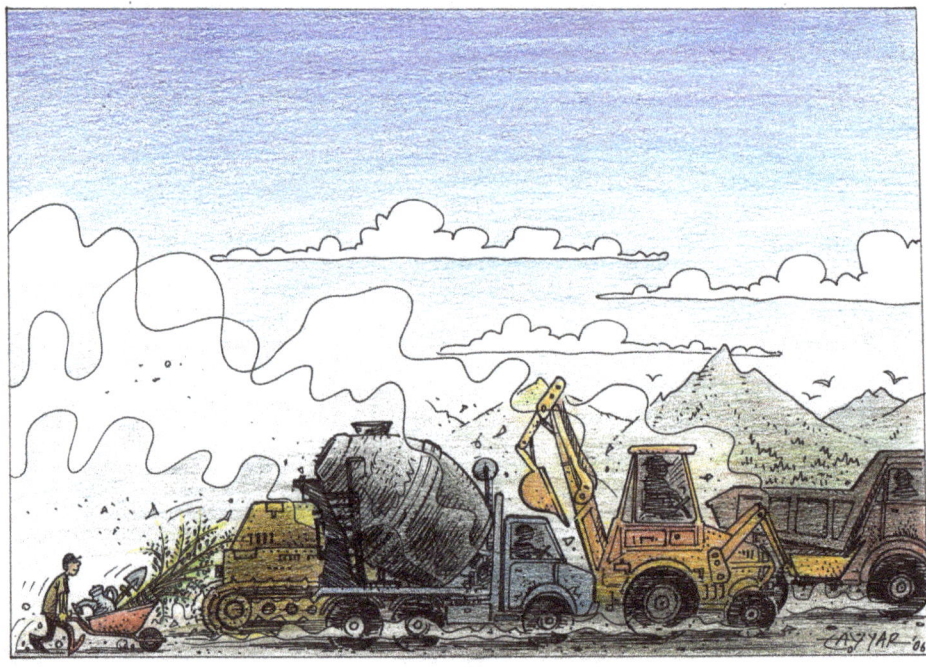

-This one got the **first prize** in **Çorum-Turkey** in 2006.

CARTOONS FOR FUN.

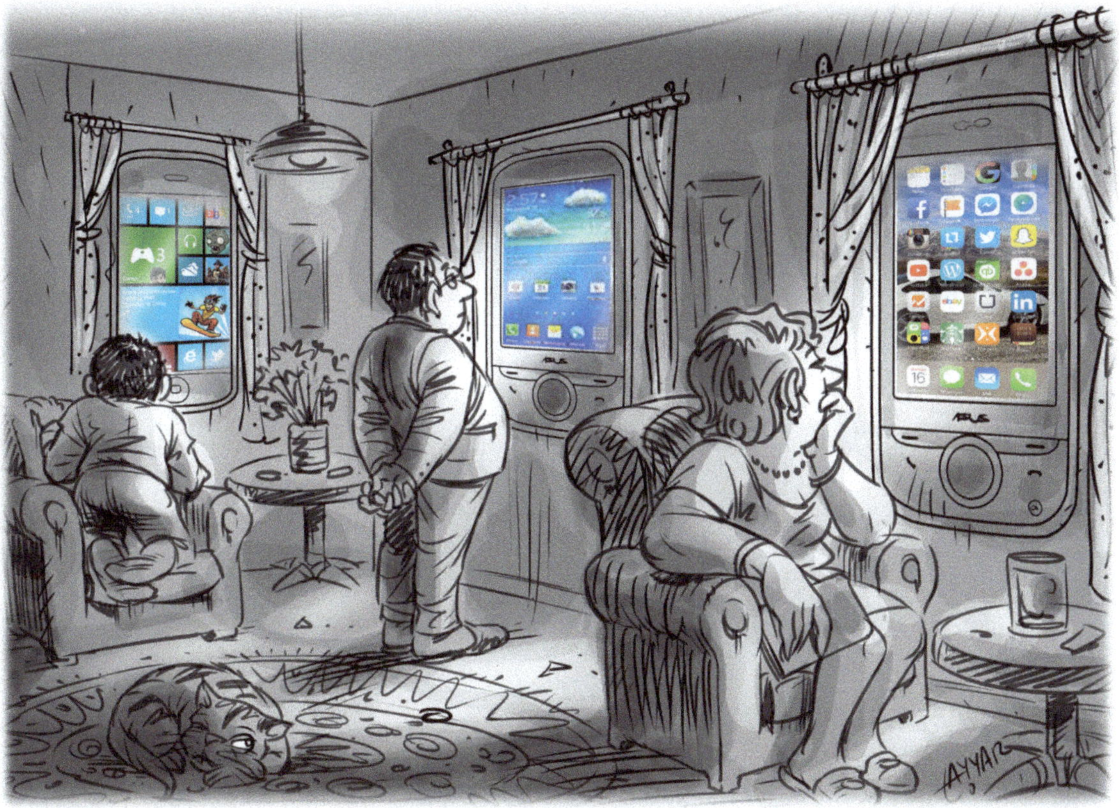

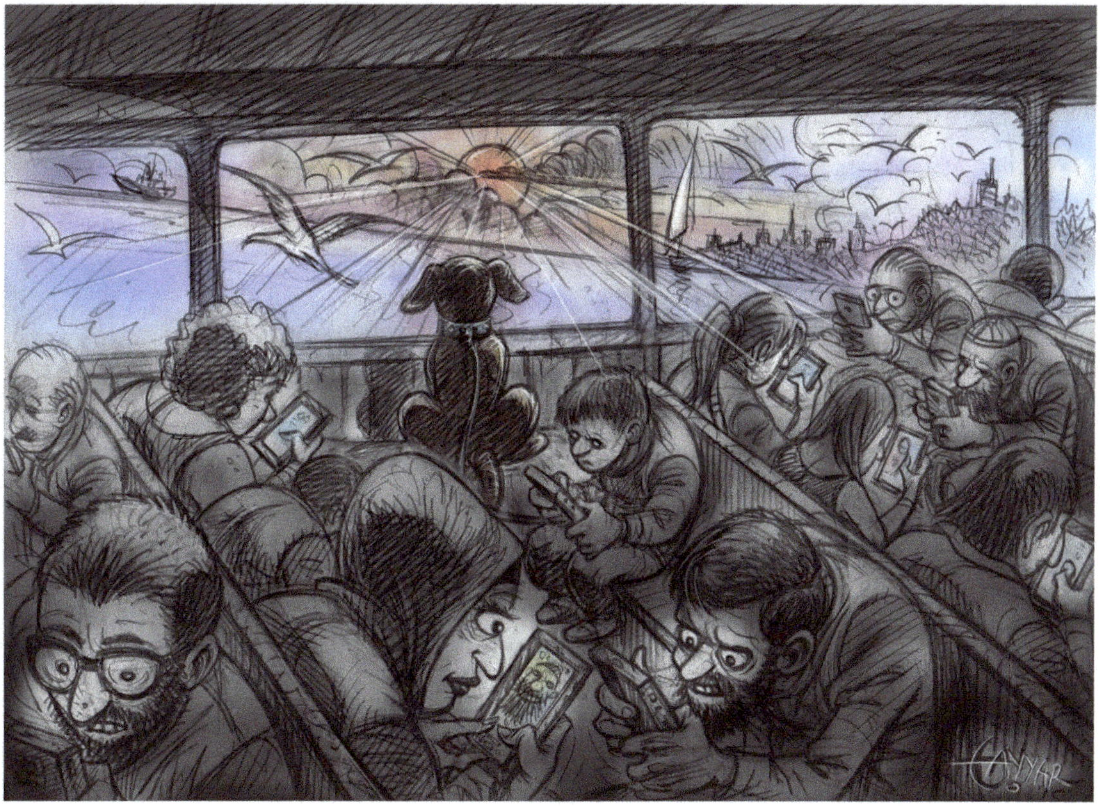

CARTOONS FOR FUN.

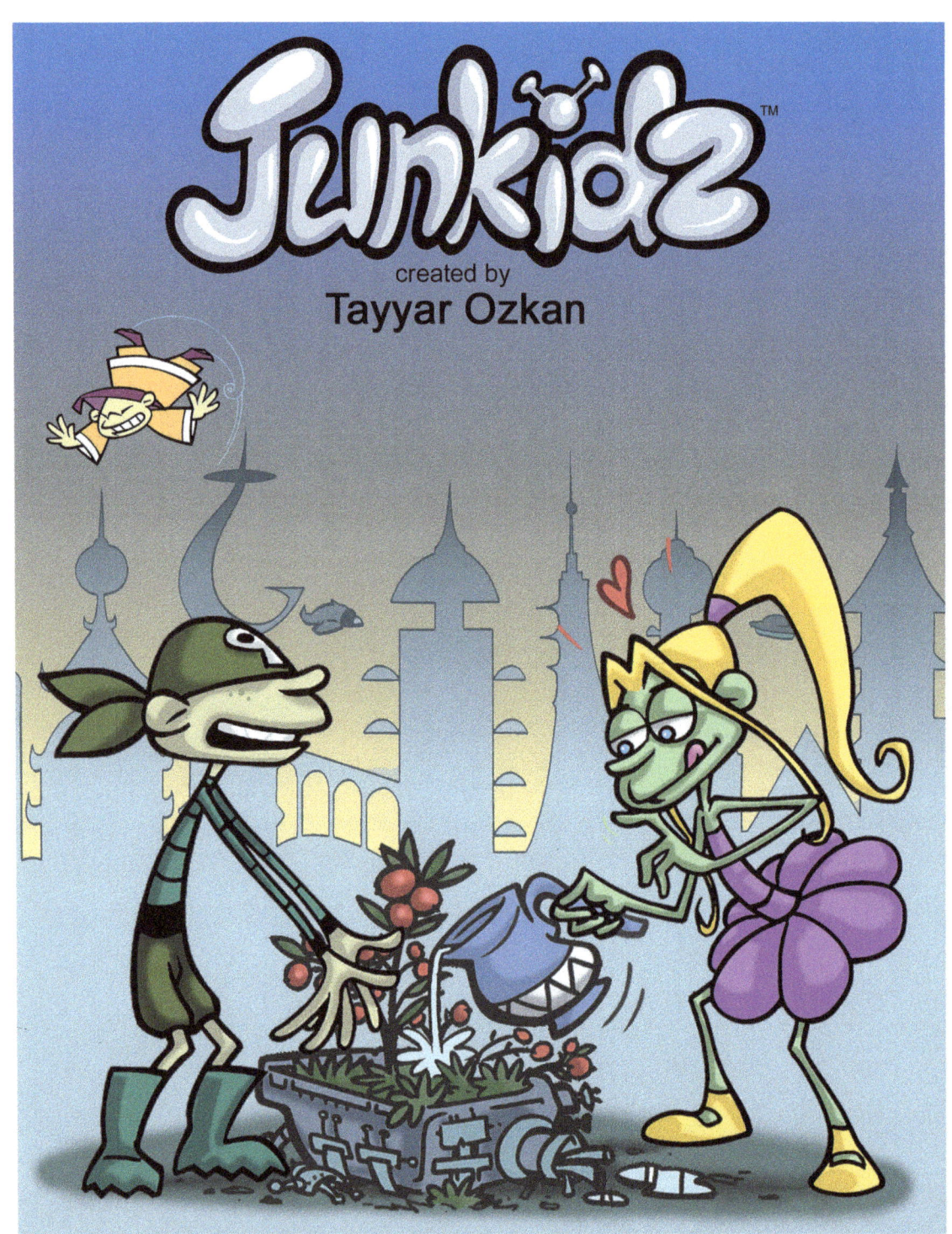

-**Junkidz** are 8 mod-archaeologist kids of the future,
discovering their past in our trash.
I've created this as an animation project for *Cartoon Network* but
hasn't happened yet. It has got *published* as a kid's *comic books* and
released as *comic strips* in some news papers.

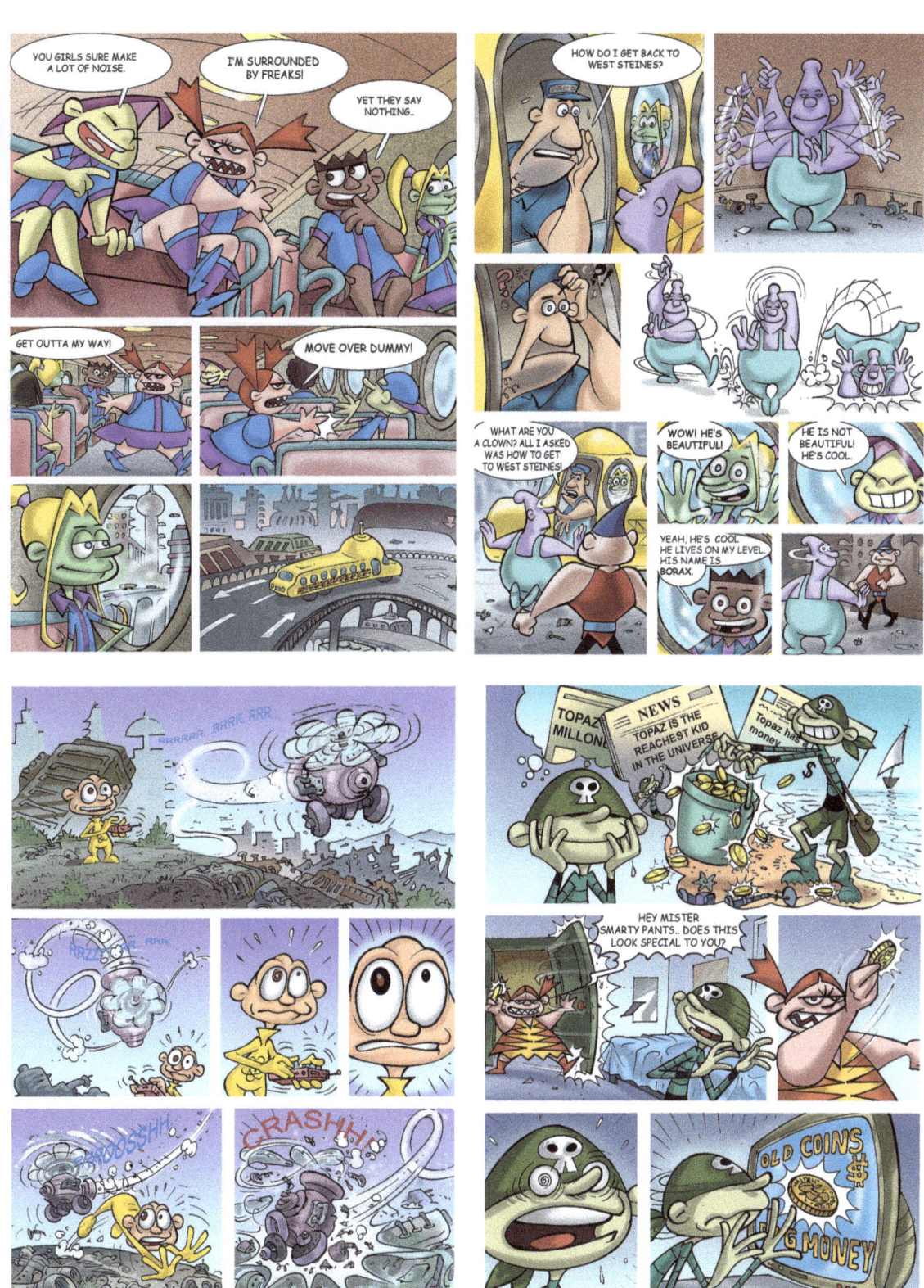

-*Junkidz* comic pages.

BORAX

He is a strong, silent leader type. He has many friends, but prefers being alone. Borax has a crush on Jade but is too shy to talk to her. He has developed an odd exercise regiment by using discarded exercise equipment.
He also has a secret agenda in visiting the junkyard, and that is to be near Jade.

JADE

She has cultivated a small patch of grass amongst the refuse, into a beautiful vegetable and flower garden.
There is also a small stream of clean water flowing near the garden.
Jade has always had a love for plants. Jade can name plants the same way other kids can name dinosaurs or pro athletes.
Jade's parents have allowed her to make their apartment into a mini-jungle.
Jade hates school because the other kids tease her about being thin and green.
Jade has a crush on Borax but she is too shy to tell him that she likes him.

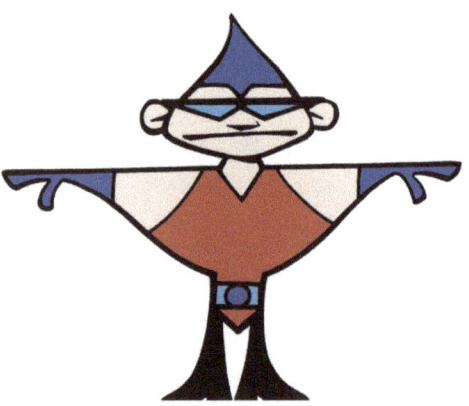

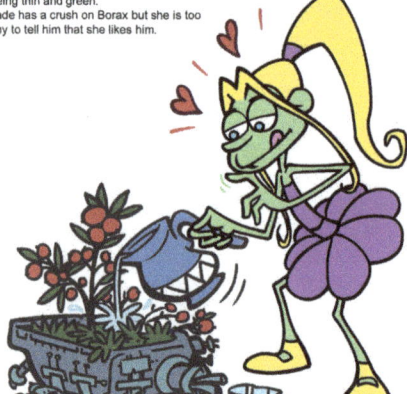

LAVA

She is always sent to the junkyard to retrieve her little brother, Topaz and bring him home.
Lava feels everyone is dumb expect for her. She fights people in school because they tease her for being big. She is also teased because Topaz is a junkid and he is her brother. That makes Lava a junkid by proxy.
Therefore, Lava really hates Topaz, Cobi, Jade, and all the others that she sees in the junkyard, because she is not a junkid.
Yet, she often sneaks huge meaty snacks down to the junkyard so she can eat them without getting in trouble with her parents.

TOPAZ

He found an old coin in the junkyard one day.
He looked it up on the Internet and found it was worth a lot of money.
His sister, Lava, took the coin from him and told him she flushed it down the drain.
Topaz believes he will find the coin again in the junkyard because he is sure that the pipe that runs through Jade's garden is the same pipe that is connected to the drains of his home.
In the meantime, Topaz searches for other treasures.
Topaz has adopted the guise of a pirate, because he believes pirates are the best treasure hunters.

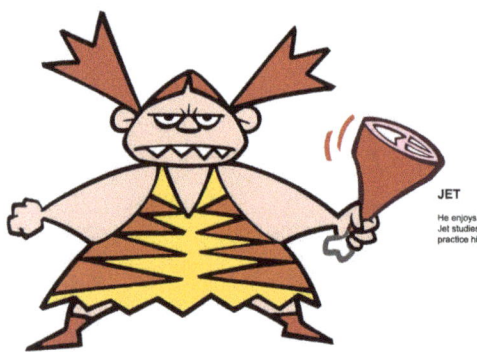

JET

He enjoys the physical challenge of negotiating the bizarre terrain of the junkyard. Jet studies the martial arts and has found the junkyard is the perfect place to practice his moves and train his reflexes.

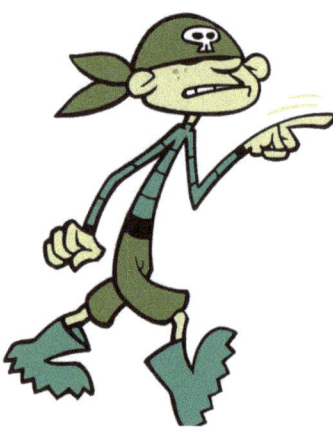

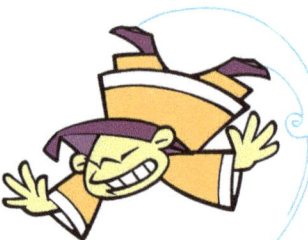

GABBRO

He is a large, mute young man. He likes going to the junkyard because it is silent like him. He studies what the refuse and tries to imagine how articles were used.

MICA

He is a musician. Mica has discovered that fusing this weird part with that strange piece opens a wide avenue for musical expression.

COBI

He is a misfit genius. He finds solace and peace in the junkyard. It is not a junkyard to Cobi; it is a free and fertile supply depot. Discarded PCs, wiring, piping, tubing, batteries, digital cameras and microwave appliances allow Cobi to indulge his limitless thirst for experimentation. Cobi creates working machines and appliances that usually fall short of his expectations.

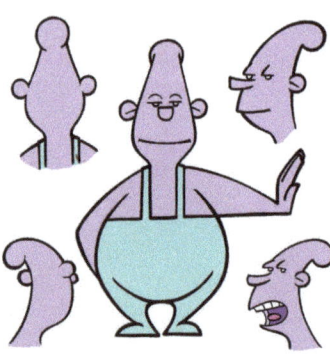

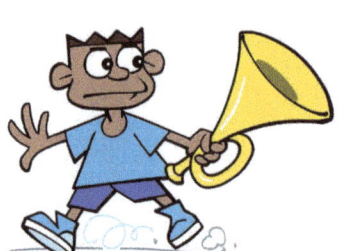

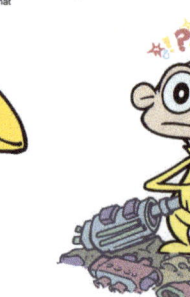

JUNKIDZ Characters

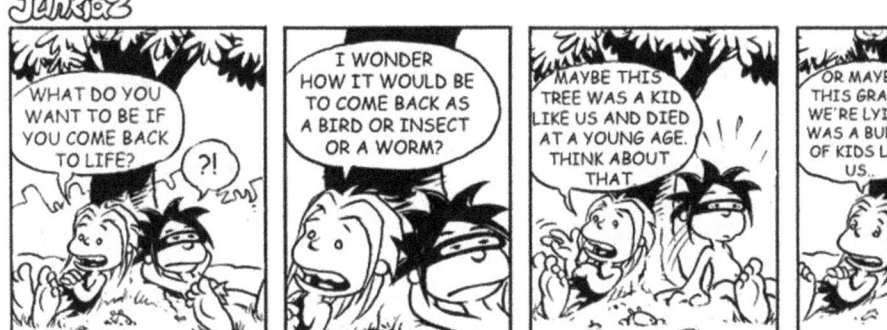

-Junkidz comic strips for the newspapers..

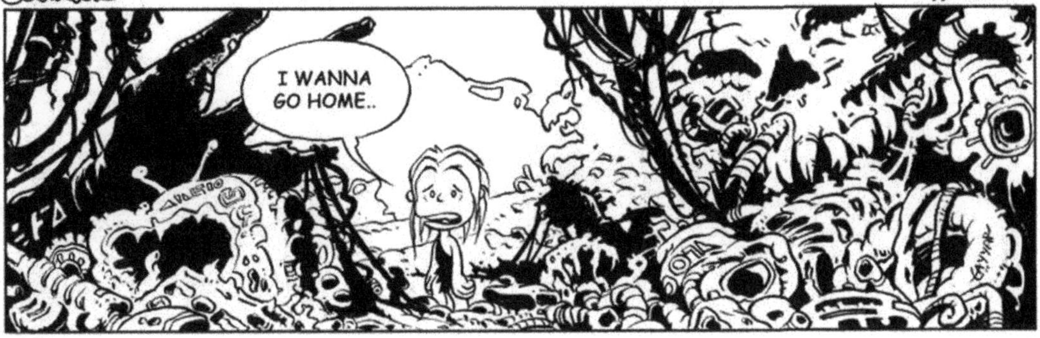

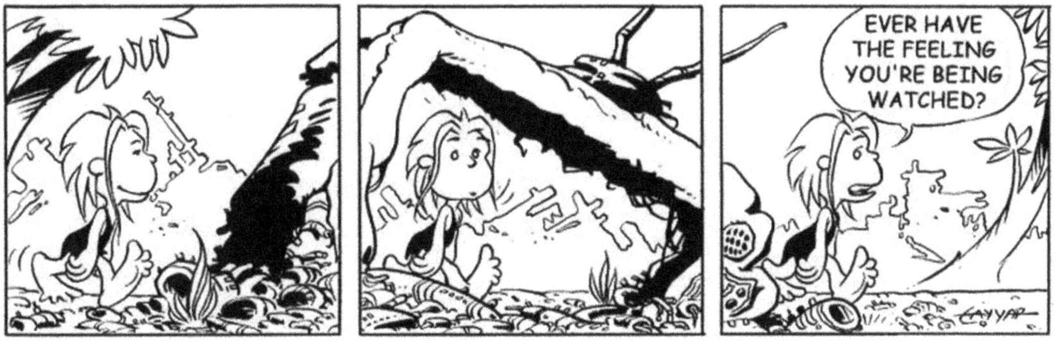

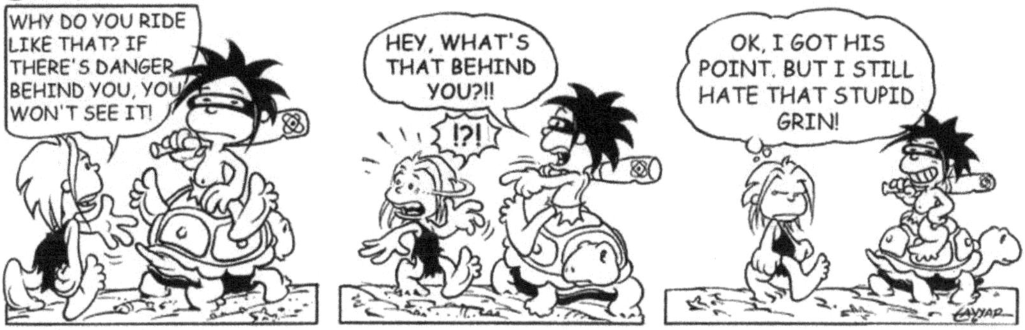

These are the first version of *Junkidz* characters I drew.
After I've got some submission feeedbacks I changed the style and
age group I've targeted.

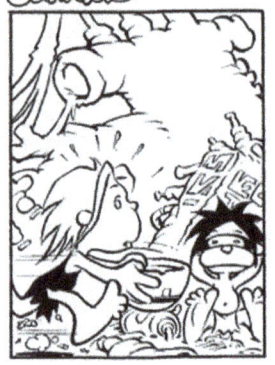
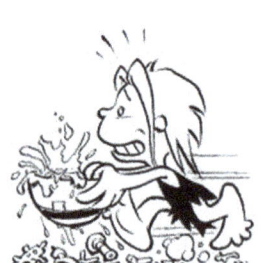
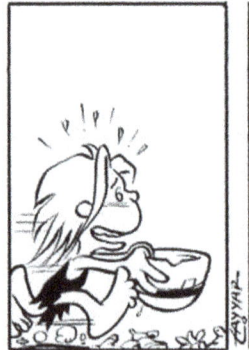
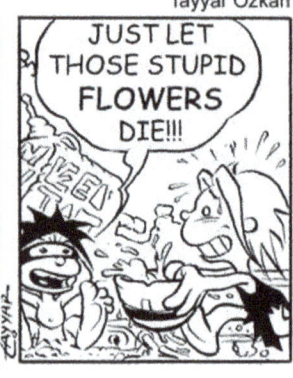

Tayyar Ozkan

JUST LET THOSE STUPID **FLOWERS** DIE!!!

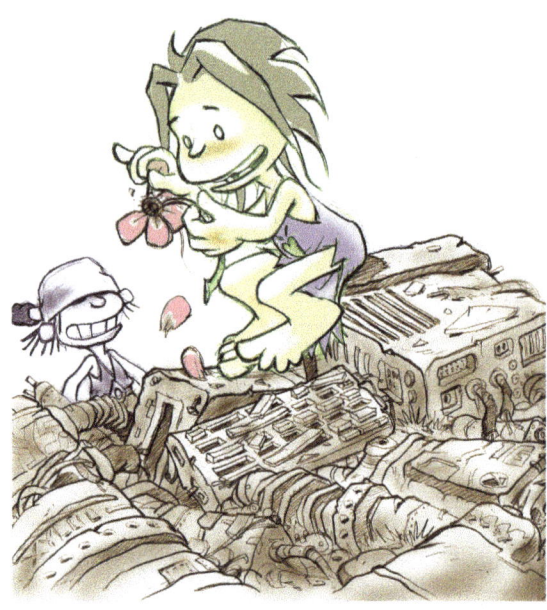
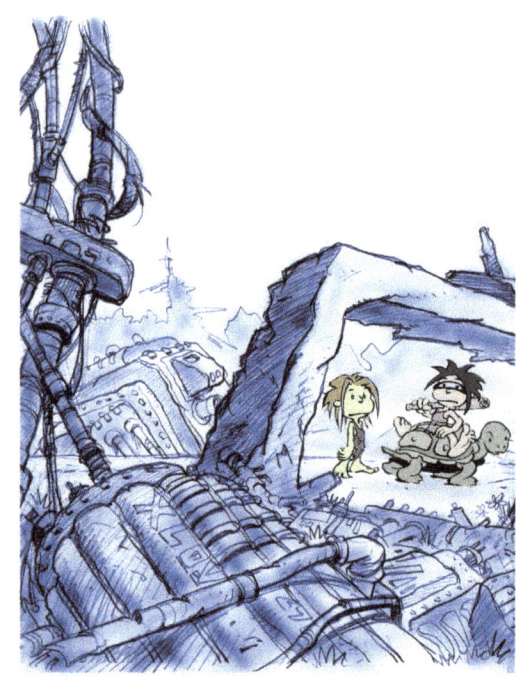
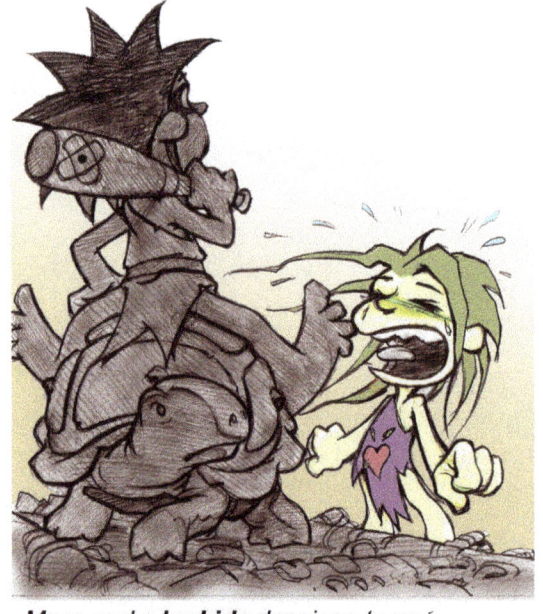
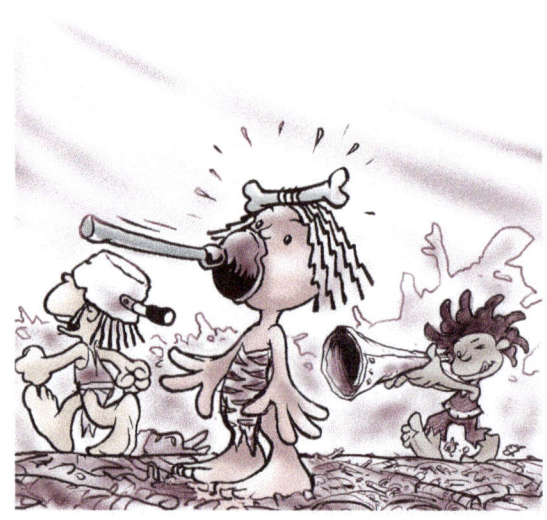

*-More early **Junkidz** drawings to go.´*

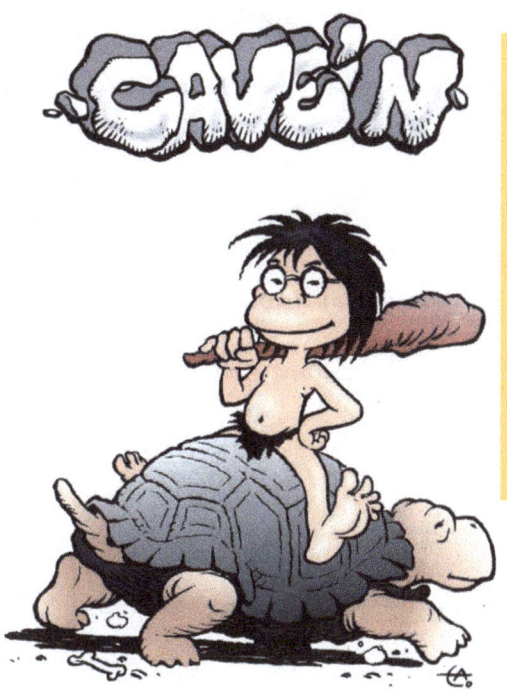

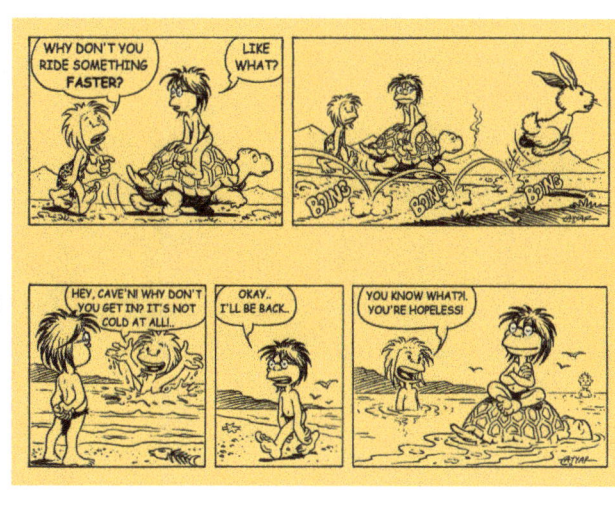

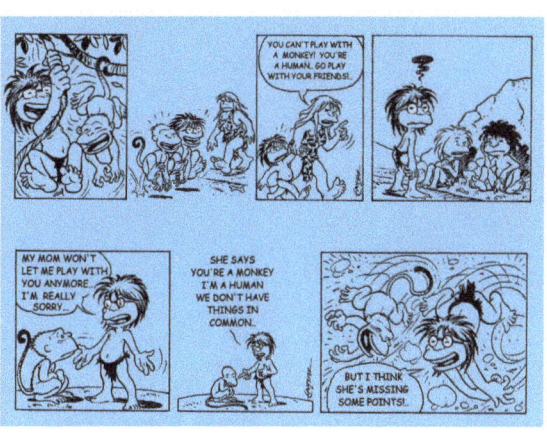

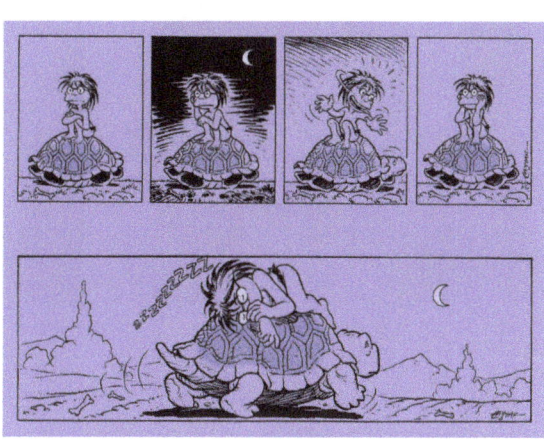

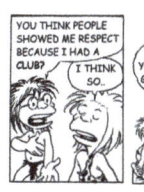
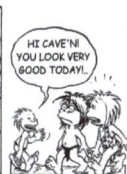
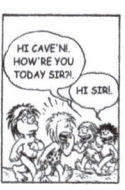
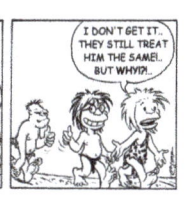
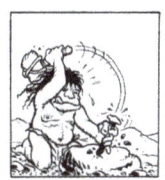
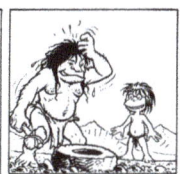
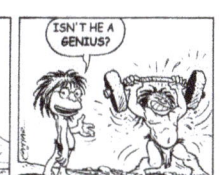

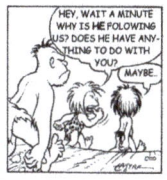
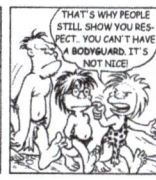
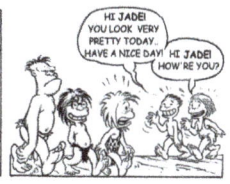
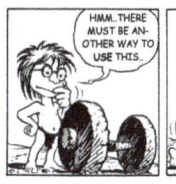
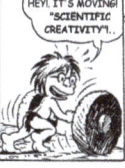
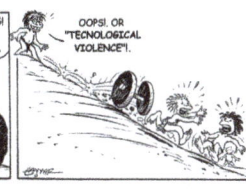

-*CAVE'N* comic strips.

I've created this *character* as a '*Cave Boy*' of Caveman.

BIG APPLE

Tayyar Ozkan

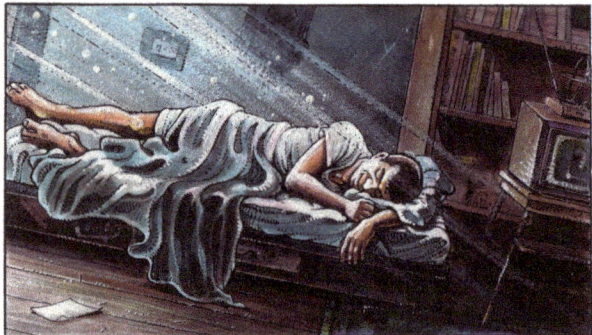
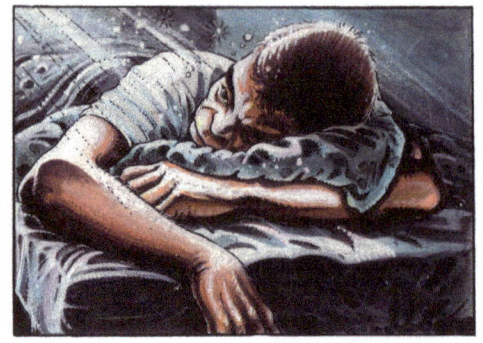

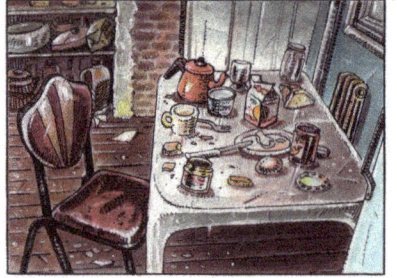
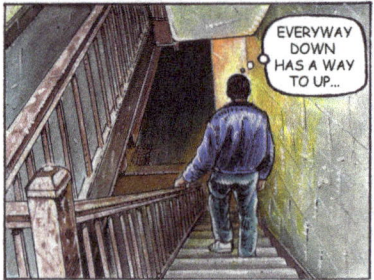
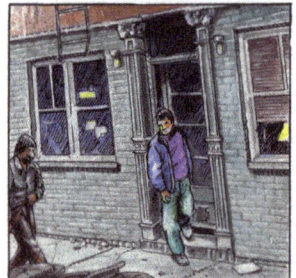

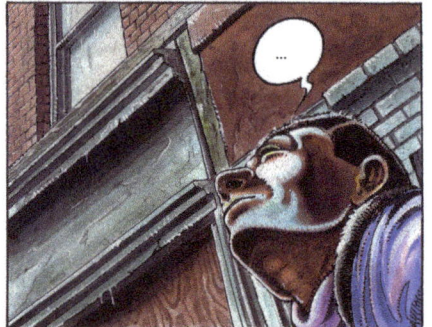
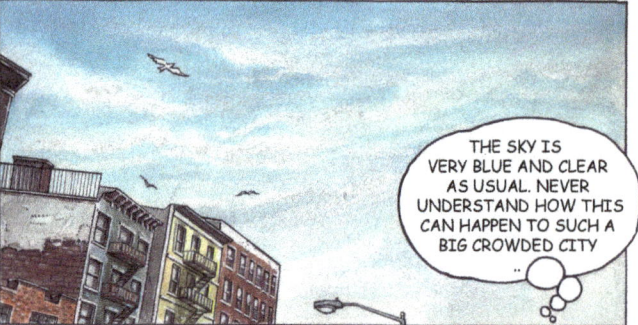

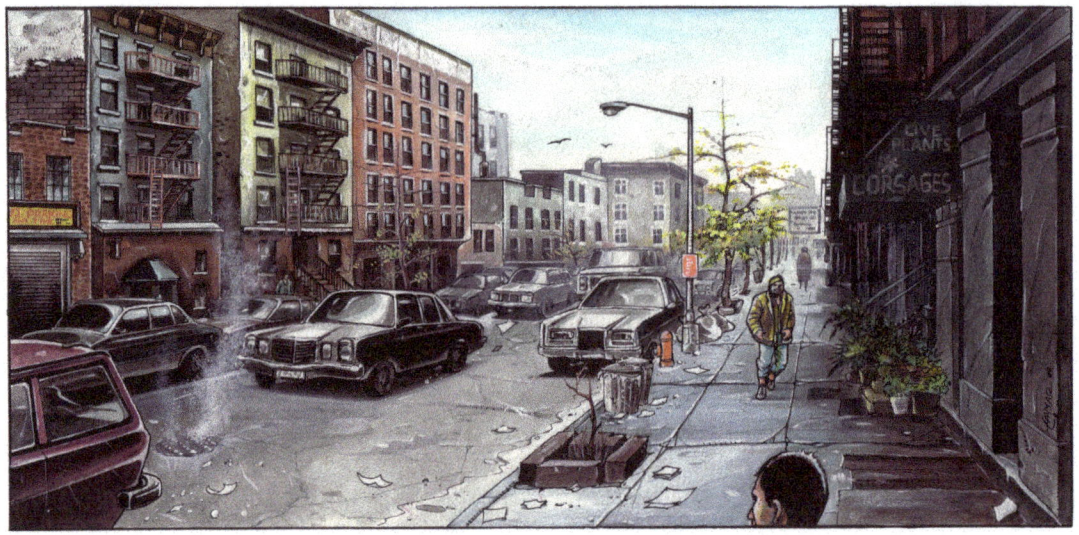

I've done this *8 pages story* just for my portfolio right after
I moved to *USA* and started to live in *Downtown NYC*.
This work got great attentions and helped me to *found* so many *jobs*
in the art market.

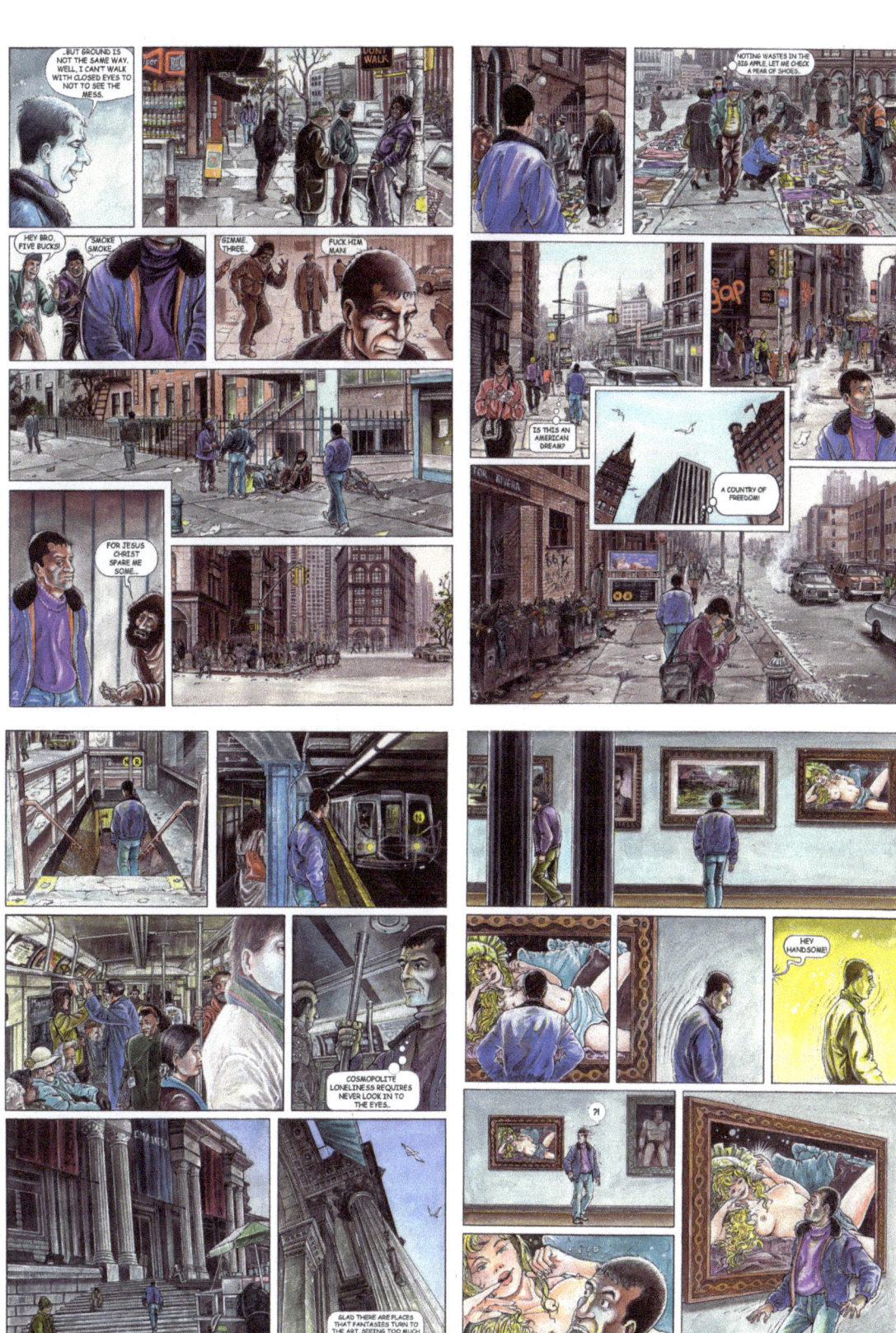

-"*BIG APLE*" pages.

PASSENGER BOARDIN BRIDGE OPERATIONS AND WORKING AT BRIDGE PARKING AREAS

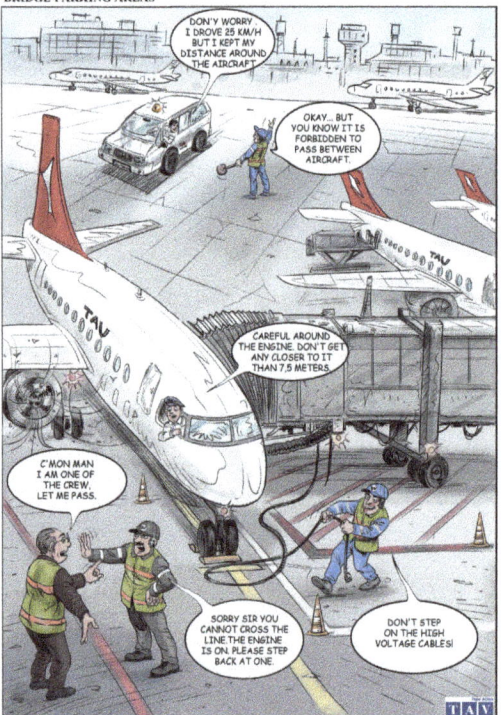

PASSENGER BOARDIN BRIDGE OPERATIONS AND WORKING AT BRIDGE PARKING AREAS

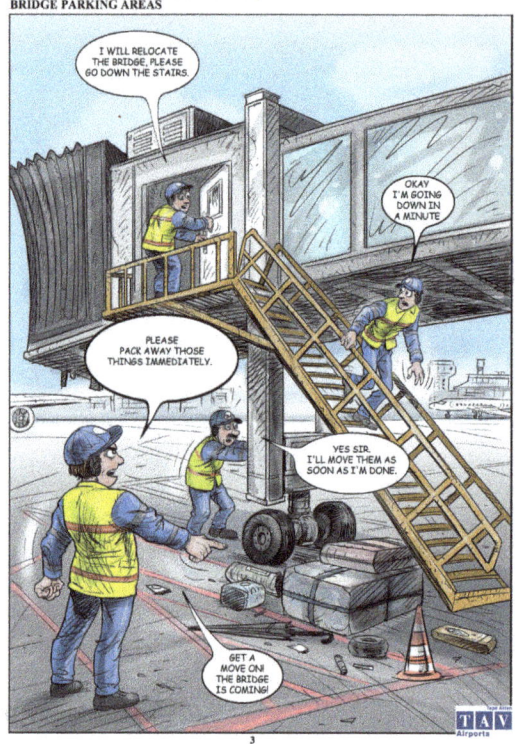

USE OF COMPANY CARS

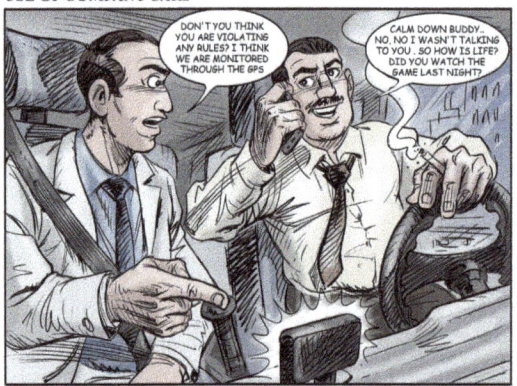

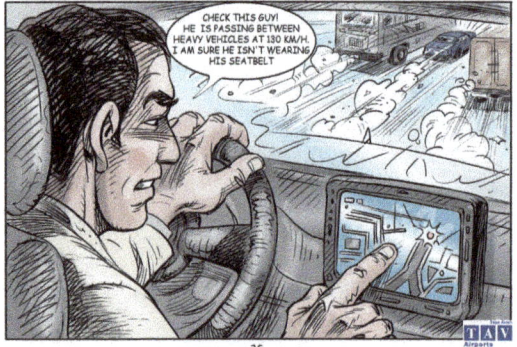

INSTRUCTIONS FOR MACHINE OPERATORS

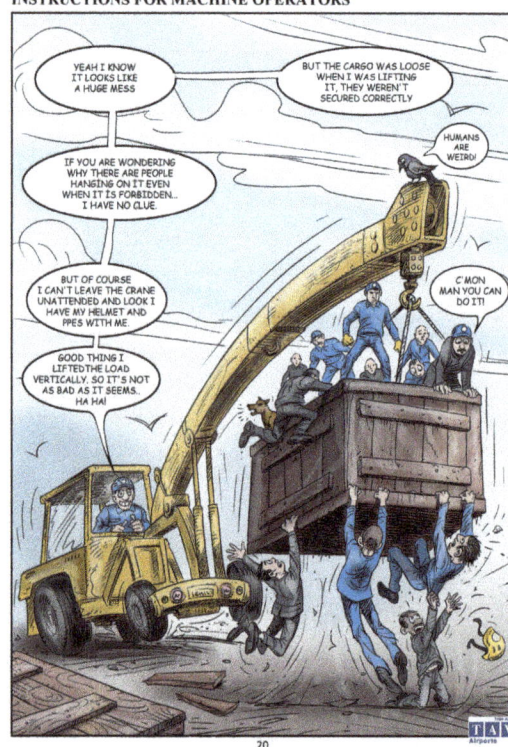

-Commission **cartoon pages** for an airport company.

Textile &
Fashion Designs

C00273

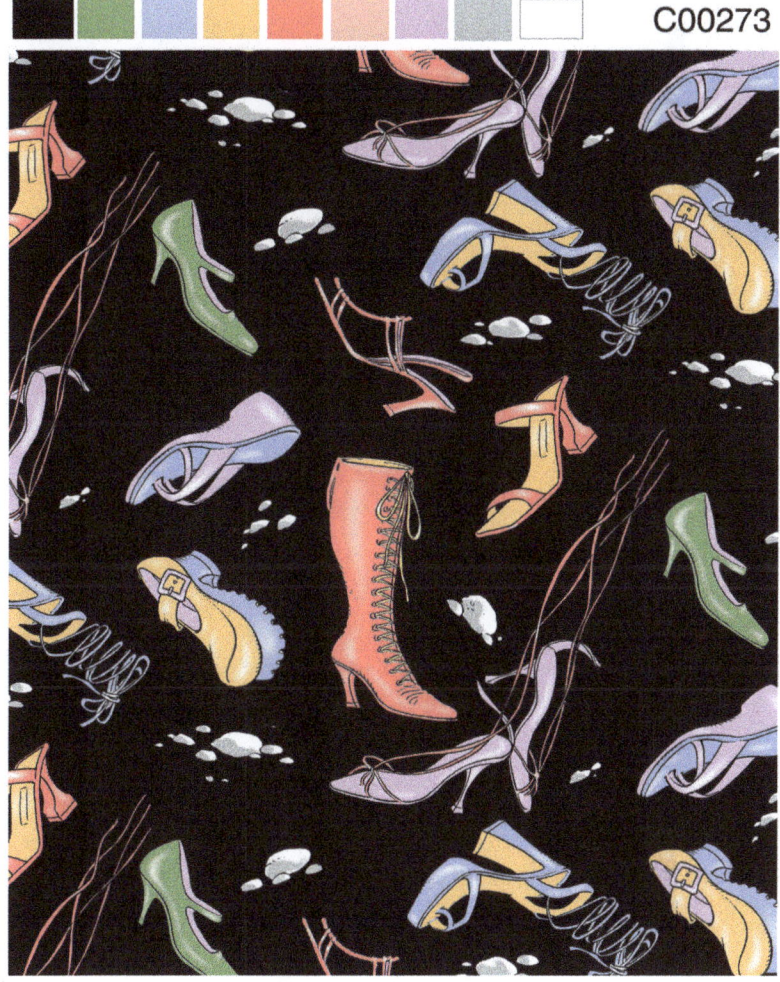

After I moved to **USA** in 1989,
I've started to work in the *textile* and *fashion* market.
These are from my print designs for textile and fabric products. I've done many
work for the top companies such as ***Tommy Hilfiger, Chaps, Polo-Ralph Loren,
Christian Dior, Joe Boxer, Intimo, Mavi Jeans, Tiffany*** and so on.

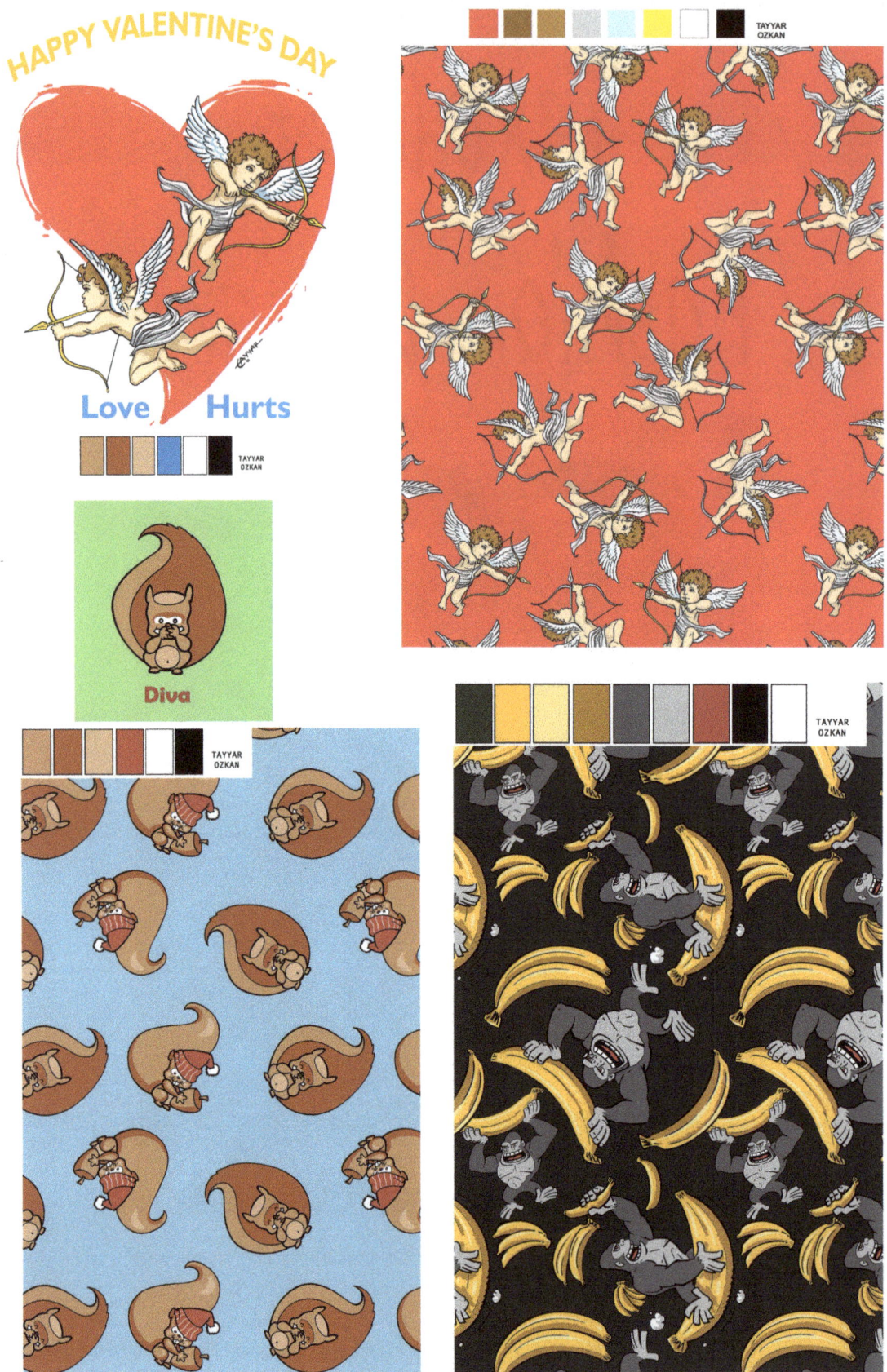

Drawings For *Textile* Design.

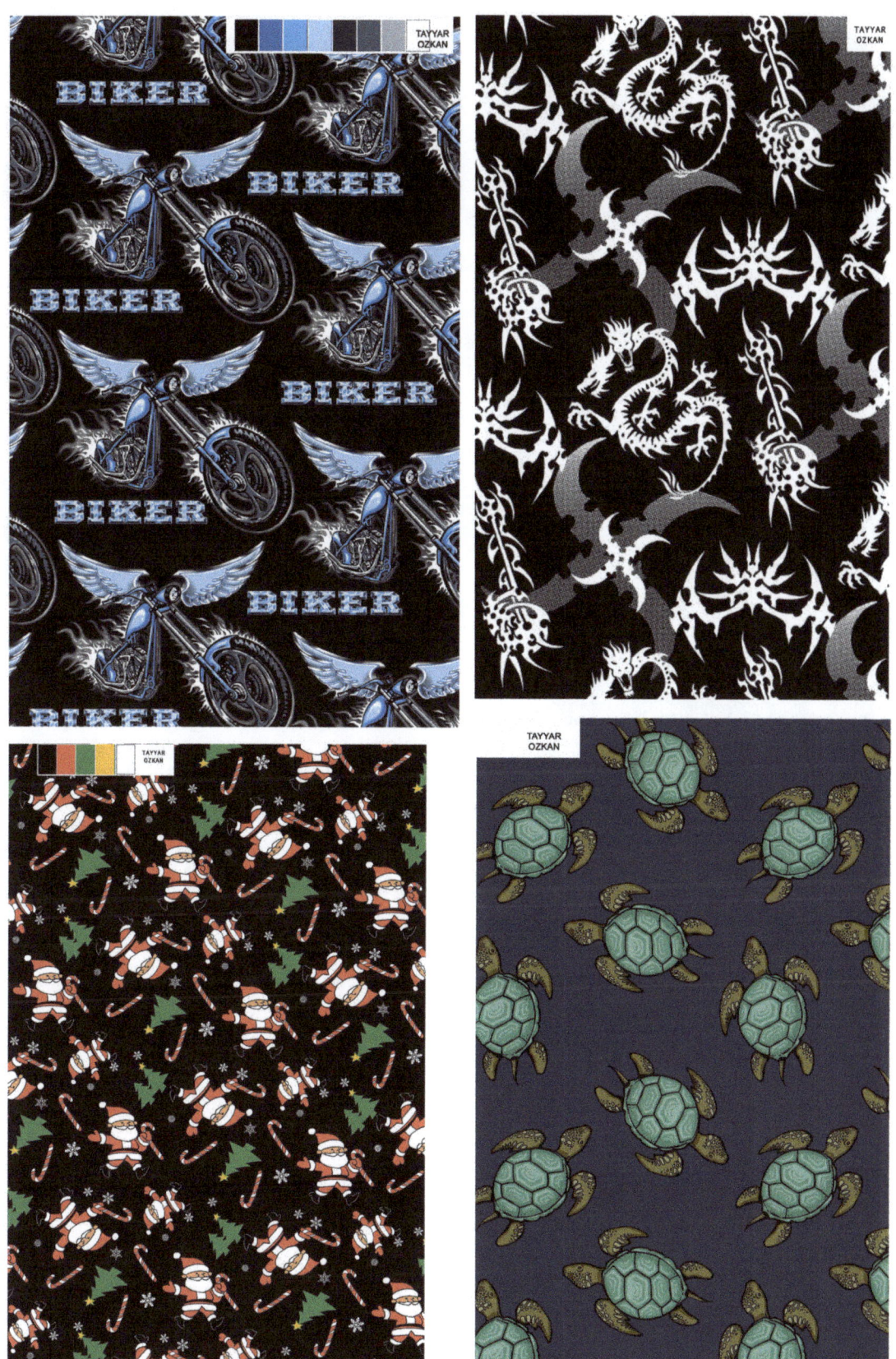

Drawings For *Textile* Design.

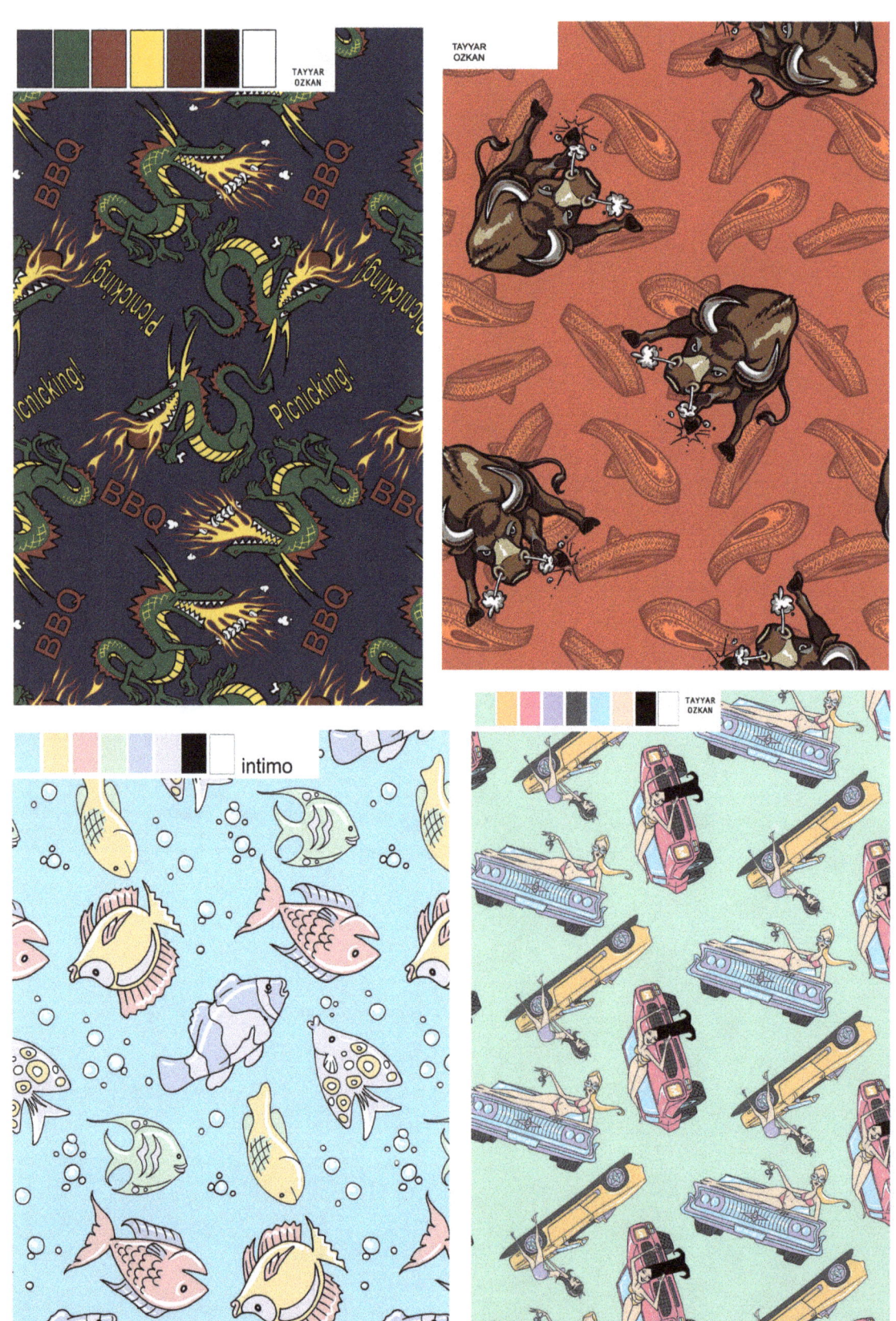

Drawings For *Textile* Design.

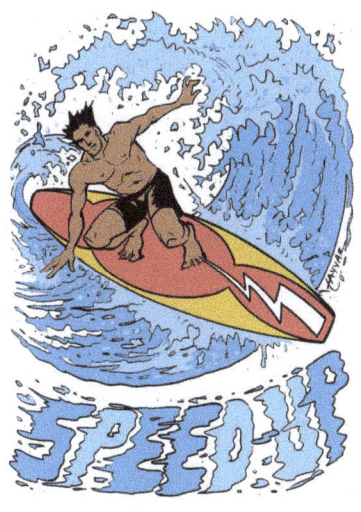
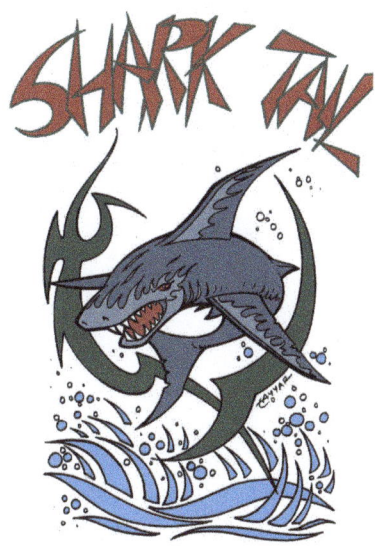
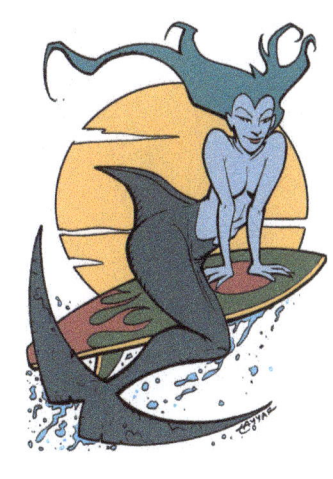

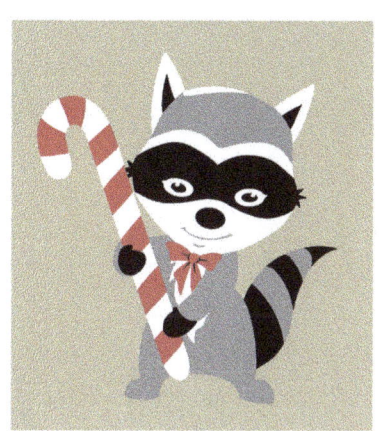
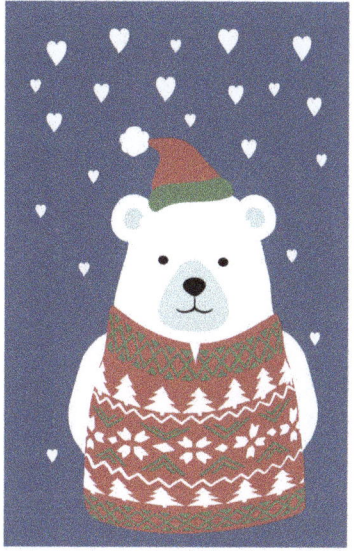
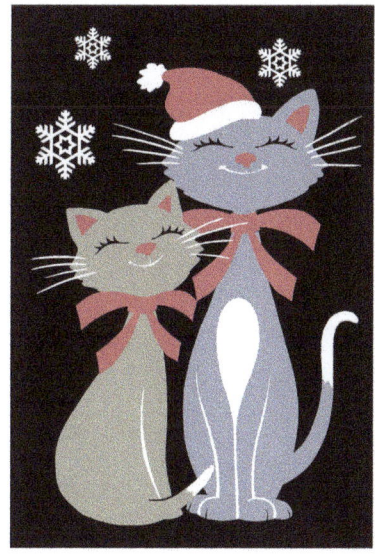
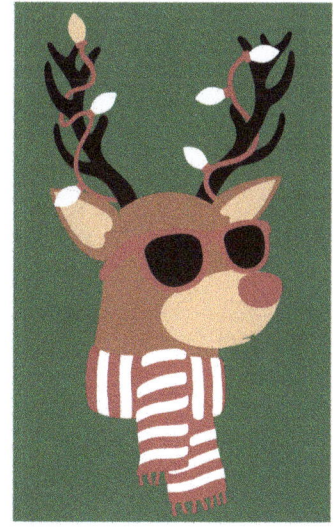
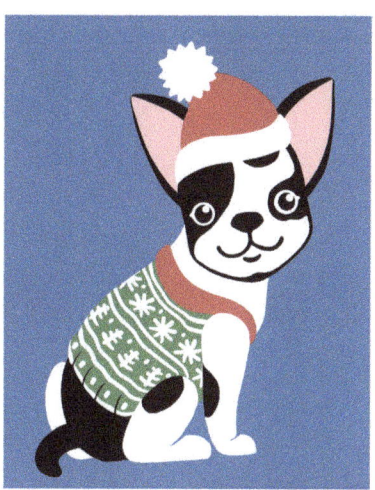

Drawings For *Textile* Design.

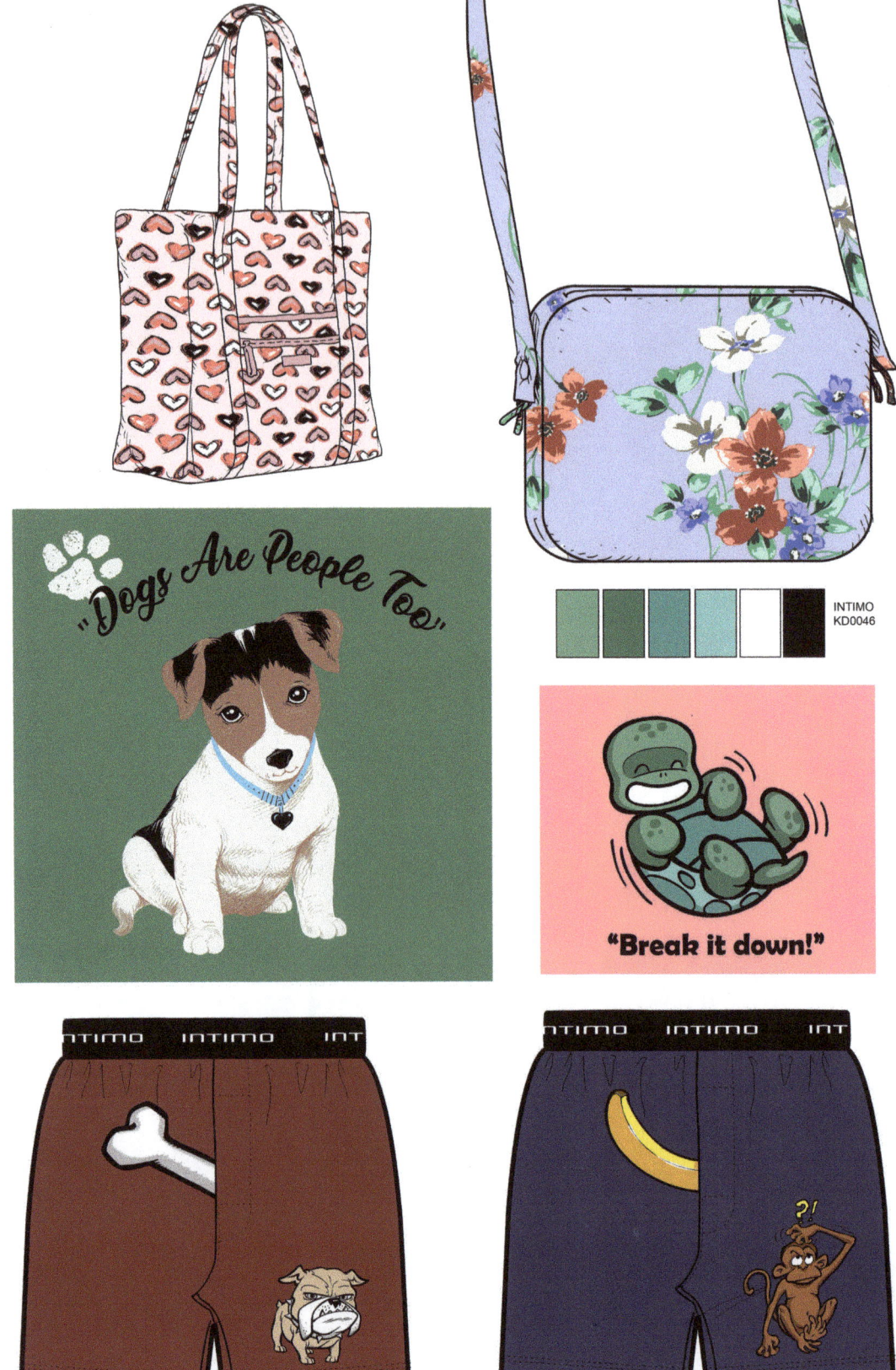

Drawings For Textile Design.

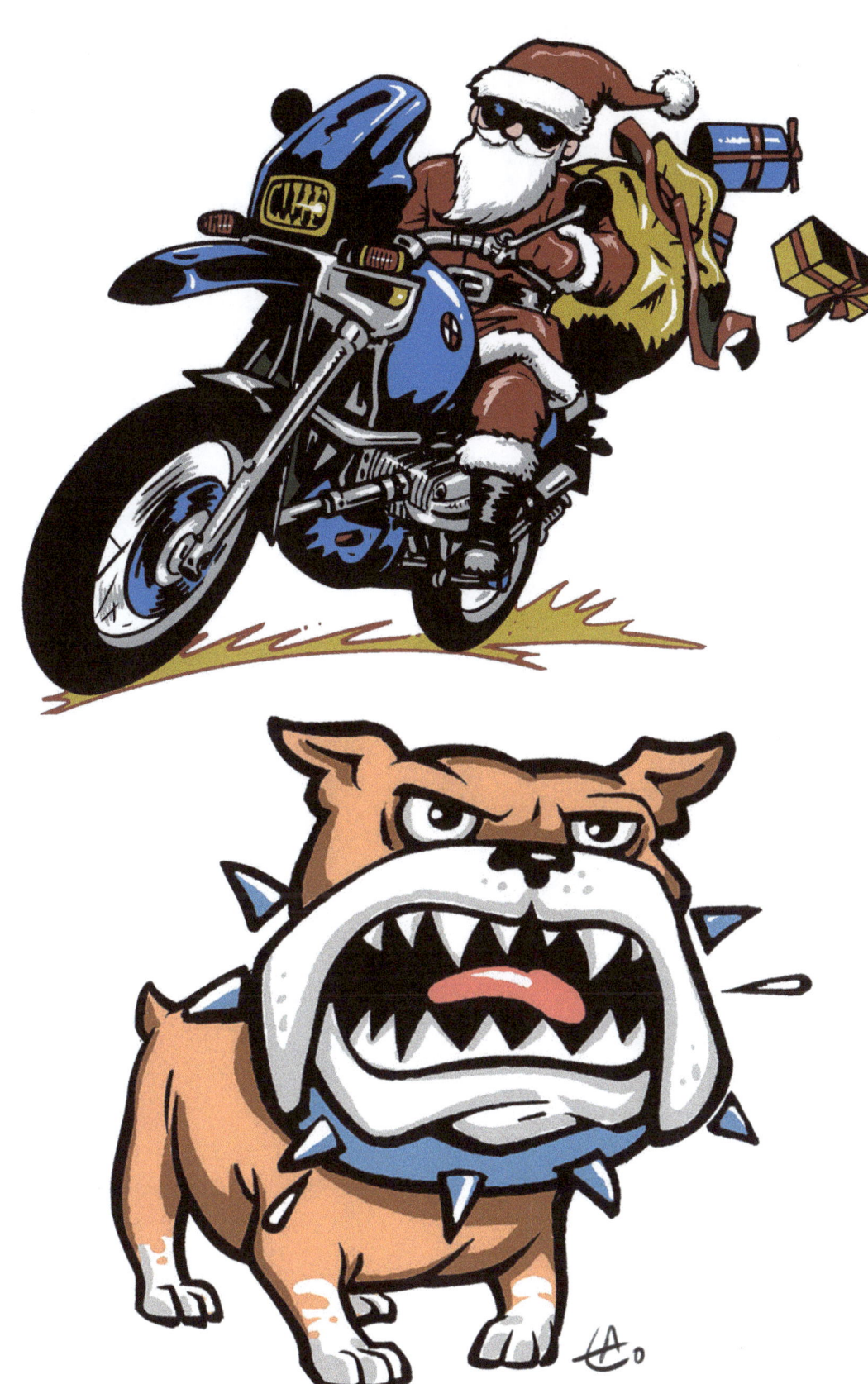

Drawings For *Textile* Design.

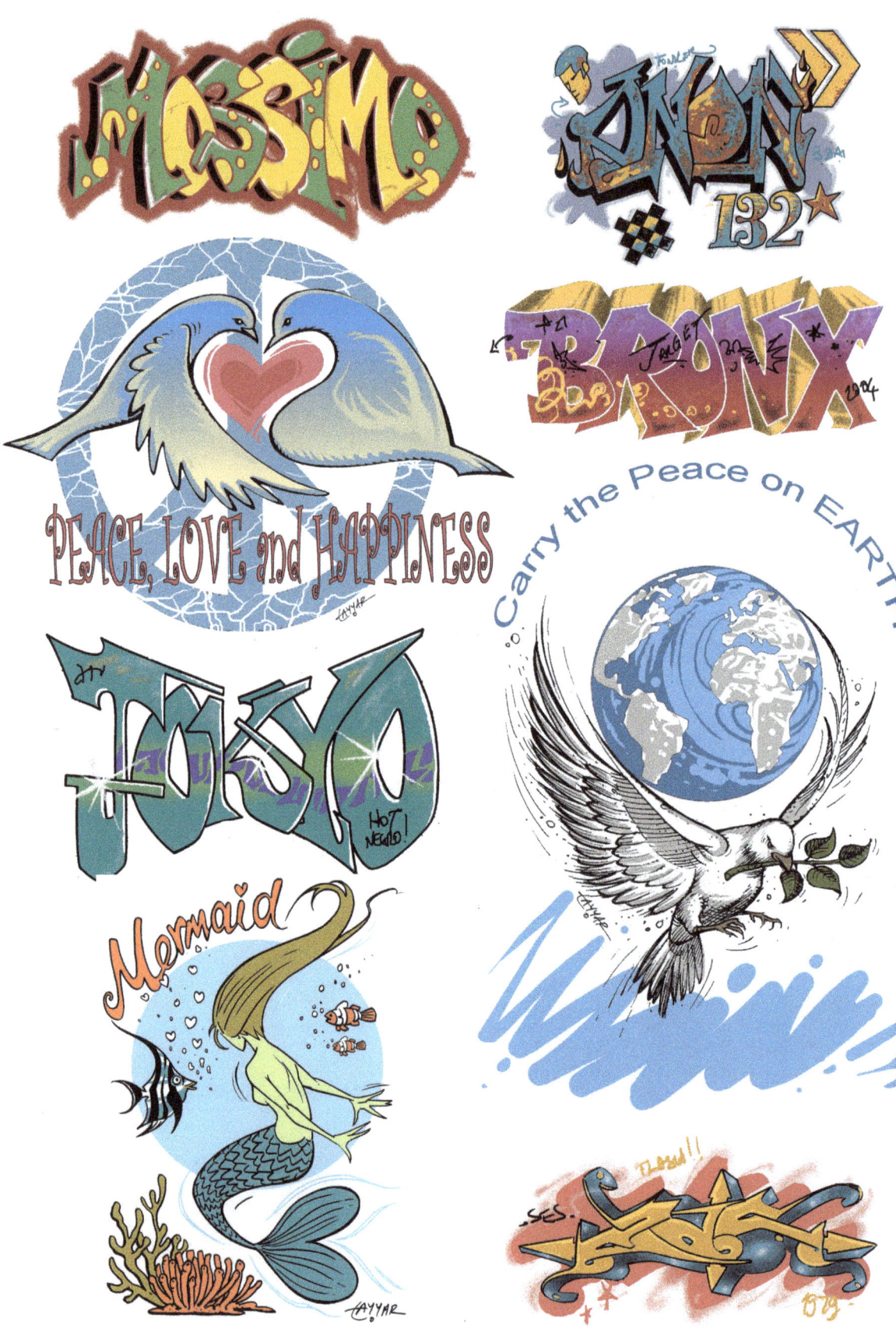

Drawings For *Textile* Design.

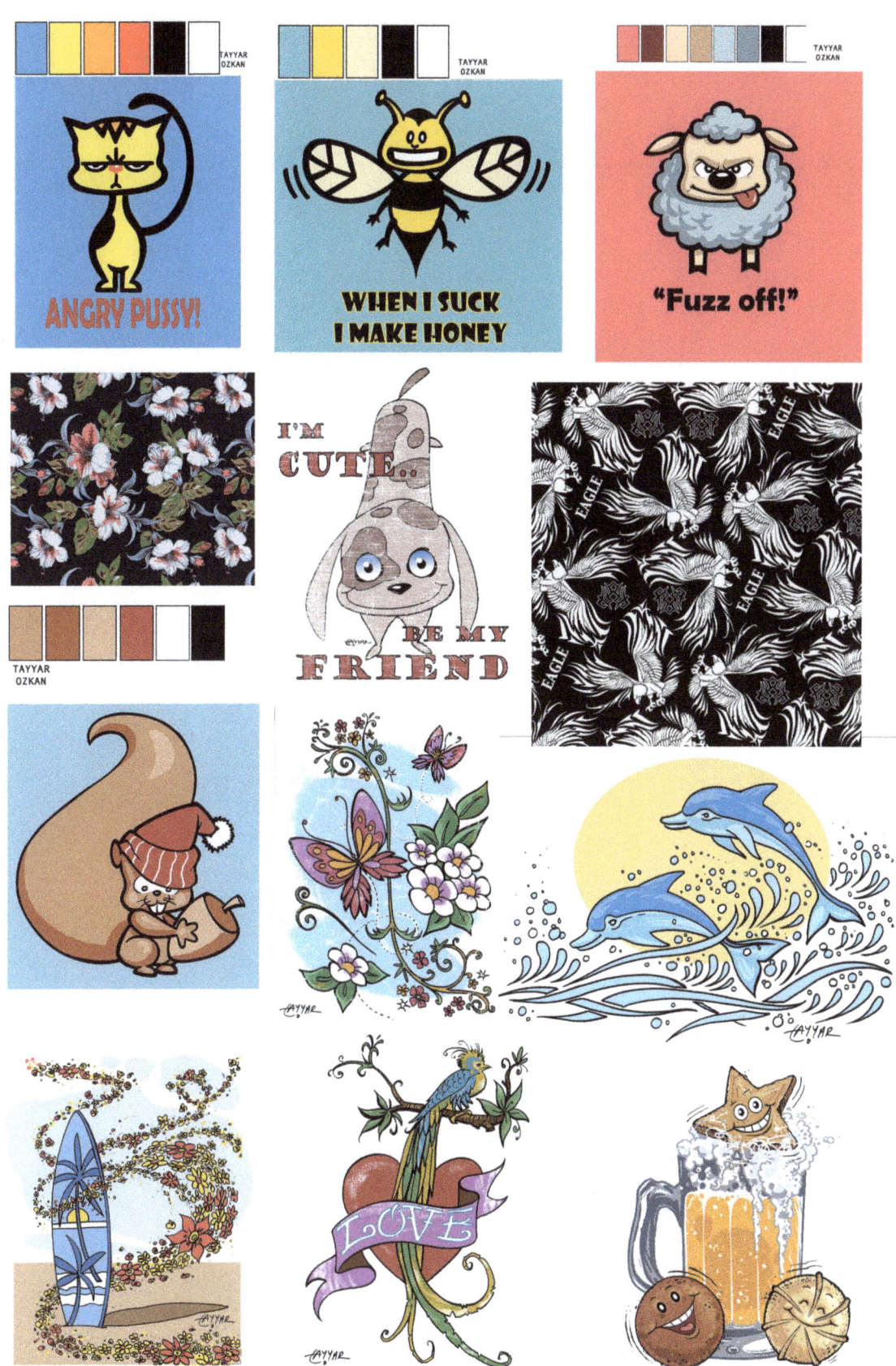

Drawings For *Textile* Design.

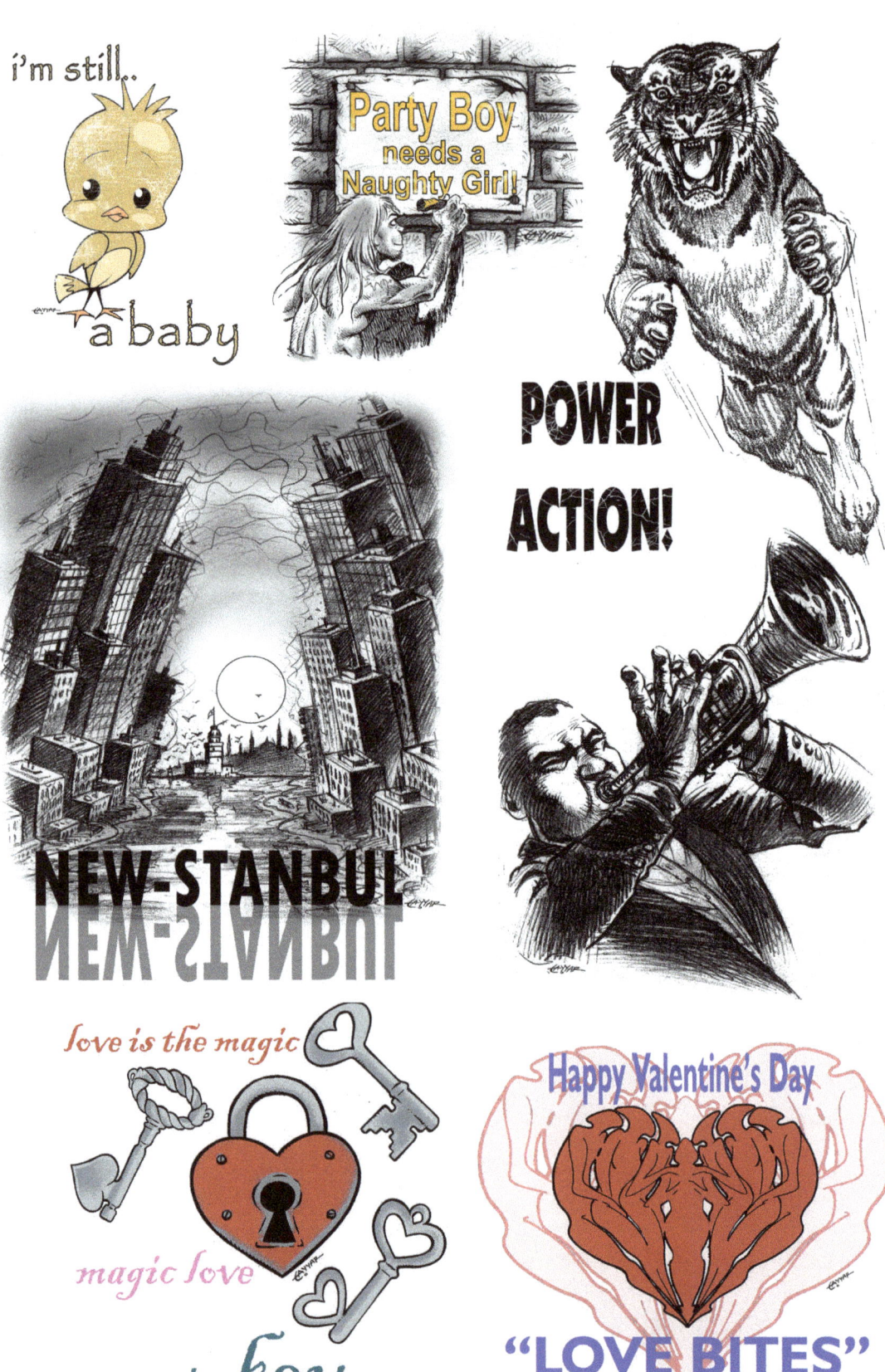

Drawings For *Textile* Design.

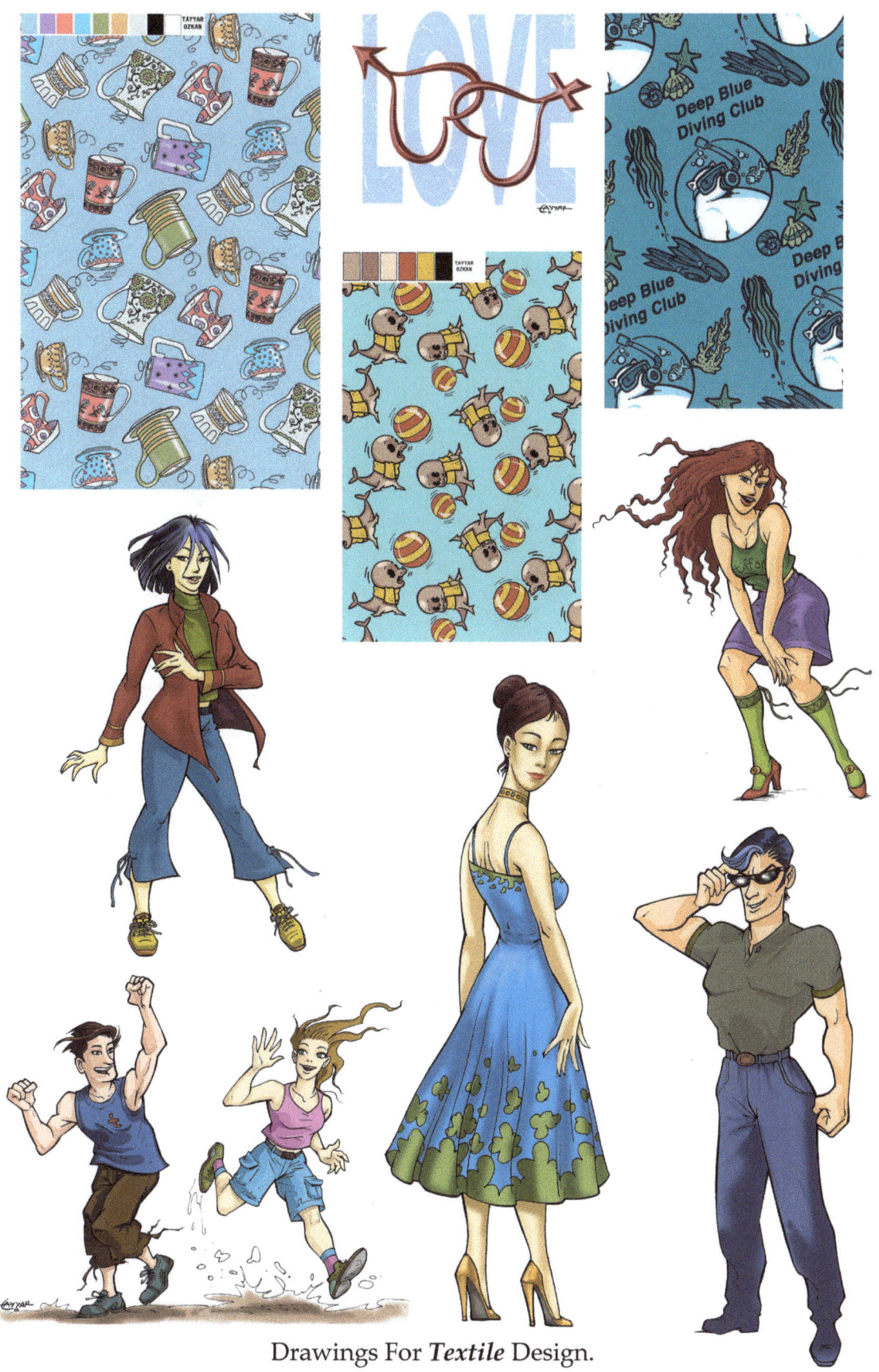

Drawings For *Textile* Design.

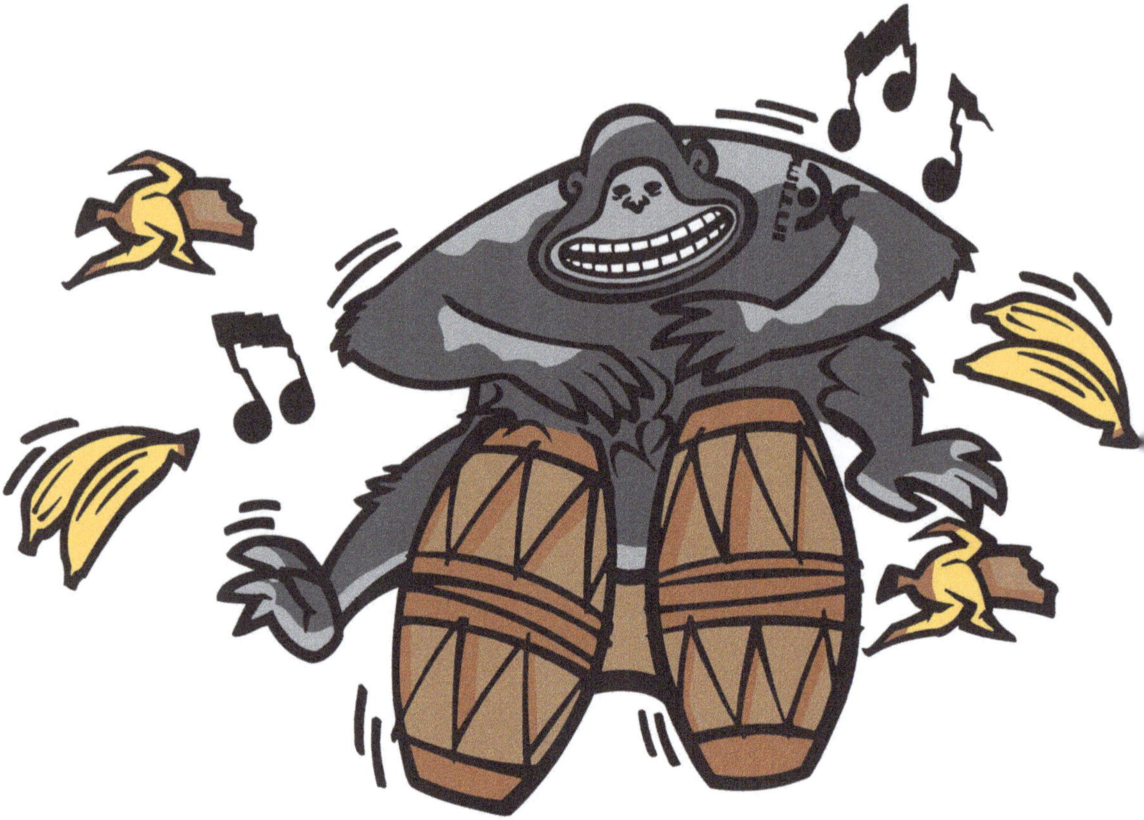

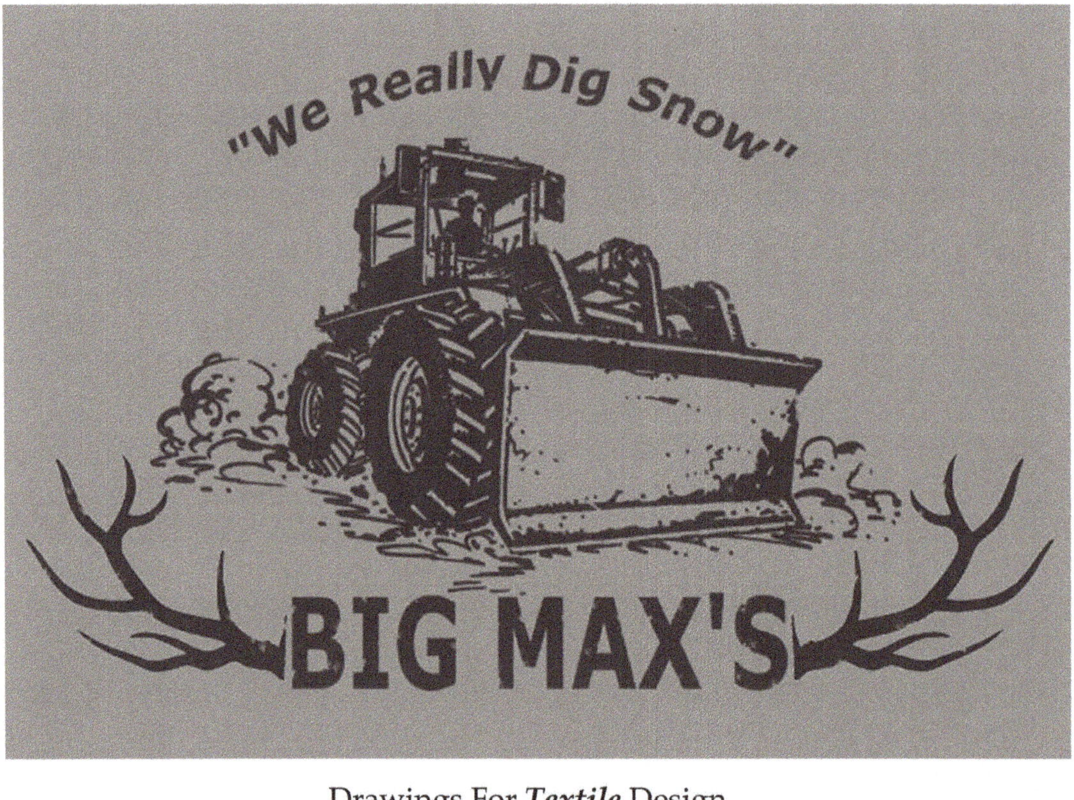

"We Really Dig Snow"

BIG MAX'S

Drawings For *Textile* Design.

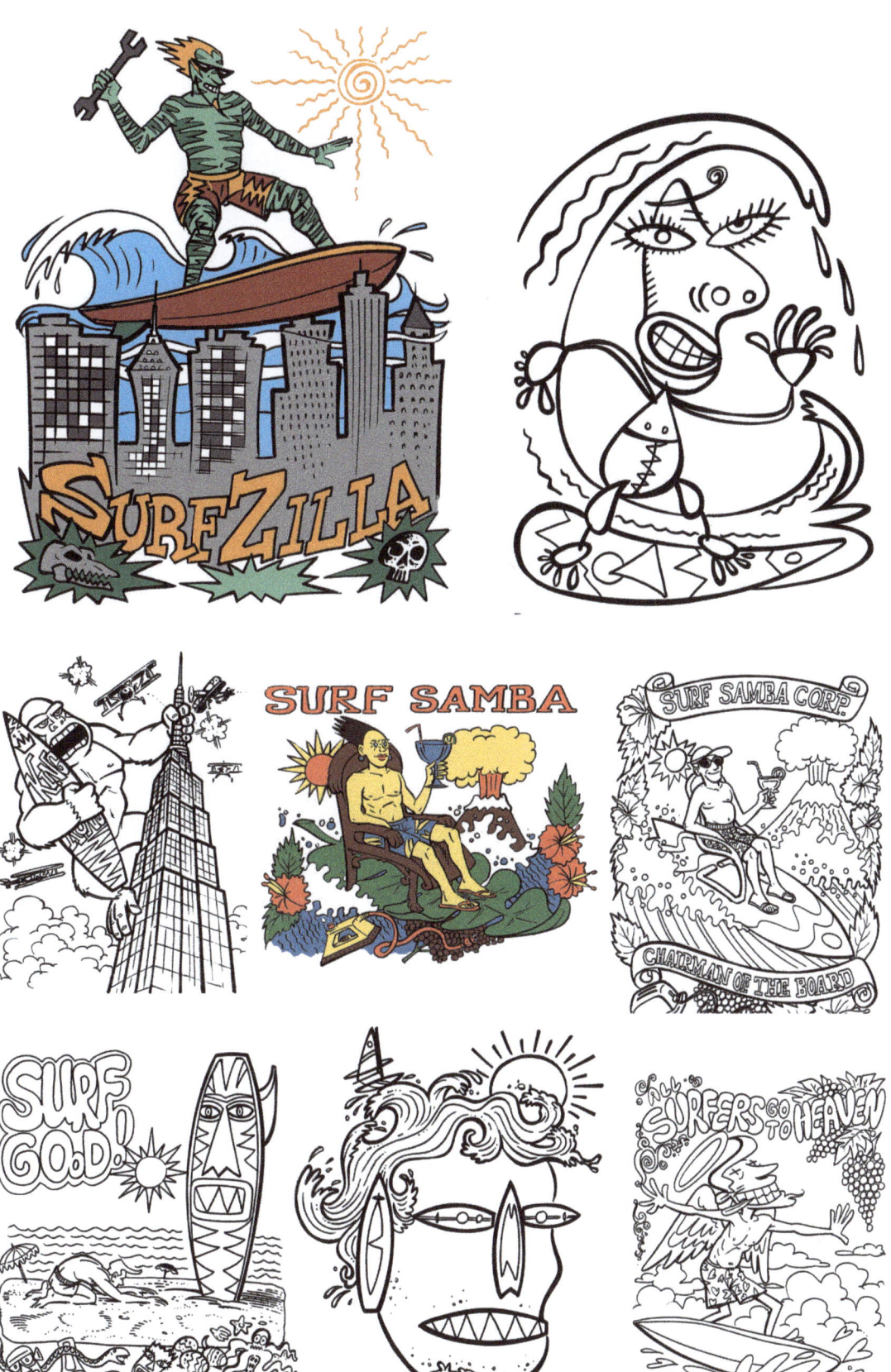

Drawings For *Textile* Design.

Character

Designs

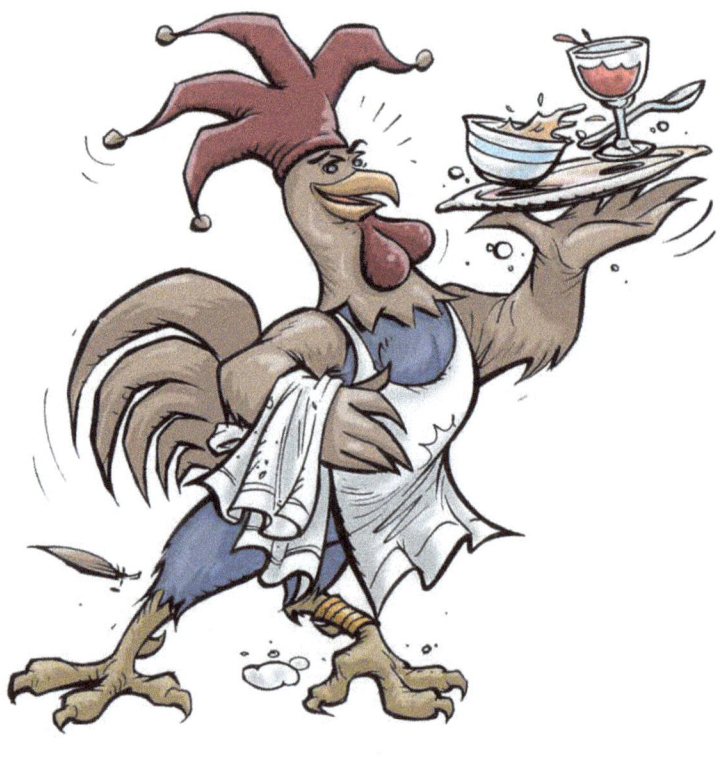

Most of the **characters** here are for TV *animation* movies and *advertising* agencies.

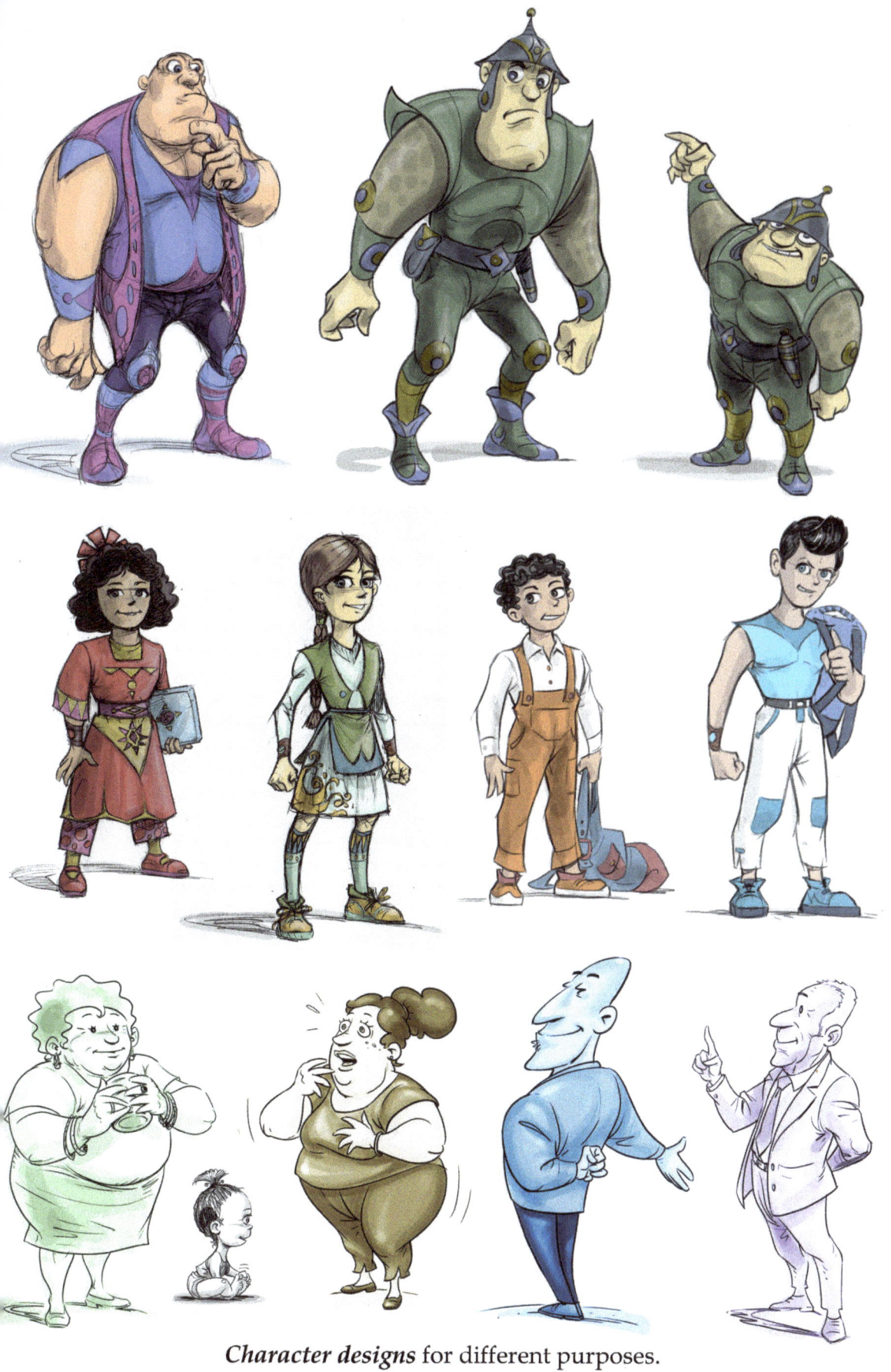

Character designs for different purposes.

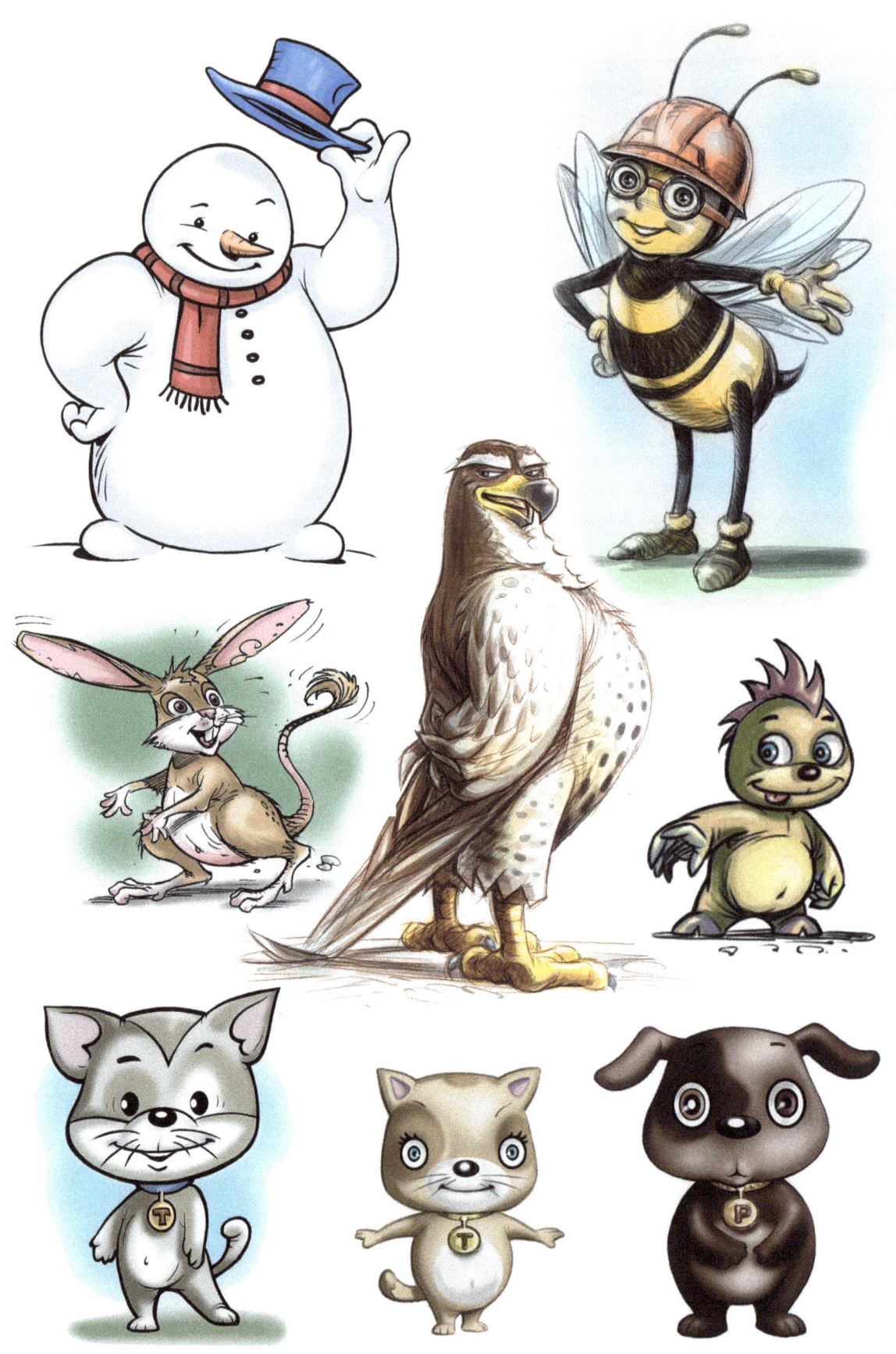

Character *designs* for different purposes.

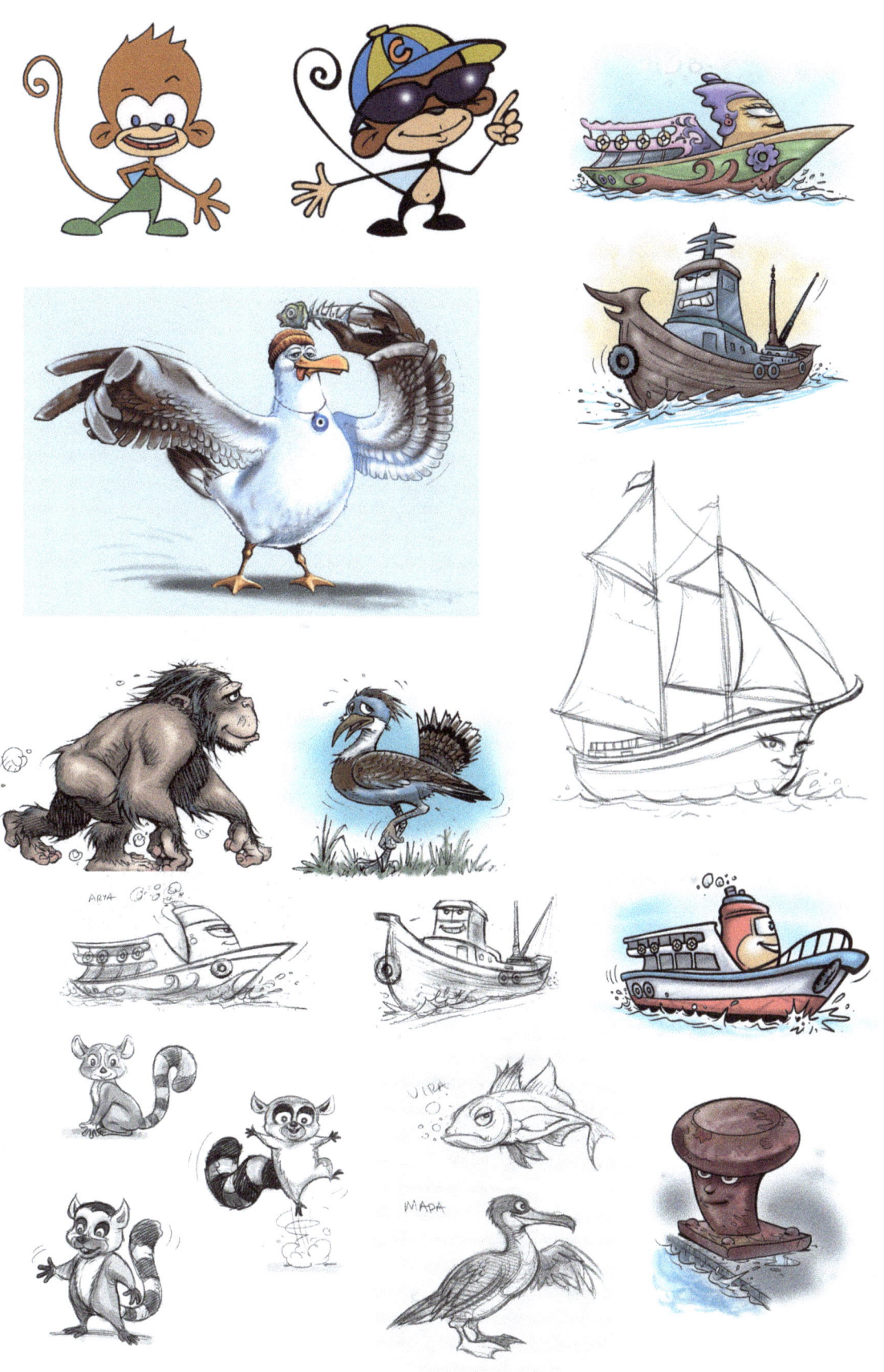

Character designs for different purposes.

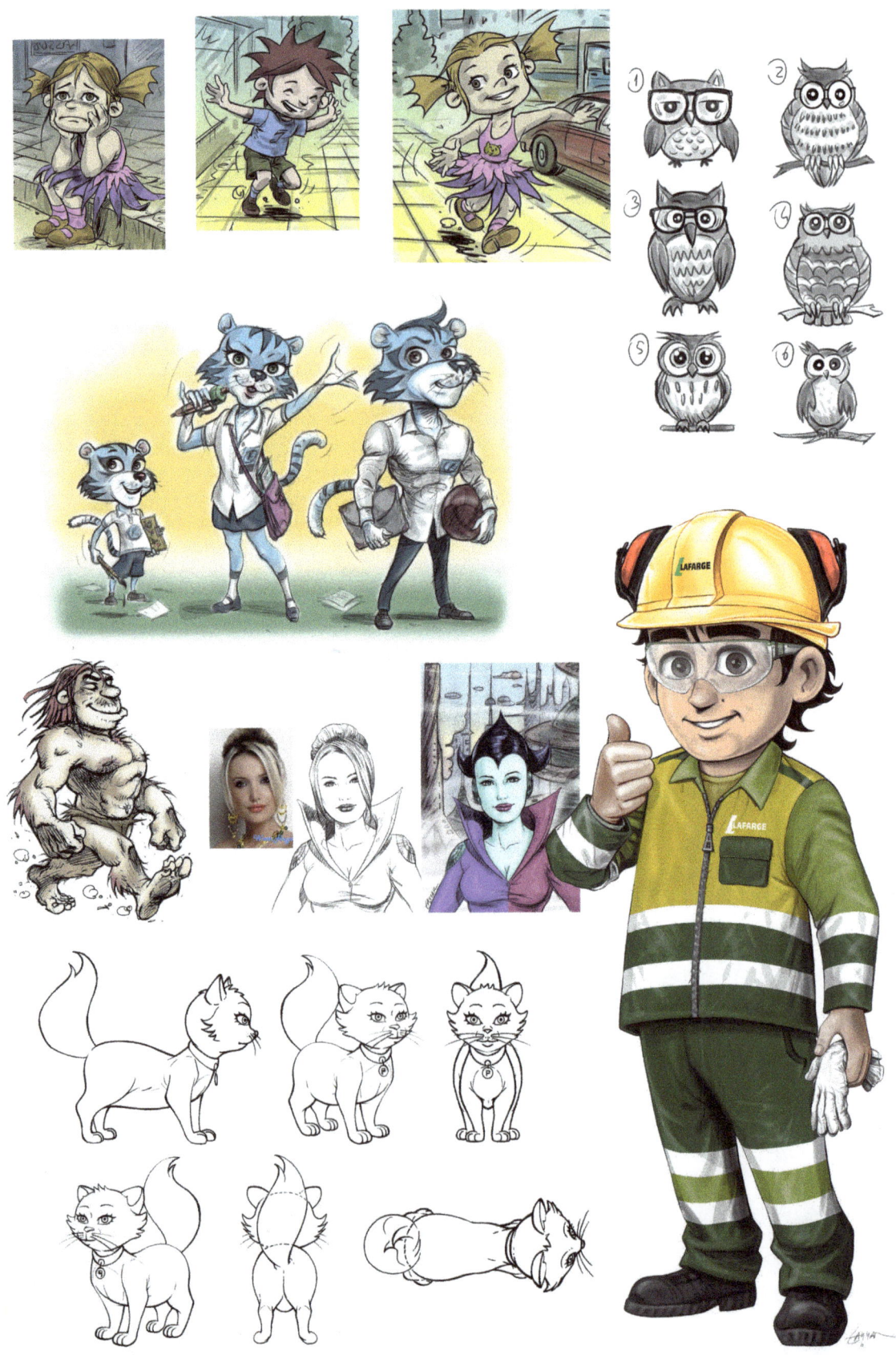

Character *designs* for different purposes.

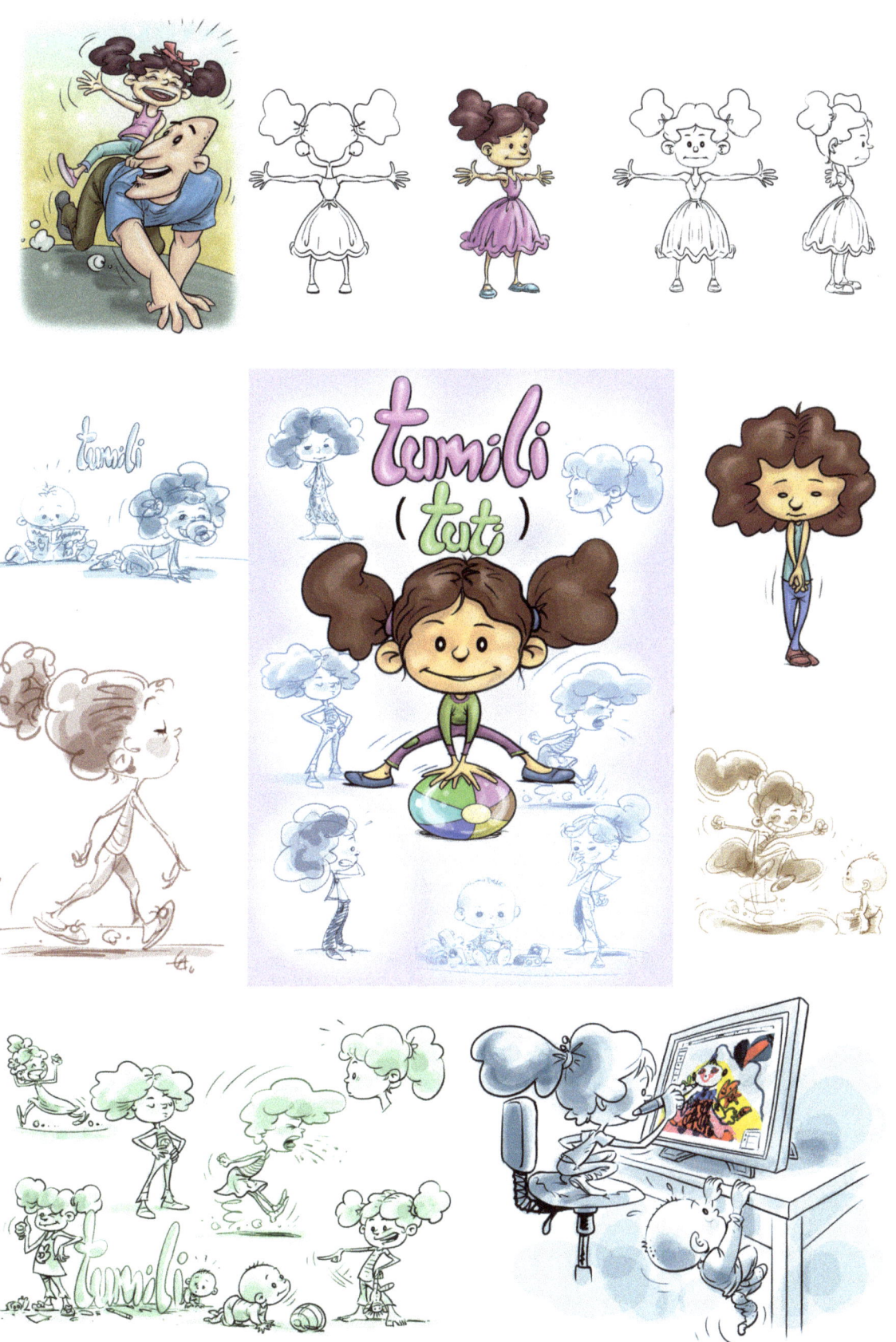

I created this *character* based on my daughters **Tutku** and Peri for an *animation* project but never happened yet..

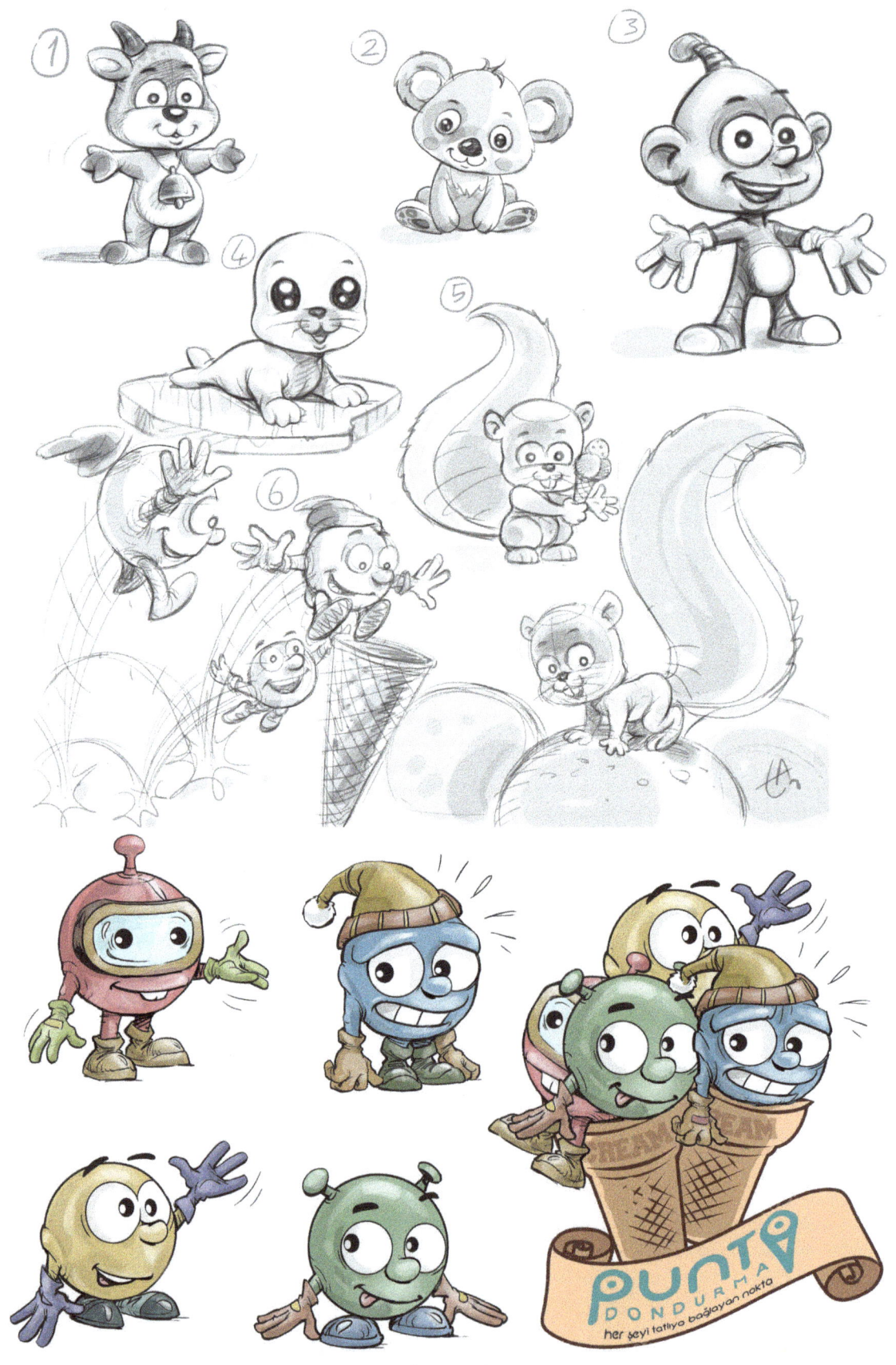

Character designs for an *ice cream* company.

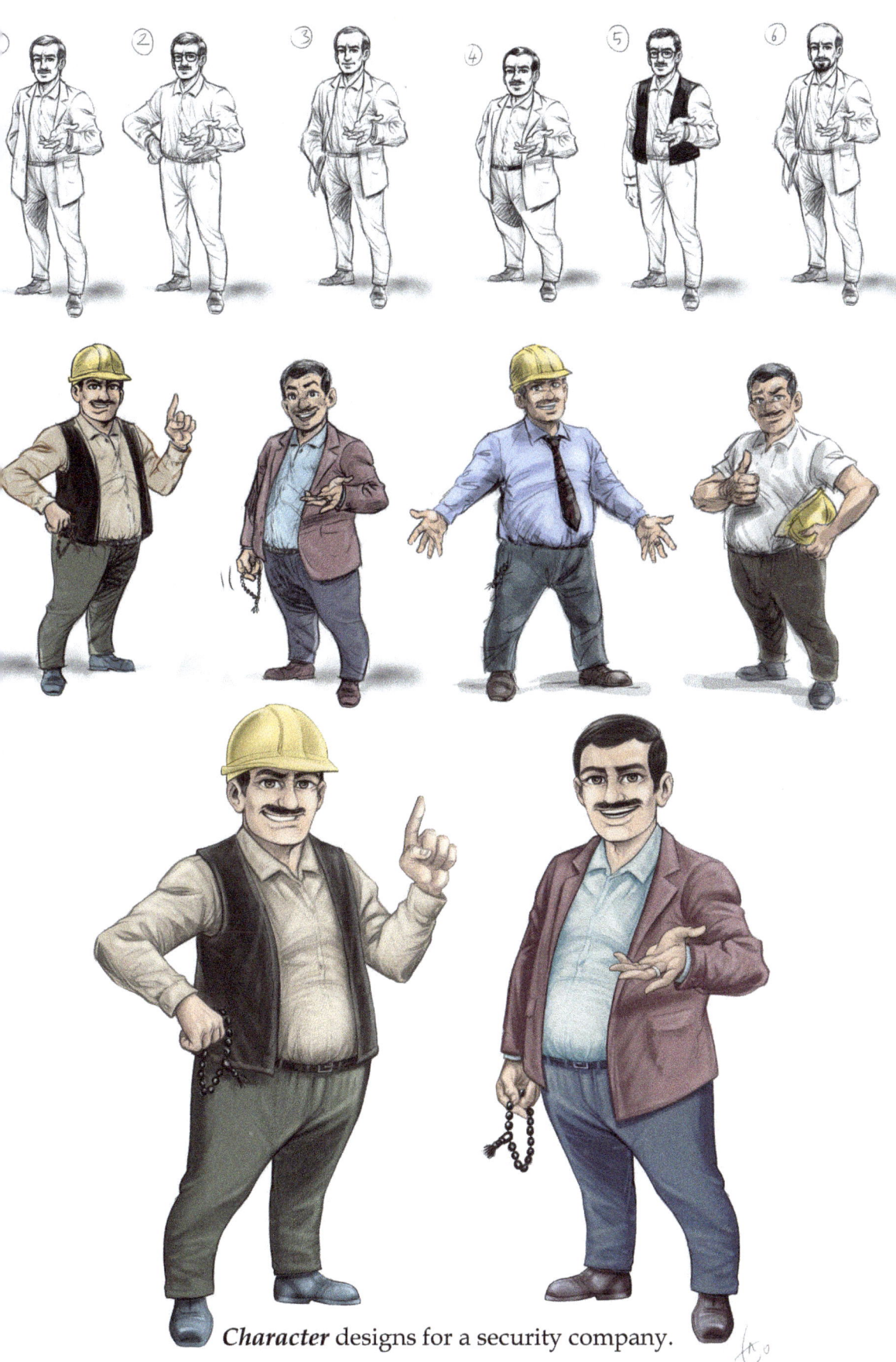

Character designs for a security company.

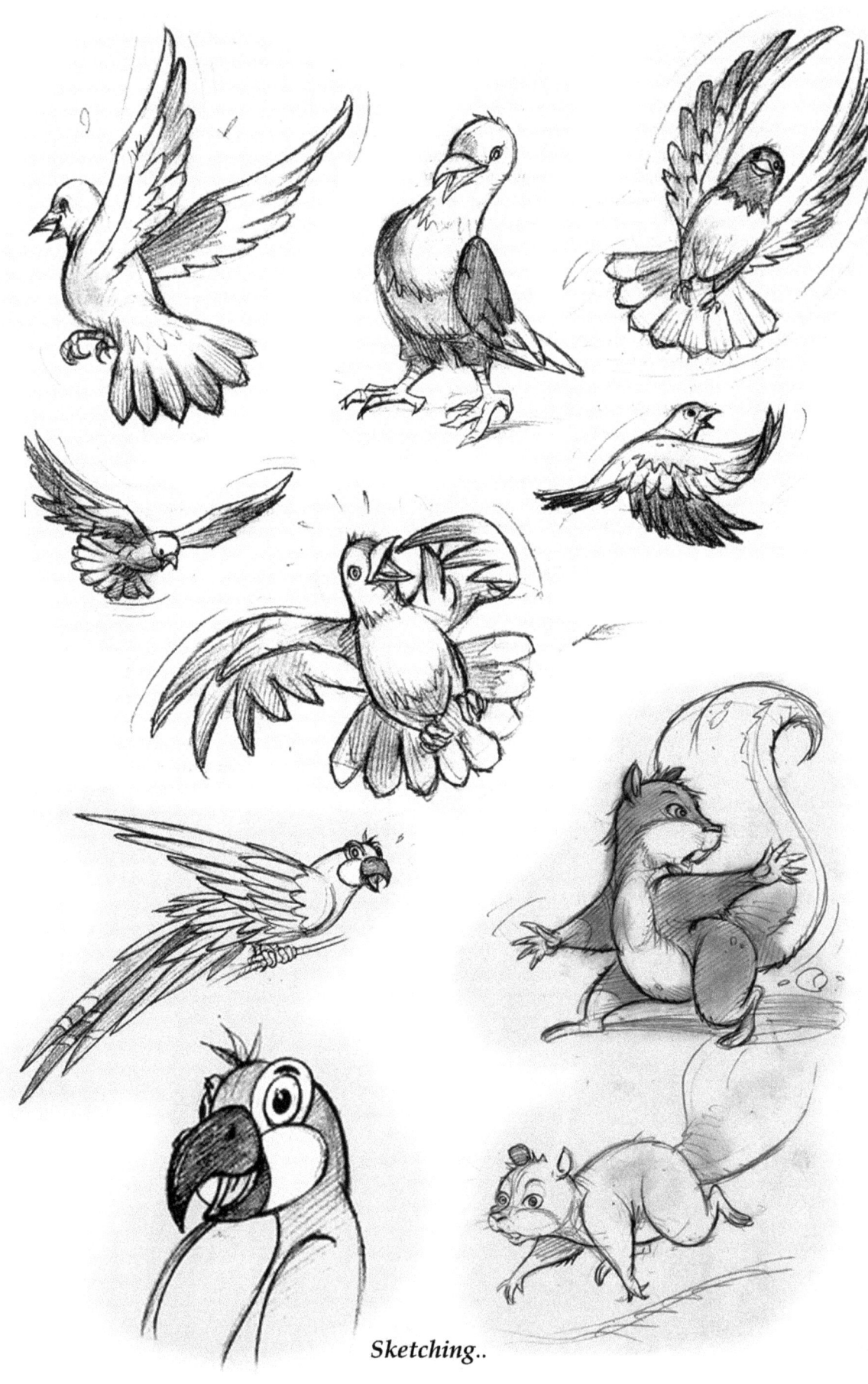

Sketching..

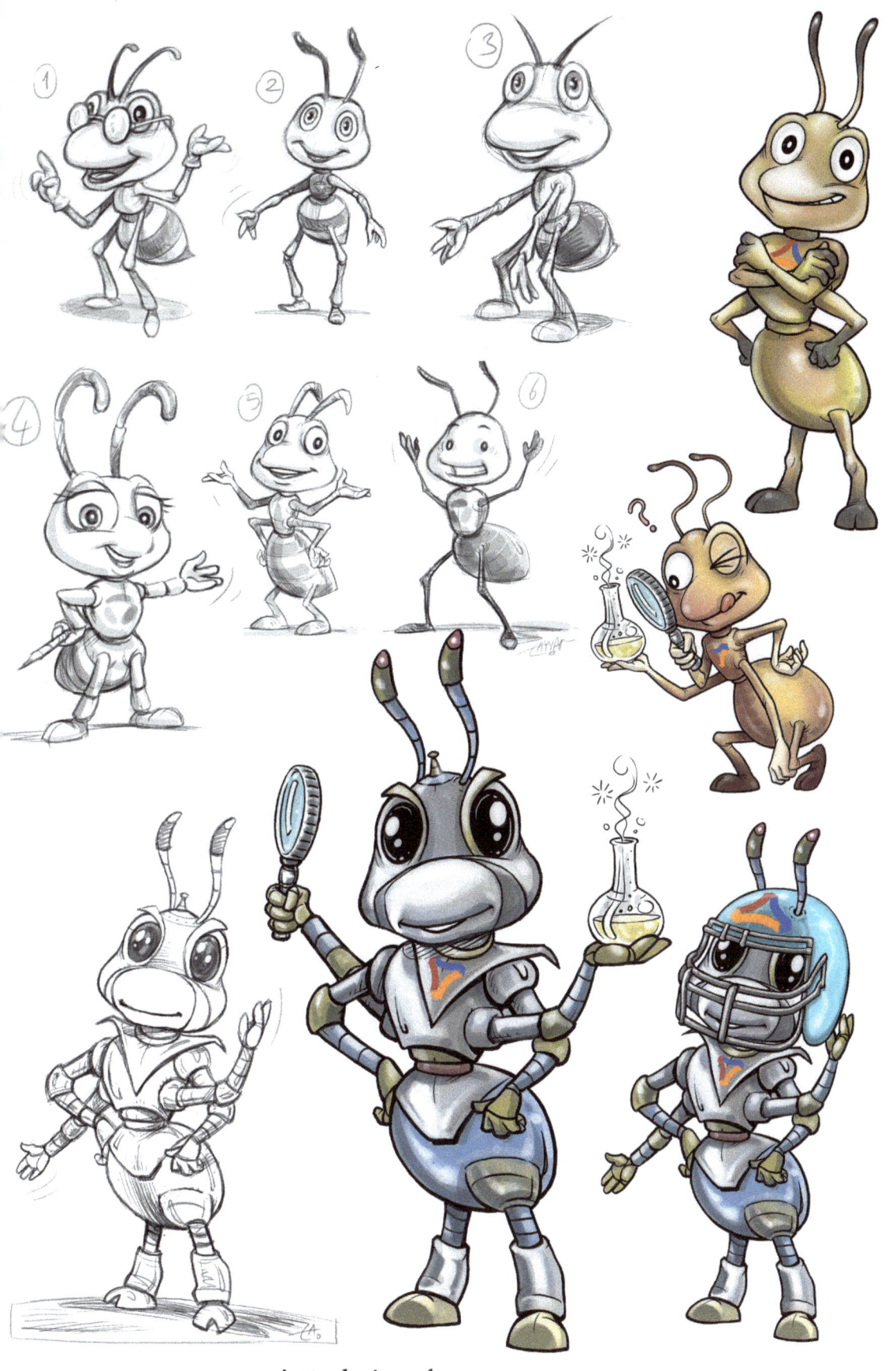

Ants designs for an agency.

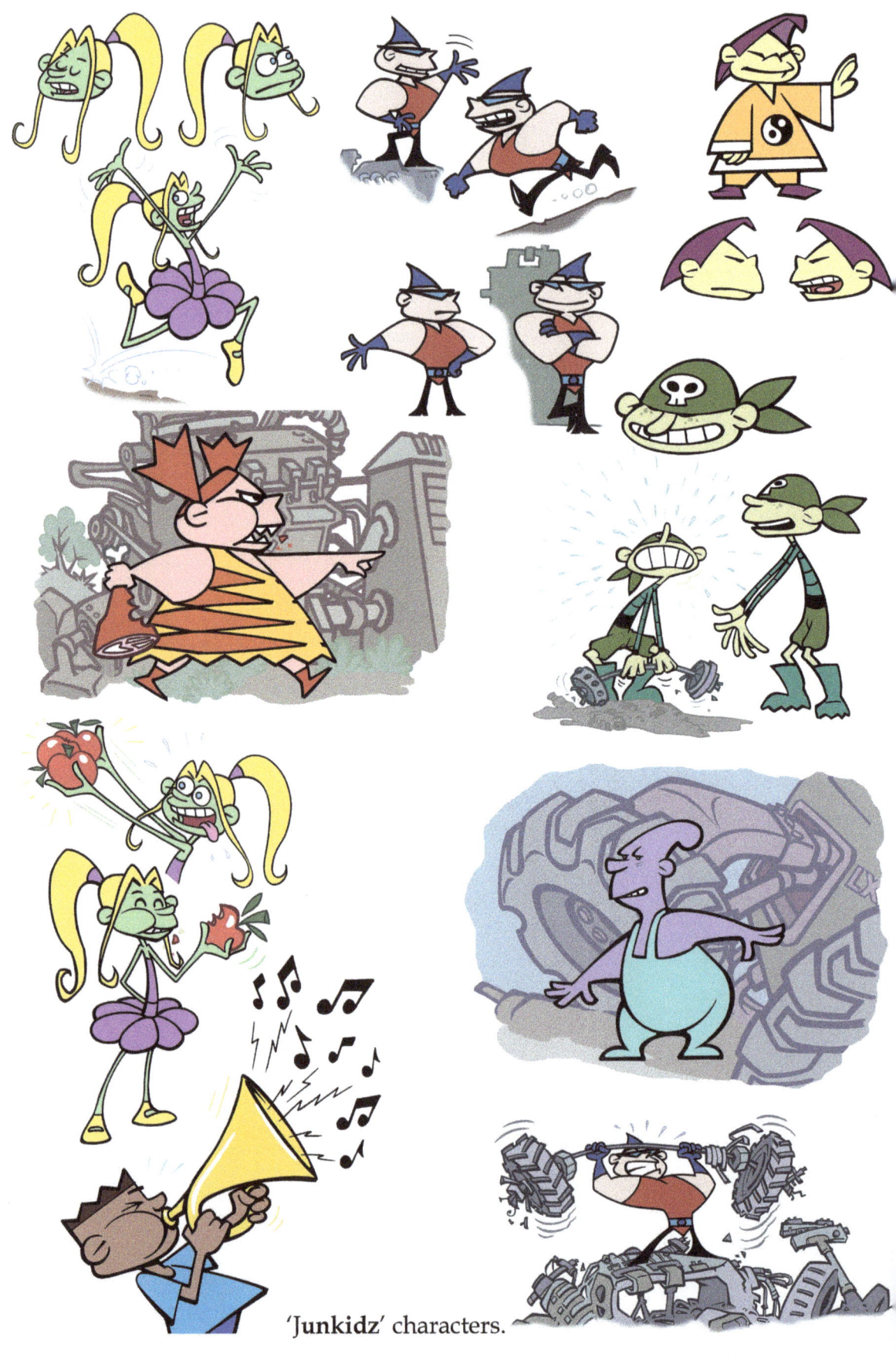

'Junkidz' characters.

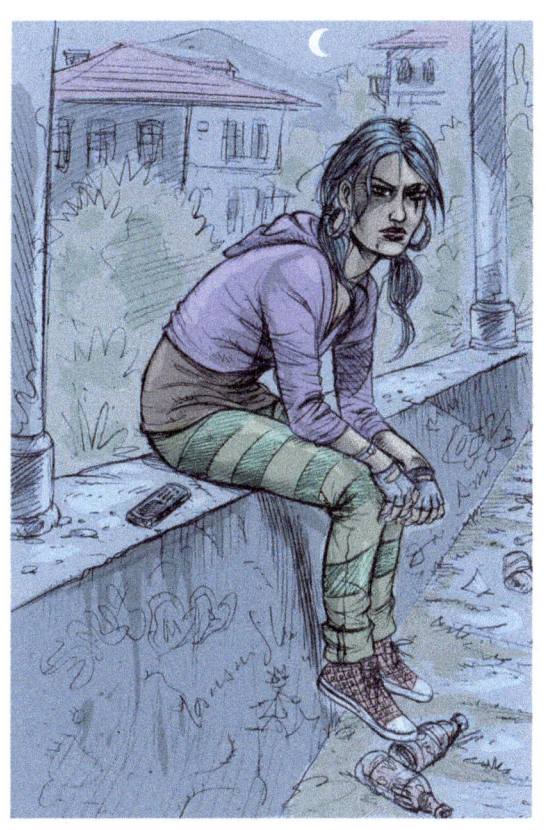
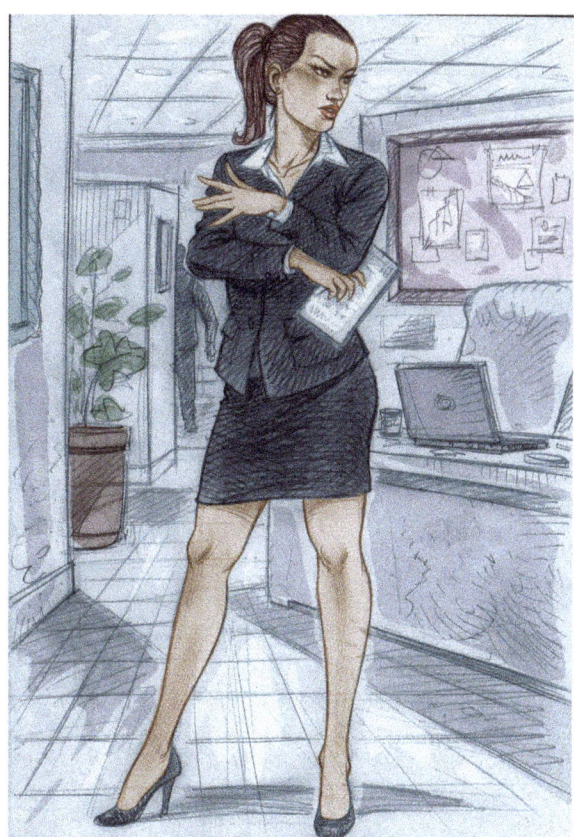
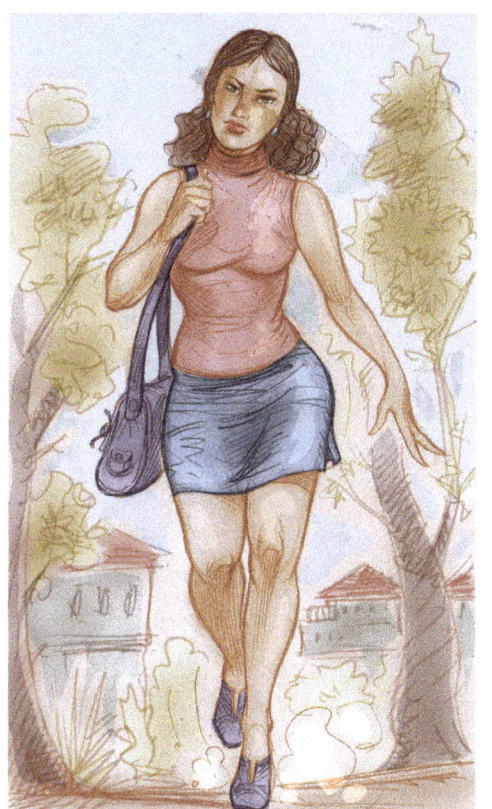
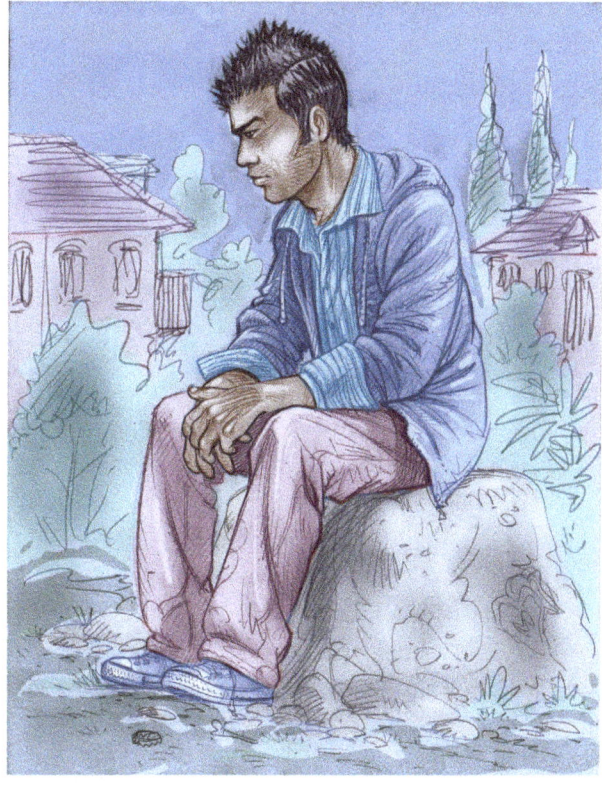

Some *character sketching* for a TV series.

Illustrations and Sketches

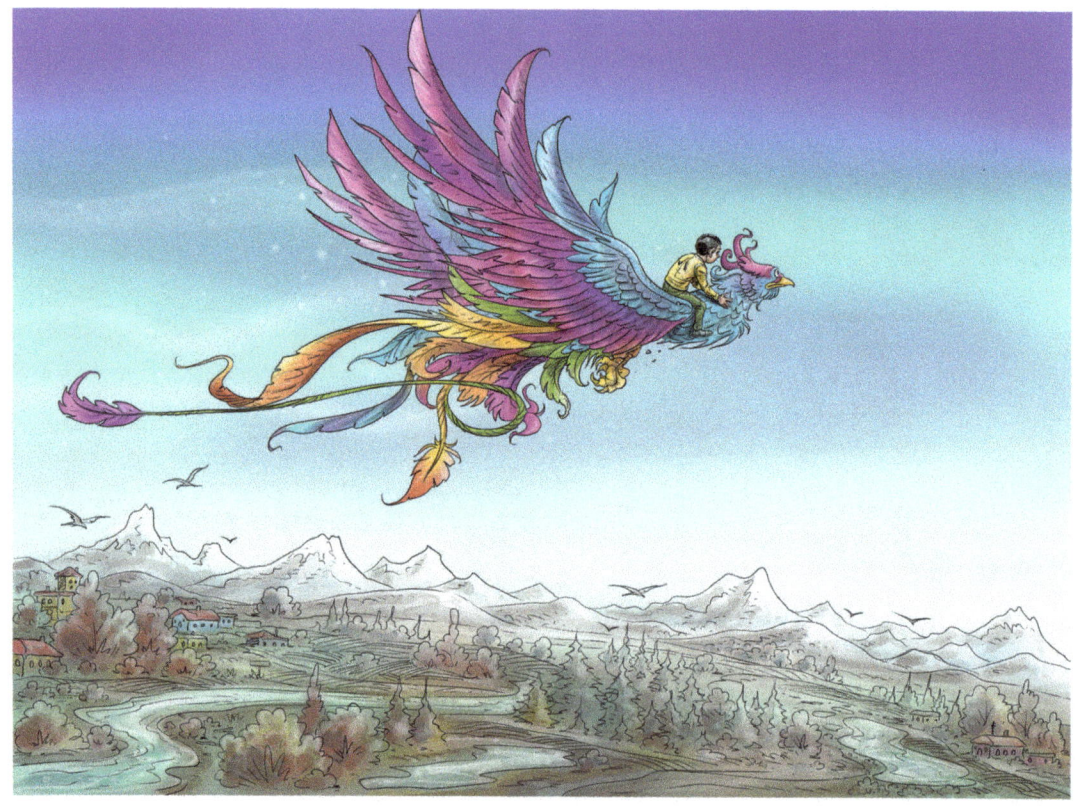

These are the *illustrations* and *sketches* for many reasons,
such as for children's books, book covers,
commissions and personal requires.

Sketches are done for fun at the *different times* and *places*.

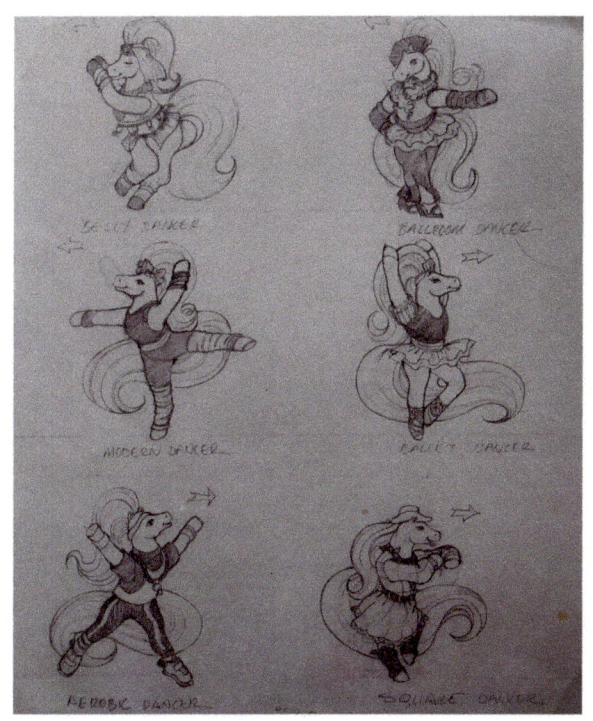

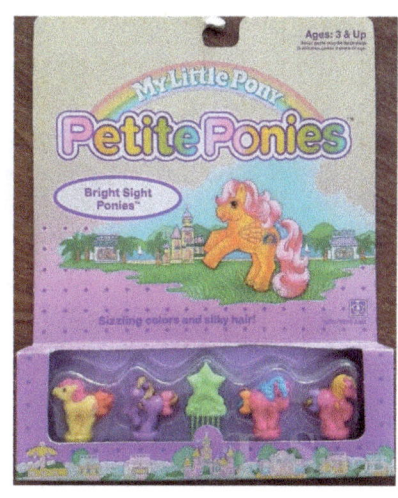

-"*MY Little Pony*".. This was the **first commission work** right after a month I moved to USA in **1989**.

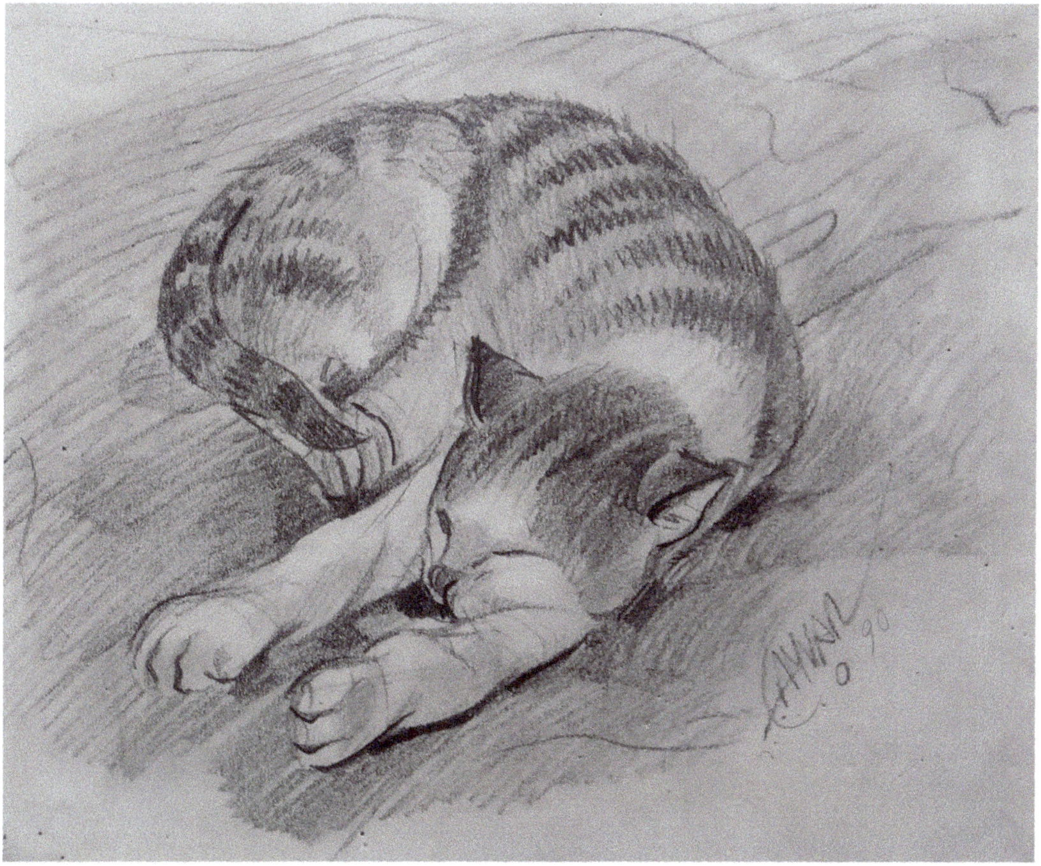

-The sketch of my **cat** in NYC in 1990.

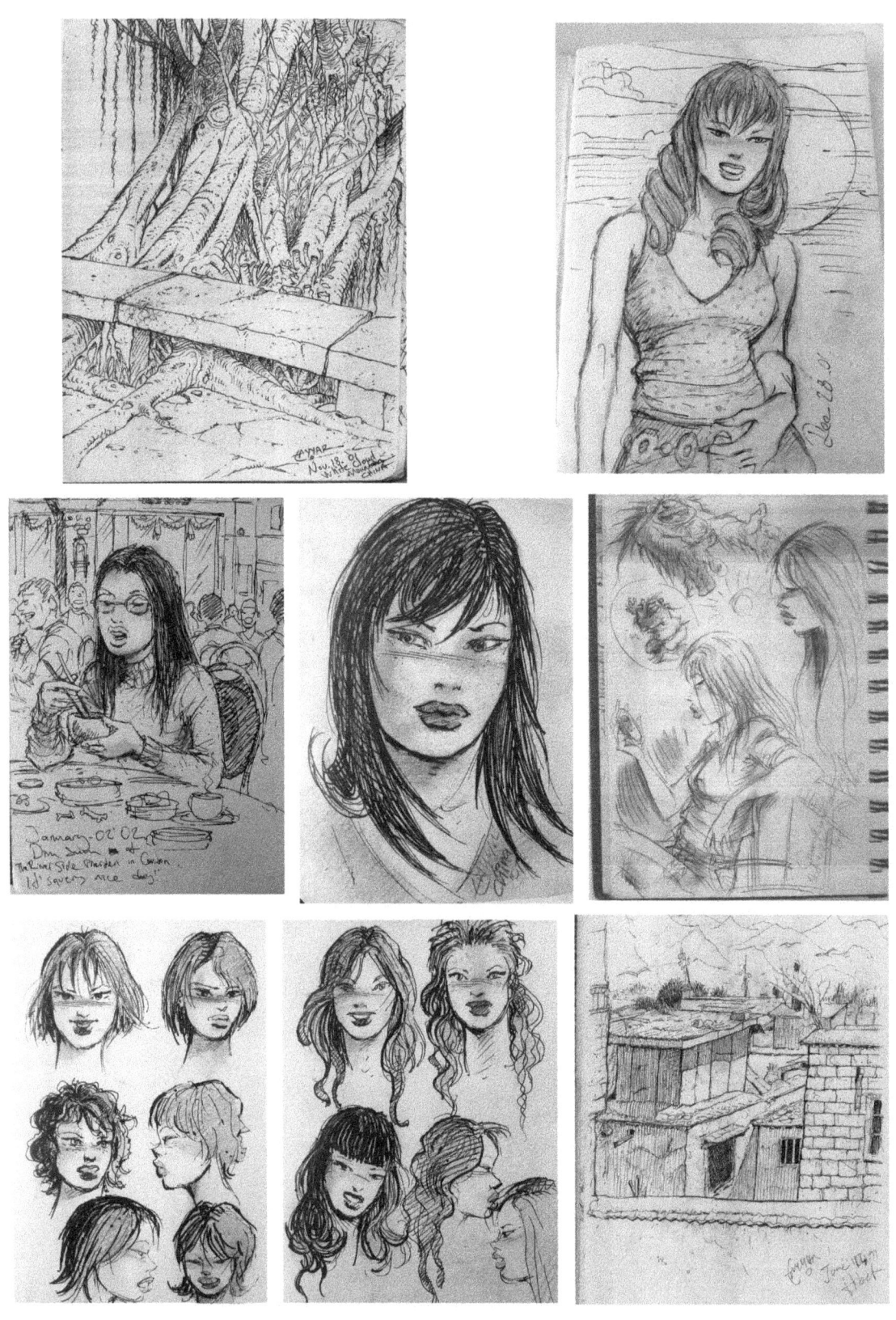

Quick *sketches* while in I was *China* during the
different times.

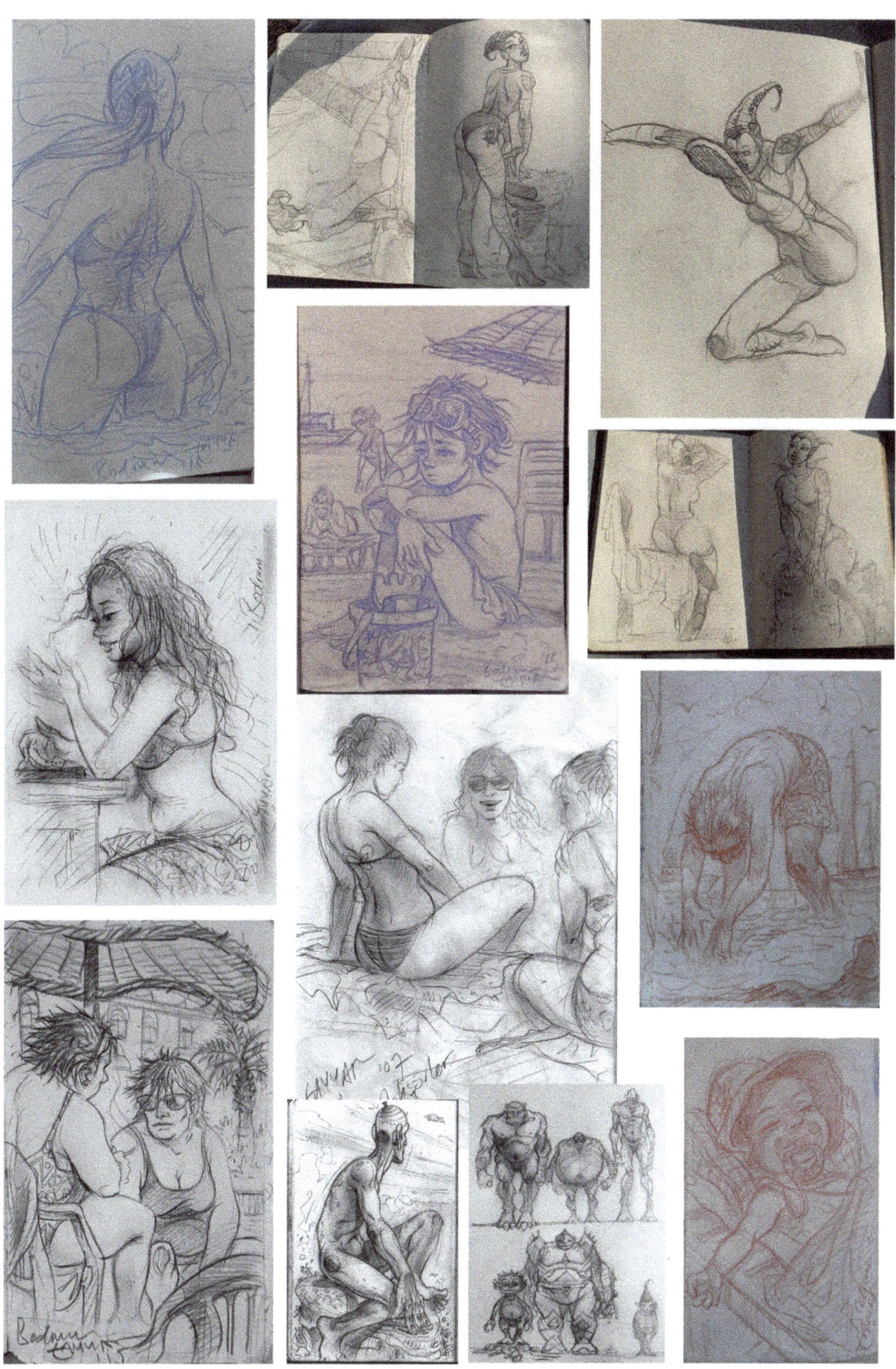

Miscellaneous *sketches*.

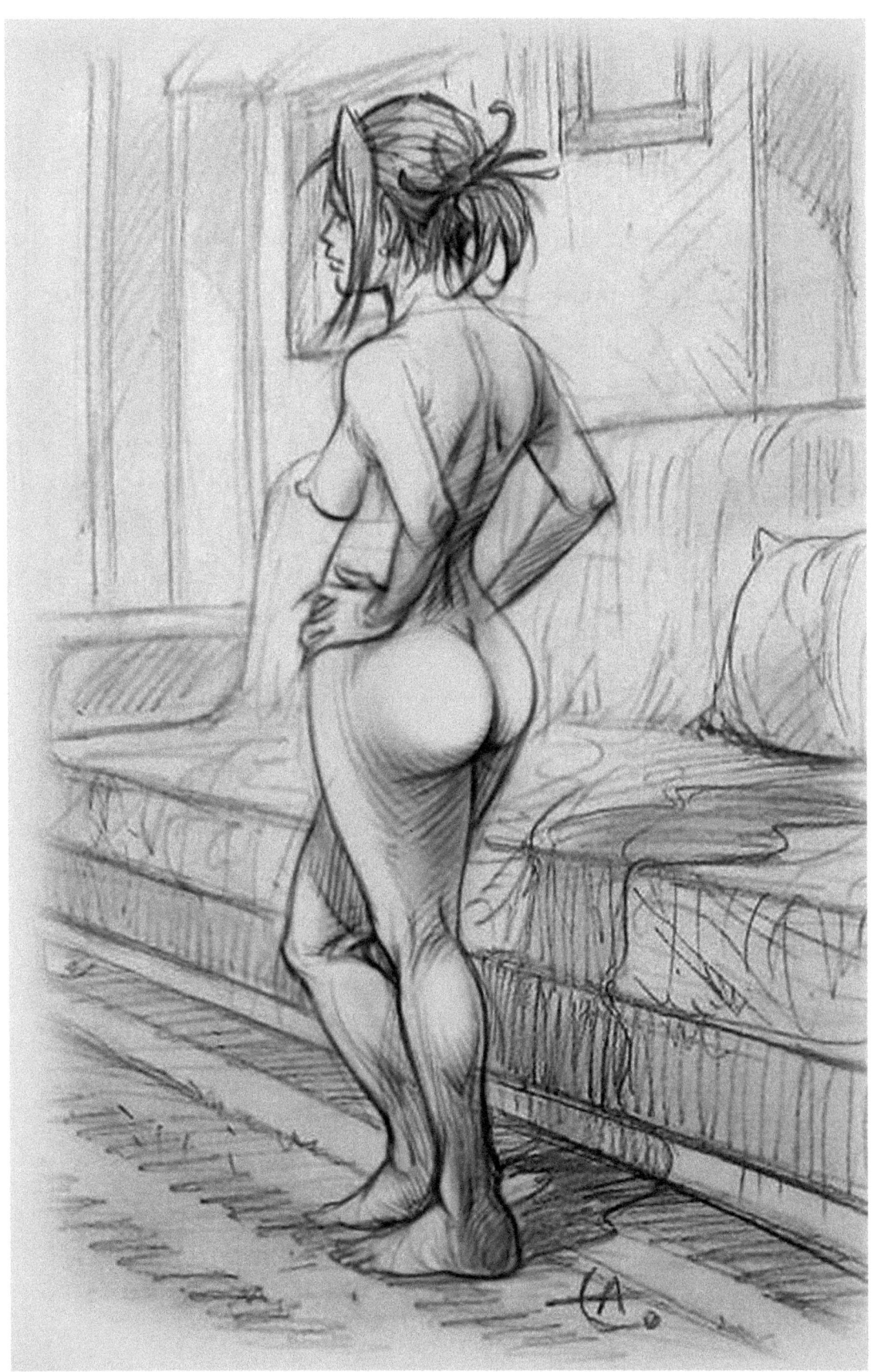

-Life drawing.

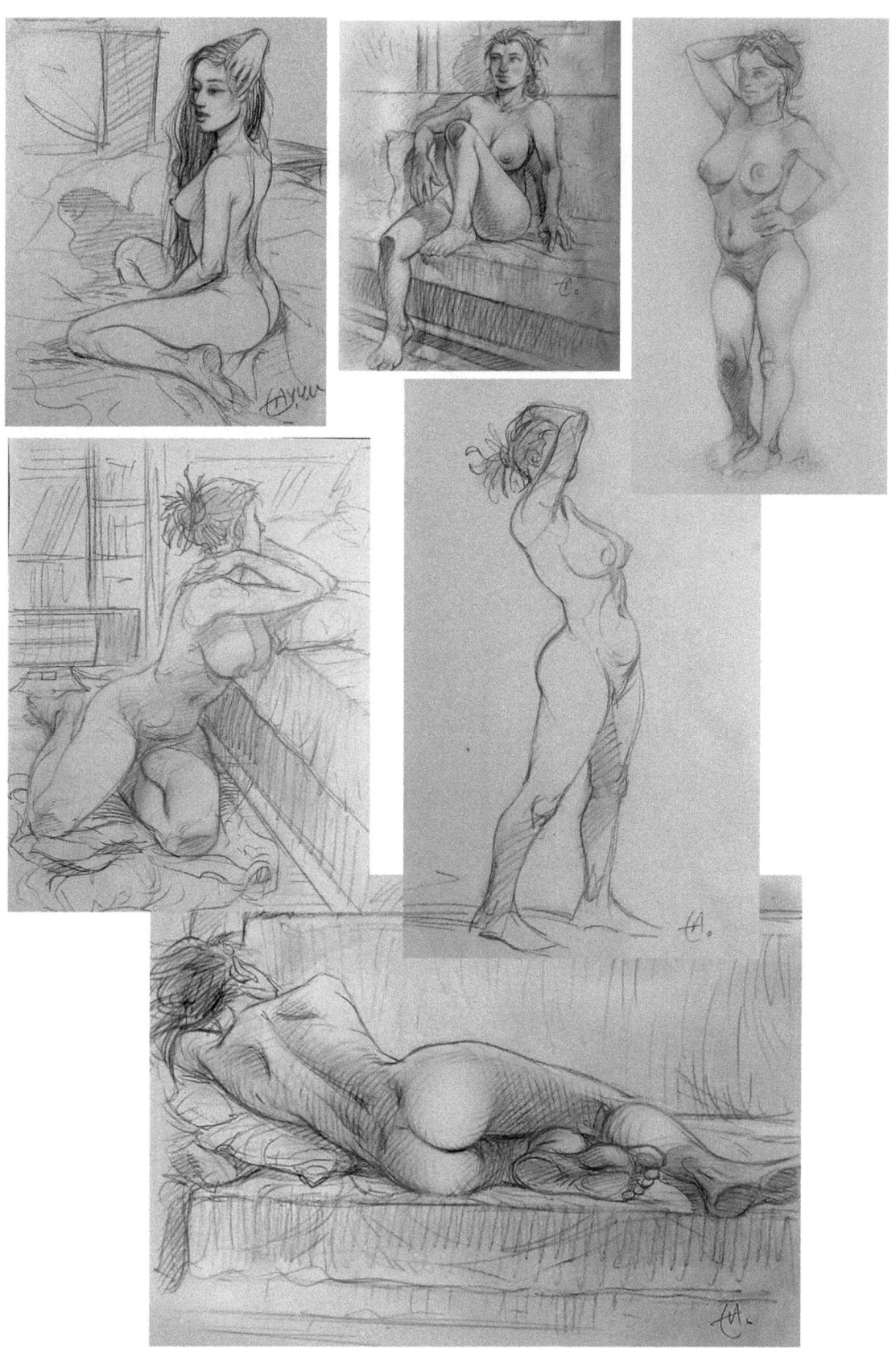

Life drawings.

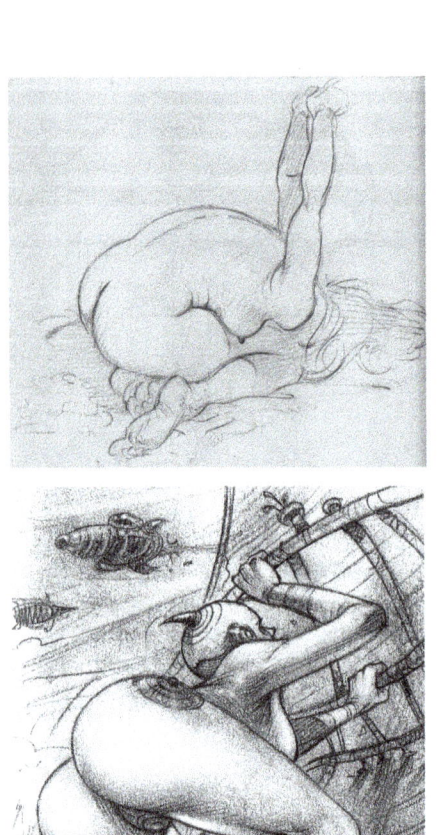
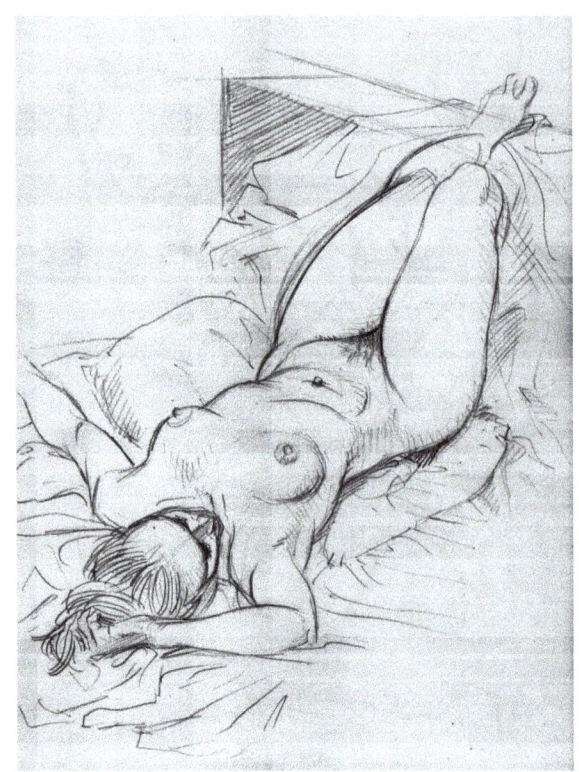
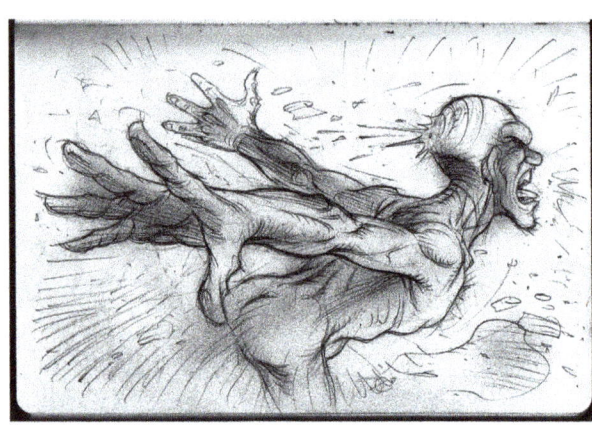
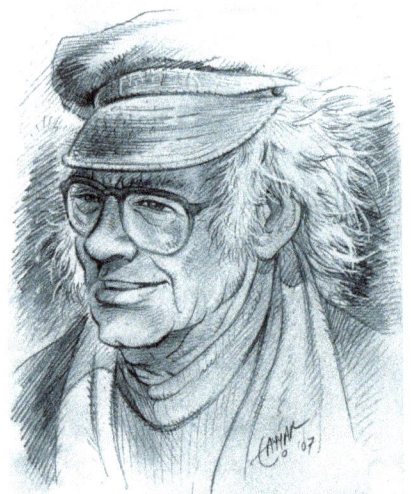
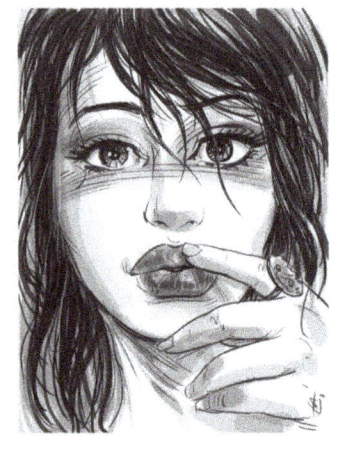
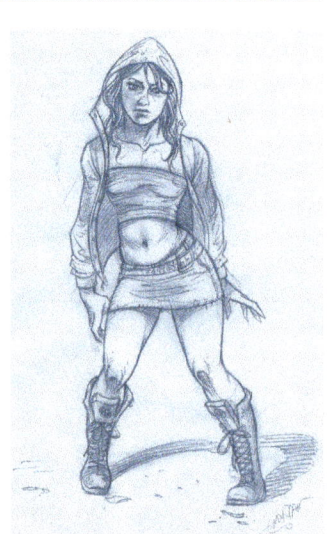

Miscellaneous *sketches*.

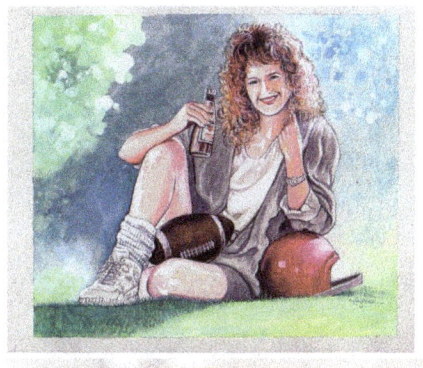
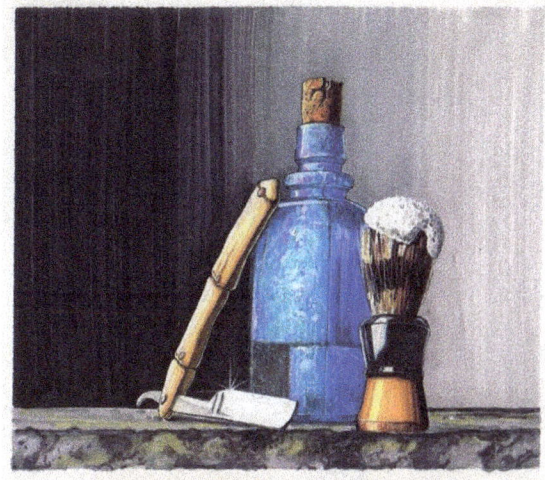
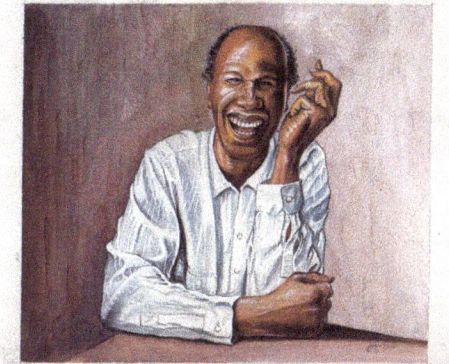
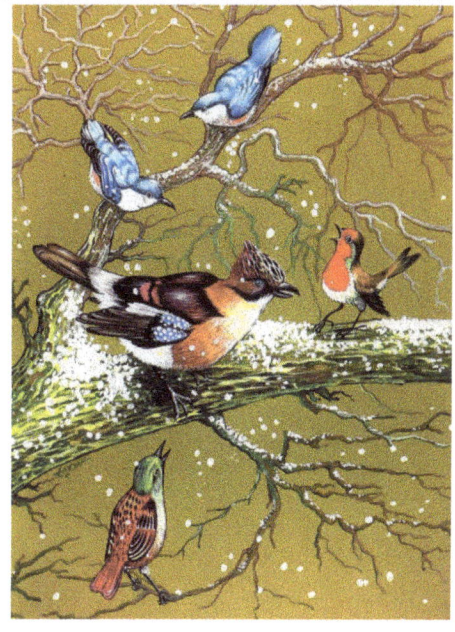
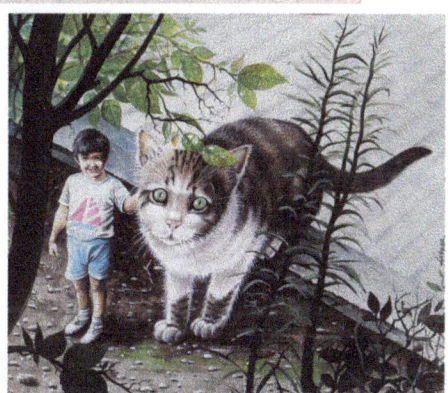
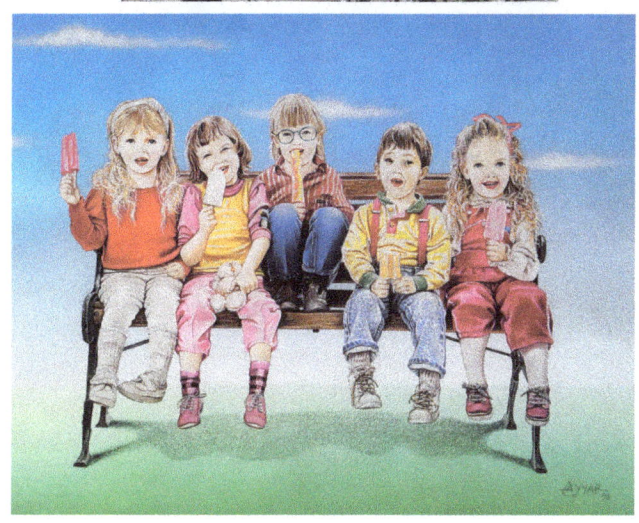
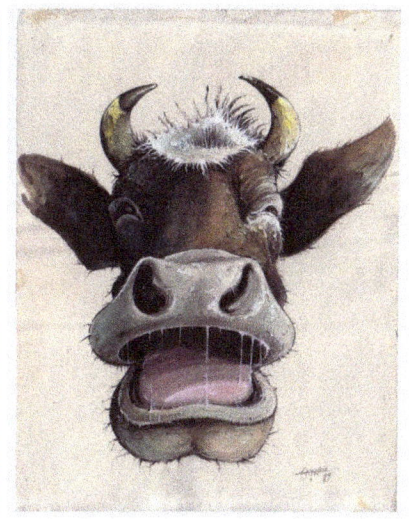

Very early *illustrations* for an *ad agencies* after I moved to USA in 1989.

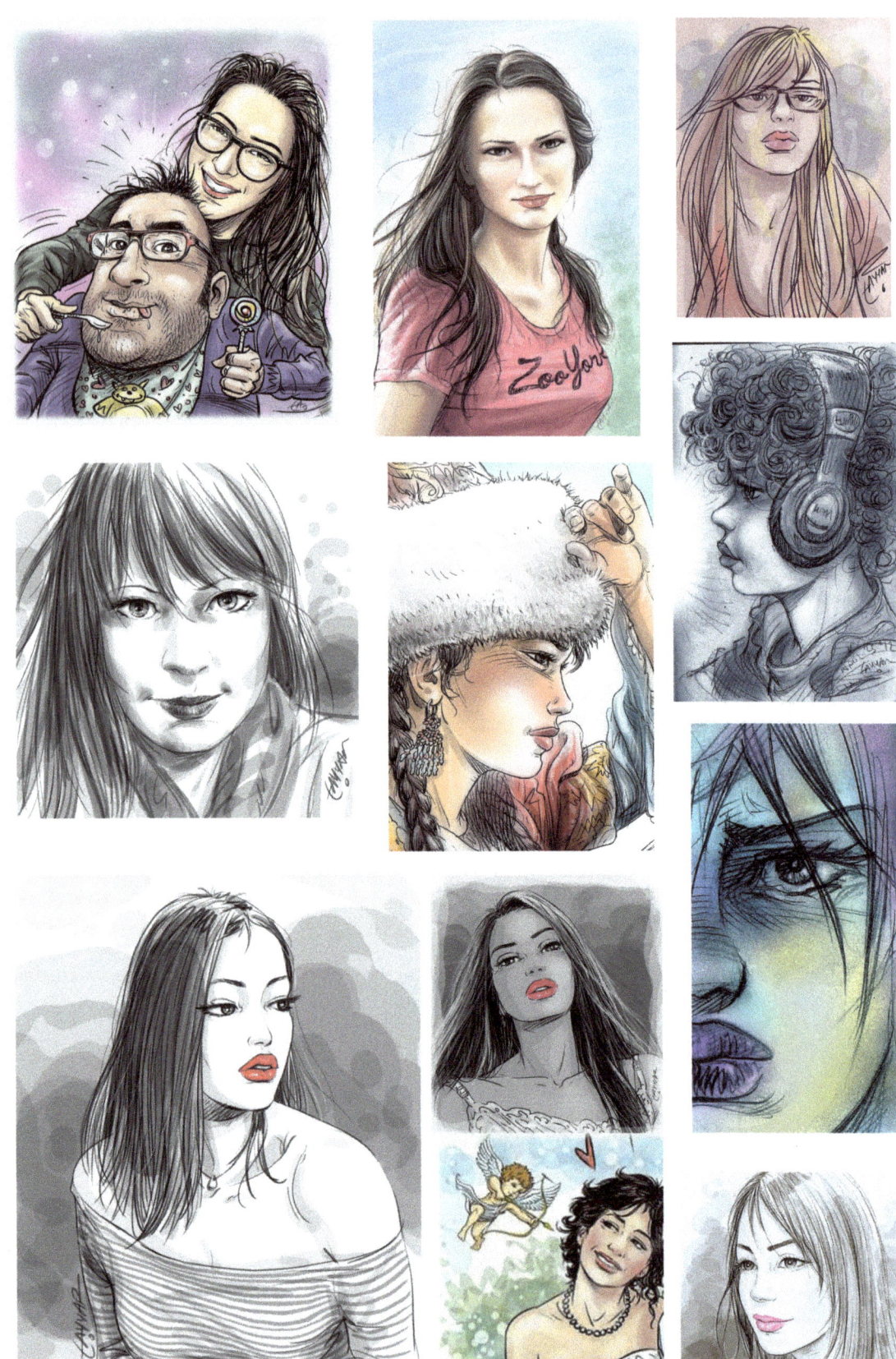

Portraits for the personal orders.

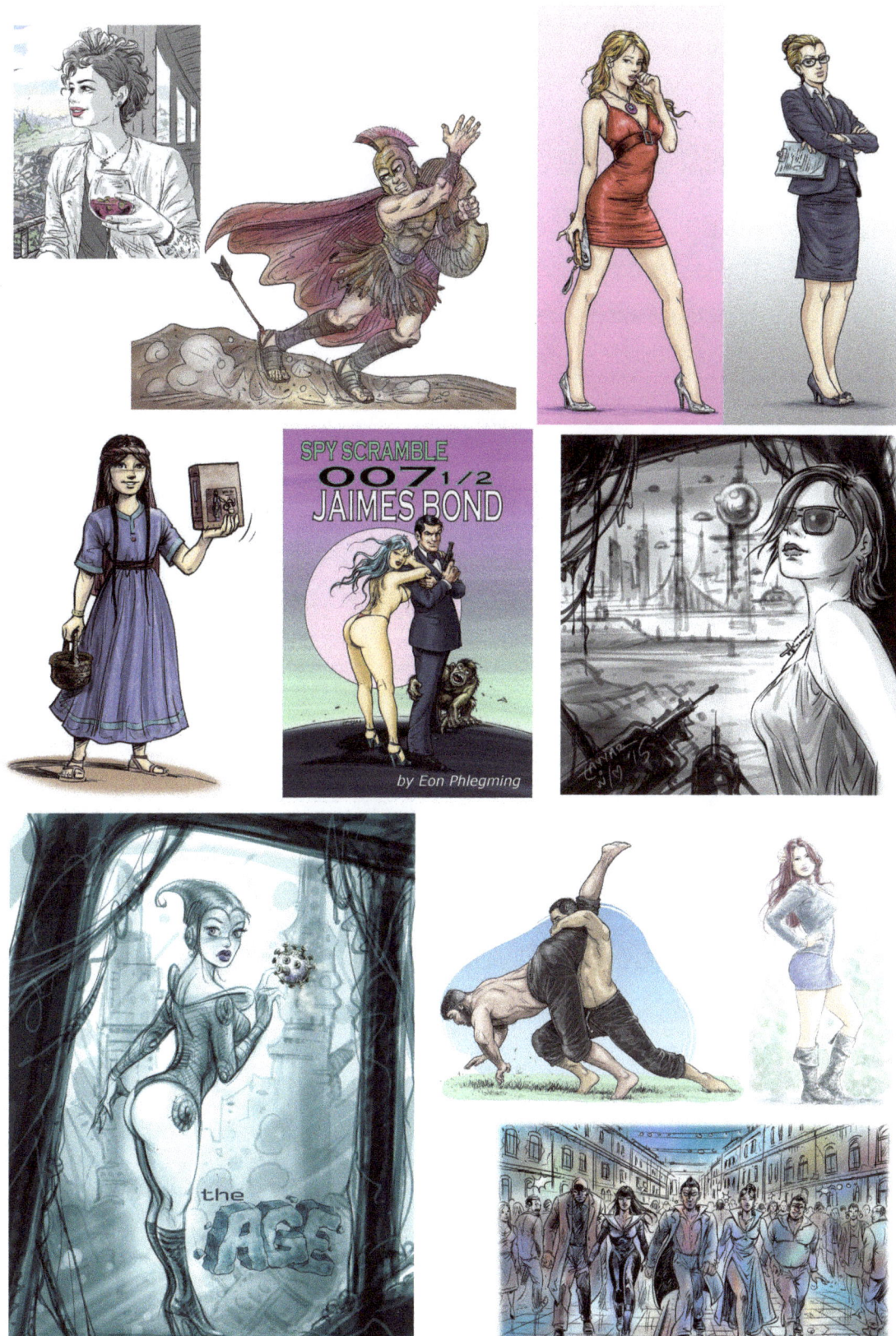

Different types of *drawings* for the marketing.

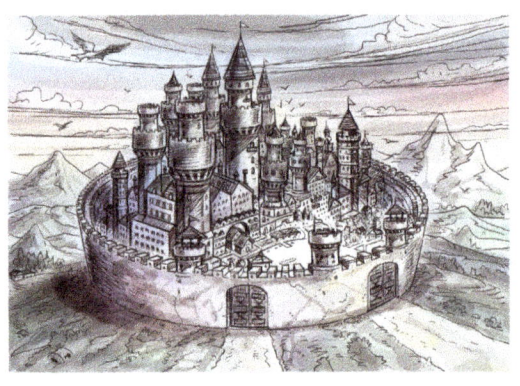
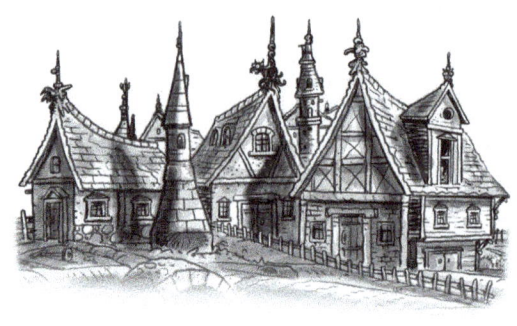
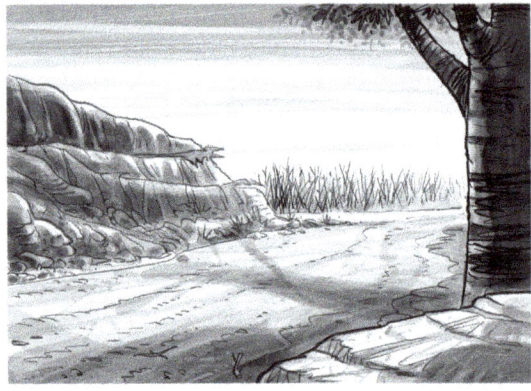
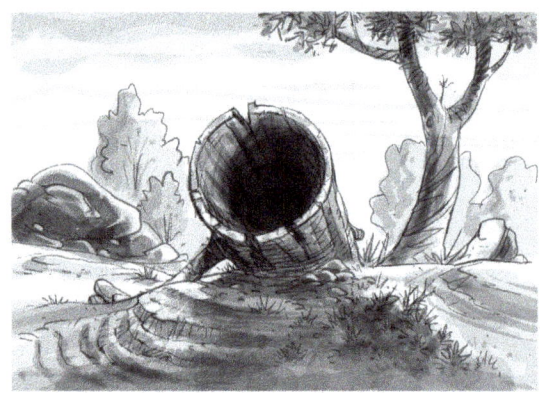
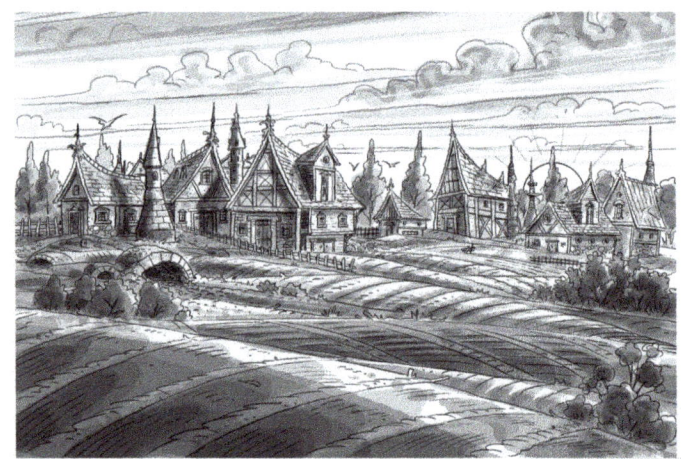
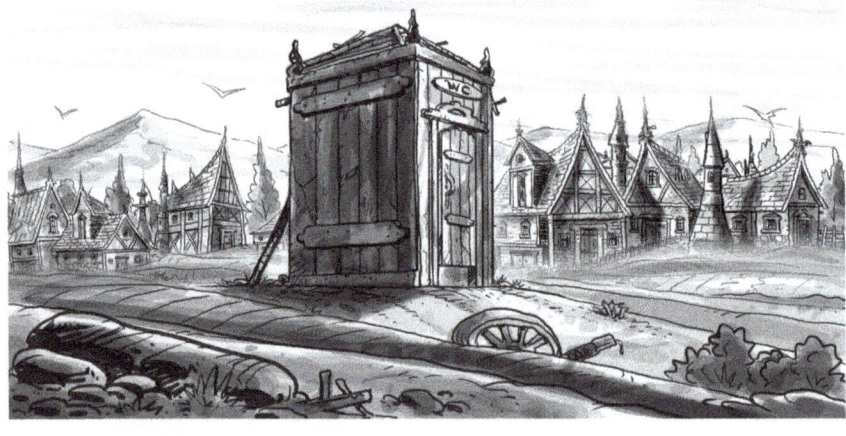

Background *designs* for an animation *movie*.

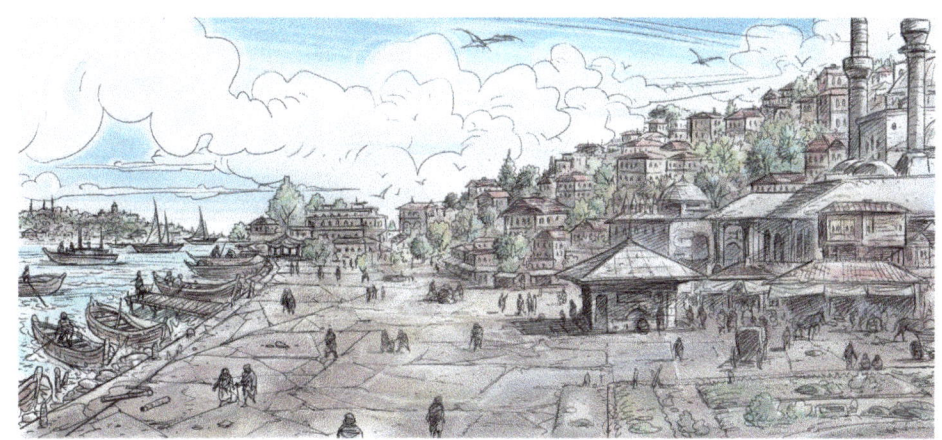

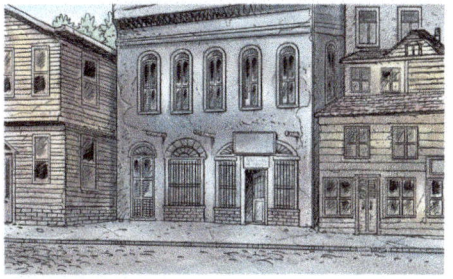

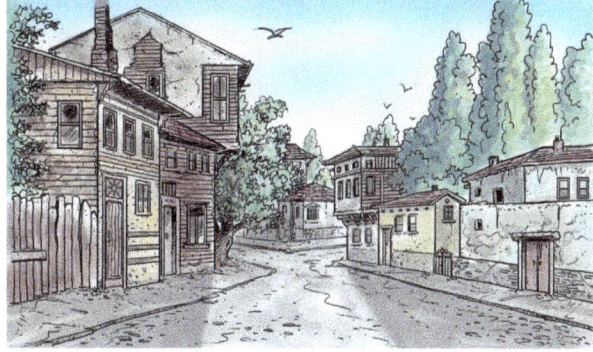

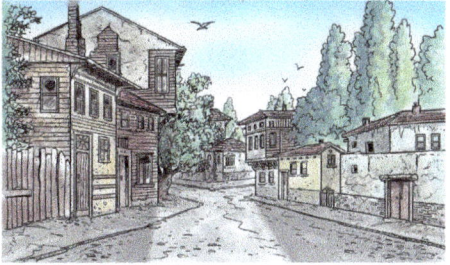

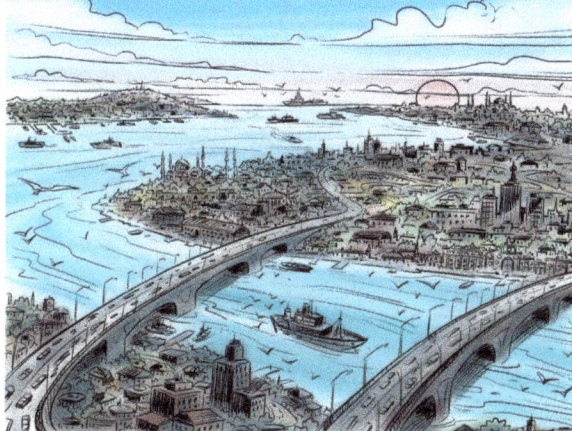

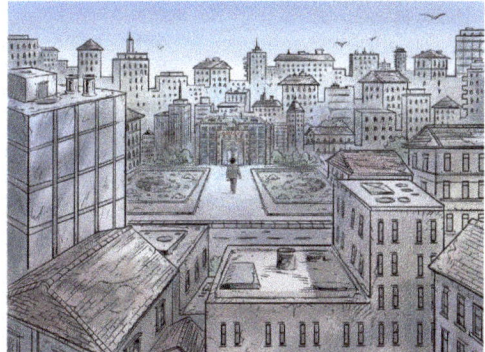

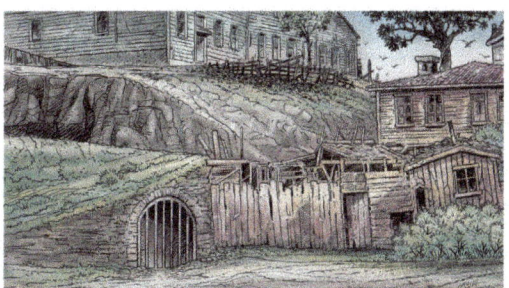

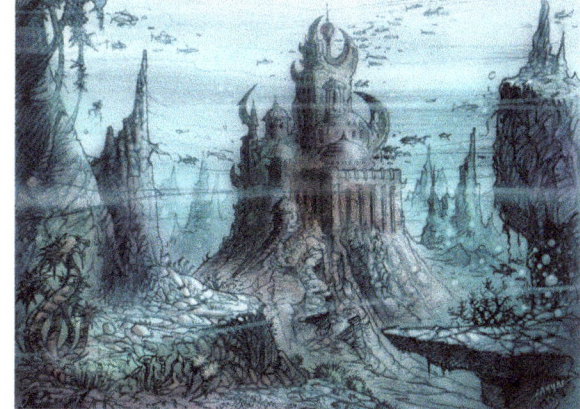

Background **designs** for an animation movie.

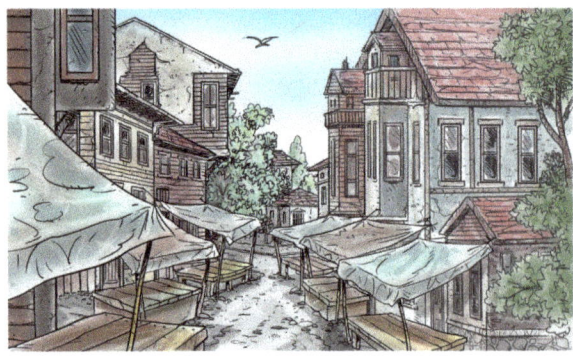
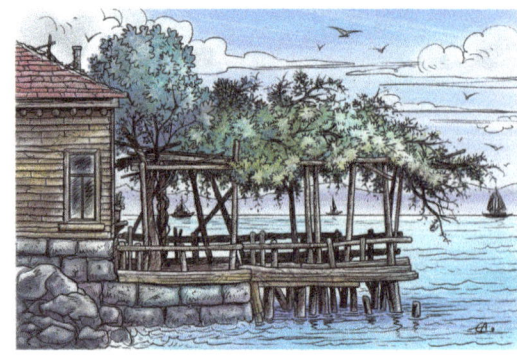
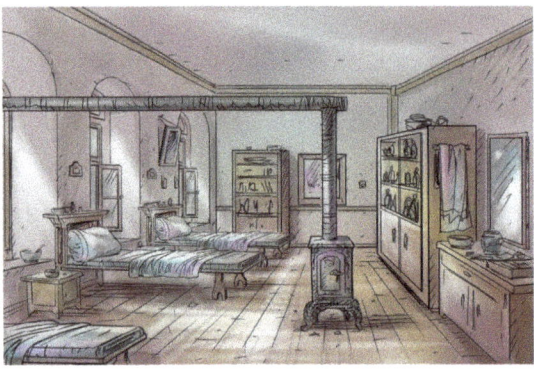
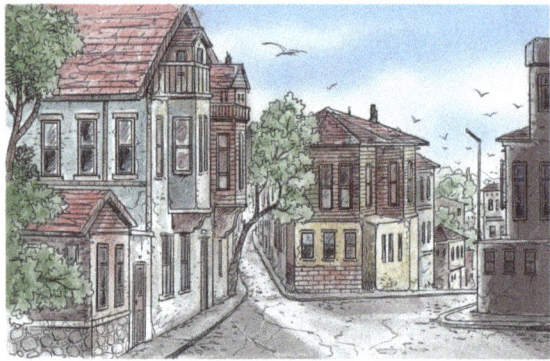
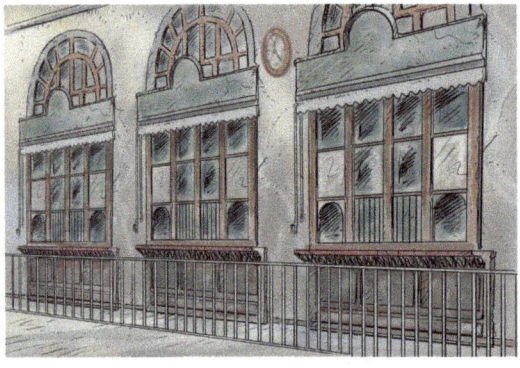
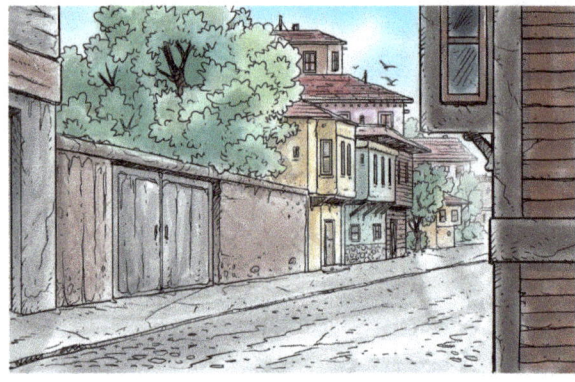
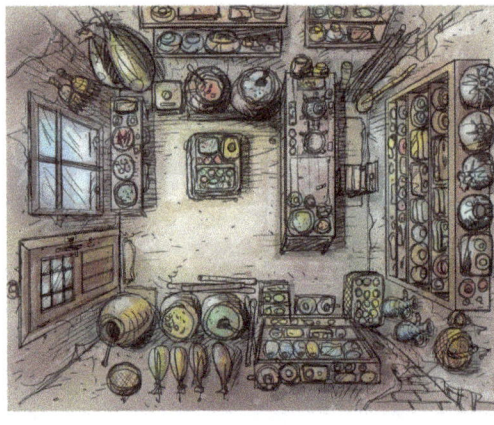
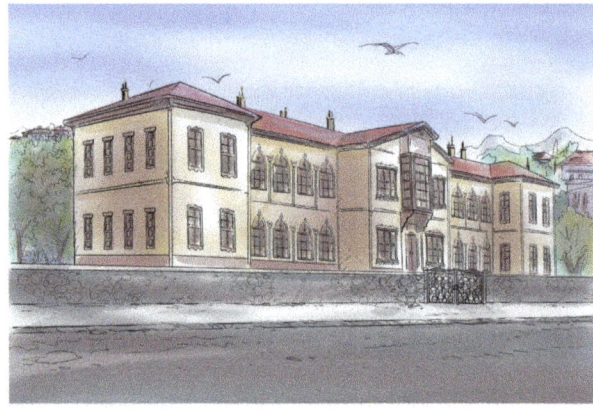

Background *designs* for a *TV animation* series.

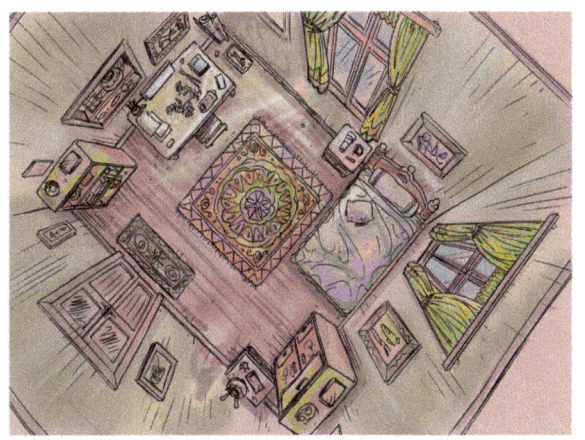
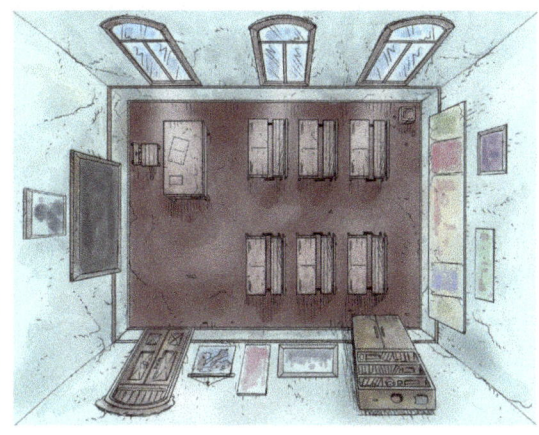
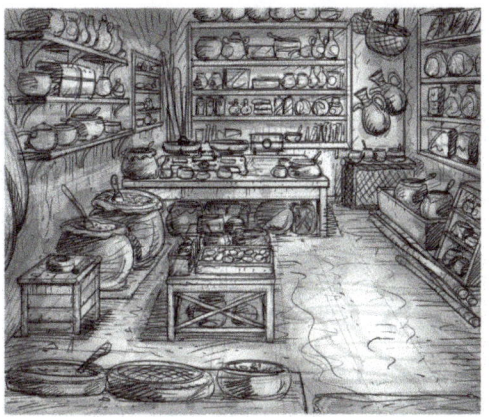
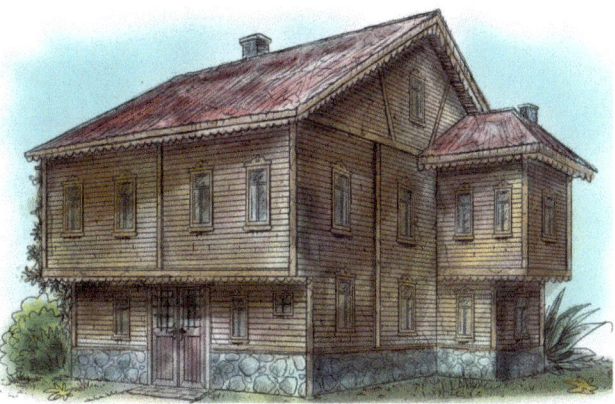
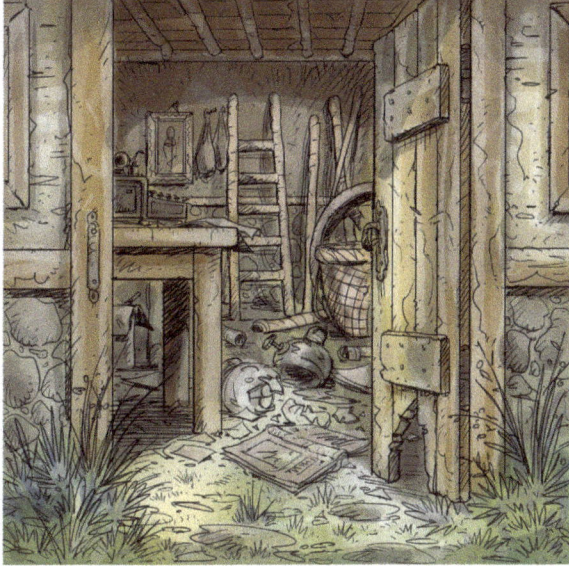
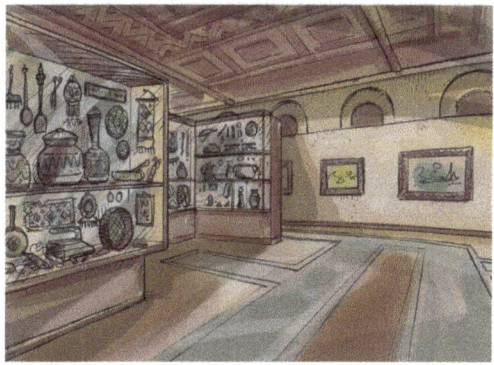
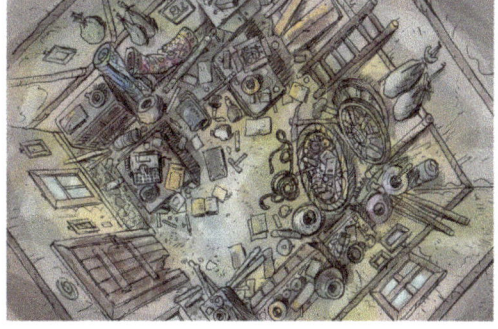

Background designs for some animation movies.

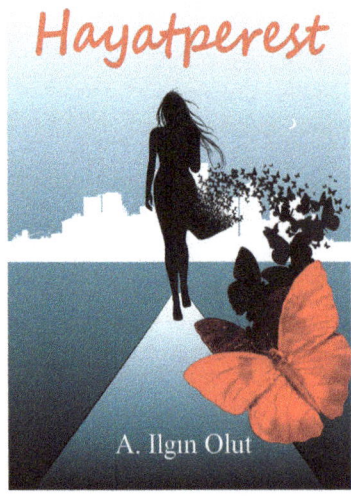

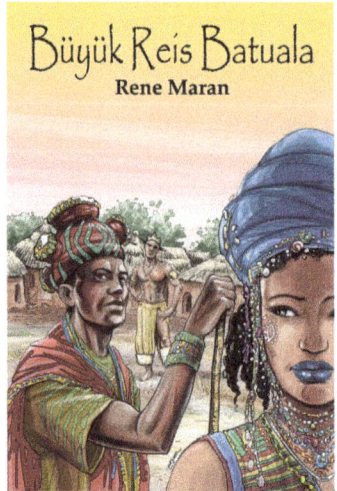

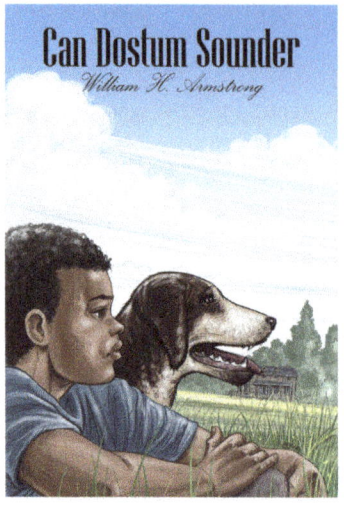

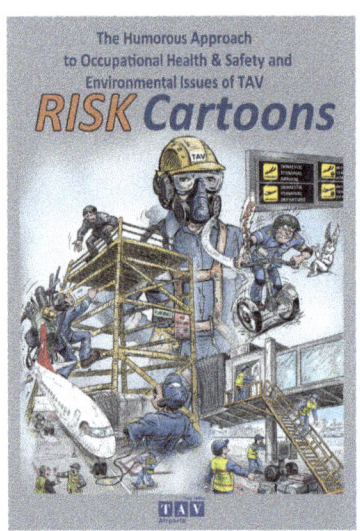

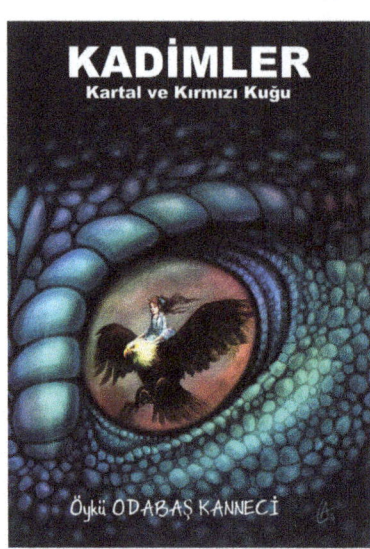

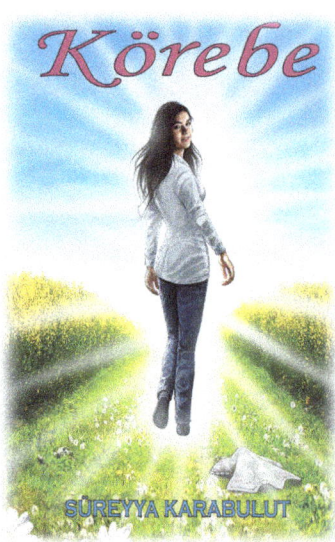

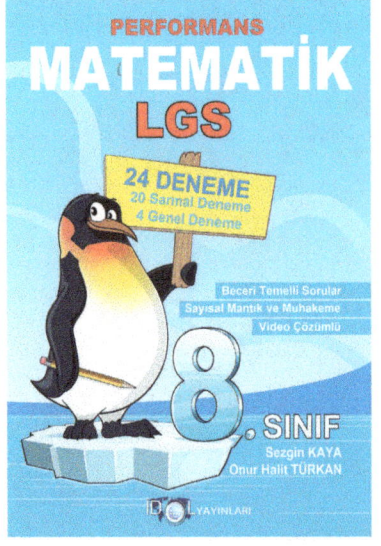

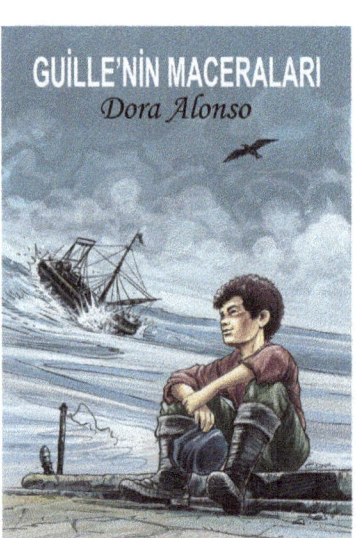

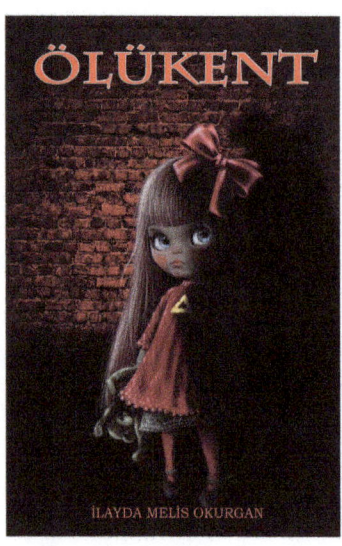

Book *covers* I've illustrated for the *different* companies..

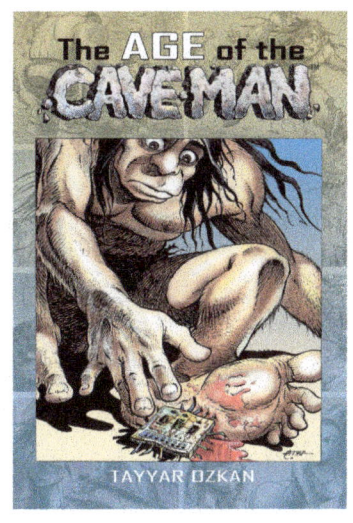

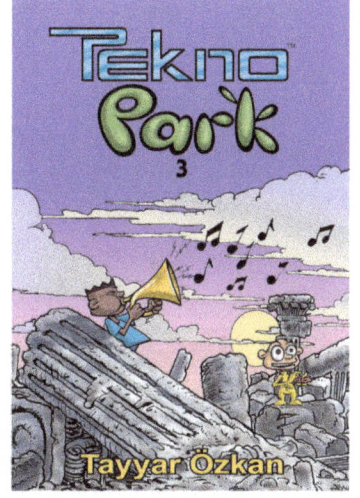

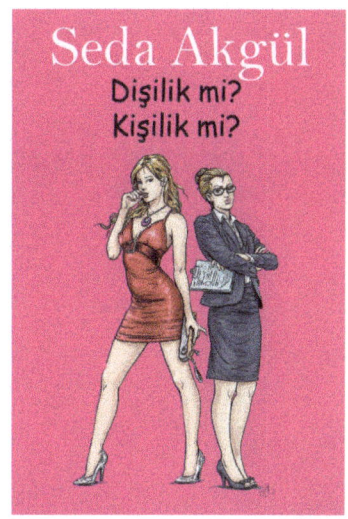

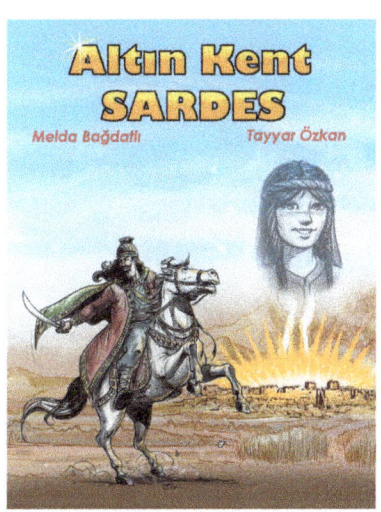

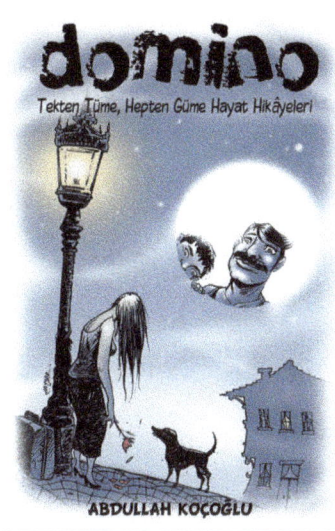

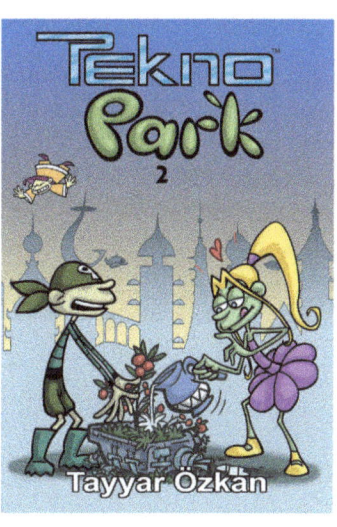

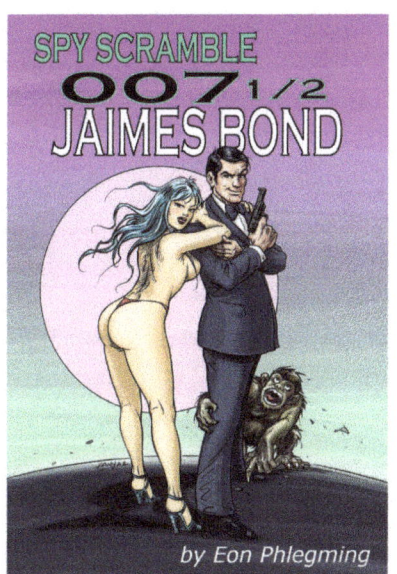

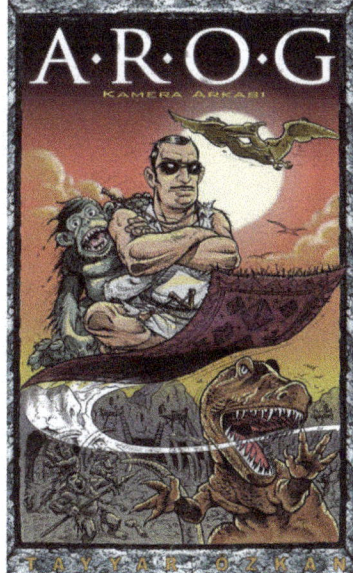

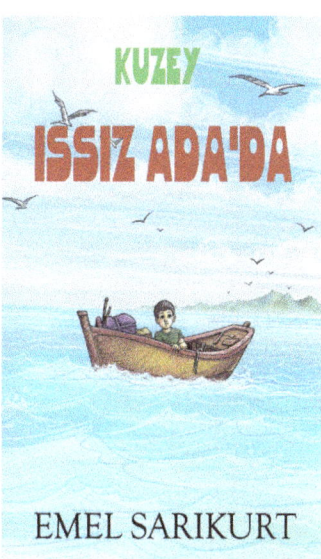

Some more *book covers* I've illustrated..

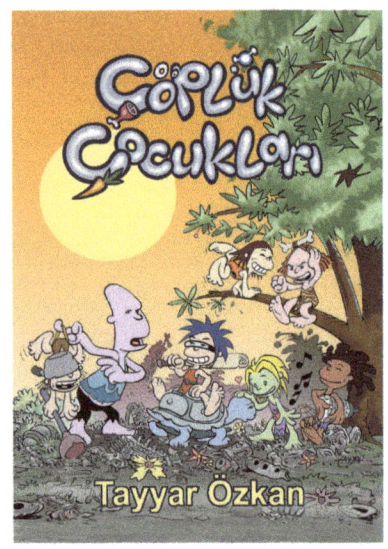

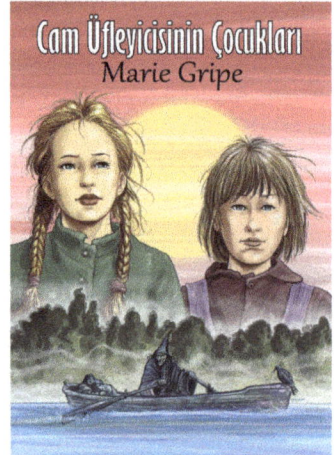

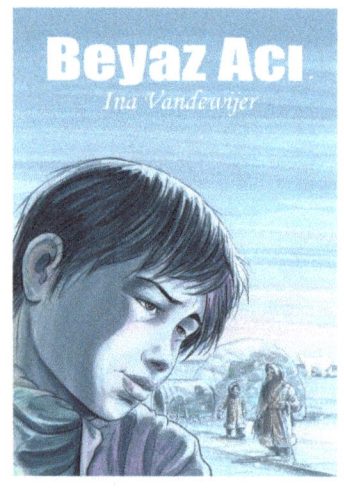

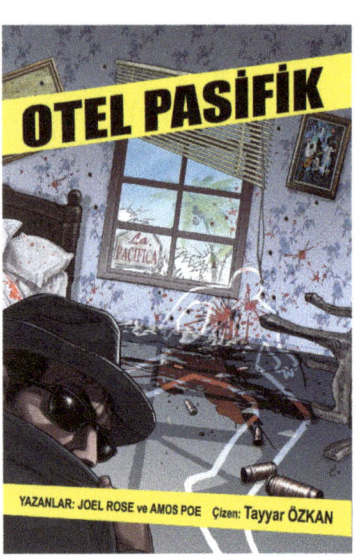

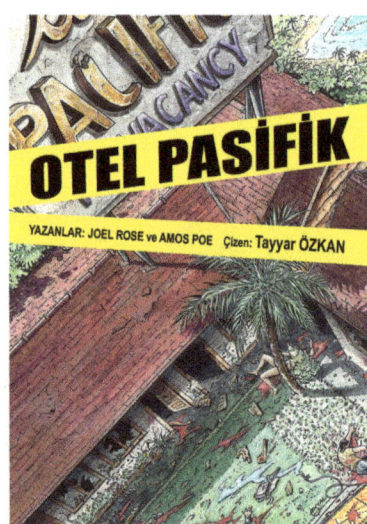

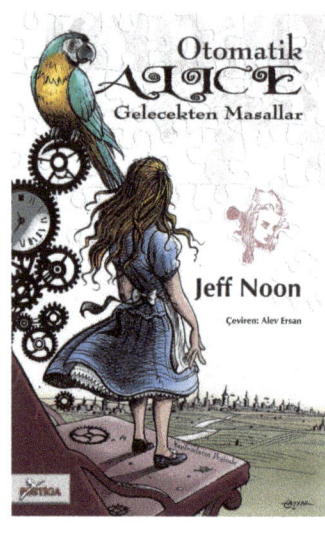

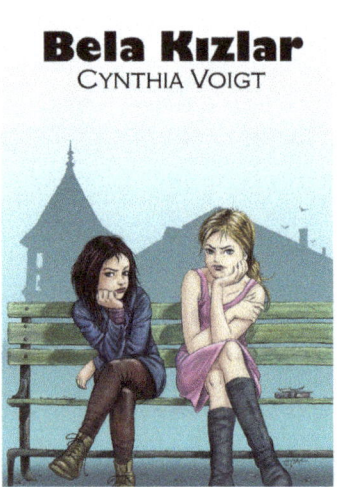

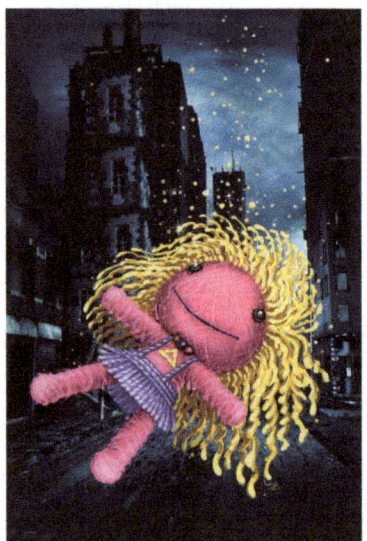

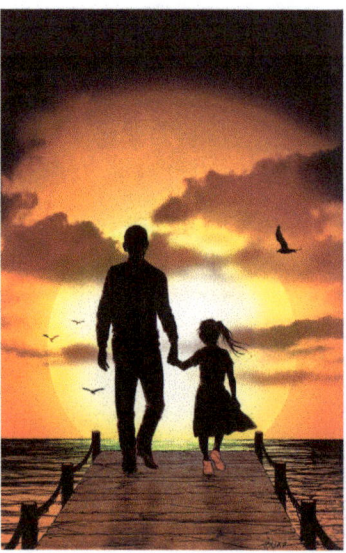

Some *book covers* I've illustrated..

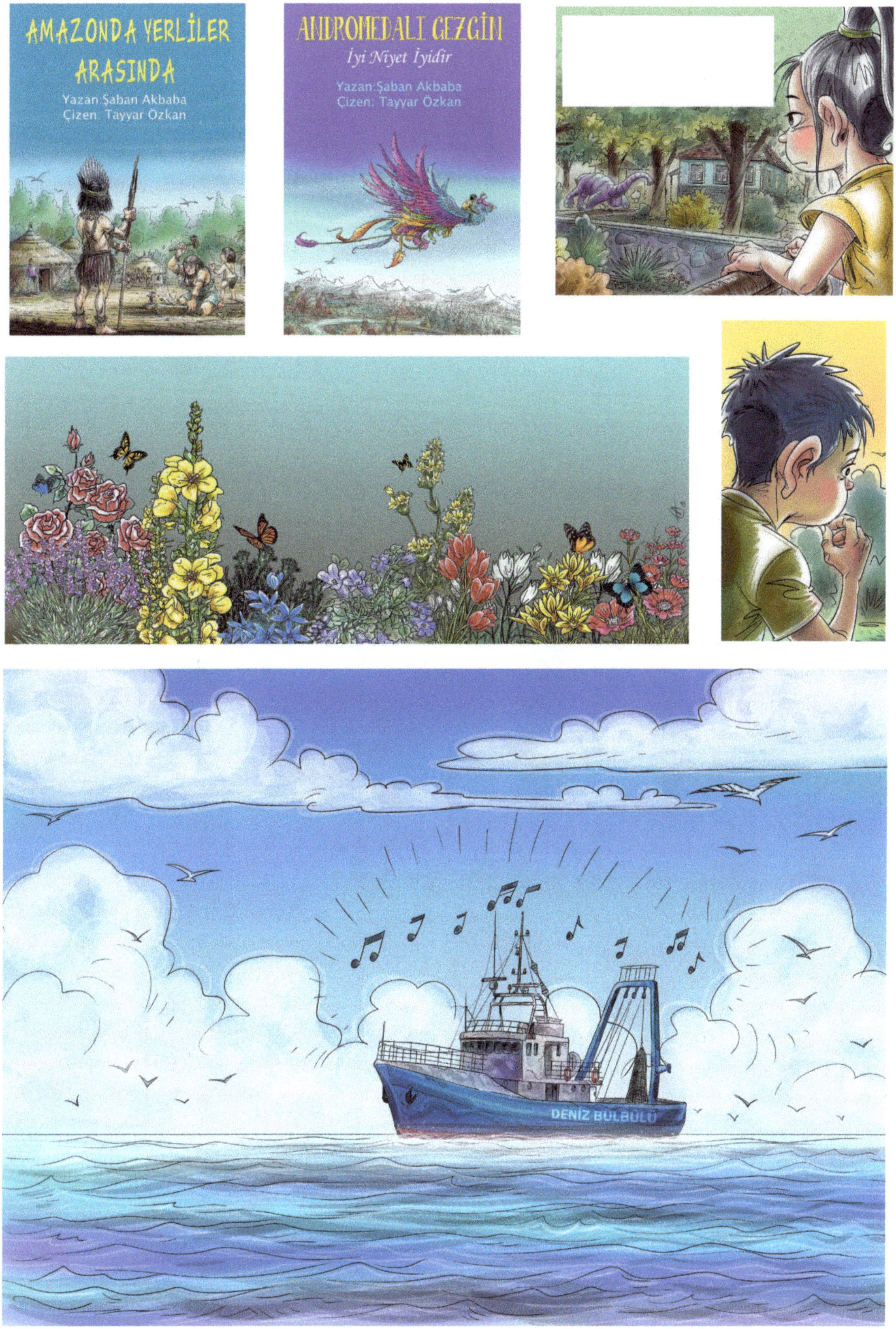

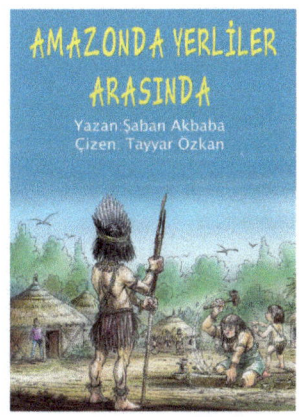

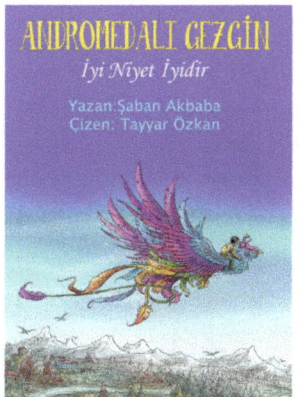

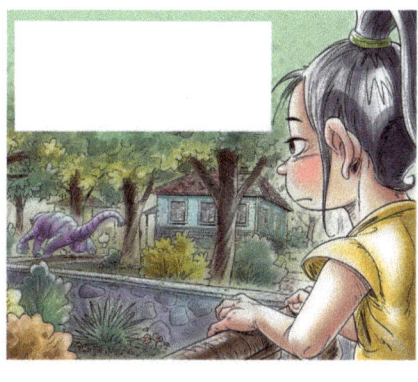

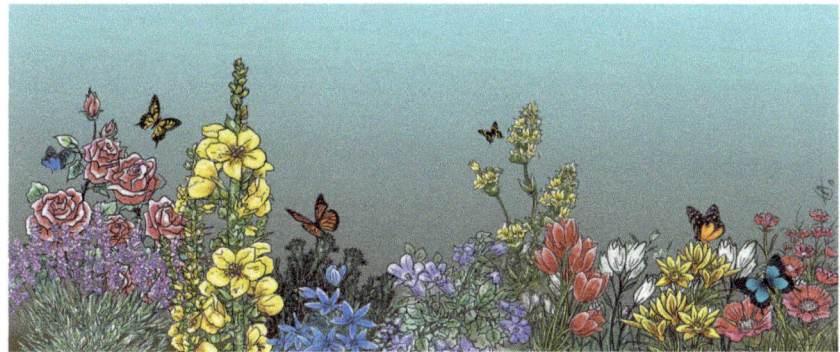

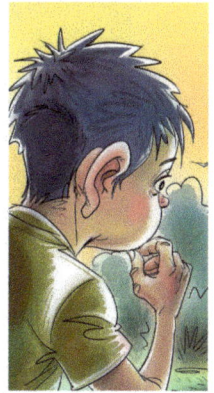

Types of illustrations for *children's books*.

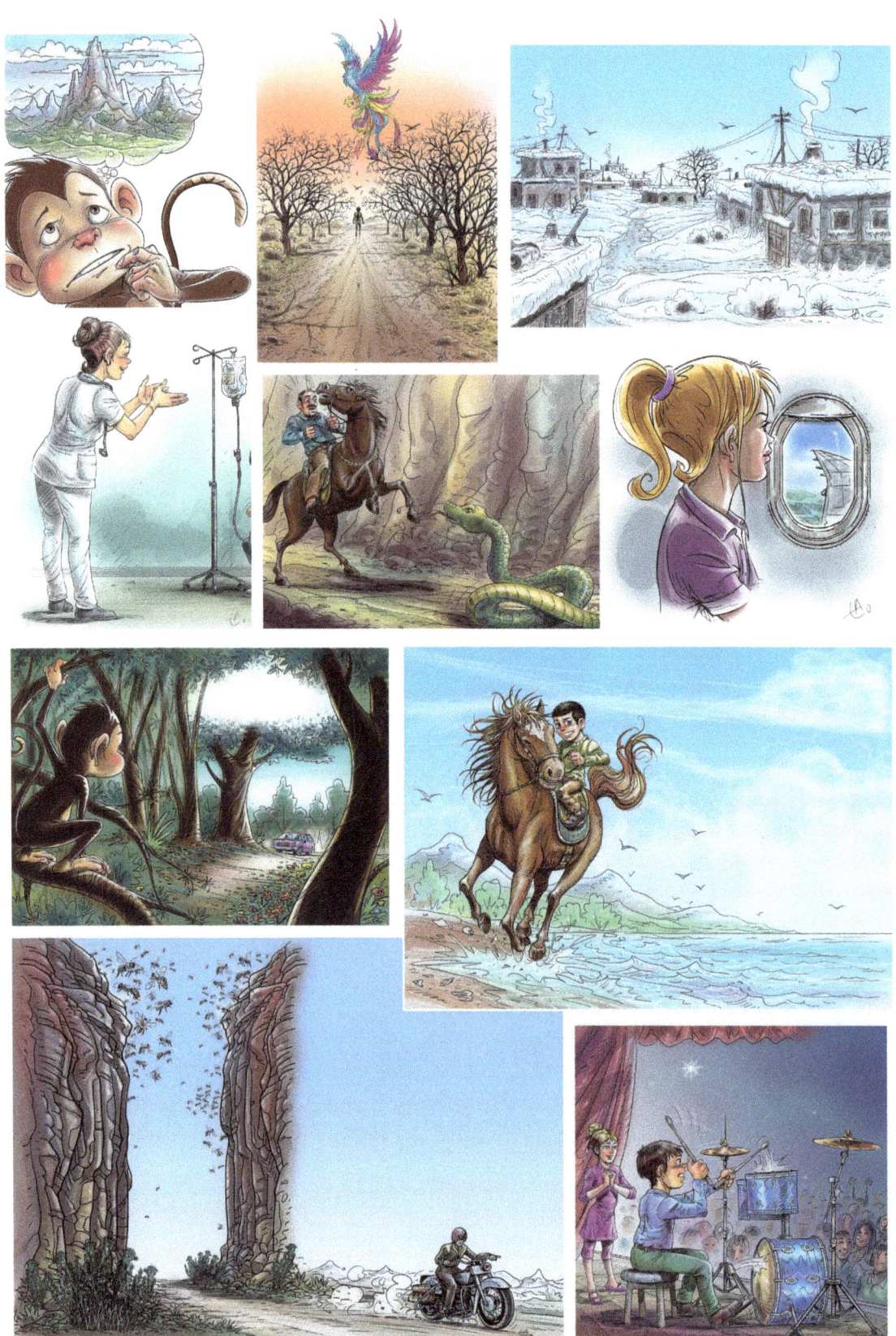

Some more *illustrations* for children's books.

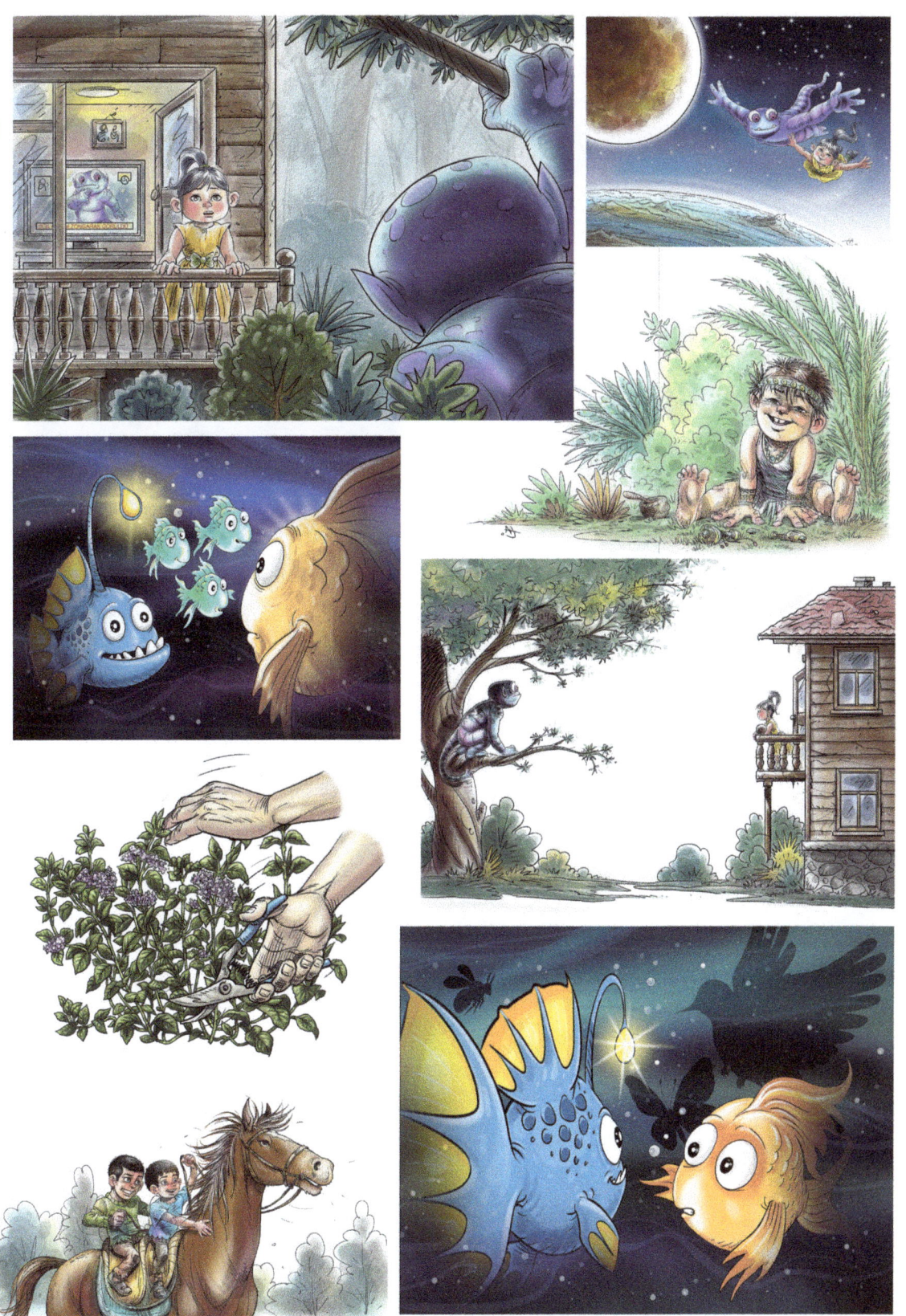

Types of illustrations for *children's books*.

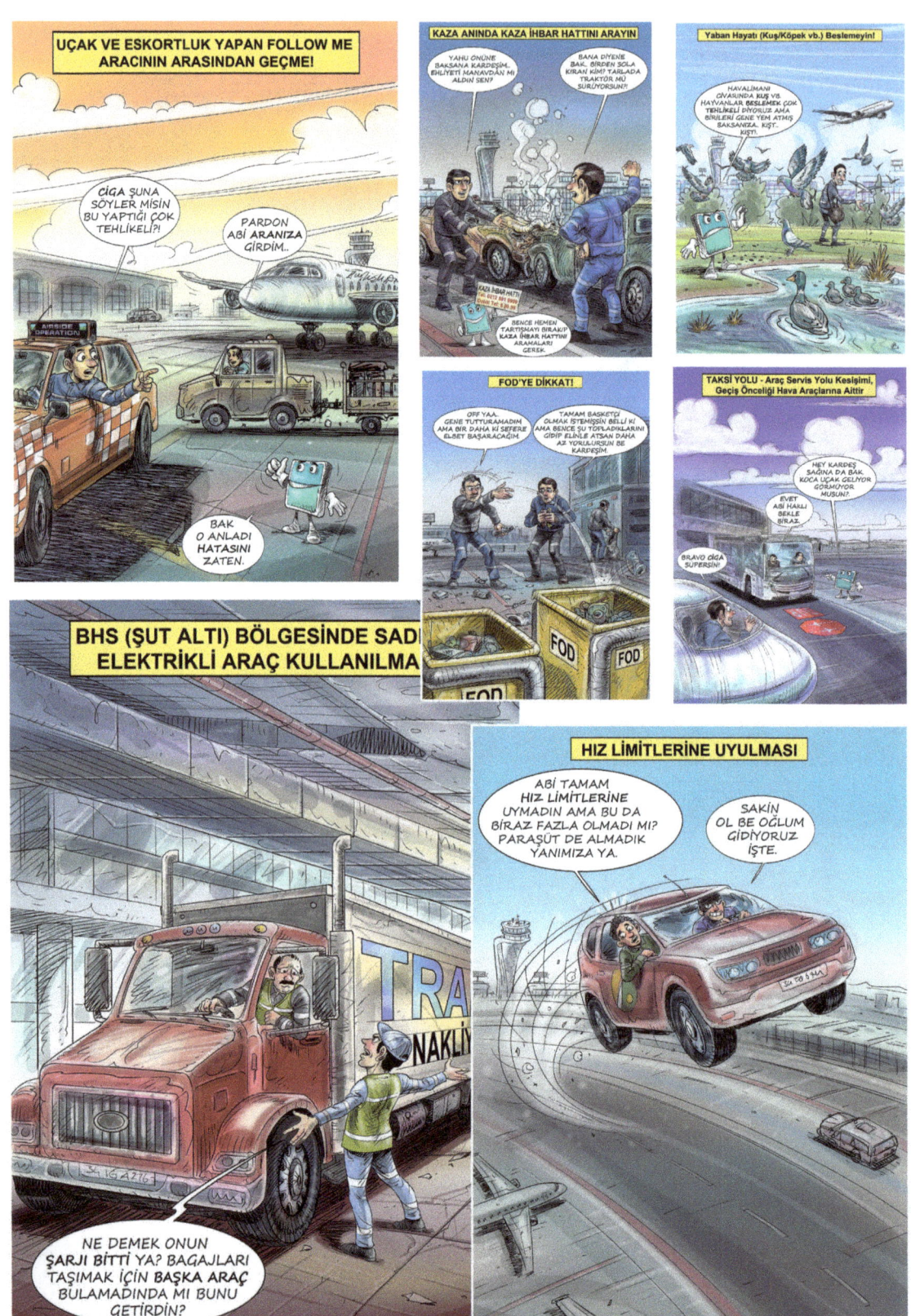

Drawings for *IGA*-Istanbul Airport's Catalog.

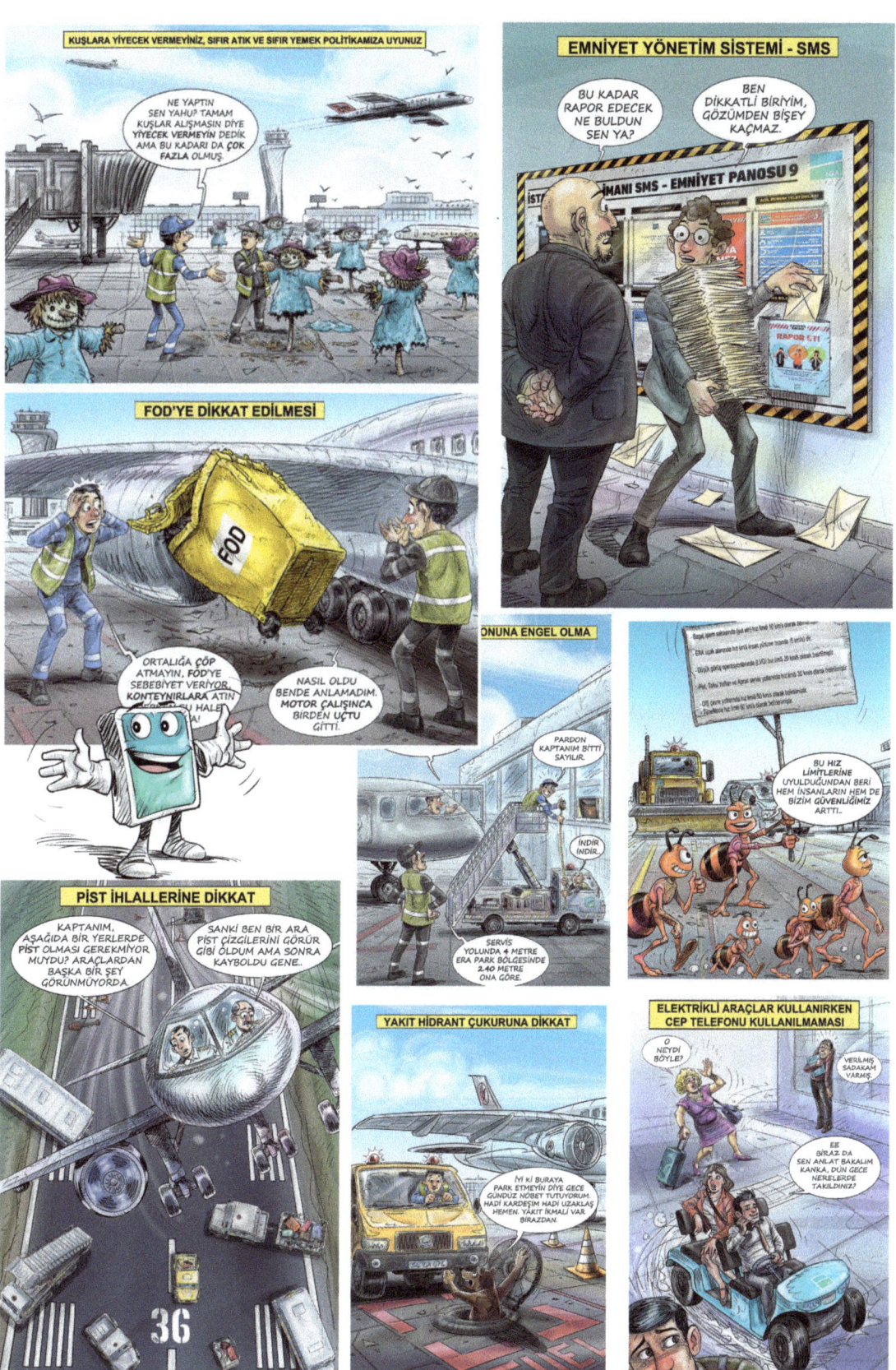

Drawings for *IGA*- Istanbul Airport's Catalog.

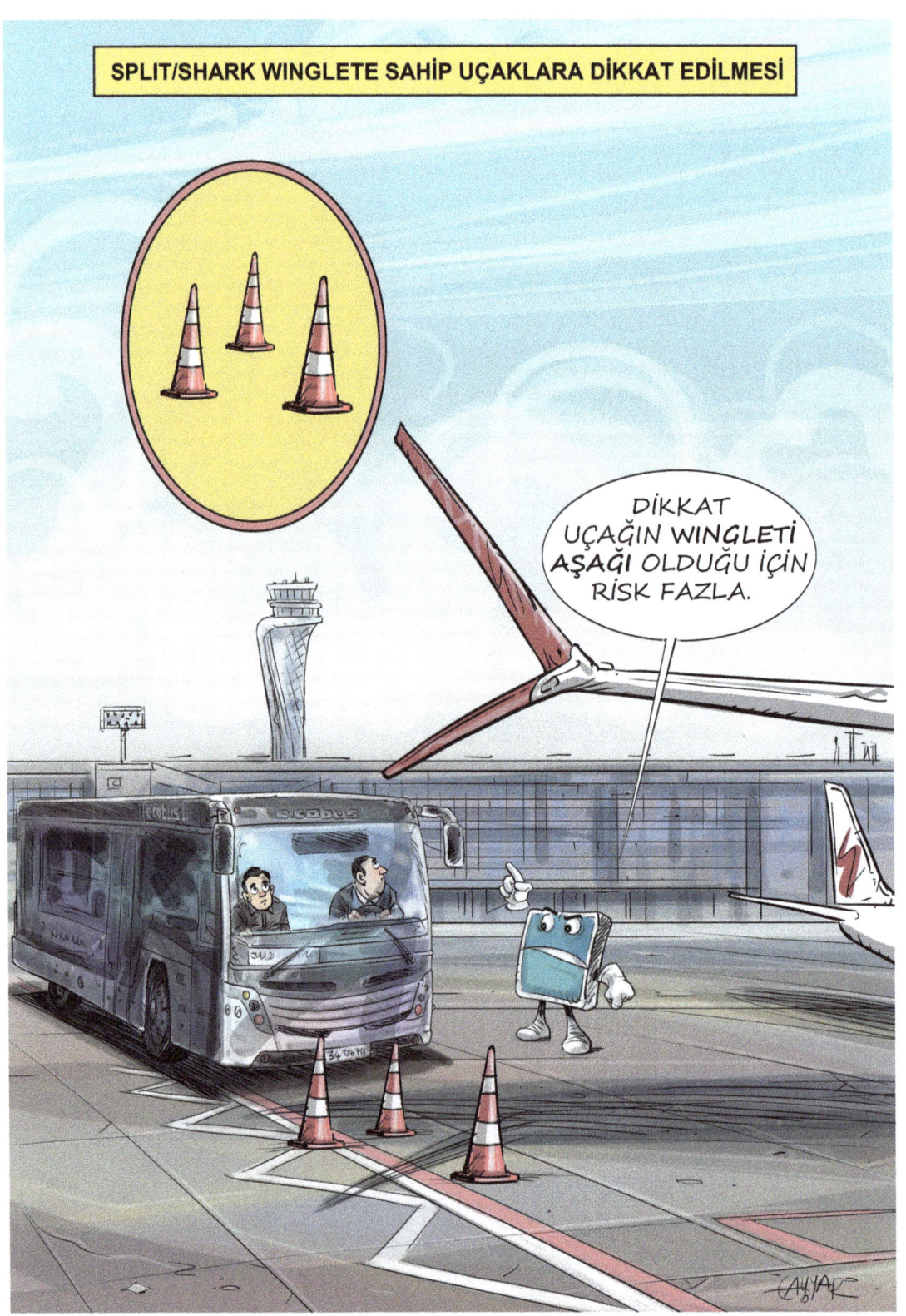

Drawing for *IGA*- Istanbul Airport's Catalog.

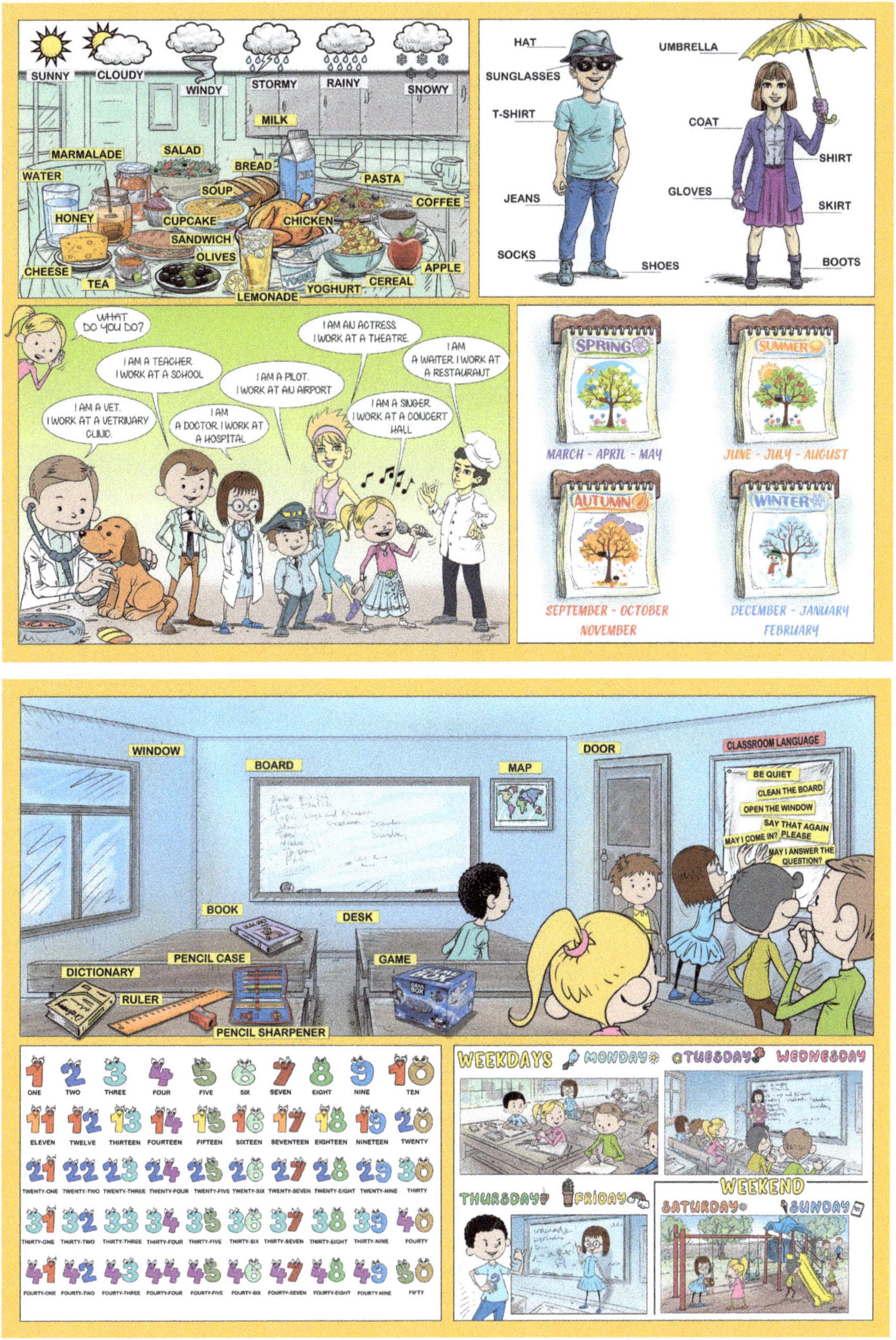

SUNNY   CLOUDY   WINDY   STORMY   RAINY   SNOWY

MARMALADE   SALAD   MILK
WATER   BREAD   PASTA
HONEY   SOUP   COFFEE
CHEESE   CUPCAKE   CHICKEN
   SANDWICH   SANDWICH
TEA   OLIVES   APPLE
   LEMONADE   YOGHURT   CEREAL

HAT   UMBRELLA
SUNGLASSES
T-SHIRT   COAT
   SHIRT
JEANS   GLOVES   SKIRT
SOCKS   SHOES   BOOTS

WHAT DO YOU DO?

I AM AN ACTRESS. I WORK AT A THEATRE.
I AM A TEACHER. I WORK AT A SCHOOL.
I AM A PILOT. I WORK AT AN AIRPORT.
I AM A WAITER. I WORK AT A RESTAURANT.
I AM A VET. I WORK AT A VETRINARY CLINIC.
I AM A DOCTOR. I WORK AT A HOSPITAL.
I AM A SINGER. I WORK AT A CONCERT HALL.

SPRING — MARCH - APRIL - MAY
SUMMER — JUNE - JULY - AUGUST
AUTUMN — SEPTEMBER - OCTOBER NOVEMBER
WINTER — DECEMBER - JANUARY FEBRUARY

WINDOW   BOARD   MAP   DOOR

CLASSROOM LANGUAGE
BE QUIET
CLEAN THE BOARD
OPEN THE WINDOW
SAY THAT AGAIN
MAY I COME IN? PLEASE
MAY I ANSWER THE QUESTION?

BOOK   DESK
PENCIL CASE   GAME
DICTIONARY
RULER
PENCIL SHARPENER

ONE	TWO	THREE	FOUR	FIVE	SIX	SEVEN	EIGHT	NINE	TEN
1	2	3	4	5	6	7	8	9	10

ELEVEN	TWELVE	THIRTEEN	FOURTEEN	FIFTEEN	SIXTEEN	SEVENTEEN	EIGHTEEN	NINETEEN	TWENTY
11	12	13	14	15	16	17	18	19	20

TWENTY-ONE	TWENTY-TWO	TWENTY-THREE	TWENTY-FOUR	TWENTY-FIVE	TWENTY-SIX	TWENTY-SEVEN	TWENTY-EIGHT	TWENTY-NINE	THIRTY
21	22	23	24	25	26	27	28	29	30

THIRTY-ONE	THIRTY-TWO	THIRTY-THREE	THIRTY-FOUR	THIRTY-FIVE	THIRTY-SIX	THIRTY-SEVEN	THIRTY-EIGHT	THIRTY-NINE	FOURTY
31	32	33	34	35	36	37	38	39	40

FOURTY-ONE	FOURTY-TWO	FOURTY-THREE	FOURTY-FOUR	FOURTY-FIVE	FOURTY-SIX	FOURTY-SEVEN	FOURTY-EIGHT	FOURTY-NINE	FIFTY
41	42	43	44	45	46	47	48	49	50

WEEKDAYS   MONDAY   TUESDAY   WEDNESDAY
THURSDAY   FRIDAY
WEEKEND   SATURDAY   SUNDAY

-Drawings for elementary school **subjects**.

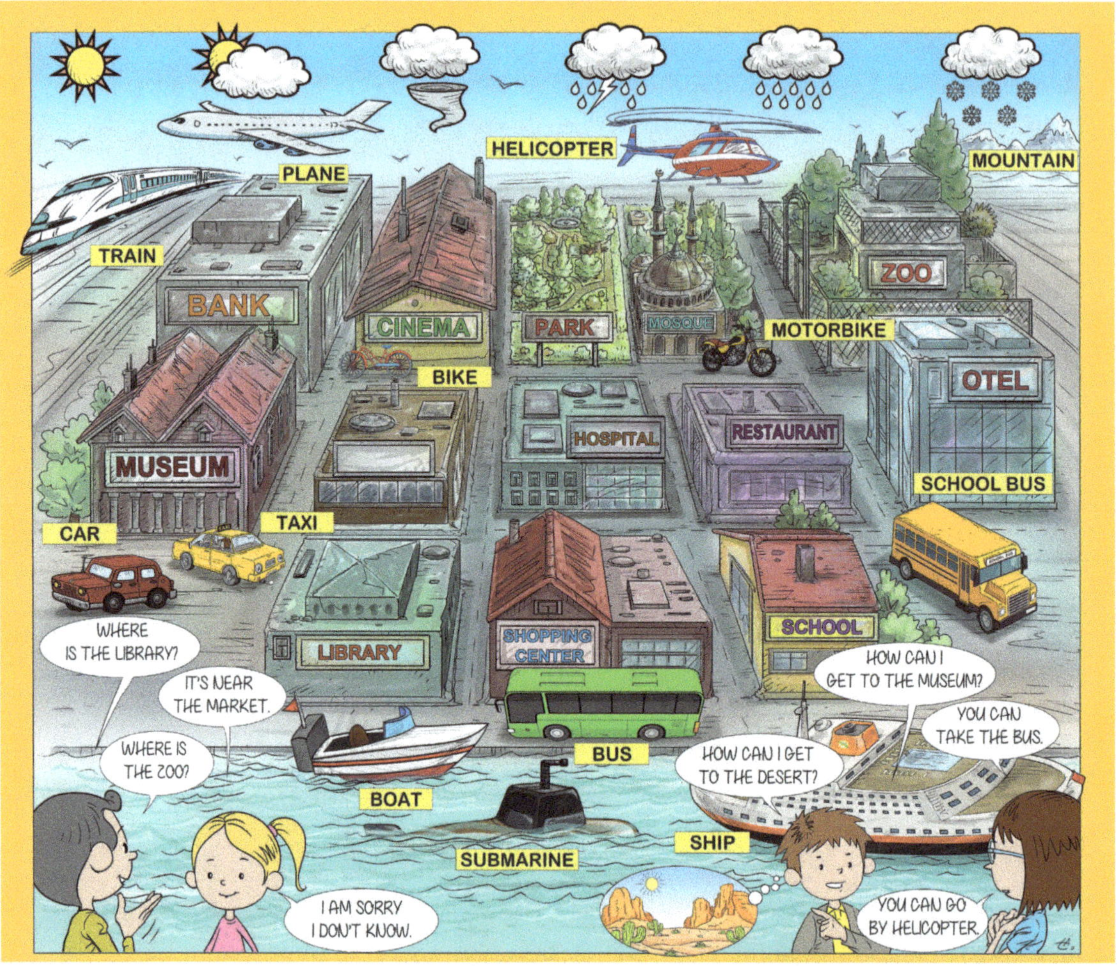

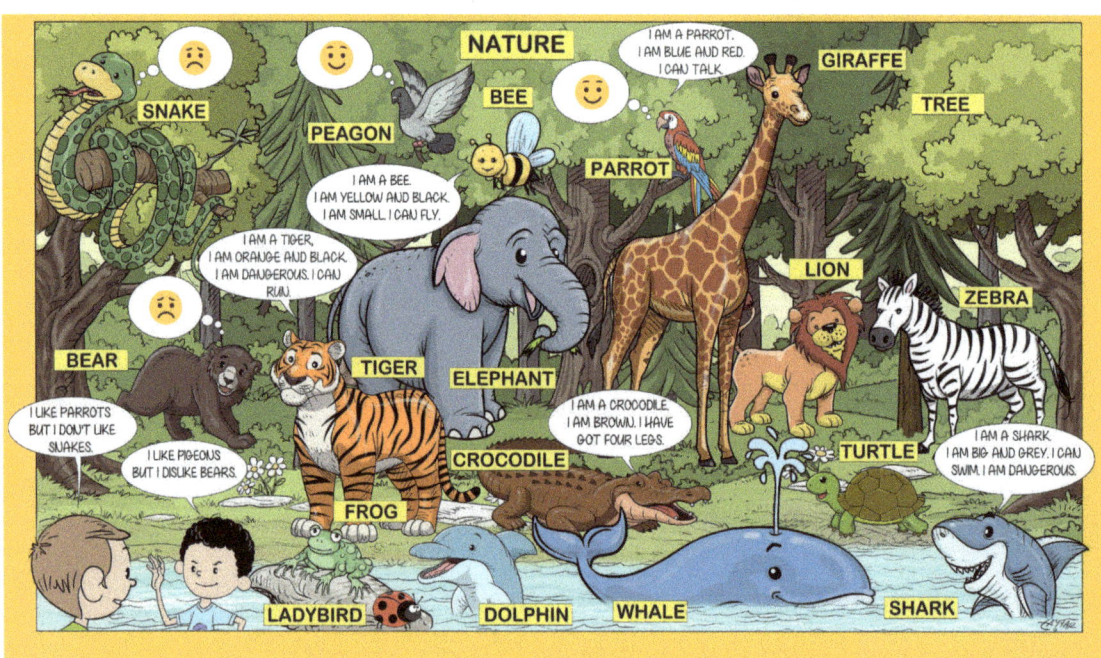

-Drawings for elementary school **subjects**.

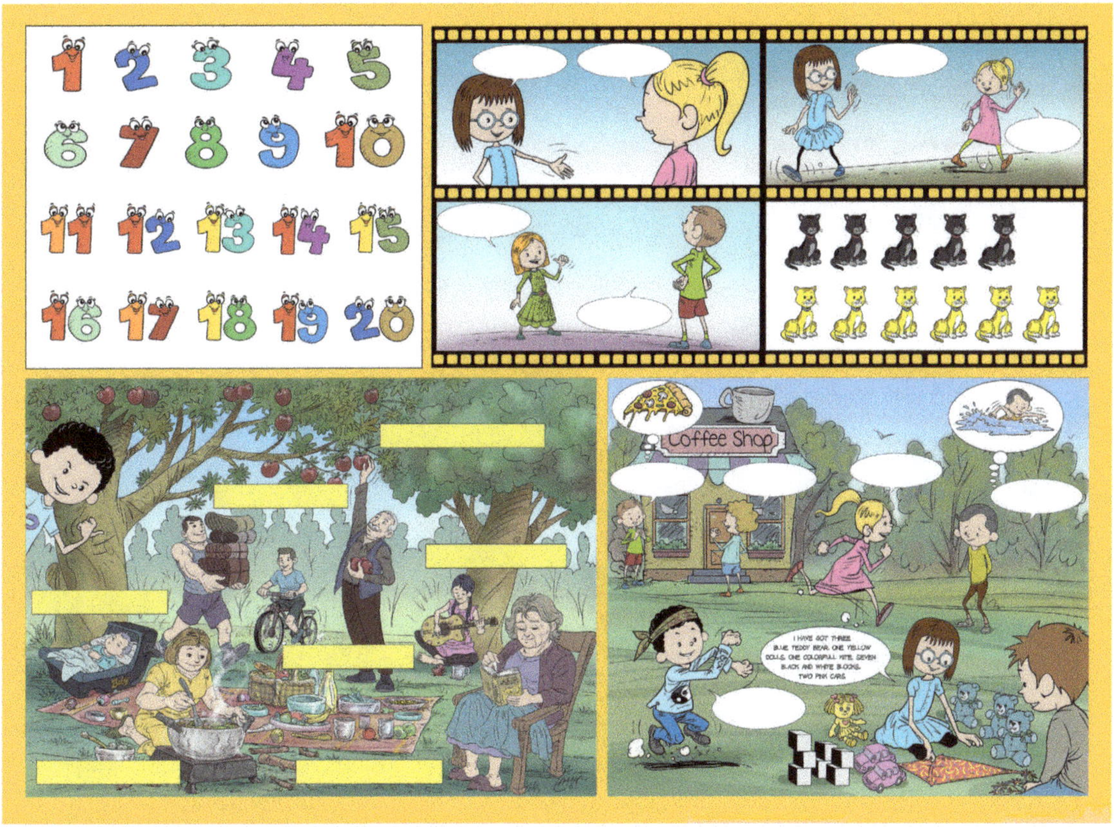

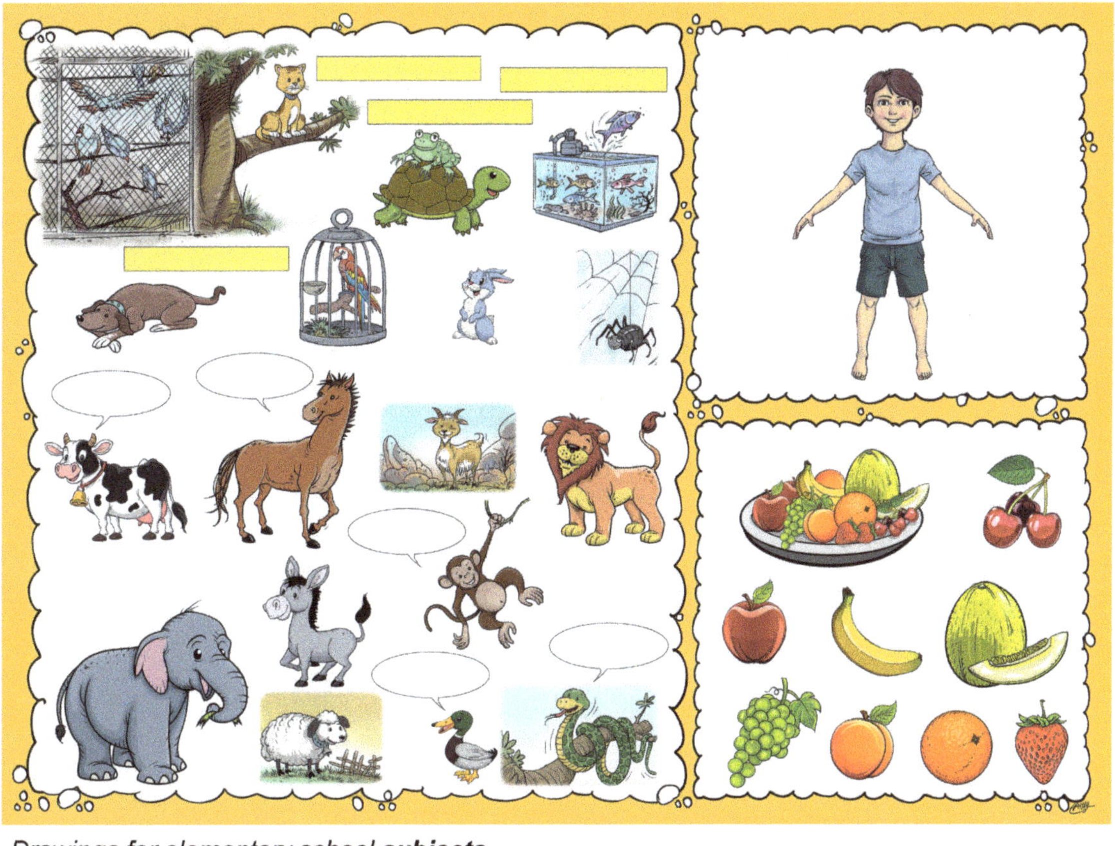

-Drawings for elementary school **subjects**.

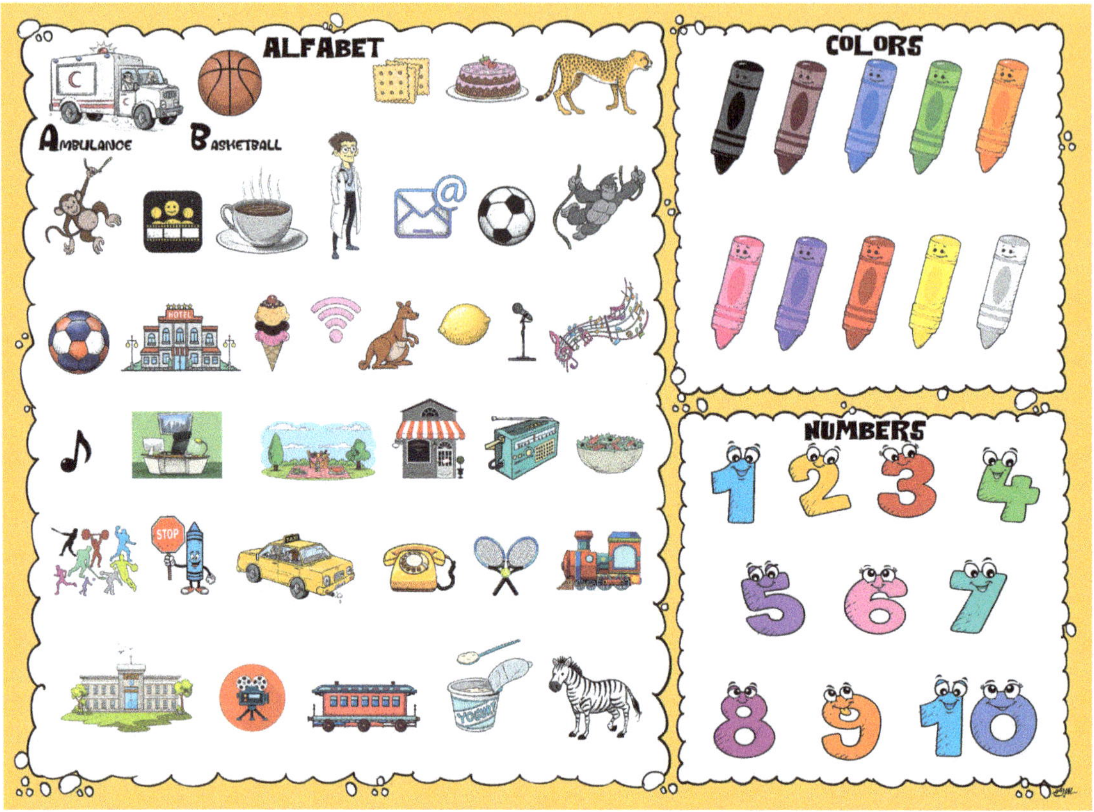

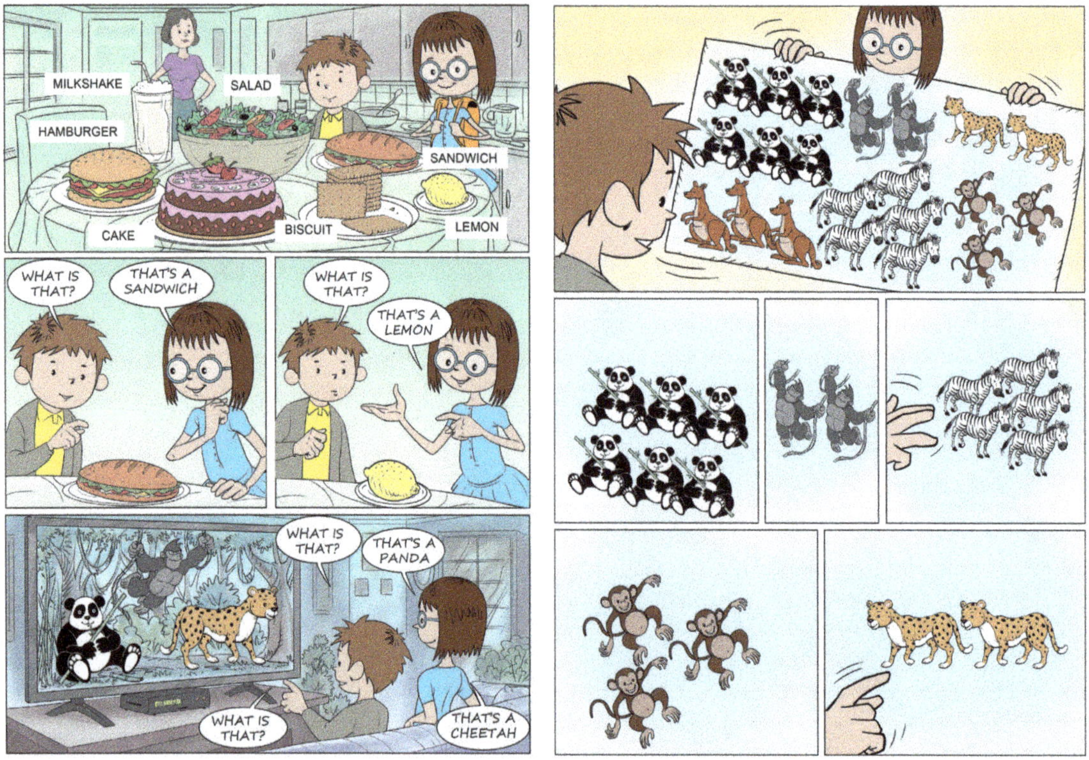

-Drawings for elementary school **subjects**.

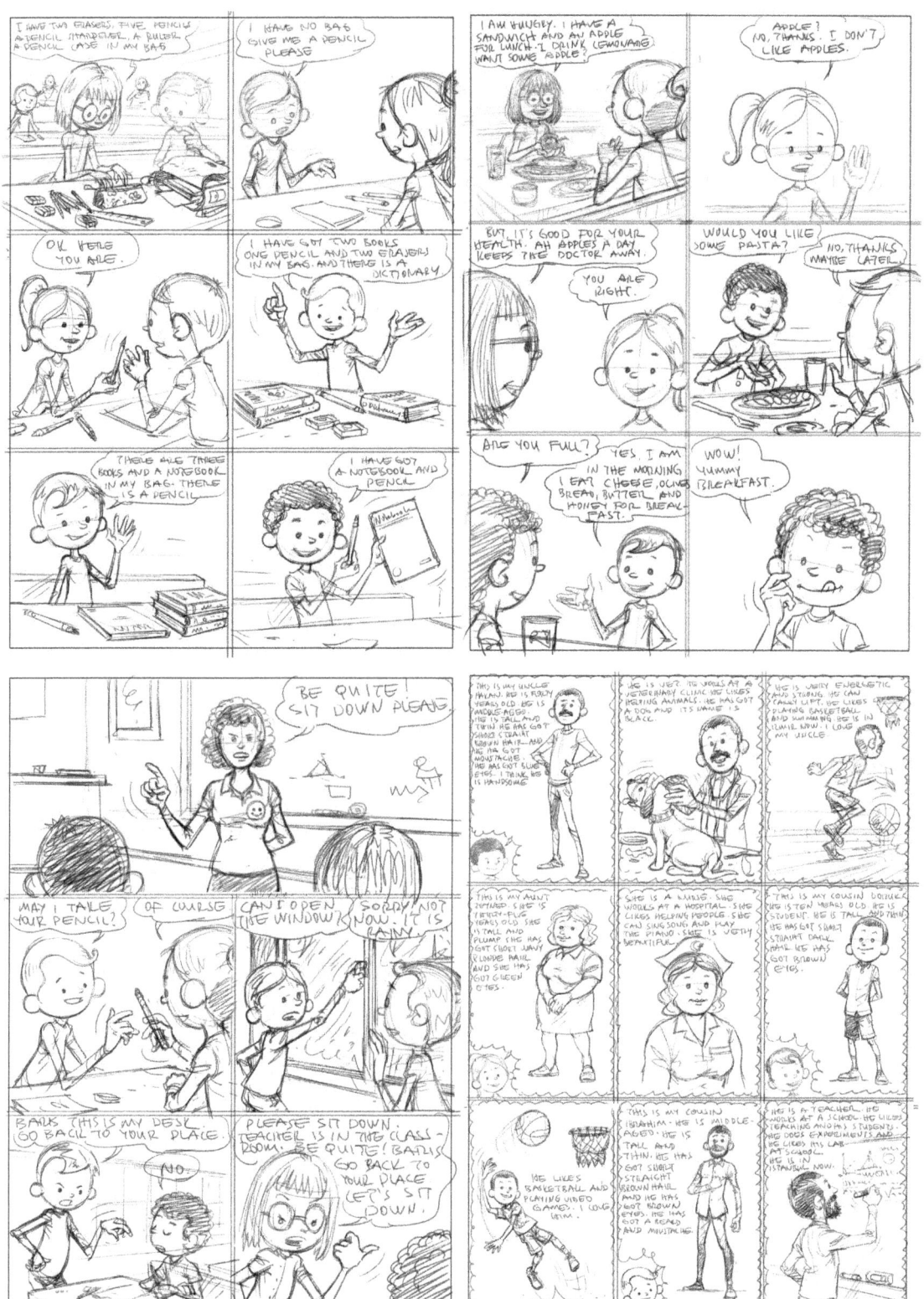

-Several comic **pencil pages** for an elementary school books.

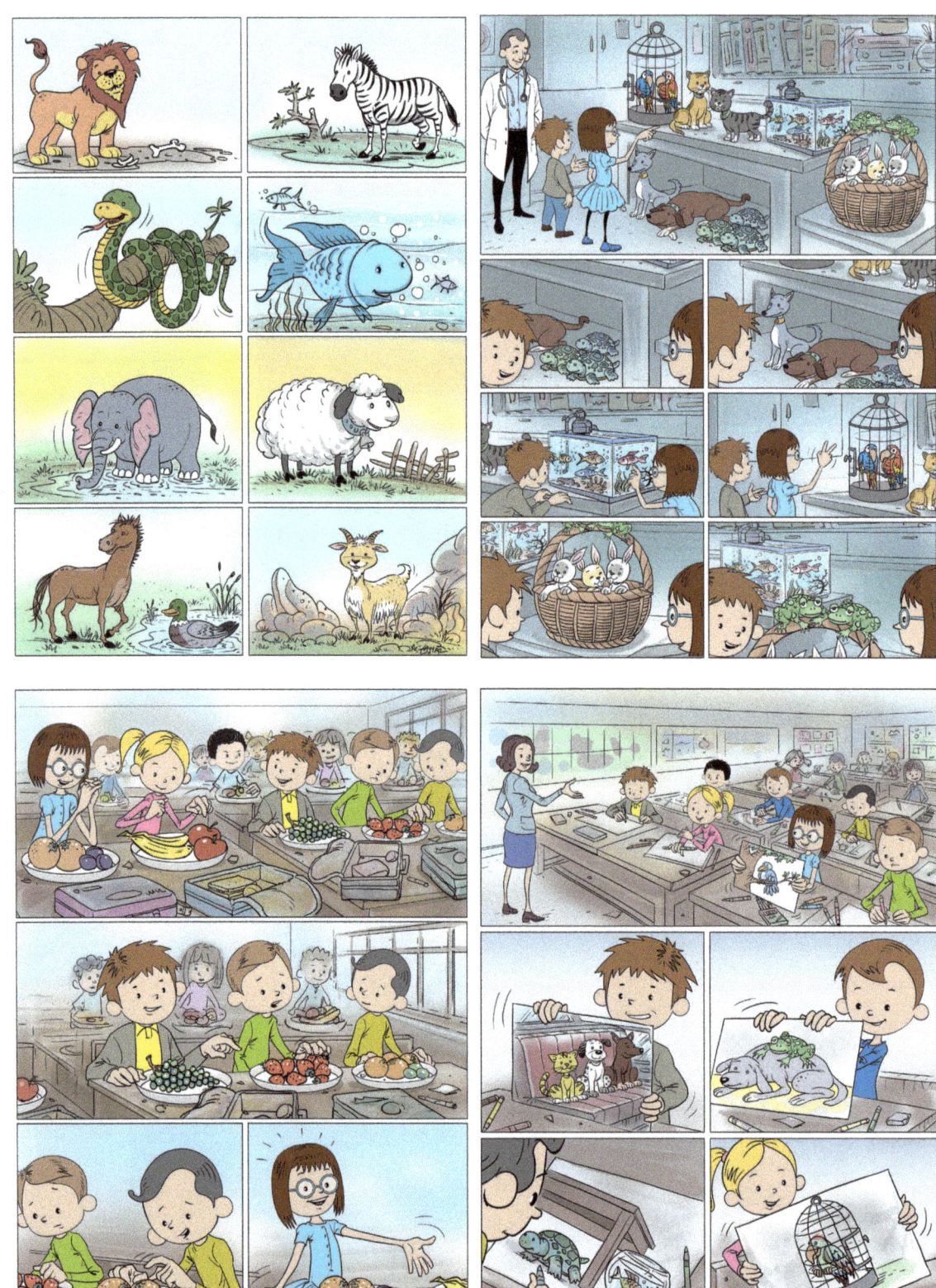

-Some **comic pages** for the school books.

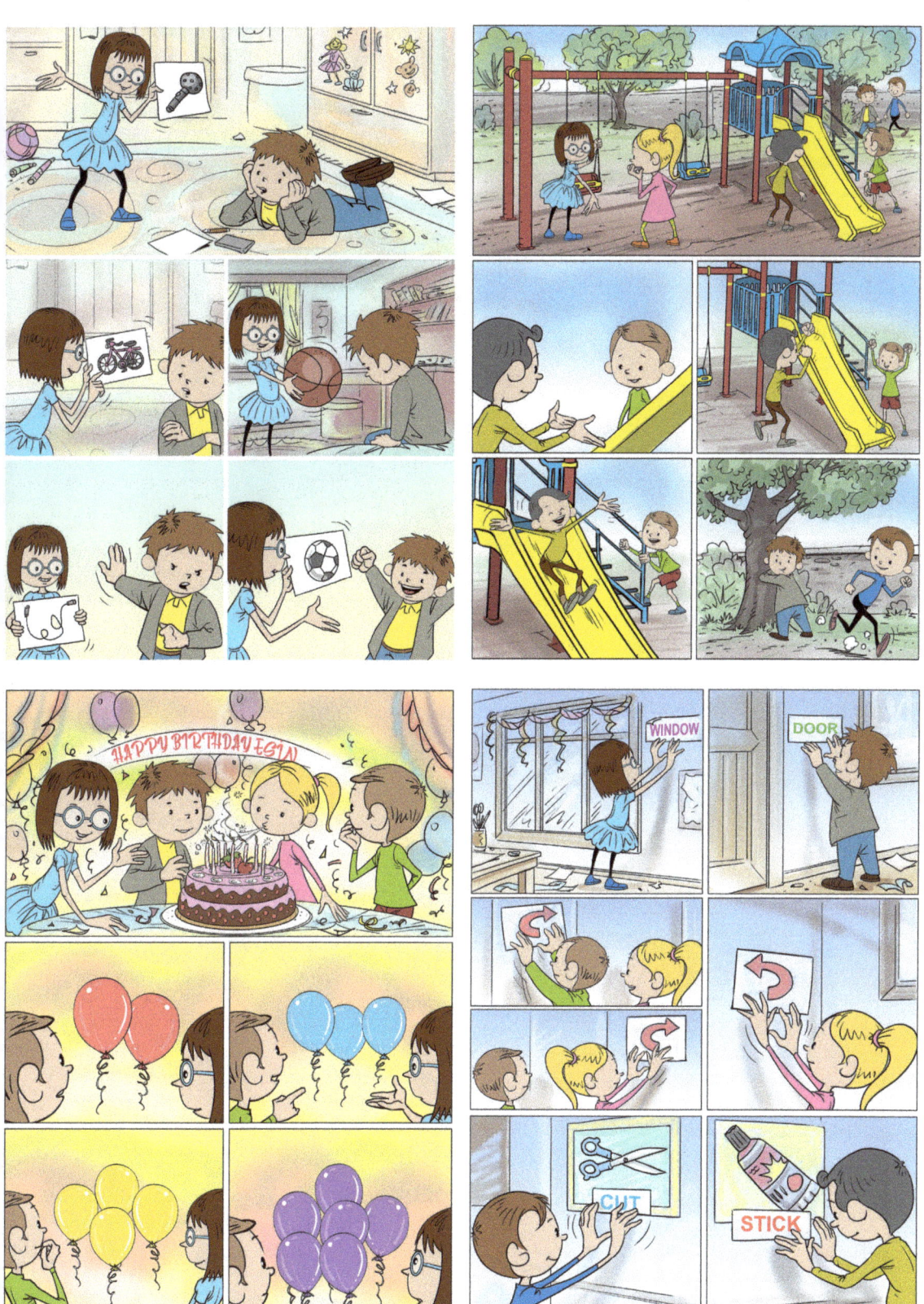

-*Comic* pages for the ***school book***.

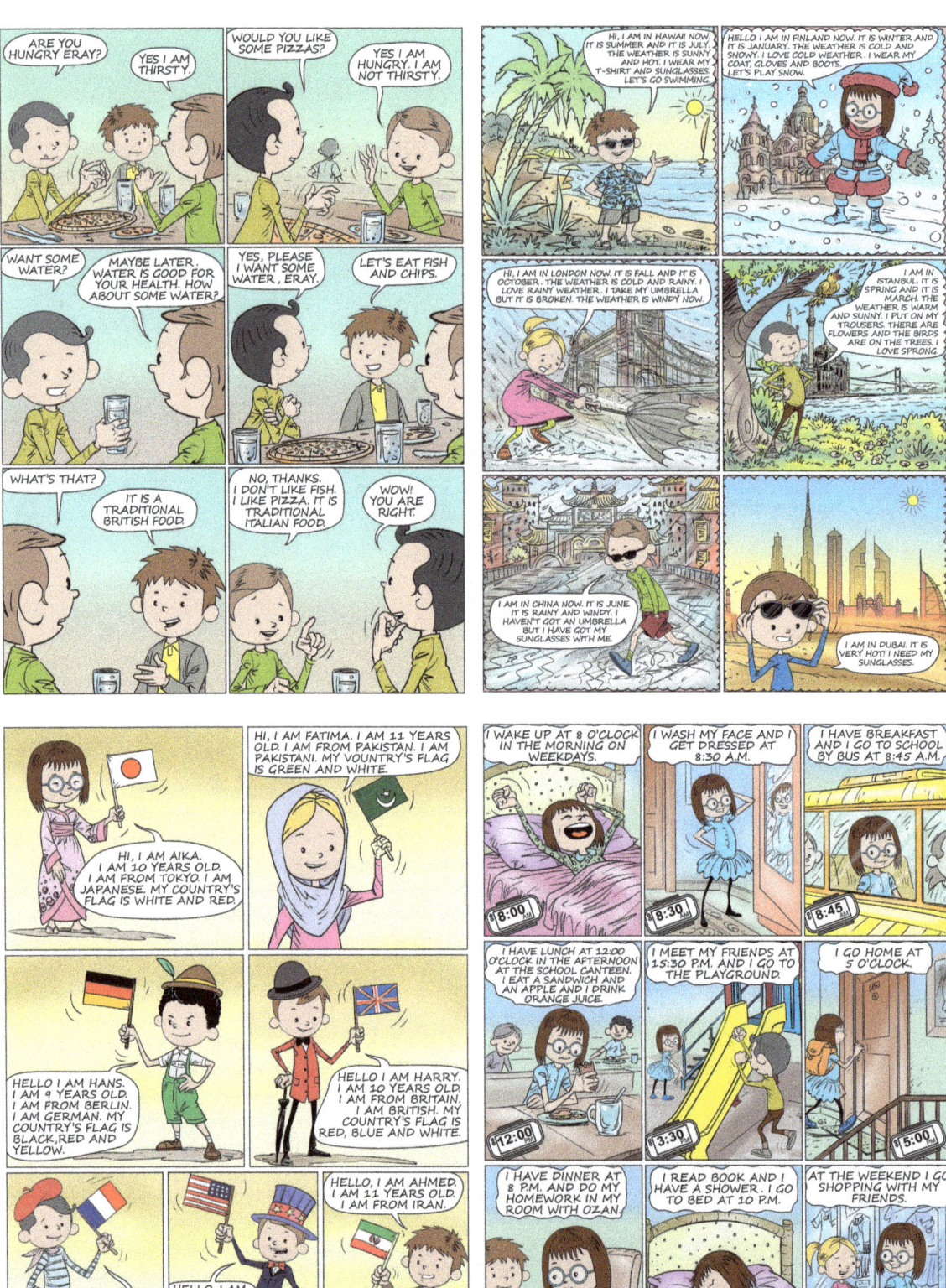

-Some more **comic** pages for the **school book**.

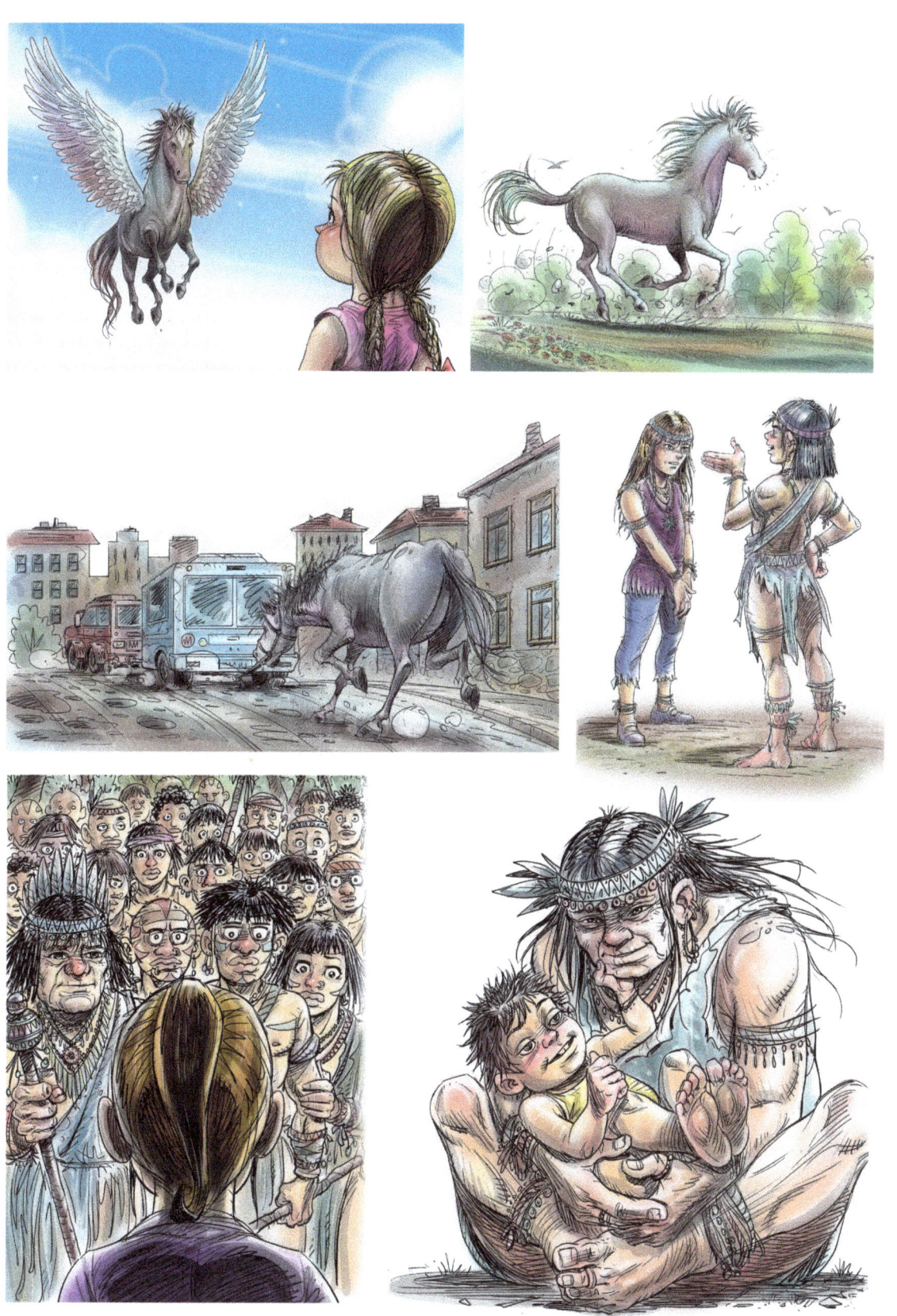

Types of *illustrations* for children's books.

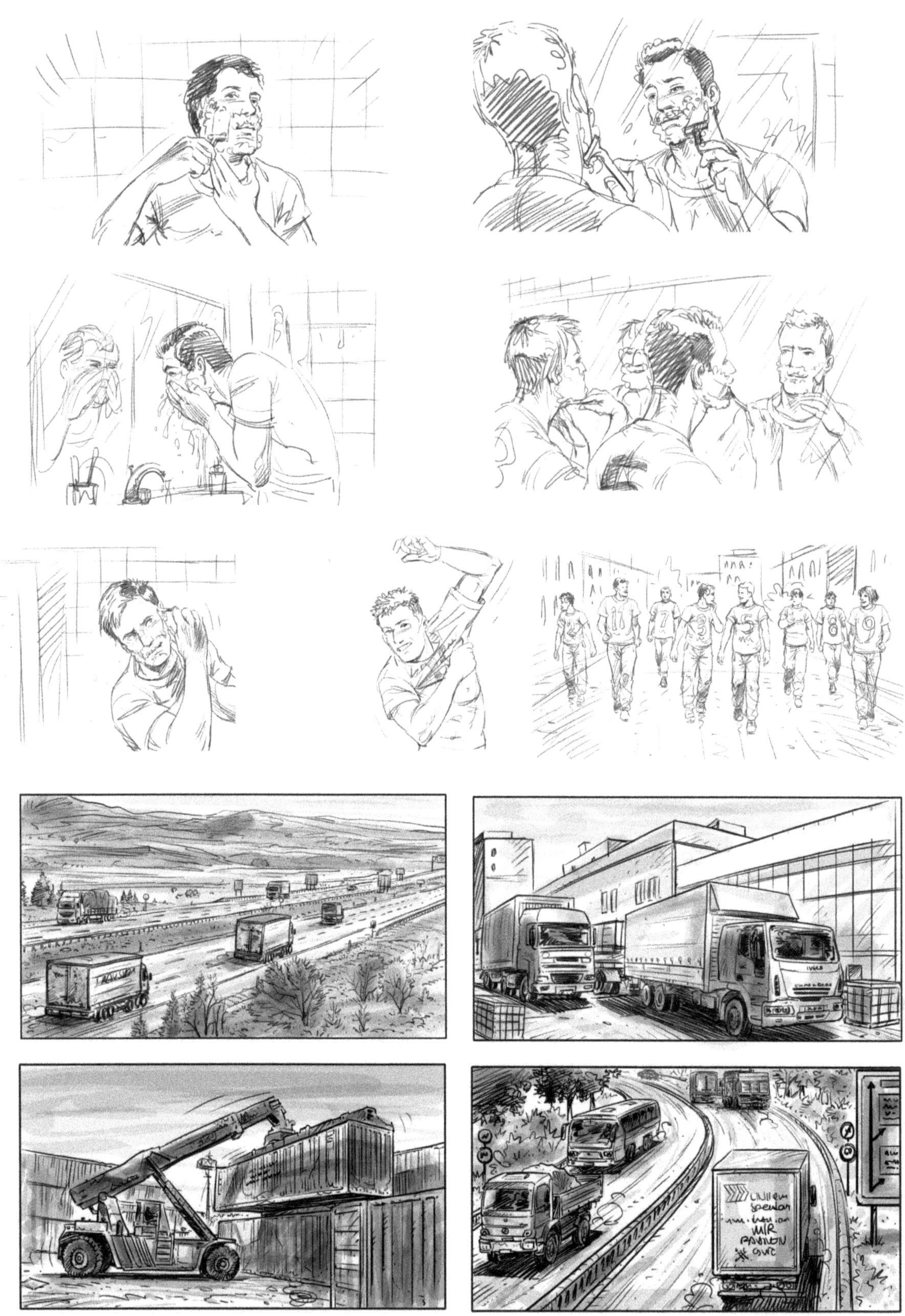

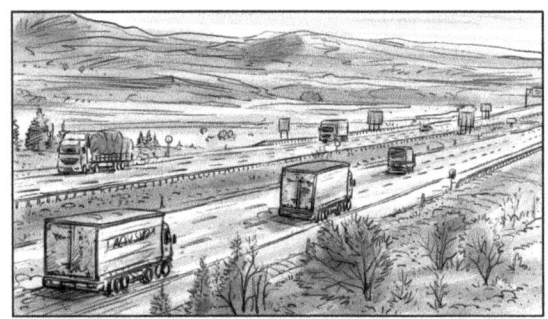
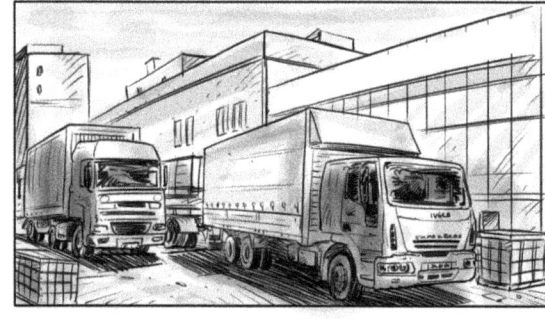
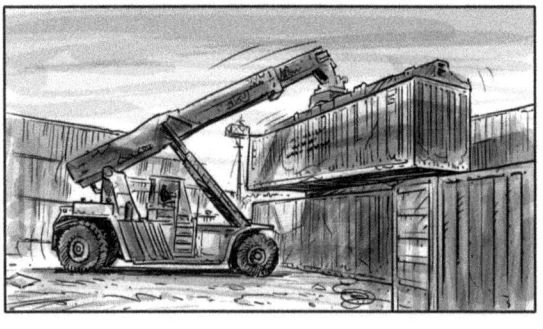
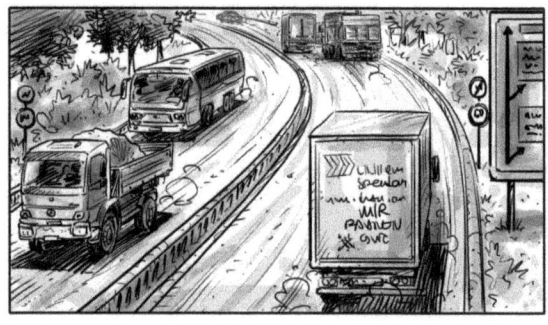

STORYBOARDS FOR TV COMMERCIALS.

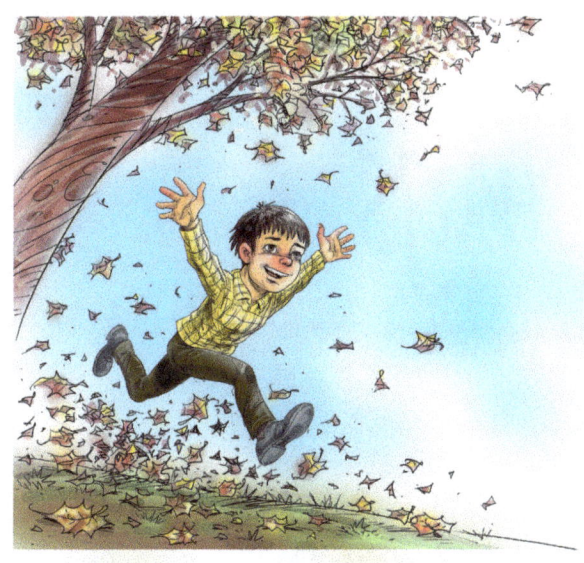
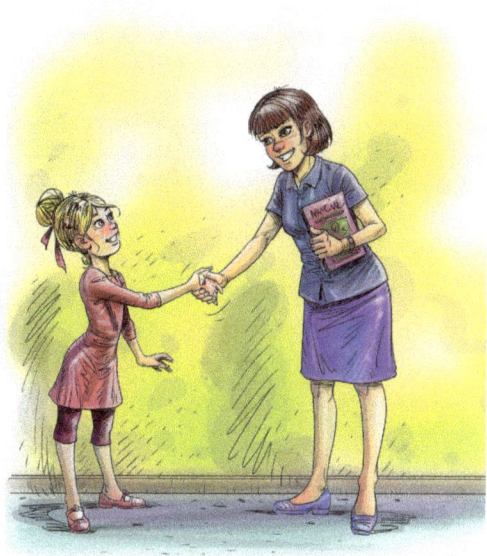
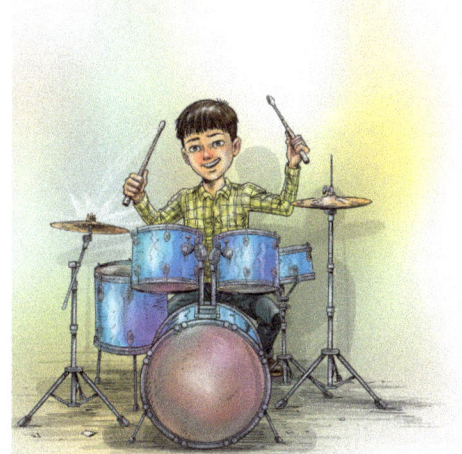
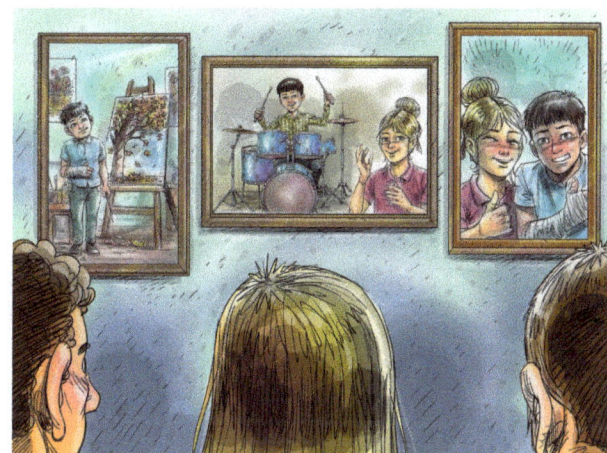
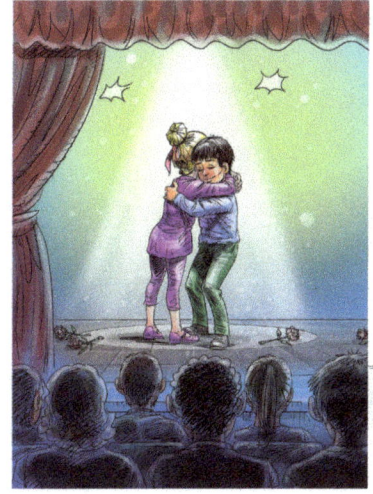
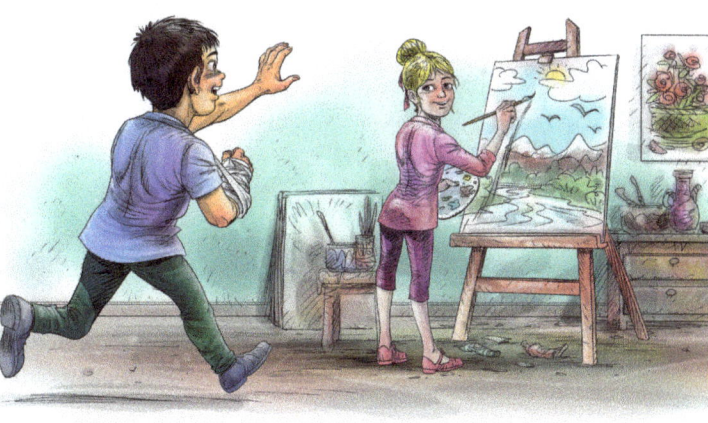

-Some **illustrations** for children's books

Paintings

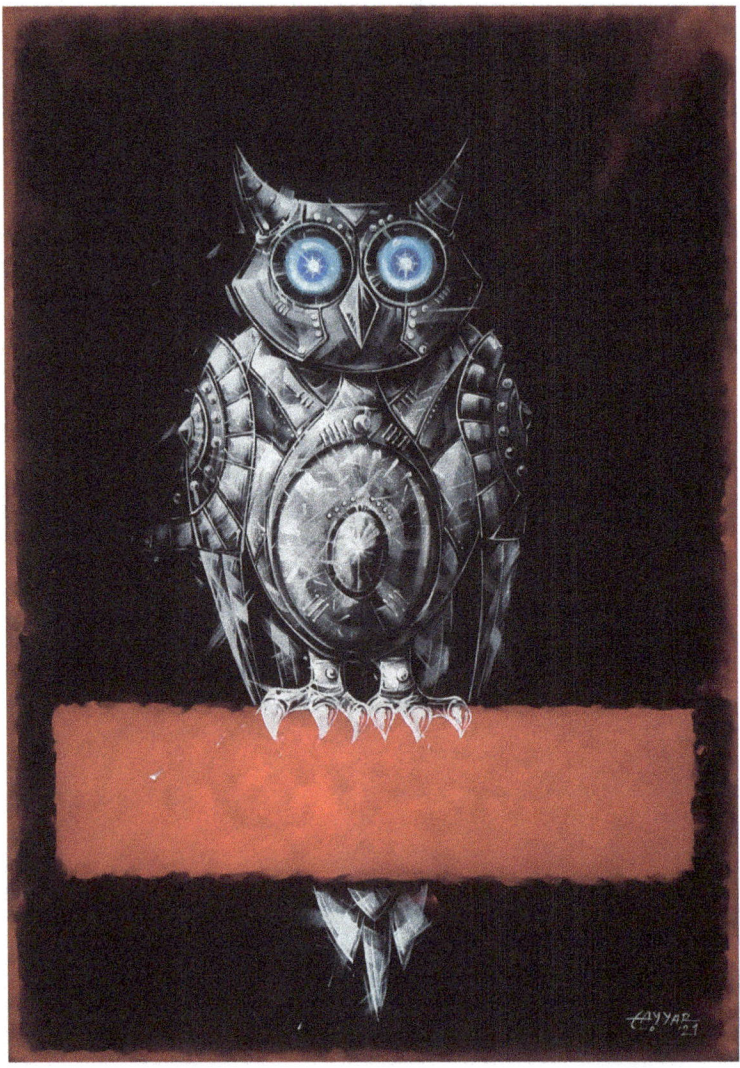

-Lately I've started to working on *acrylic paintings*
for my new *career*. The concepts of these paintings are
about the conflict of *AI* and the *nature* we live in.
The whole idea here is *controversy* of protecting the nature
aganist to growing technology.

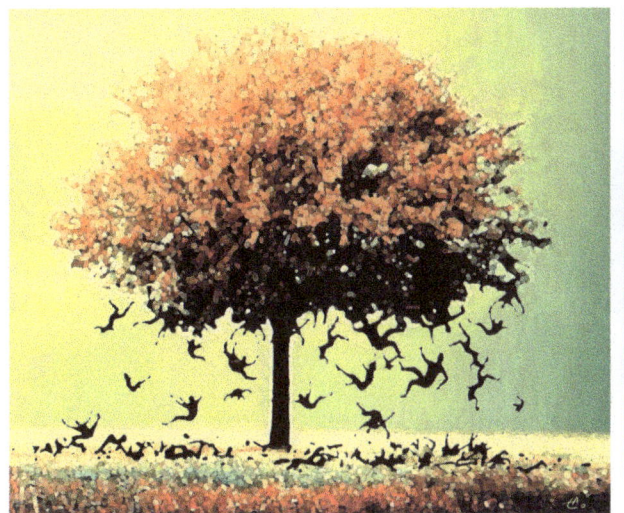
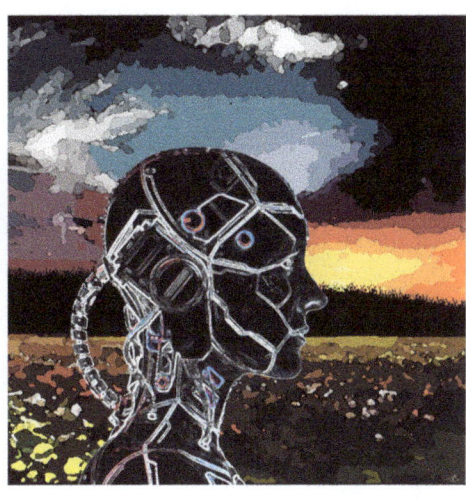
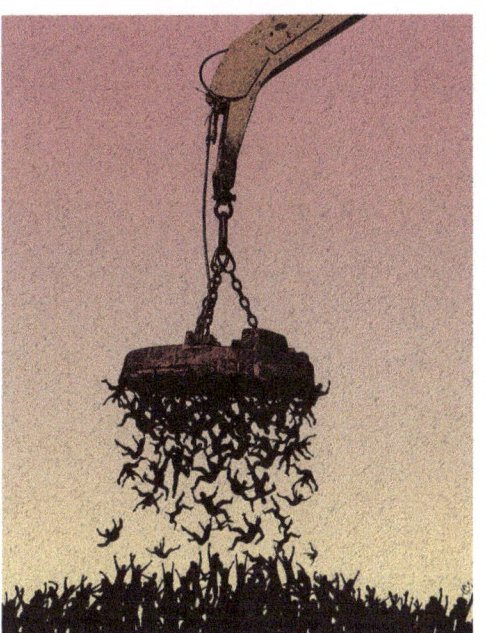
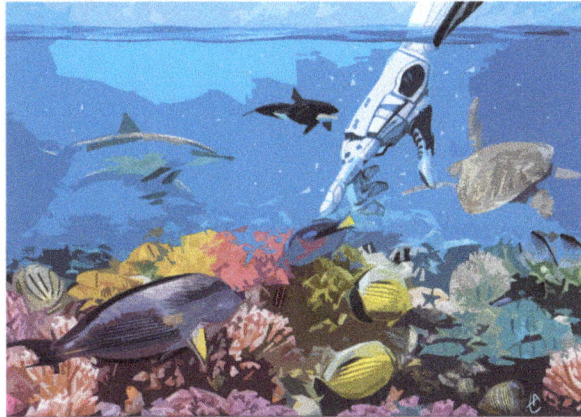
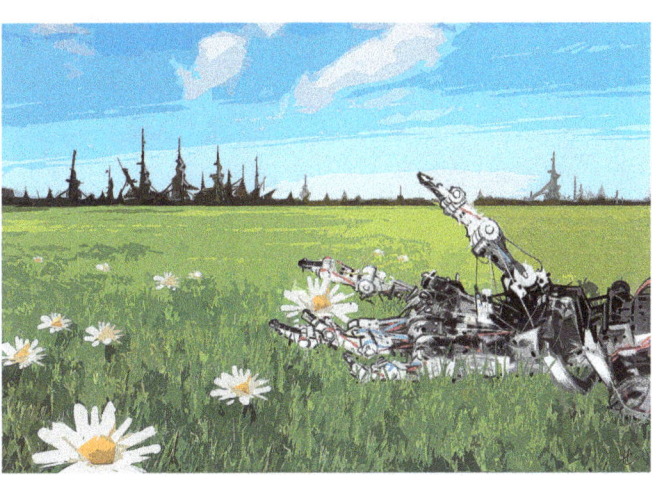
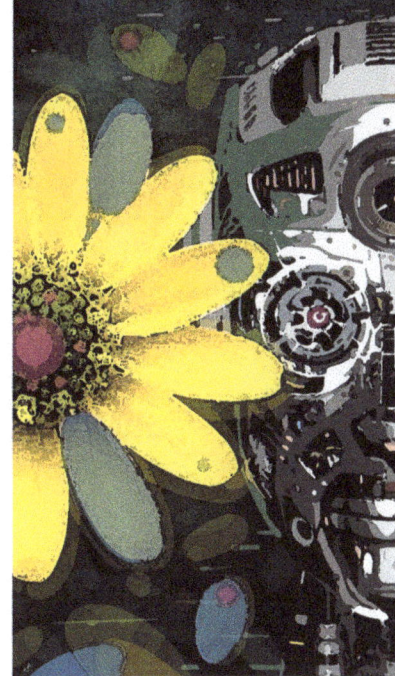

Digital work before doing acrylic paintings.
I'm very concerned about the upcoming *technology* versus *nature*.

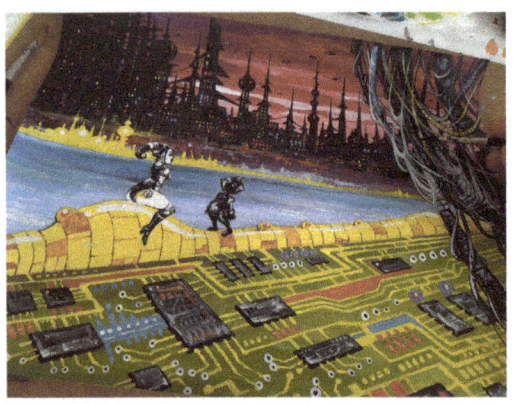

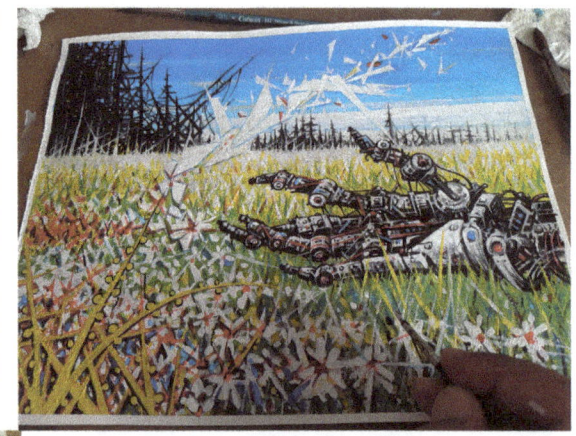

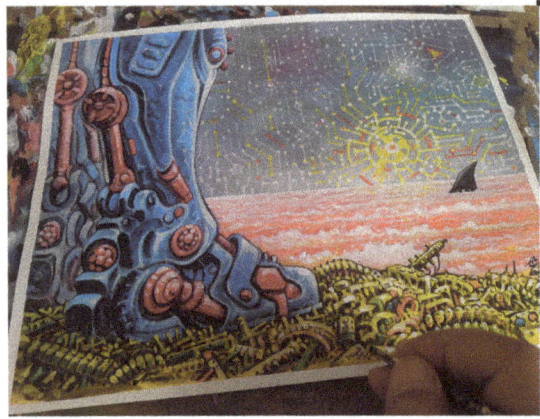

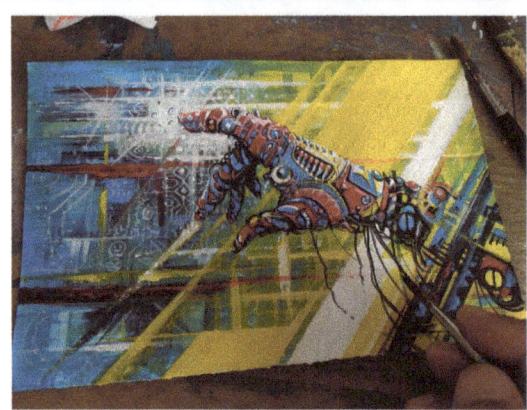

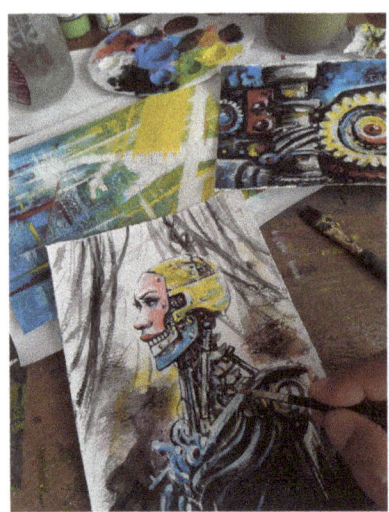

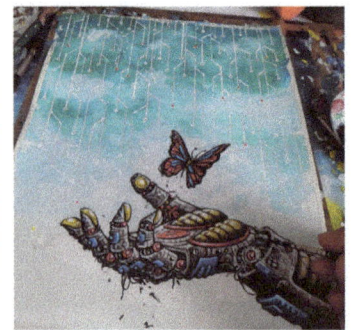

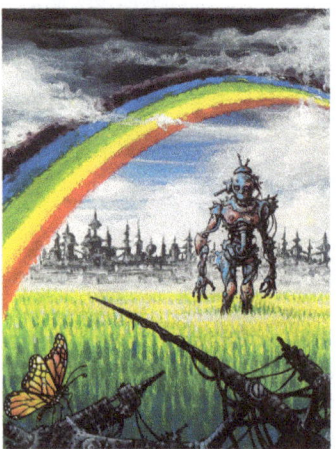

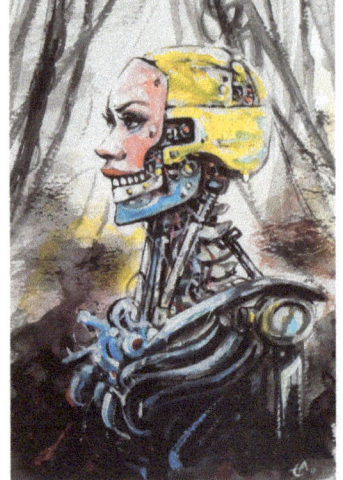

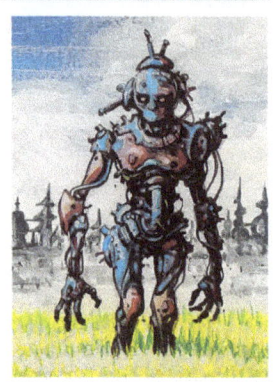

*These are my **small** acrylic **practicing** on papers before I started for painting on canvas.*

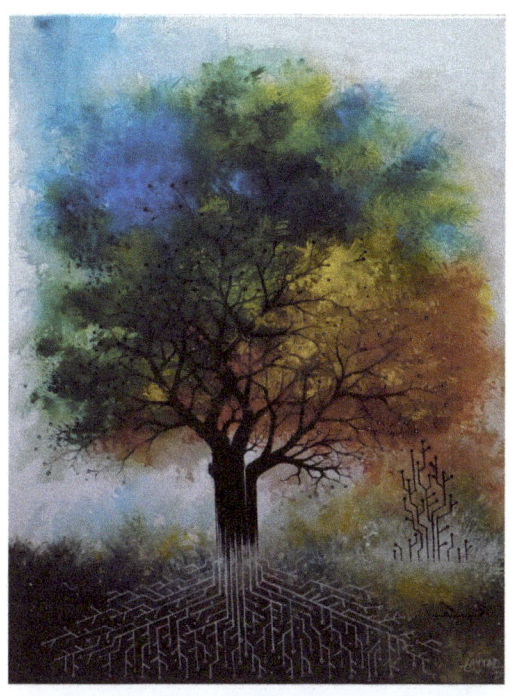
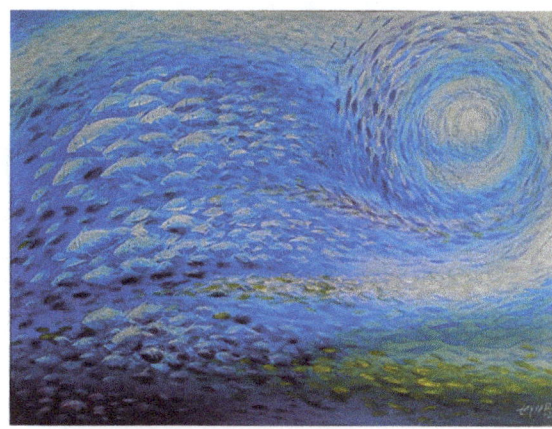
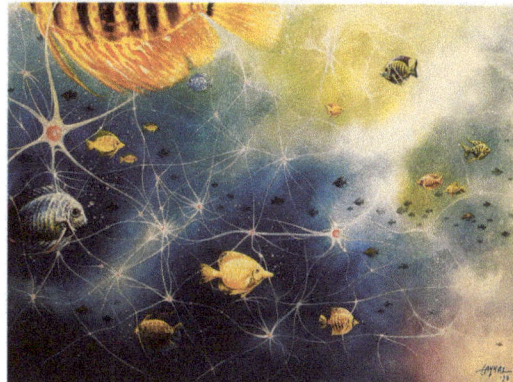
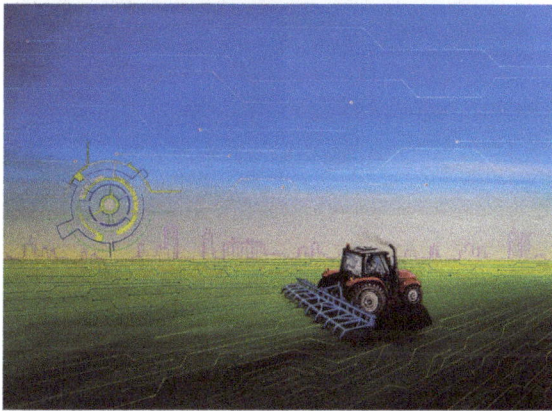
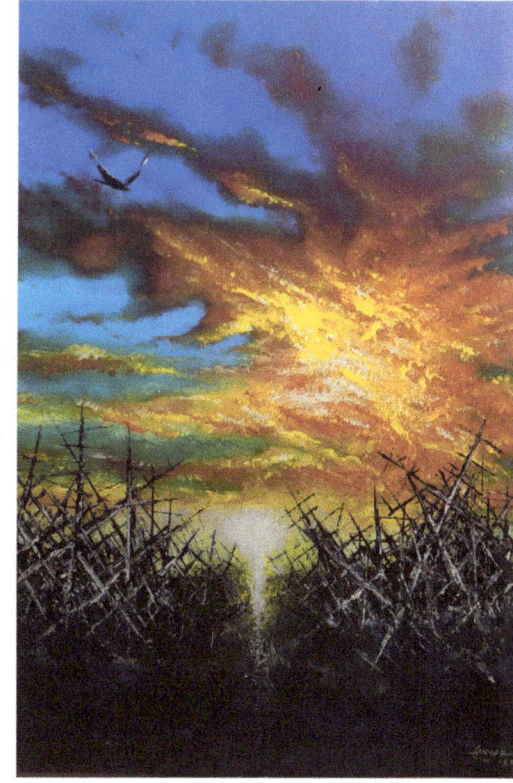
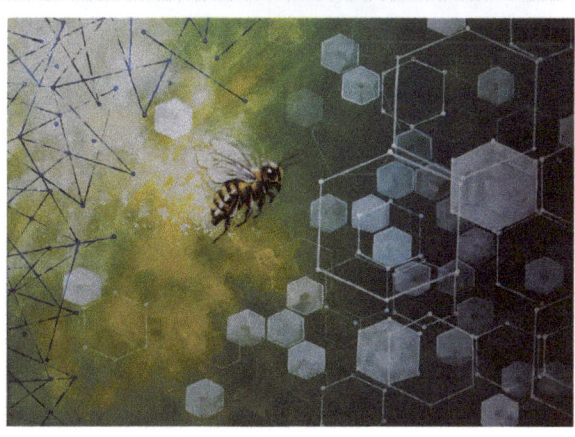

-Early acrylic *paintings* on canvas.
All sizes here are 50x70cm.

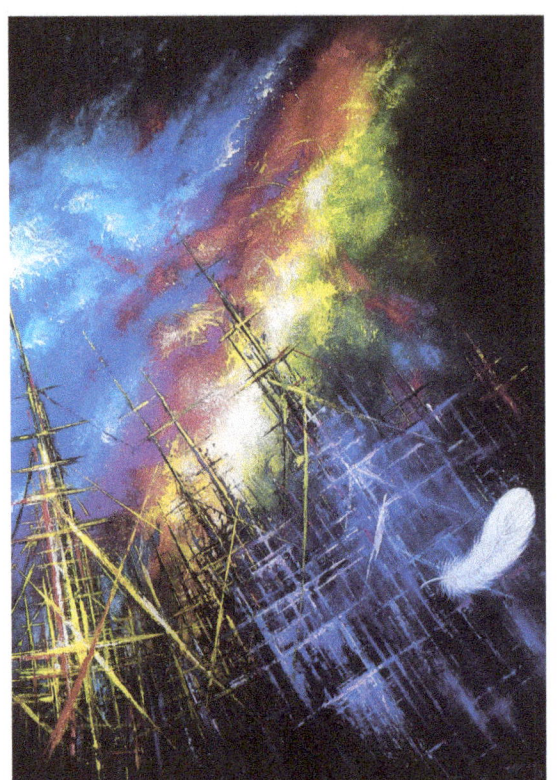
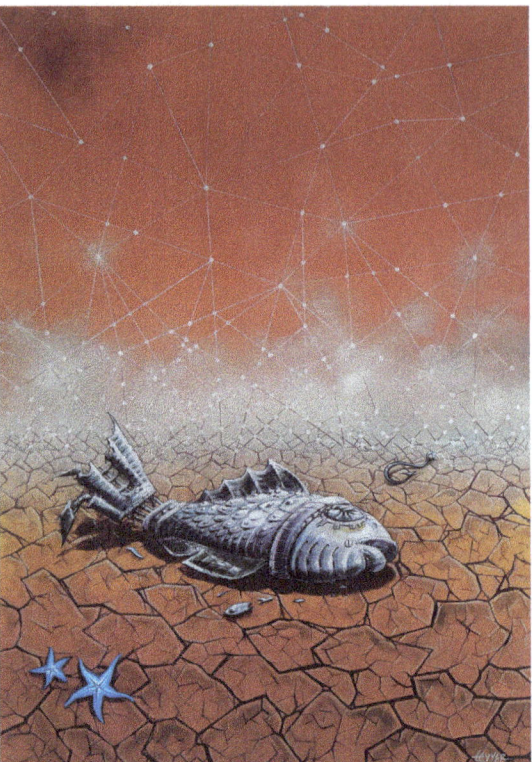

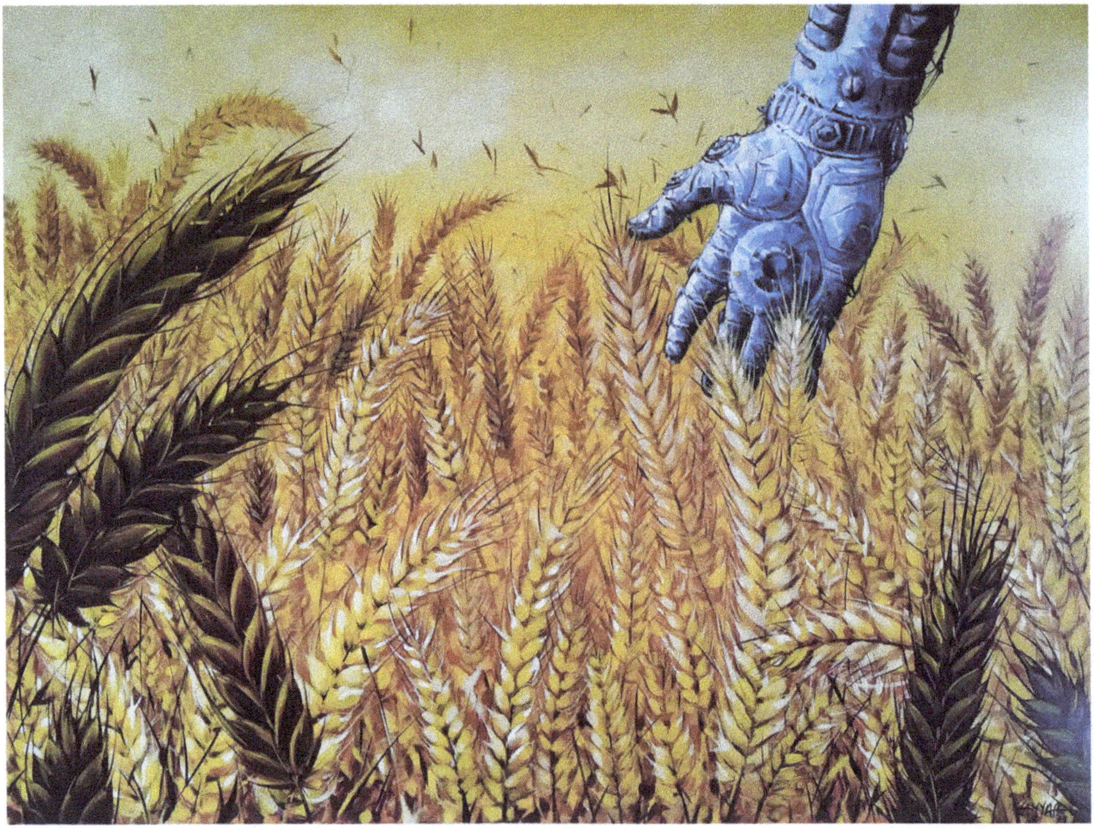

Early acrylic *paintings* on canvas.
They all are 70x100cm.

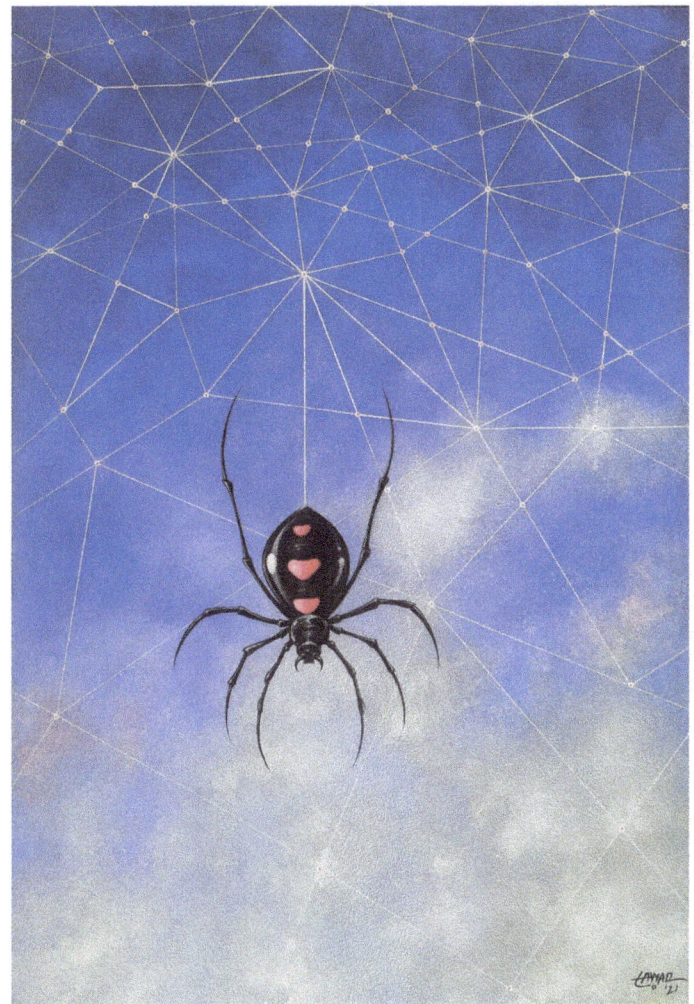

70x100cm.

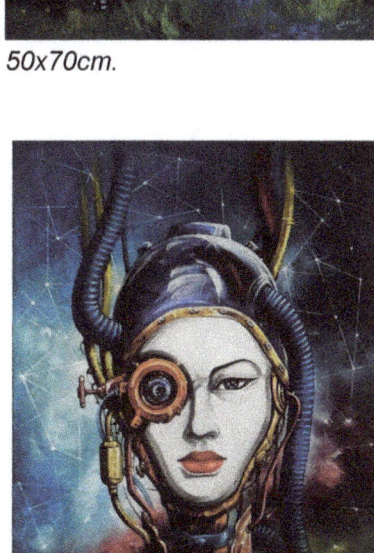

50x70cm.

50x70cm.

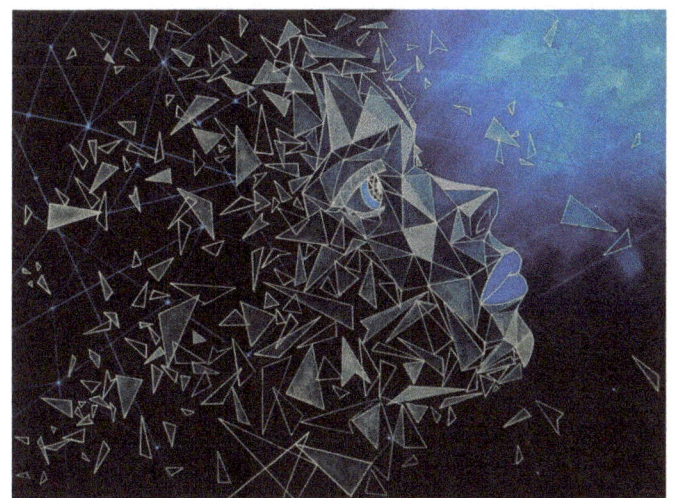

50x70cm.

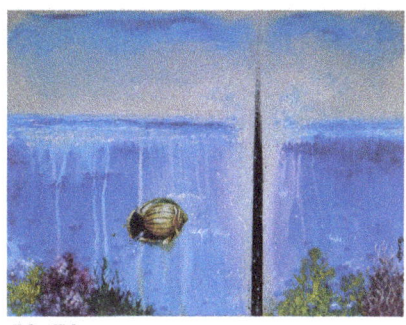

50x70cm.

Early acrylic *paintings* on canvas.

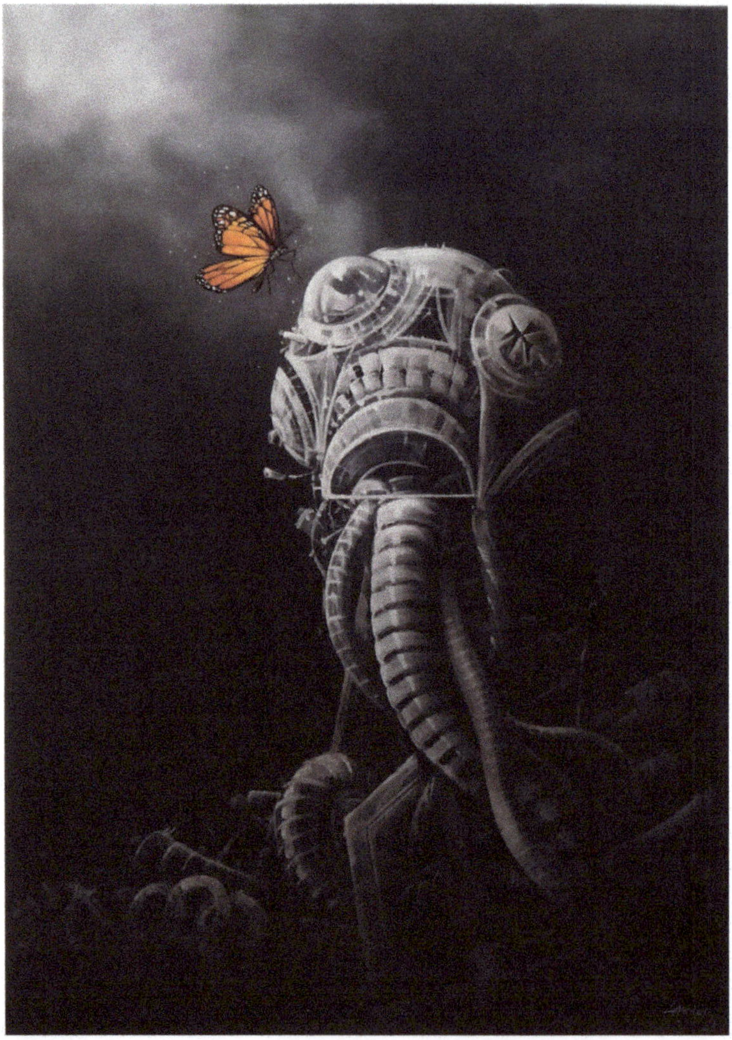

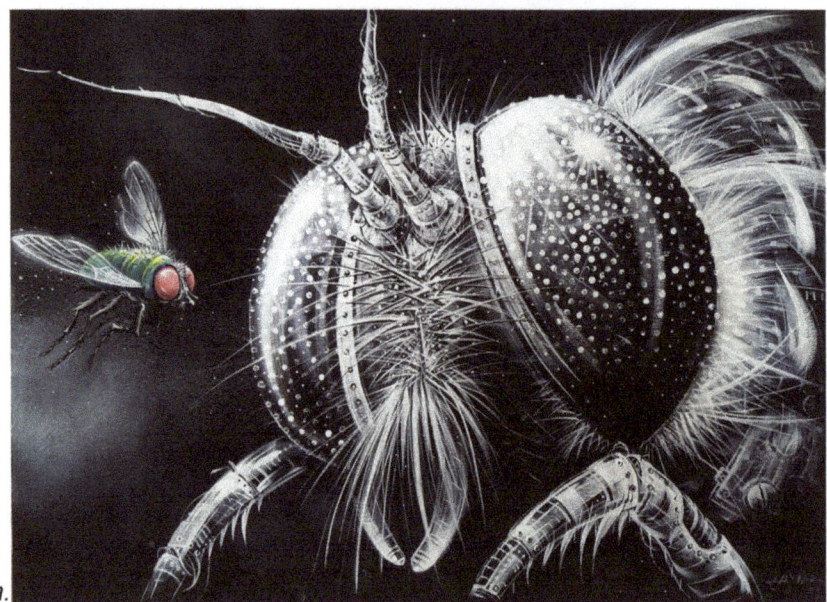

54x80cm.

50x70cm.

Early acrylic *paintings* on canvas.

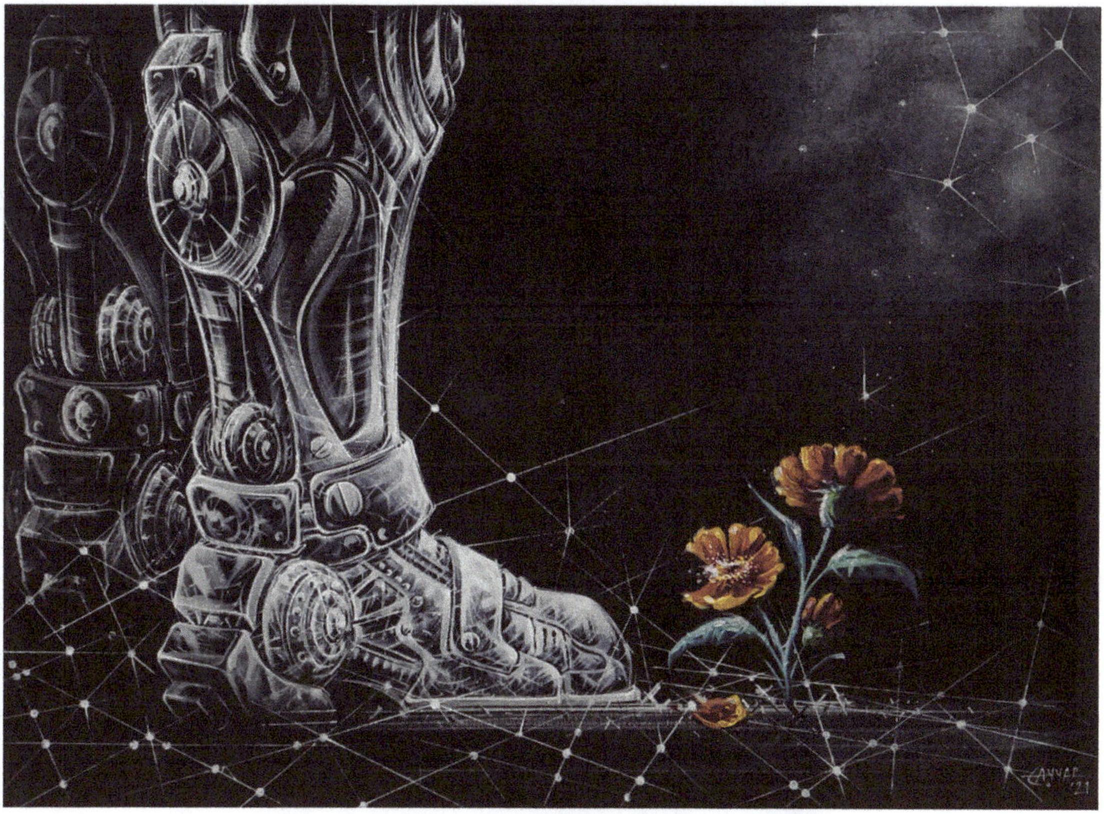

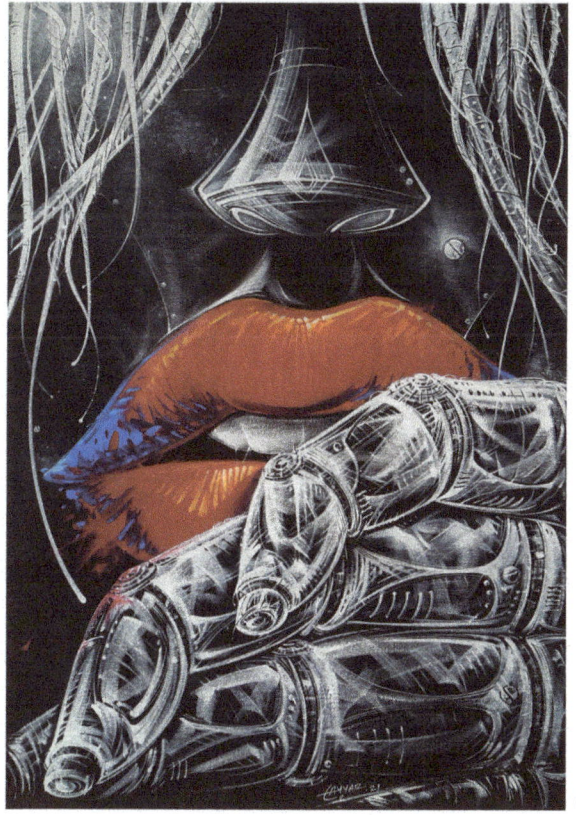

50x70cm.

50x70cm.

Acrylic *paintings* on canvas.

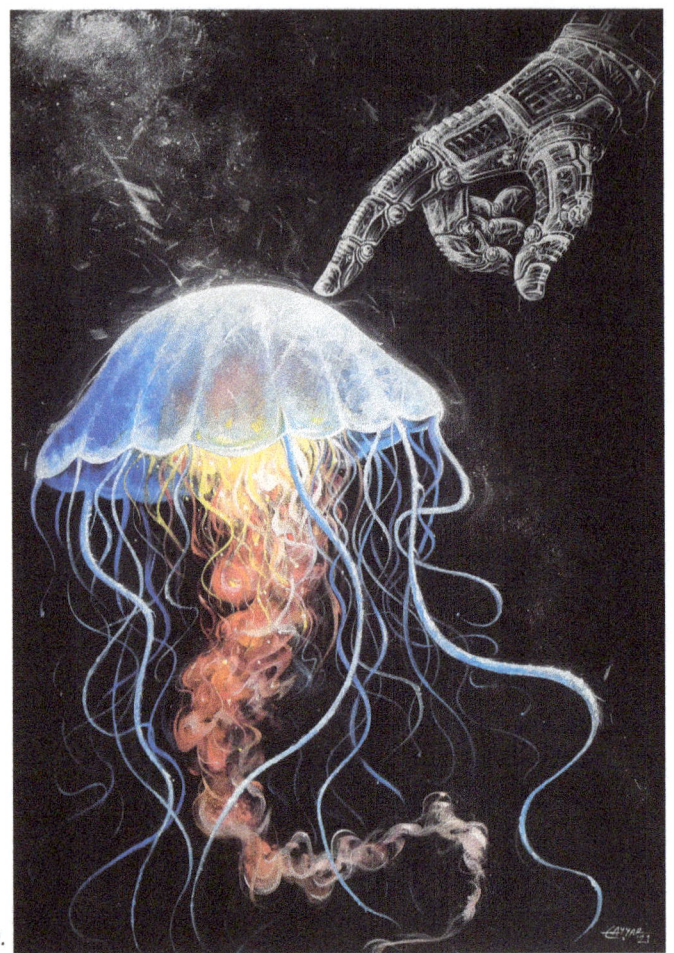

70x100cm.

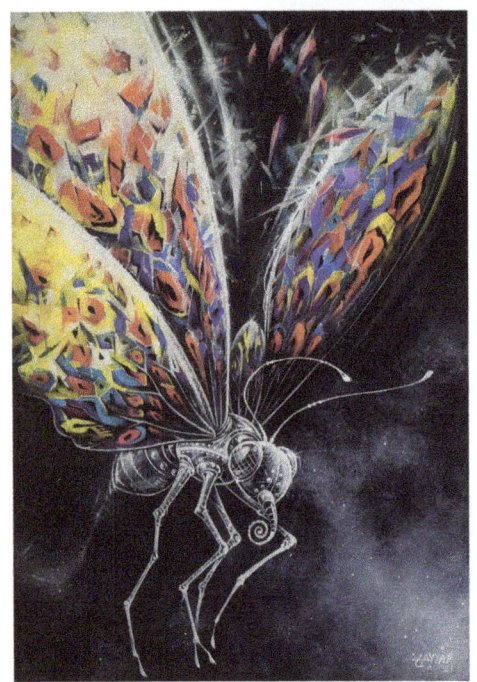

50x70cm.

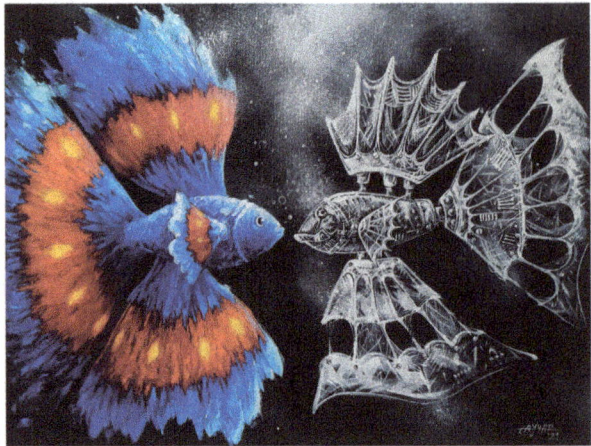

50x70cm.

Acrylic *paintings* on canvas.

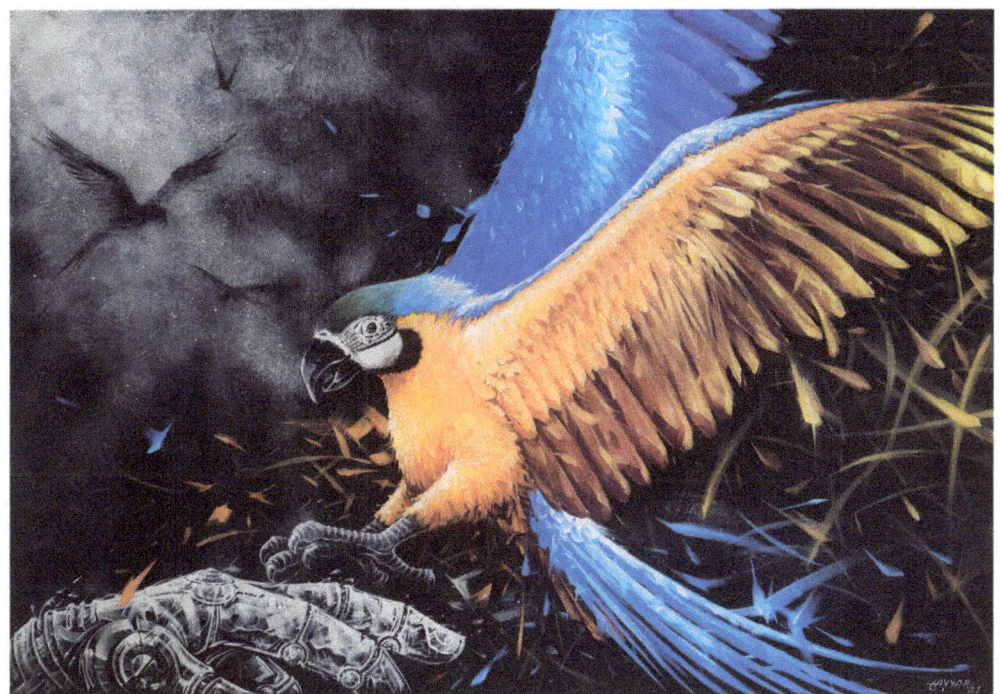

70x100cm.

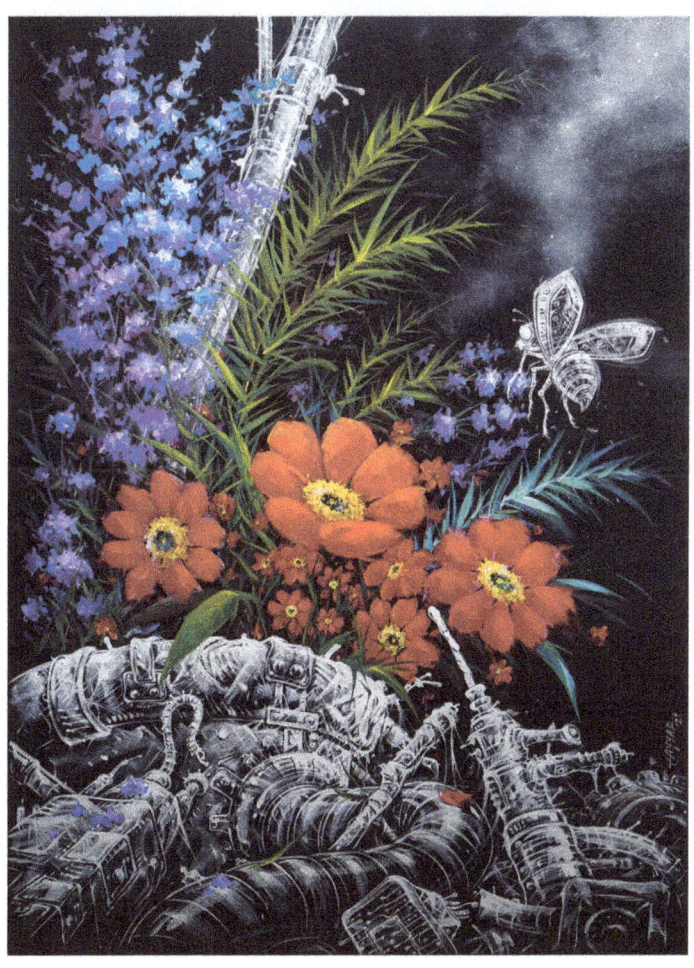

70x100cm.

Acrylic *paintings* on canvas.

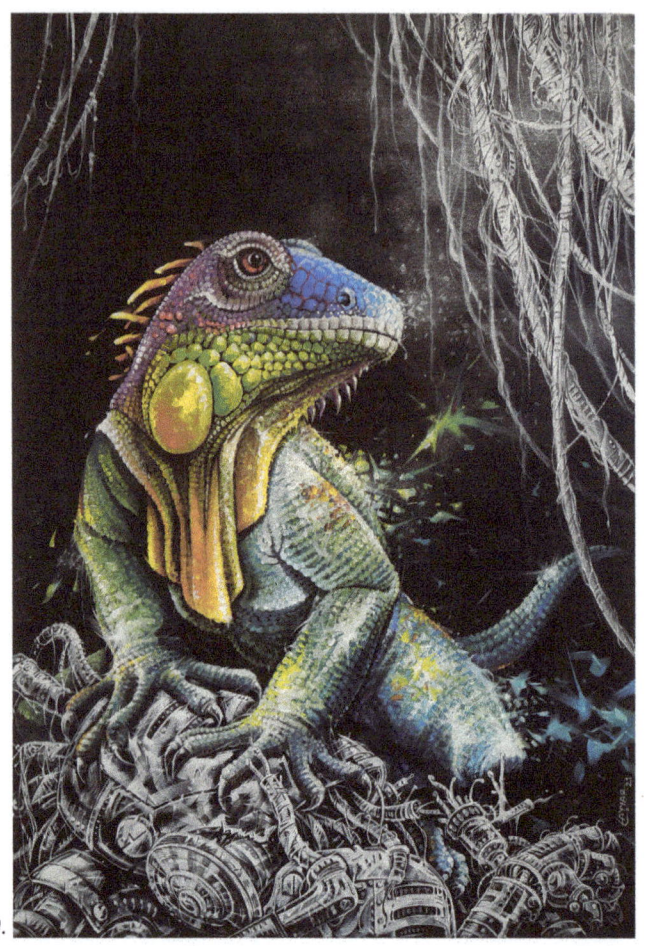

-70x100cm.

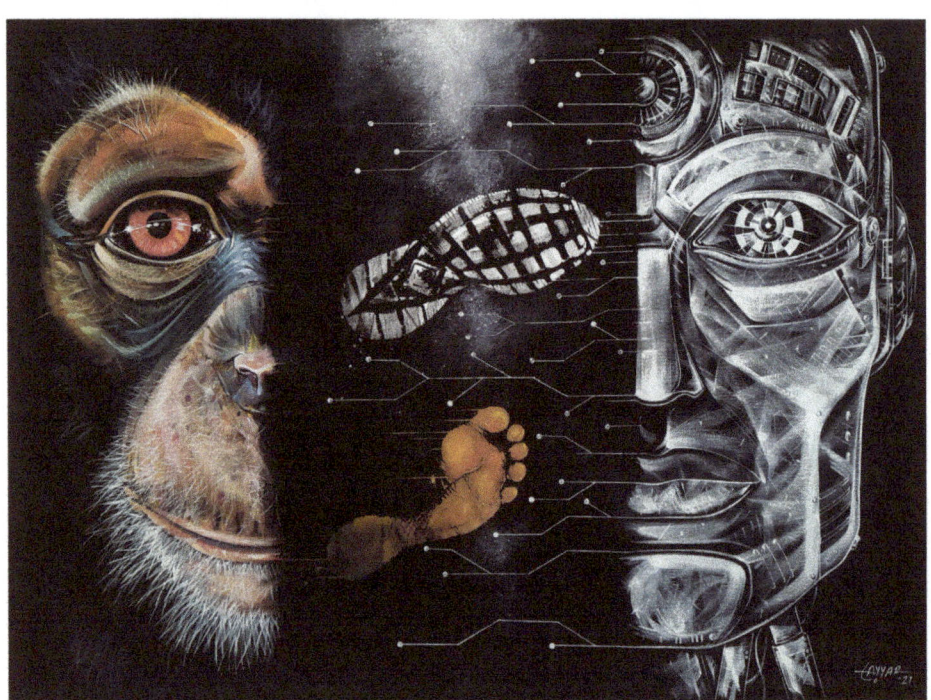

-70x100cm.

Acrylic *paintings* on canvas.

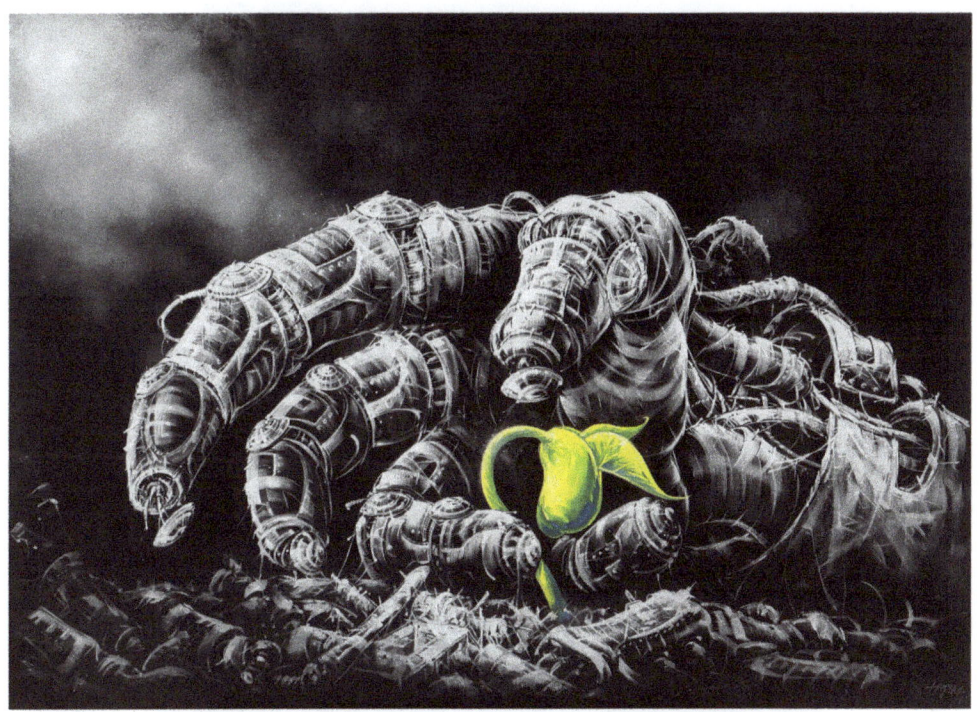

70x100cm.

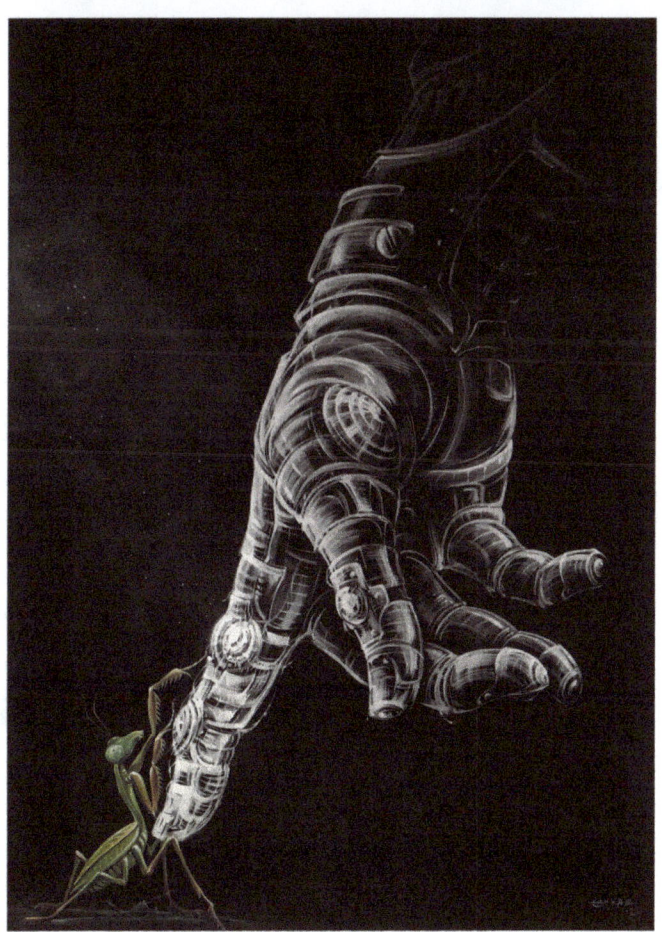

70x100cm.

Acrylic *paintings* on canvas.

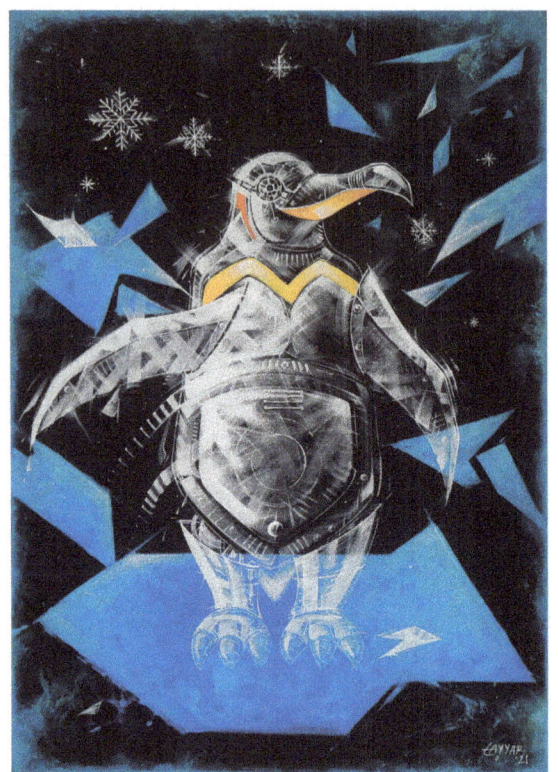

50x70cm.

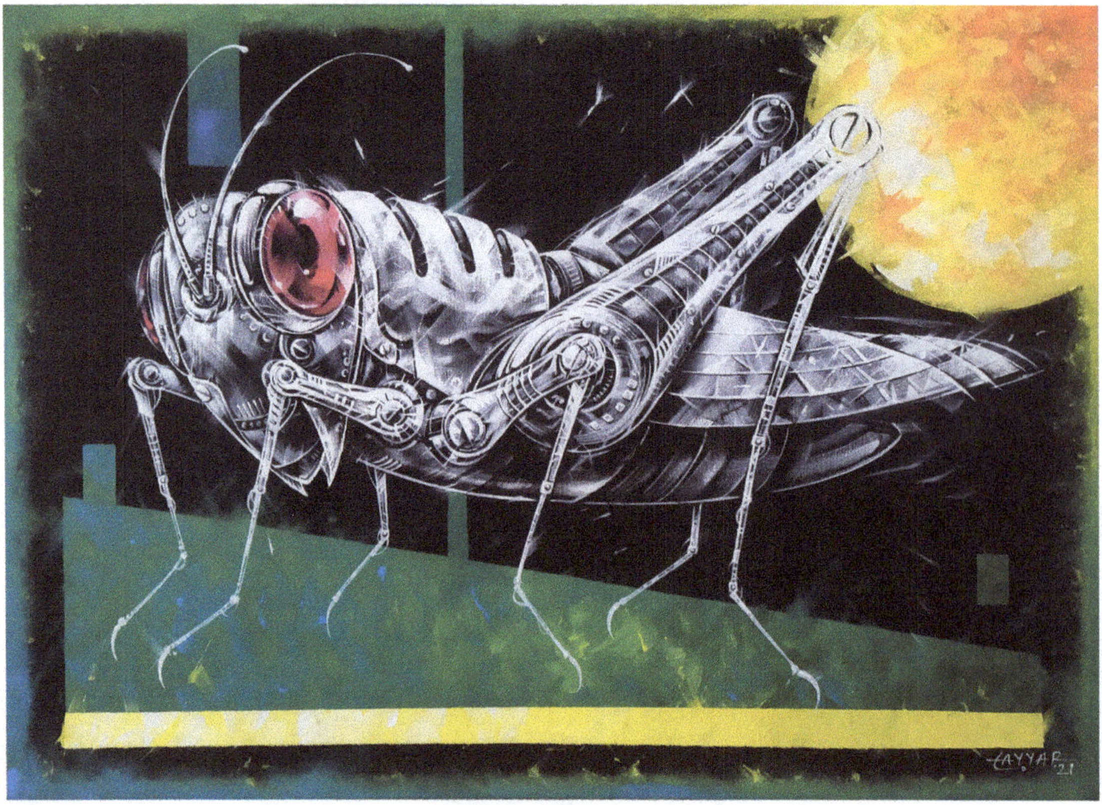

50x70cm.

Acrylic *paintings* on canvas.

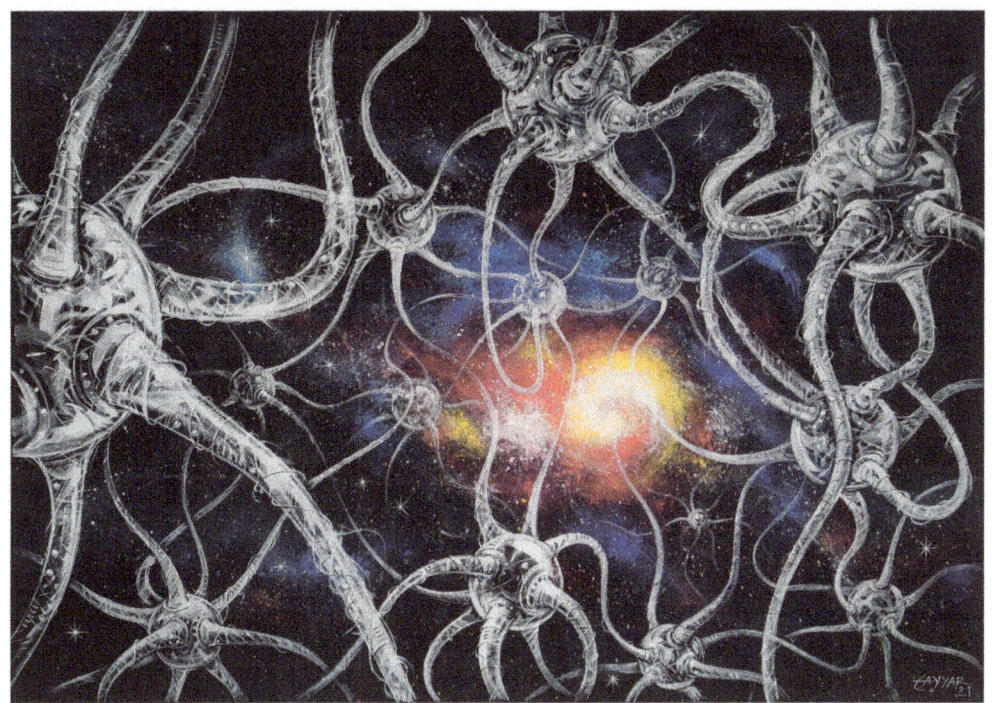

70x100cm.

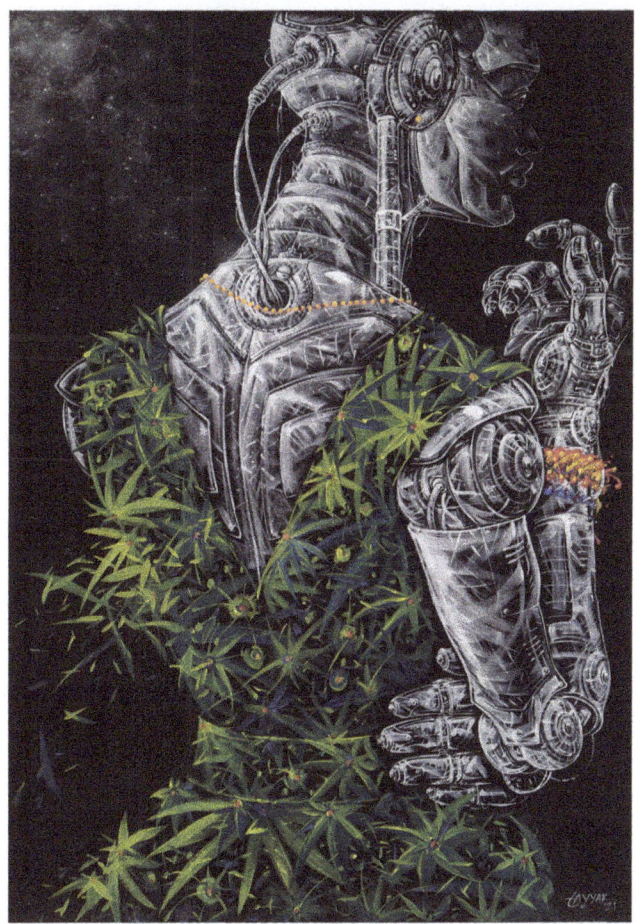

70x100cm.

Acrylic *paintings* on canvas.

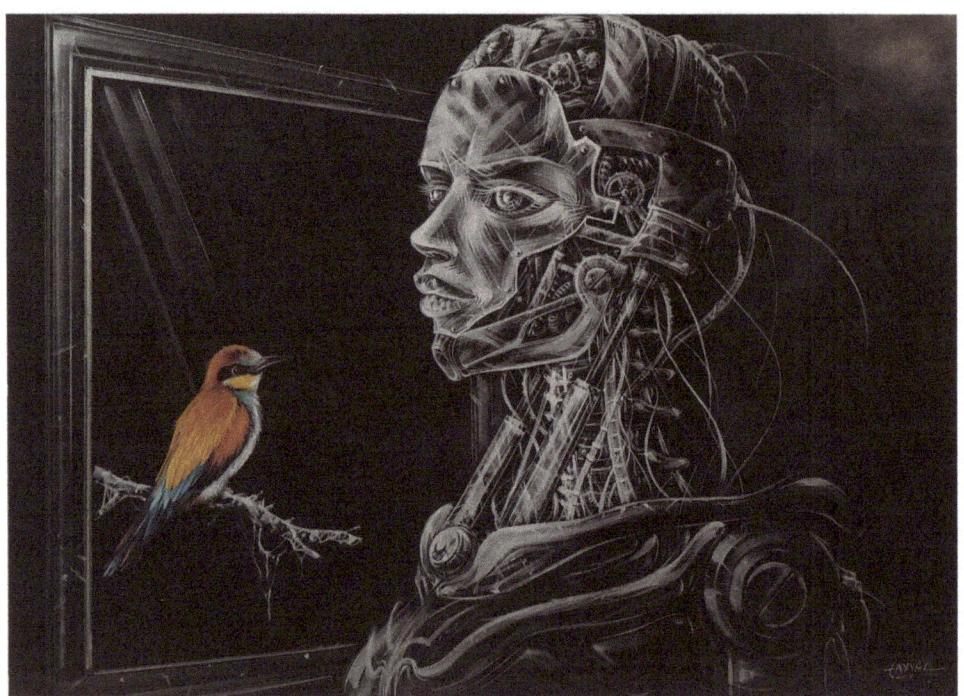

70x100cm.

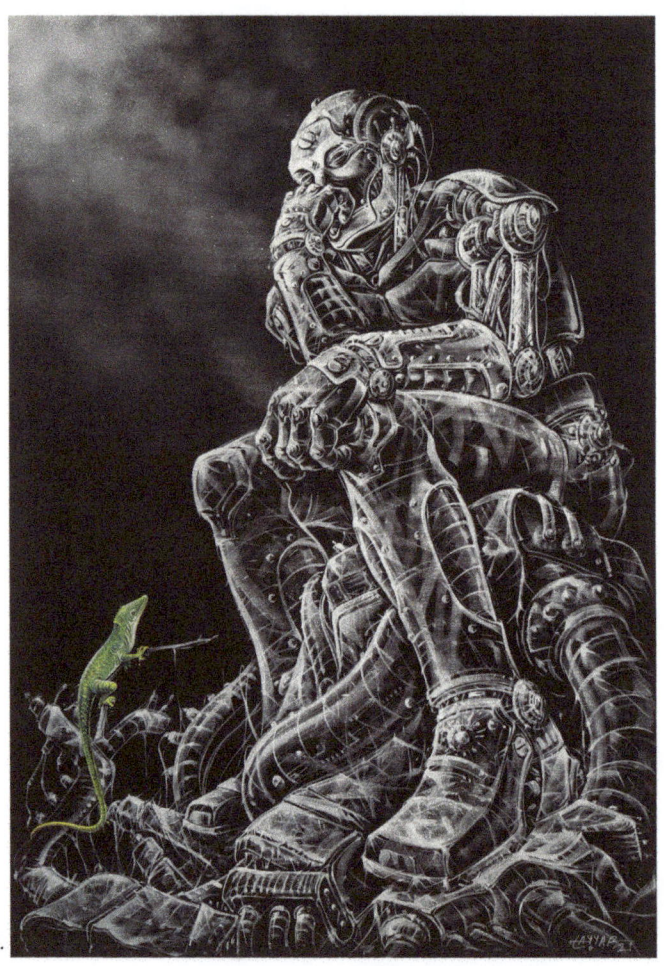

70x100cm.

Acrylic *paintings* on canvas.

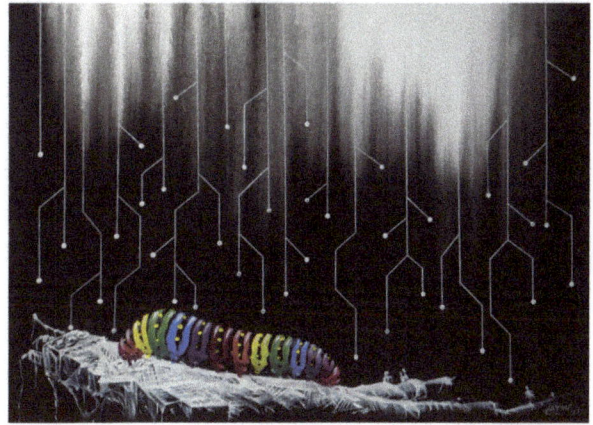

50x70cm.

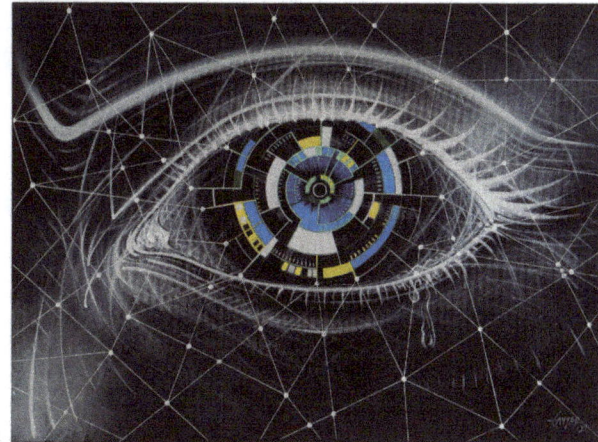

50x70cm.

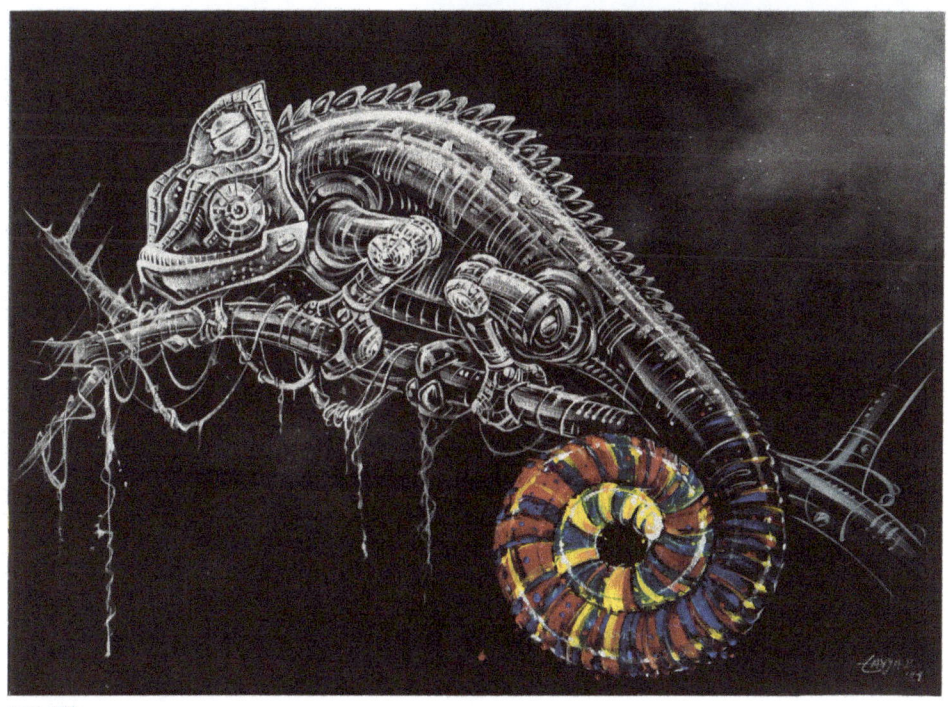

50x70cm.

Acrylic paintings on canvas.

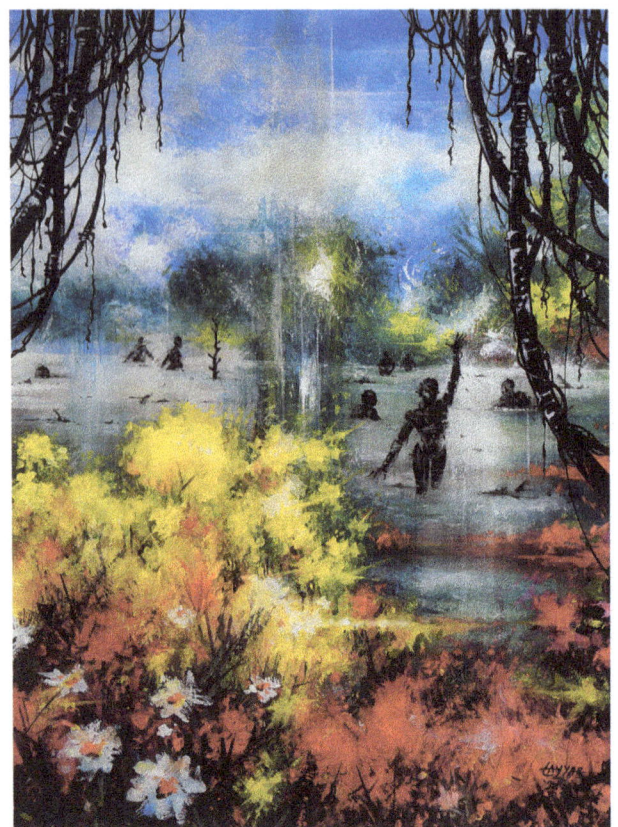

-Acrylic painting on paper.   46x61cm.

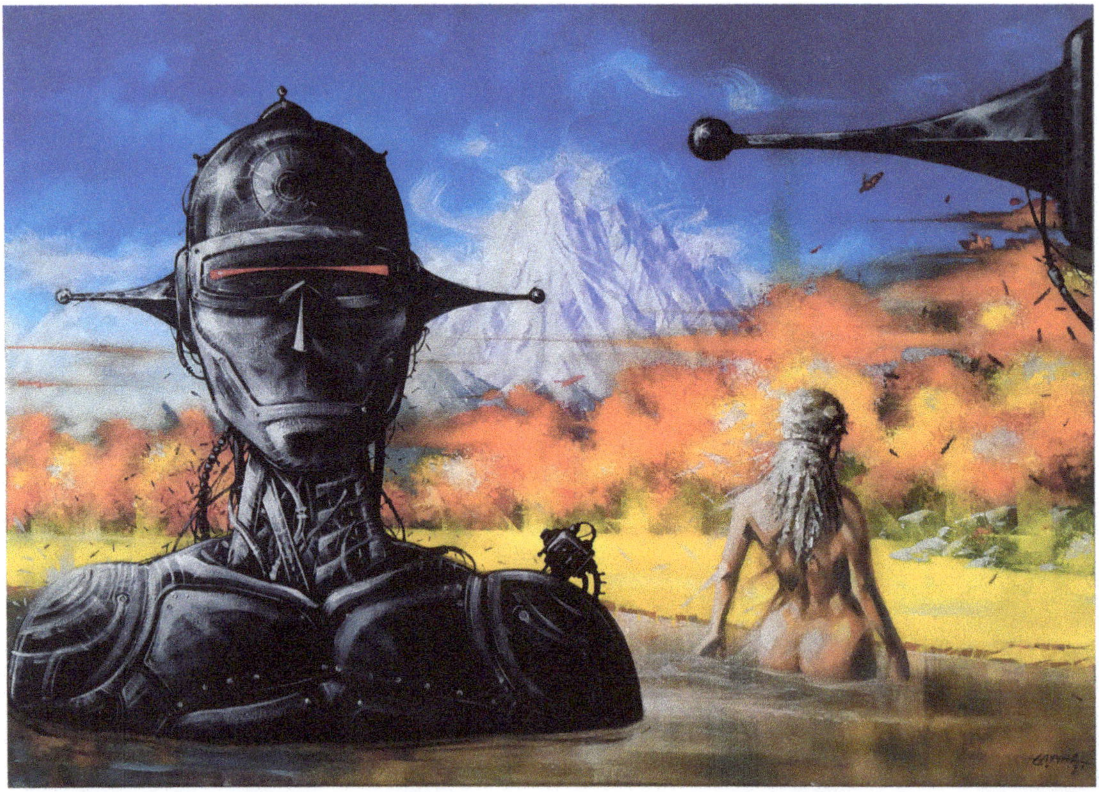

-Acrylic **painting** on canvas.   70x100cm.

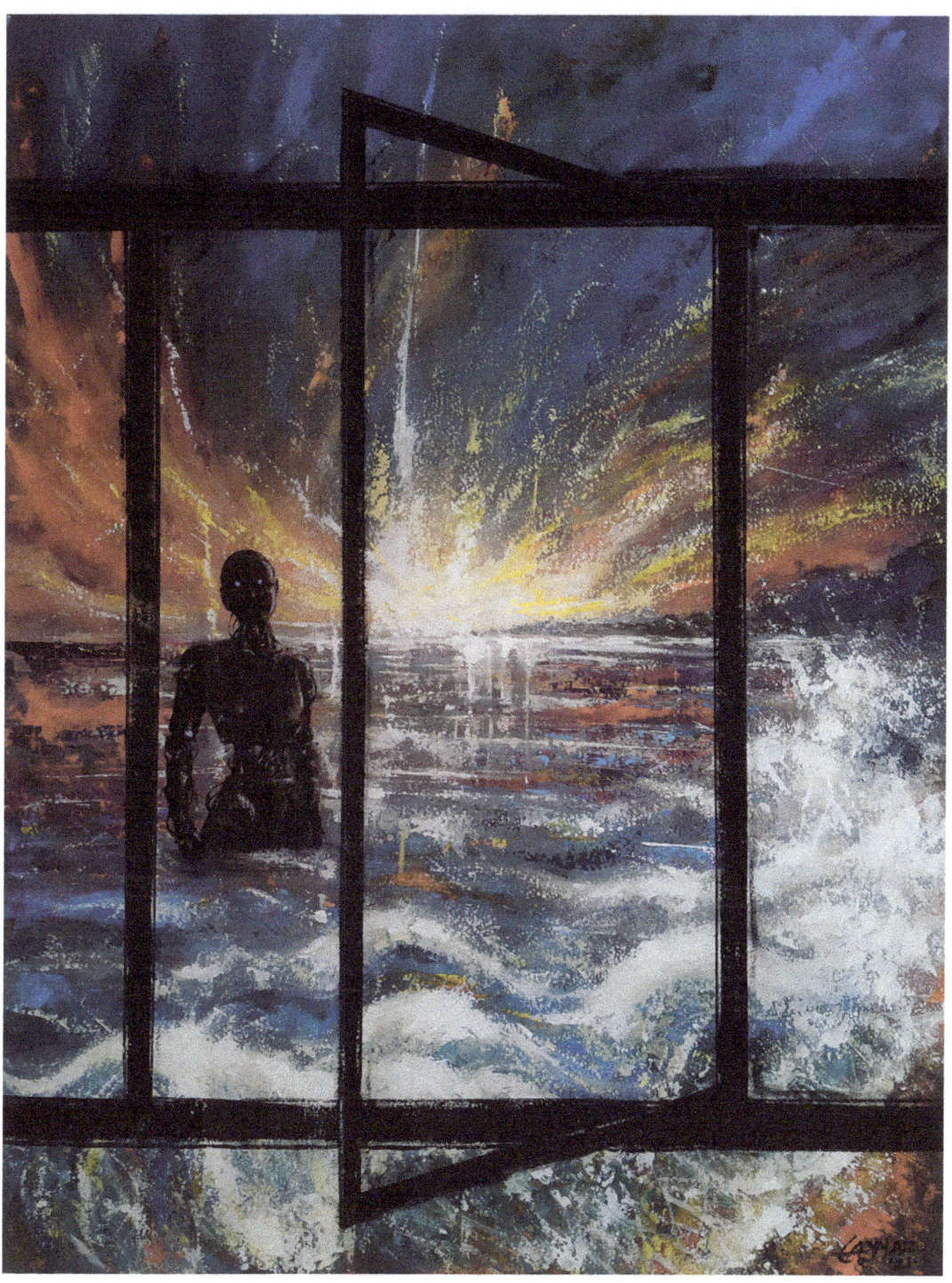

-Acrylic **painting** on paper.

46x61cm.

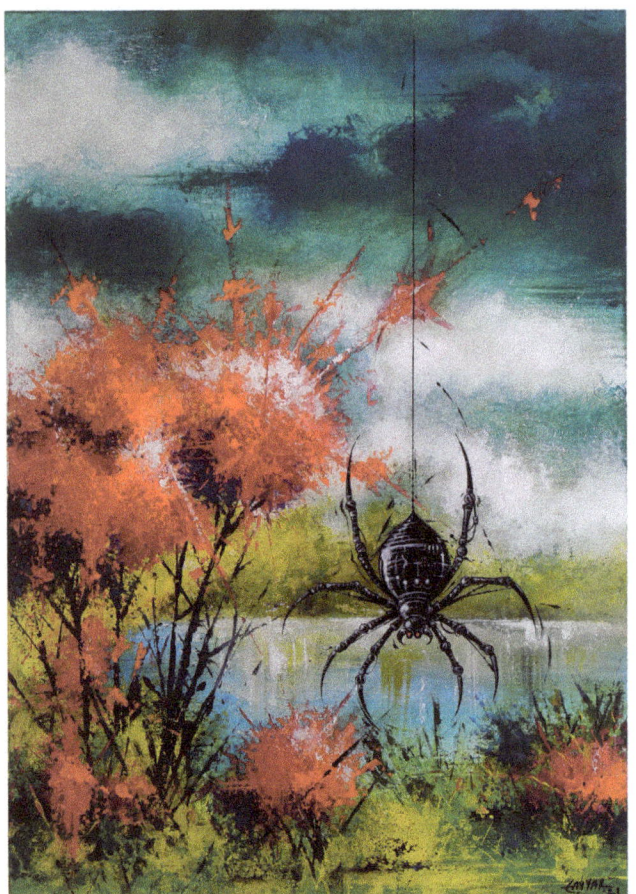

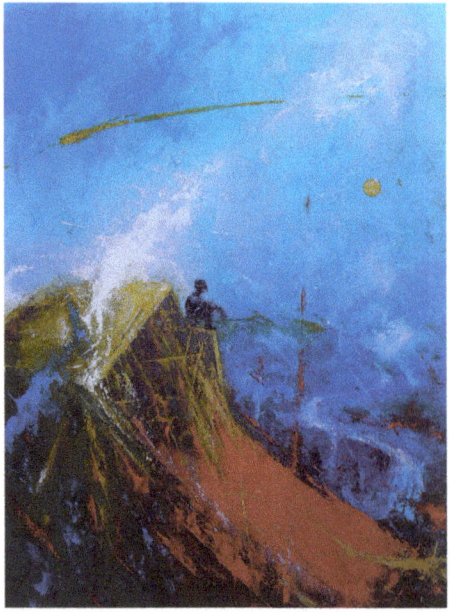

46x61cm.

46x61cm.

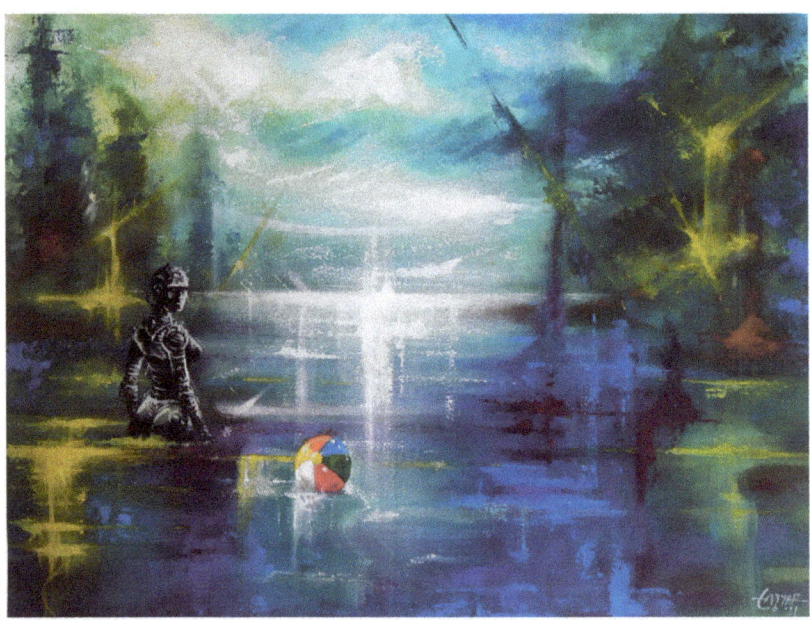

46x61cm.

Acrylic *paintings* on paper.

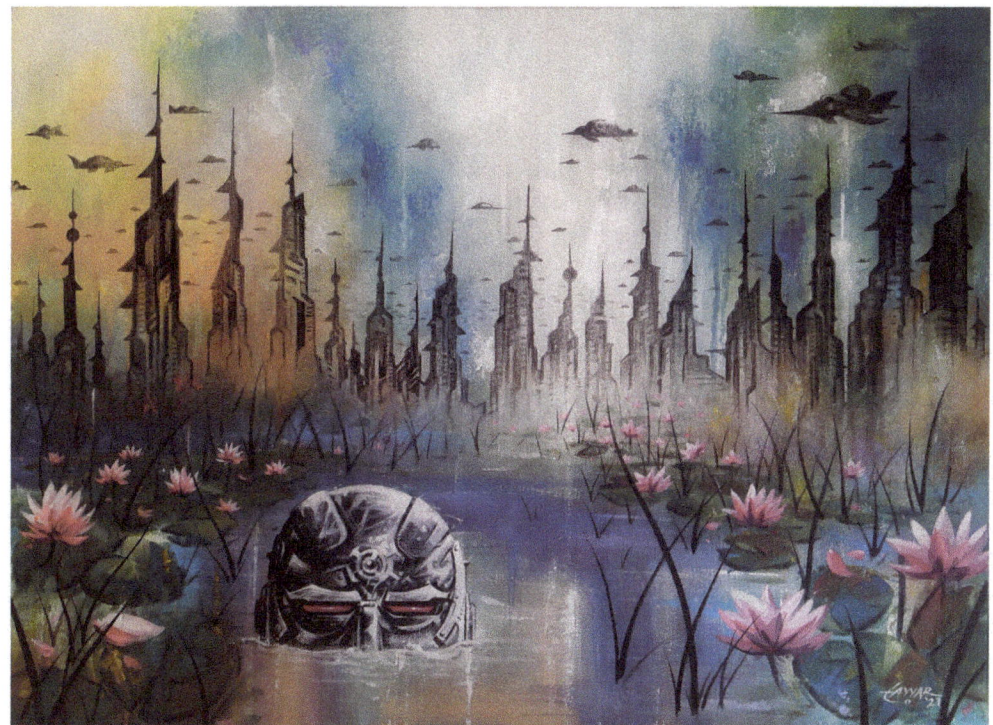

50x70cm.

*-**Acrylic** painting on canvas.*

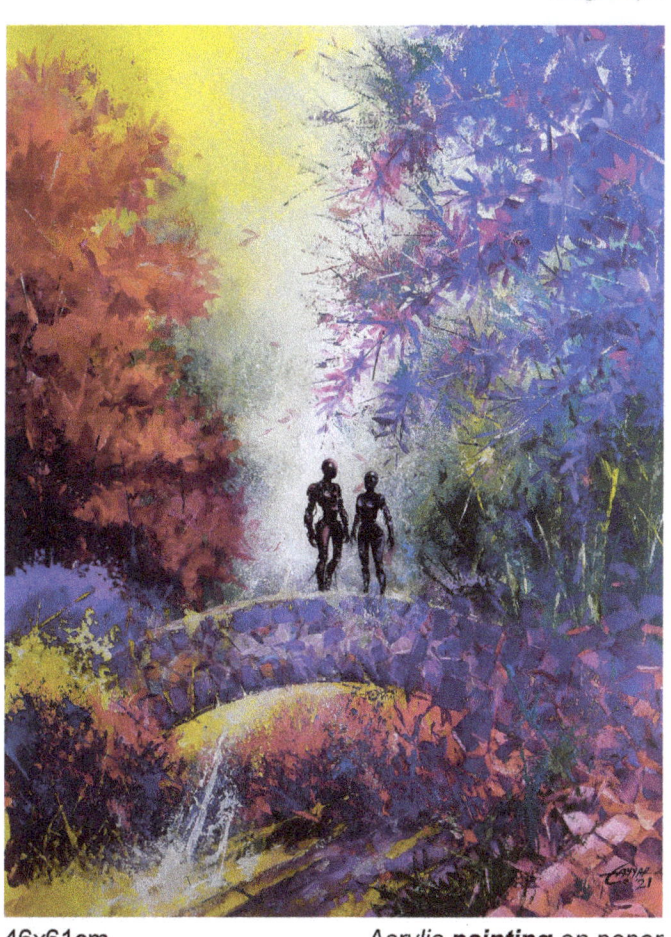

46x61cm.

*-Acrylic **painting** on paper.*

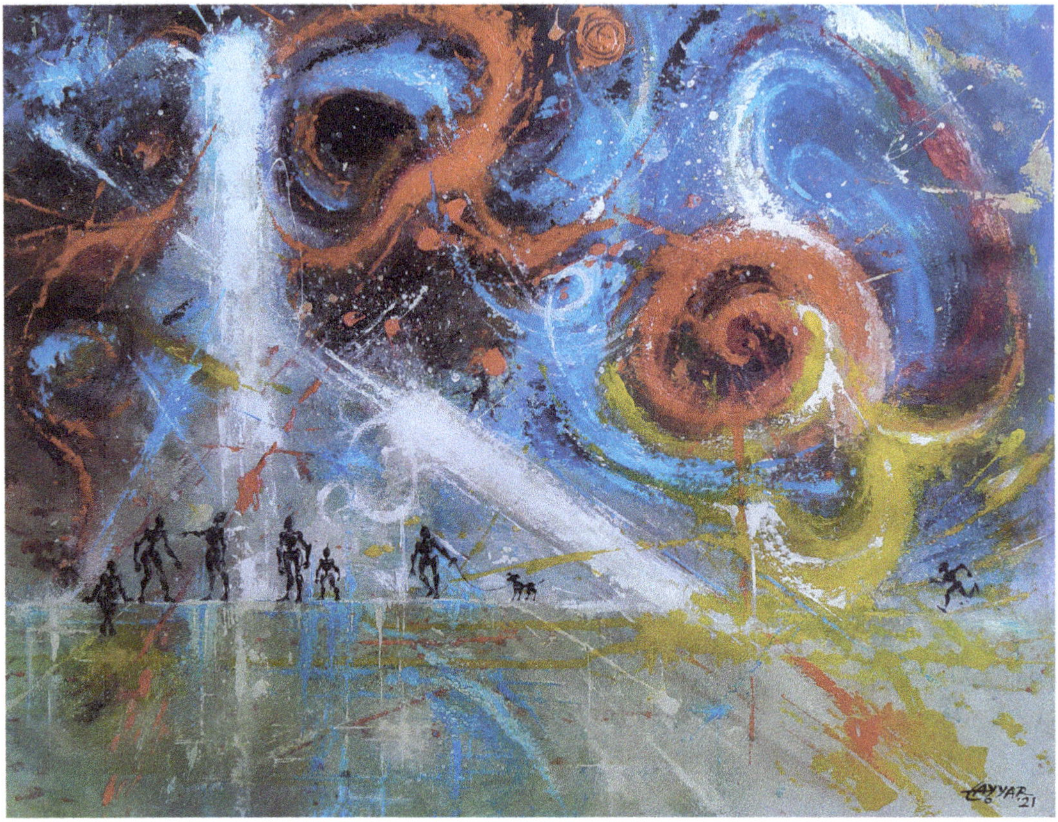

46x61cm.

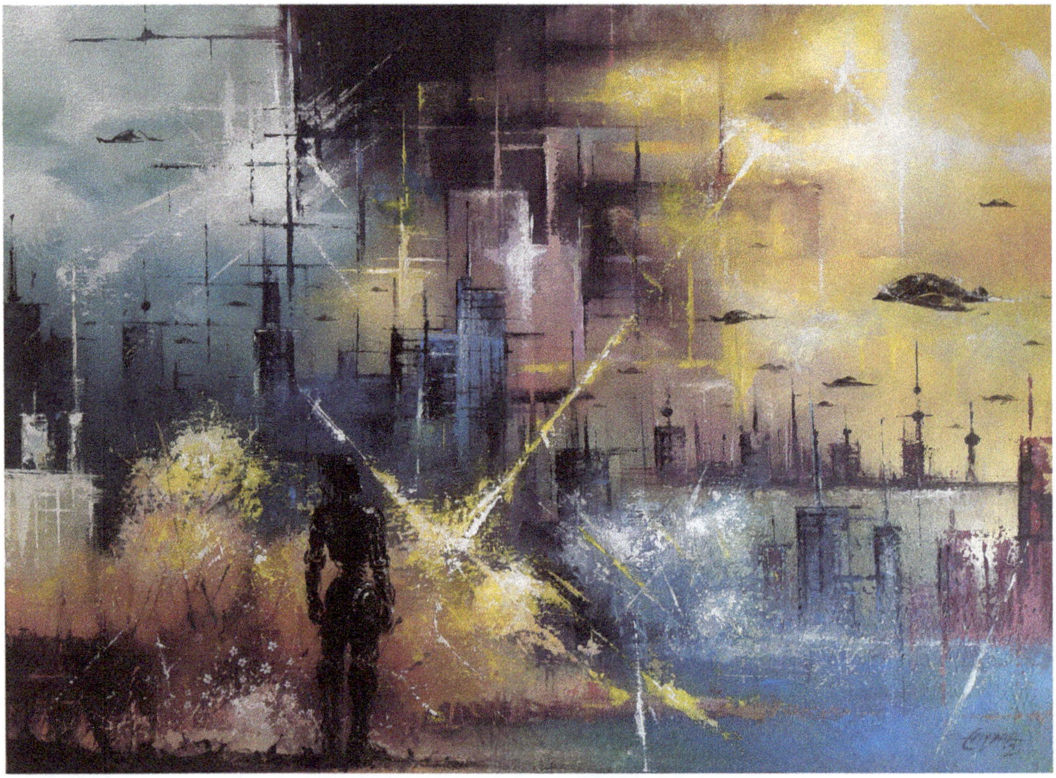

46x61cm.

Acrylic *paintings* on paper.

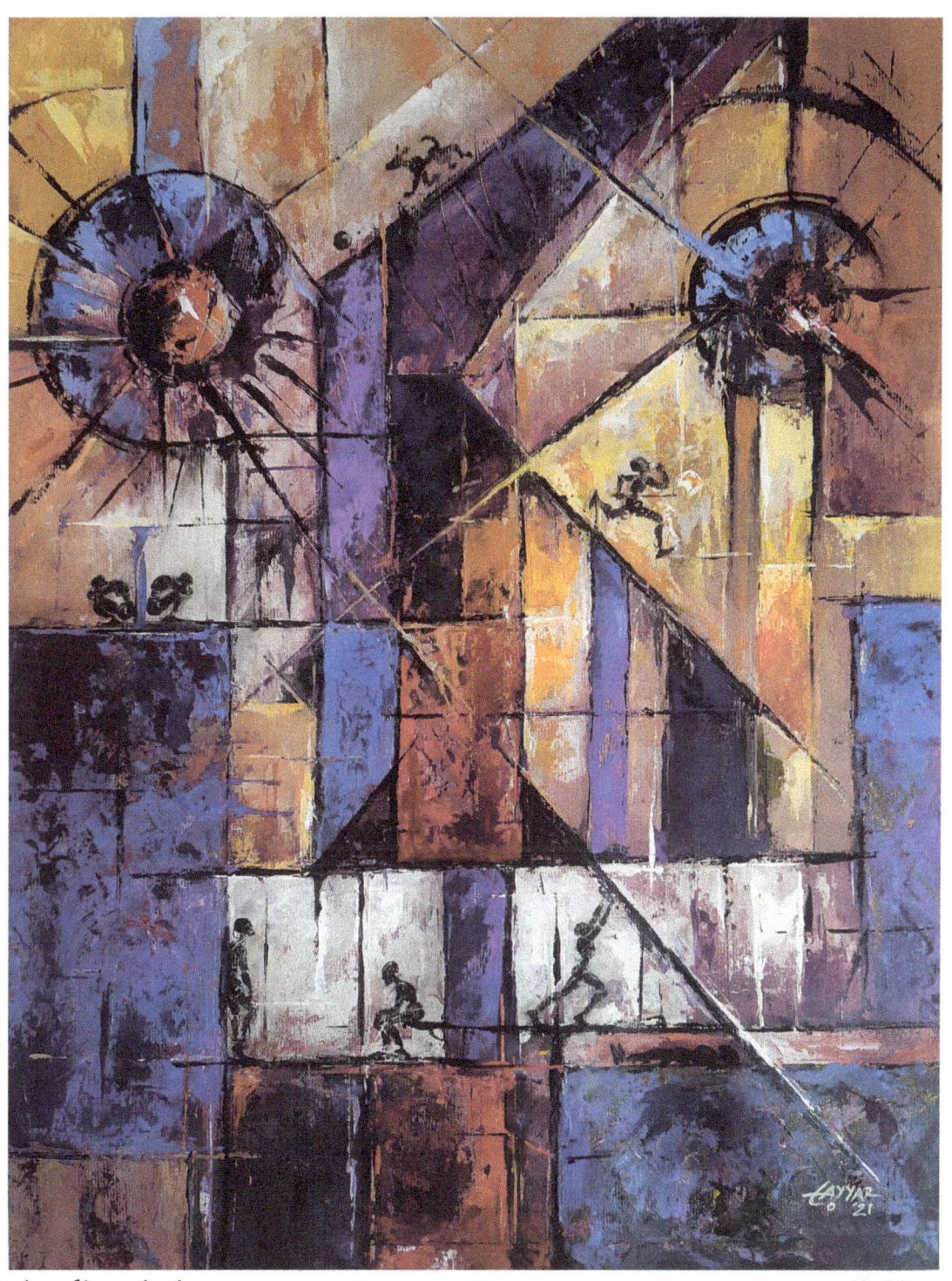

-Acrylic *painting* on paper. 46x61cm.

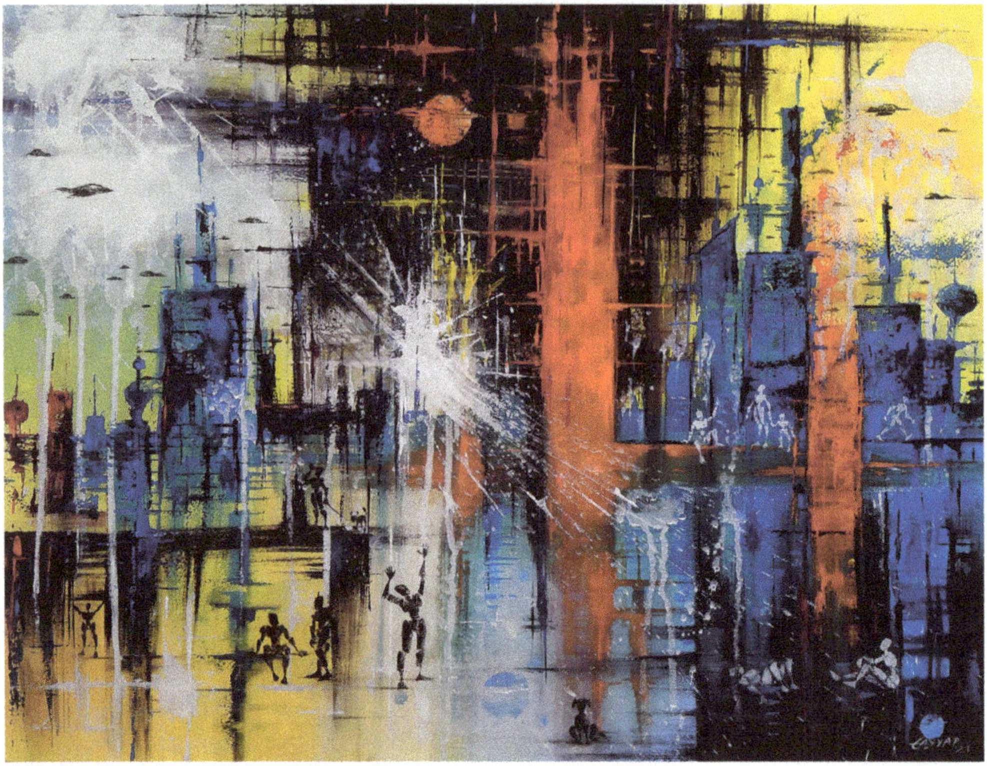

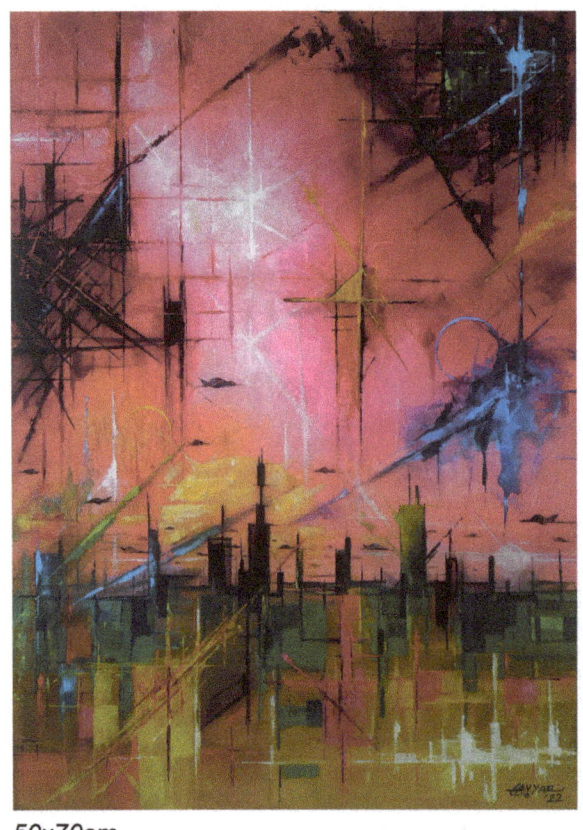

50x70cm.

50x70cm.

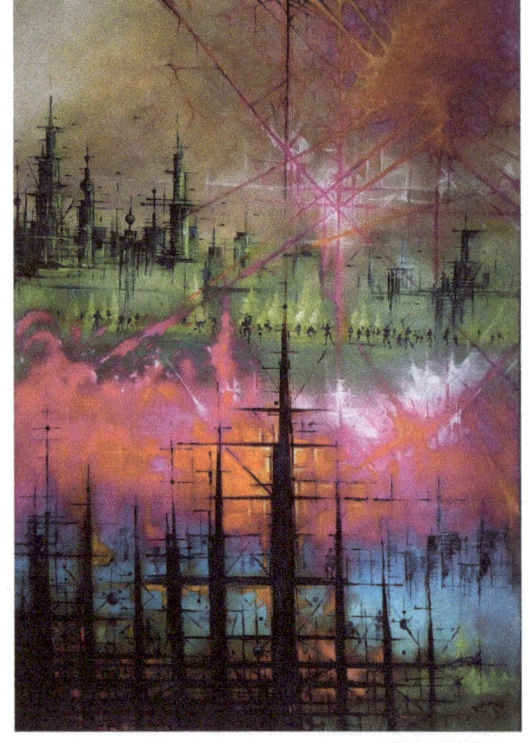

70x100cm.

Acrylic *paintings* on canvas in 2022.

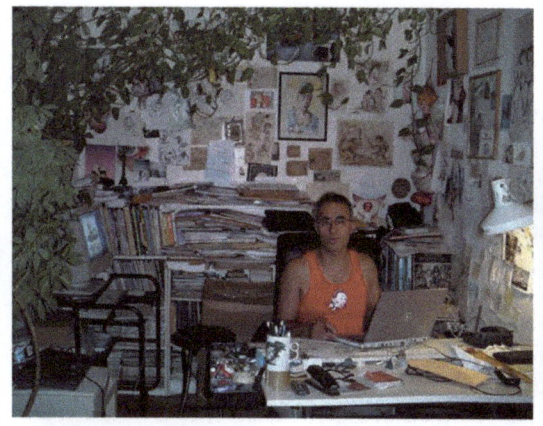
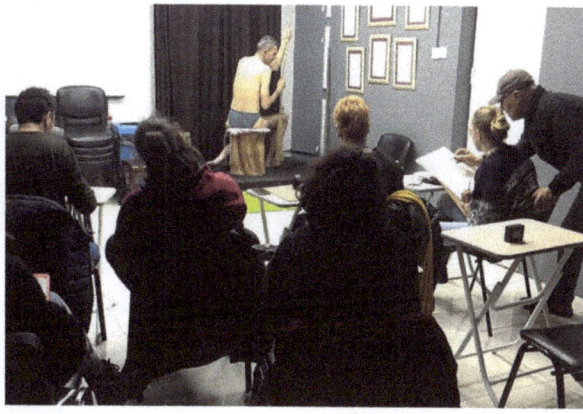
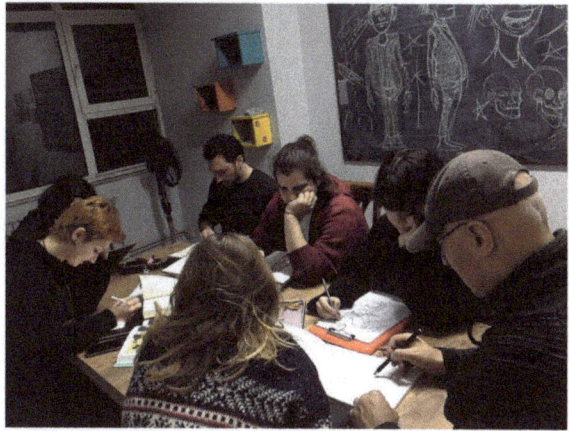
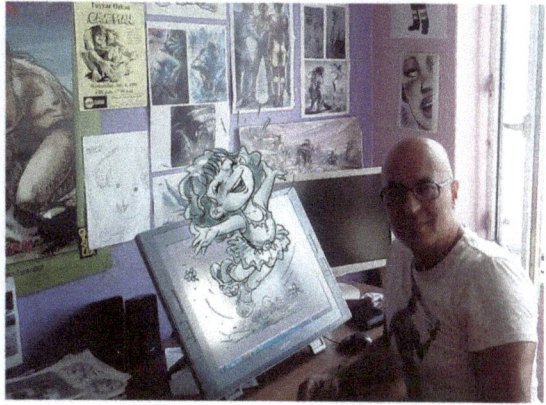
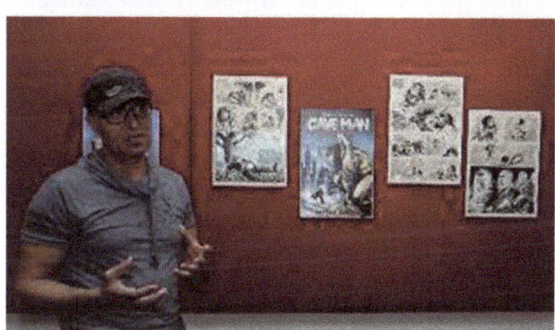
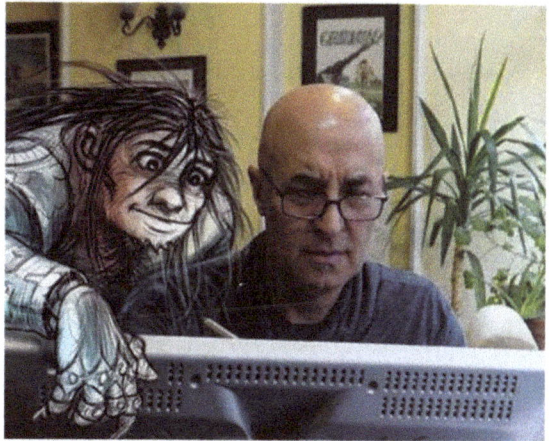
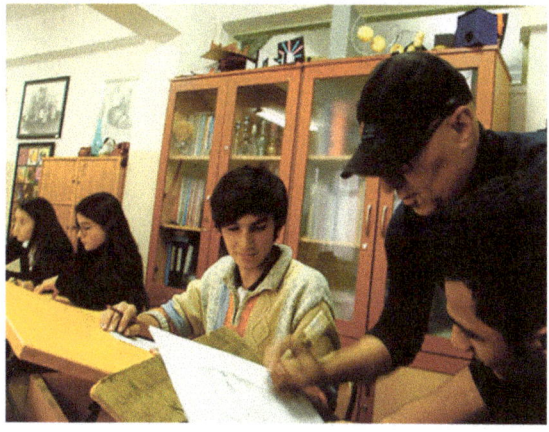
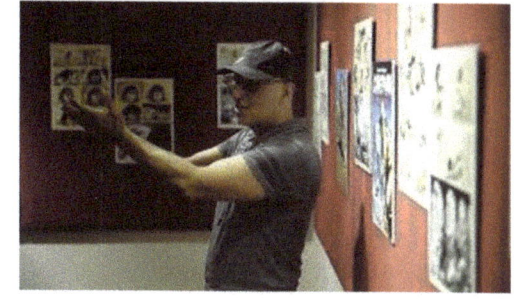

Photos at work with the *different times* and places.

TAYYAR OZKAN

--Born in Anatolia in 1962. He published his first cartoon in local newspapers and magazines in between 1975-78. In the following years he also illustrated many children's books and greeting cards.

After he moved to USA in 1989;
He worked on graphic and textile design for **Tommy Hilfiger, Chaps, Polo Ralph Lauren, Christian Dior Joe Boxer, Intimo, Tiffany, Mavi Jeans** and many others between 1989-2018.

His first comics in USA were published in WORLD WAR 3 Illustrated in 1991. His ongoing creation **CAVEMAN** appeared in *HEAVY METAL* in 1993. In 1997 first CAVEMAN stories are collected as a graphic novel by *NBM*. His collaboration with writer Joel Rose and Amos Poe produced the mystery book **LA PACIFICA** (282 pages) for *Paradox/DC Comics* in 1994. He inked 4 issues of **The DREAMING** for VERTIGO/DC. Meanwhile, work of his can be found in all Paradox The BIG BOOK OF... collections. His erotics books B*USHWHACKED, CAVE BANG #1, #2, #3, #4, PET, FLESHPOT, LEWD MOANA and ORIENT SEXPRESS #1, #2, #3, #4* have been published by **EROS COMIX**. He also produces erotic drawings for several magazines in U.S. (*Screw, Hustler* etc.) and in Europe (*Penthouse COMIX* in Spain, *Blue* in Italy, *Playhouse* in Holland and *Part-Time* in Germany.. etc).

He has self published 4 CAVEMAN comic books. A hard cover graphic novel (as it has been picked as "a book of month" by **FNAC** in France) has been published by French publisher *2L PRODUCTIONS*. Caveman comic book also released in Spain in 2001 by *DUDE Comics* and in 2007 by *Diartgroup*. In Holland by *Libripress Publishing House* in 2007. Also in Turkey, CAVEMAN series has been published in several major newspapers such as *YeniYuzyil, RADIKAL, FHM, Esquire and Cumhuriyet*. Caveman published in Spain in 2001 by **DUDE Comics** and in 2007 by Diartgroup. In Holland by **Libripress Publishing House** in 2007 Full Color Caveman Graphic novel released by **Gerekli Şeyler** in Turkey in 2011. Two books of **"The AGE of the Caveman"** published in UK by **Markosia Enterprises** in 2020 and 2021.

He created an other comic strip character called **Junkidz** (several books and comic strips had also released as a title of **Tekno Park**).

He taught a course on Sequential Art: How Comics Rule at the *School of Visual Arts* in New York in 1997-1999 and many other schools in Turkey. He still teaches an art class online.

-Also Caveman strips published in *Guangzhou Daily* newspaper in **China**!

He has done many character designs for animation projects, private companies and movies. His comic strips called "the AGE" appeared in Heavy Metal illustrated magazine in USA in 2012-13.

He directed animation films, drew storyboards, created many characters for TV commercials, films, video games and animated movies. He still works in the same field as a freelencer.

He is still working on his new project **"The AGE of the Caveman"**.

Lately he 's been working on **acrylic paintings** for his new career.

tayyar@tayyarozkan.com
http://www.tayyarozkan.com
https://www.artstation.com/tayyart
http://bencaveman.deviantart.com/

www.ingramcontent.com/pod-product-compliance
Lightning Source LLC
Chambersburg PA
CBHW052135170526
45162CB00003B/24